THE SUPREME COURT
ON RACIAL DISCRIMINATION

The
Supreme Court
on Racial Discrimination

Edited by
JOSEPH TUSSMAN

New York
OXFORD UNIVERSITY PRESS
1963

Copyright © 1963, by Oxford University Press, Inc.

Library of Congress Catalogue Card Number: 63–7870

Second printing, 1967

PRINTED IN THE UNITED STATES OF AMERICA

TABLE OF CONTENTS

Introduction

"Preoccupation by our people with the constitutionality, instead of with the wisdom, of legislation or executive action is preoccupation with a false value."

These words of Justice Frankfurter, emerging, as they do, from a lifetime of involvement with the theory and practice of government in America pose something of a challenge to anyone who sets about to increase that preoccupation. No one, I suppose, would argue that we should not be concerned with the wisdom of our actions, and perhaps the warning is only against excess. But when all allowances are made the suggestion still remains that constitutional-mindedness is something of a spiritual disorder.

This, of course, raises some questions about the place of the Supreme Court in American life, and I think it would not be unfair to Justice Frankfurter's position to see in it the suggestion that if, indeed, all were well with us the Supreme Court would be a far less interesting and significant institution than it is.

But questions of wisdom and of constitutionality are not so easily separated, and it is because he is aware of this that Justice Frankfurter is also a leading advocate of judicial "self-restraint." The relation of constitutionality to wisdom is a complex problem. Some degree of folly is "legitimate" and the remedy is not the court but the "political" process. But it is also the case that, on occasion, what we think wise may be unconstitutional; and there we chafe at the restraint of rule and principle, robe and parchment. Here is all our twentieth-century electronic equipment, there the encumbering legacy of the eighteenth century. Are we then, where we are concerned with constitutionality, preoccupied with a false value?

In the end the answer to this question takes us to the heart of the theory of the state and the theory of moral behavior. And it is because it takes us there that the study of the Supreme Court is especially rewarding.

Foreign observers, Tocqueville among them, have been struck with our constitutional preoccupation. It is a fact of American life. But its significance has not always been grasped. Some countries seem old countries even when their governments are new. But ours seems young even as it ages. Put shortly, they have traditions; we have a charter. We are a people of the Text and the Gloss.

It is not through perversity or accident that constitutionality looms large in our lives. It is a reflection of the fact that our political life has not floated easily on a stable, homogeneous cultural foundation. We have not had the deep-rooted moral consensus based in centuries of a common history; we have not had an established church. The result is that we have had to pay more explicit attention to the moral basis of political life.

The constitution, the idea of constitutionality, has thus come to occupy a crucial position. It stands somewhere between the daily products of political machinery and the moral sense of a culture; it is a peculiar merging of the political and the moral, and it gives to our politics a moral flavor and to our moral controversies a political form. On the one hand it keeps politics always subject to moral demands and prevents it from moving off on its own into a condition in which it would need to rest more heavily on sanction or coercion. On the other hand, providing the common ground on which our political life is played, it makes less urgent the drives for religious and moral orthodoxy and sustains such separation as is possible of church and state.

The constitution is thus both a political and a moral charter and, seen in this light, our preoccupation with it is hardly an addiction to a false value. There are, to be sure, diseases into which it is all too easy to fall. We can worship the letter at the expense of the spirit or presume too much in the name of the spirit. We can disguise our self-serving as law-mindedness or can develop casuistry to the point of shamelessness and hypocrisy. These are tendencies to which moral life is always prone, and it is just at this point that the Supreme Court has a special, guiding role.

We look to the Court as the arbiter of constitutionality. Whether intended or not, it has established this position and holds it against recurrent challenge and even, at times, its own misgivings. Day in, day out, it faces the question of whether the actions of government are within the bounds of constitutional propriety. The particular problem may be about the meaning of free speech, or double jeopardy, or equal protection, or due process, and this is interesting enough. But as it deals with these problems it must also deal with questions about the nature of rules and principles, the proper art of interpretation, and the role of a constitution in a democratic society. Thus the court deals not only with the principles of the constitution but also with the principles of constitutionalism; and I know of no better way of coming to grips with the fundamental problems of political life than by sharing in these preoccupations of the court.

I am not sure that the Supreme Court is not more important as an educational institution than as a governing tribunal. It is, of course, important for what it does. But it is even more important for what it thinks and says as it does it. Decade after decade some of our most powerful minds have grappled with the most urgent and perplexing issues of American life. Its judicial character—although it is far from being simply a "court"—brings it within the tradition of adversary proceedings and requires that it support its decisions with carefully stated opinions. These are subjected to a powerful barrage of criticism and analysis, professional and amateur, from many points of view. The court must give reasons for what it does. It must display its wisdom. It must demonstrate capacity to grasp the baffling details of a concrete situation, give meaning to principles which seem applicable, make difficult consequential decisions—and do all this with the awareness of the implications of its activity for the theory of the state and for democratic political life. Moreover, the tradition of dissenting opinions makes publicly apparent the conflicting strains within the court, develops counterargument of great power, and pushes the court into greater depth of analysis—to everyone's profit.

In the course of its way of life the Supreme Court produces a body of literature quite unique in quality and significance. It welds fact and theory in a context of action. The study of this literature is exciting and rewarding. Unfortunately, however, several things contribute to the fact that it remains, for most people, an unexplored domain.

First, because it is a court its activity brings it within the purview of the legal profession which, to some extent, guards it as a mystery which only the elect can approach. It is of special concern to lawyers, and they study it in a special way. But it is not entirely *their* oracle, although the habit of seeing it this way tends to warn others off.

Political scientists also deal with the court, generally in the form of the study of "constitutional law"; and it is in this form that most nonlawyers who read or have read opinions come to do so. In spite of the variety of approaches, it is a testimony to the intrinsic quality of Supreme Court opinions that such courses almost invariably stand as a highpoint in college education. But even here, the dominance of a professional attitude does little to dispel the technical and professional aura which shrouds the court. So that it is generally assumed, incorrectly I believe, that only after hard technical training can one understand what the court is talking about or profitably read its opinions.

Second, not unrelated to what has just been said, is the astonishing unavailability of Supreme Court opinions. There are, of course, complete sets of Supreme Court reports—in three different editions—available in law libraries and even general libraries. But these are forbidding to the non-expert and are not really available for convenient and leisurely perusal. In addition, there are various collections of opinions or of selections from opinions, volumes of "great" or "leading" decisions or the collected opinions of some Justice of unusual stature or interest. These are all useful, especially for the particular purpose for which they have been created. But they do not serve the general purpose at which this series aims.

Suppose, for example, that one would want to read the great controversy over the Smith Act as it bears on the communication activities of communists; or the great case involving the use of public funds to pay transportation costs for parochial school children. These are generally available only in fragments in extant collections. One is driven to the sets of complete reports, and these, as I said, are generally inaccessible and forbidding. The Dennis and Everson cases do not deserve this fate and we cannot afford this form of burial.

It is the intention of this series to help remedy this situation. The plan is to bring together in a single volume the significant opinions of the court on a problem of interest and importance. In this, the second volume of the series, we present cases dealing with racial discrimination.

Since those who read this have the volume in hand it is only necessary to comment on a few of its features.

1. Most of the cases, certainly all of the chief cases, are presented in full.

2. Citations and footnotes have been omitted. As for the citations, they are of use only for technical purposes of legal research, and anyone engaged in such research will be working with the regular sets of reports.

The footnotes have been omitted for the same reason. Some have purely technical import. Some do contain material of general interest, but they have been judged by the opinion writers themselves as not an integral part of the opinion.

3. The selection of cases for inclusion has posed some difficult decisions. It would be impossible to include all of the several hundred cases dealing with race. It is with regret that we decided to exclude most of the cases of the decades immediately following the adoption of the Fourteenth Amendment. The cases included have been organized in eight different categories; other classifications are certainly possible. We have thought it better to present fewer cases, generally in full, than to provide shorter excerpts from more cases.

Amendments to United States Constitution

AMENDMENT XIII.

SECTION 1. Neither slavery nor involuntary servitude, except as a punishment for crime whereof the party shall have been duly convicted, shall exist within the United States, or any place subject to their jurisdiction.

SECTION 2. Congress shall have power to enforce this article by appropriate legislation.

AMENDMENT XIV.

SECTION 1. All persons born or naturalized in the United States and subject to the jurisdiction thereof, are citizens of the United States and of the State wherein they reside. No State shall make or enforce any law which shall abridge the privileges or immunities of citizens of the United States; nor shall any State deprive any person of life, liberty, or property, without due process of law; nor deny to any person within its jurisdiction the equal protection of the laws.

SECTION 2. Representatives shall be apportioned among the several States according to their respective numbers, counting the whole number of persons in each State, excluding Indians not taxed. But when the right to vote at any election for the choice of electors for President and Vice President of the United States, Representatives in Congress, the Executive and Judicial officers of a State, or the members of the Legislature thereof, is denied to any of the male inhabitants of such State, being twenty-one years of age, and citizens of the United States, or in any way abridged, except for participation in rebellion, or other crime, the basis of representation therein shall be reduced in the proportion which the number of such male citizens shall bear to the whole number of male citizens twenty-one years of age in such State.

SECTION 5. The Congress shall have power to enforce, by appropriate legislation, the provisions of this article.

AMENDMENT XV.

SECTION 1. The right of citizens of the United States to vote shall not be denied or abridged by the United States or by any State on account of race, color, or previous condition of servitude.

SECTION 2. The Congress shall have the power to enforce this article by appropriate legislation.

Table of Cases

THE SUPREME COURT
ON RACIAL DISCRIMINATION

State Action and Private Preference

"The question," said Chief Justice Taney in the case of Dred Scott, "is simply this: can a negro, whose ancestors were imported into this country and sold as slaves, become a member of the political community formed and brought into existence by the Constitution of the United States, and as such become entitled to all the rights, and privileges, and immunities, guaranteed by that instrument to the citizen . . ."

The men who framed the Declaration of Independence, Taney concluded, "perfectly understood the meaning of the language they used, and knew how it would be understood by others; and they knew that it would not, in any part of the civilized world, be supposed to embrace the negro race, which, by common consent, had been excluded from civilized governments and the family of nations, and doomed to slavery. They spoke and acted according to the then established doctrines and principles, and in the ordinary language of the day, and no one misunderstood them. The unhappy black race were separated from the white by indelible marks, and laws long before established, and were never thought of or spoken of except as property, and when the claims of the owner or the profit of the trader were supposed to need protection."

But the Civil War and the Thirteenth, Fourteenth, and Fifteenth Amendments set the stage anew. "In that struggle," said Mr. Justice Miller in the Slaughter House Cases, "slavery, as a legalized social relation perished." And, speaking of the amendments, he adds that "no one can fail to be impressed with the one pervading purpose found in them all, lying at the foundation of each, and without which none of them would have been even suggested; we mean the freedom of the slave race, the security and firm establishment of that freedom, and the protection of the newly made freeman and citizen from the oppressions of those who had formerly exercised unlimited dominion over him."

The ending of slavery as a "legalized social relation," the admission of men once treated as property into the ranks of persons and citizens is not, however, the end of the story. It is possible to be a citizen and yet a second-class citizen; a person unequal in status to other persons. Almost a century has passed since the adoption of the Civil War amendments and we are still deeply and bitterly involved in working out their implications in theory and in practice.

The cases collected in this volume show the Court at work in a variety of situations involving charges of racial discrimination or of unequal treatment because of race. They tell a significant story of the forging and testing of law, of the struggle of a society to meet the demands of its ideals and commitments in the face of its own deep-seated anxieties and animosities. In the presence of a record that speaks so well for itself I shall not attempt to sum up or expound what it contains nor to state the law as it is now formulated and applied. I shall attempt, however, to pose briefly a fundamental problem which is both pervasive and complex and which, I believe, will come increasingly to the fore.

The injunction that no state shall deny to any person within its jurisdiction the equal protection of the law has, from the beginning, been interpreted in the light of a distinction between state action and private action. What is prohibited is discriminatory state action; the amendment does not reach private action.

This distinction seems, at first glance, both clear and proper. Clear, because we are familiar enough with the distinction between governmental or official action and non-governmental, unofficial, private action, and easily identify state action with the official actions of public officials or public tribunals. Proper, because on the one hand it recognizes that the official agents of the whole community may not wield the authority of the community in ways that discriminate against some of its members, while, on the other hand, it implicitly recognizes that a person in his private life is not to be called to account by government for his likes and dislikes, his preferences or antipathies, his whims or prejudices. He may in private life and in private association consult only his own tastes— although, indeed, he may subject them to the uneasy test of his own conscience, the analysis of his psychiatrist, or the judgment of his moral or religious leaders.

But consider "state action" more closely. Undoubtedly, the act of a legislature is the act of the state and is subject to the demand that it be non-discriminatory. So also is the action of the executive or administrative branch of government. And it seems obvious that the state acts also through its judicial organs, that the action of a state court is state action and must not be discriminatory. Thus, if a judge excludes otherwise qualified persons from jury duty solely because of race this would be regarded as forbidden discrimination by a public official.

Suppose, however, that a court is called upon to enforce the terms of a private contract. It is being asked to put the power of the state behind the contract, to "enforce" it. The court's action is state action, and, if the contract is not illegal, in so acting it is doing what it is supposed to do. But suppose that the contract is discriminatory in the sense that a party buying a house agrees not to sell it to a non-Caucasian. The court by its enforcing action would be marshaling the power of the state in support of an action which, if done by a public official—a zoning authority, for example—would be unconstitutionally discriminatory. Is the court's action discriminatory or not?

The judicial enforcement of discriminatory private undertakings can be seen in two ways. It can be regarded as simply sustaining and protecting the integrity of the system of private agreements which gives scope to private preference. Or it can be seen as state action which is imbued with the quality of the agreement it enforces and therefore, under the equal protection clause, as prohibited state action.

The situation is complicated by the fact that the making of discriminatory or racially invidious private agreements—restrictive covenants, for example—is not itself illegal. But such agreements, the court has held, are unenforceable. We seem, then, to have a vaguely defined class of non-enforceable although not illegal private agreements. And the rationale seems to be that court enforcement would be state action which would share the discriminatory character of the private action.

Thus the notion of state action seems, when judicial action is considered, to burgeon suddenly into the denial of enforcement to, or support of, a range of private agreements which are discriminatory but not illegal. Moreover, the rationale seems to call into question a great deal more than private agreements like restrictive covenants. Does it not suggest that the state action involved in granting a license or permit or in providing protection against trespass modifies the right of the license holder or property owner to discriminate in the conduct of an enterprise thus sustained within a framework of state action? And what about the "corporation," an entity created by and given its powers by the action of the state. Is the action of this creature of the state to be regarded as state action and without more ado subjected to the requirement that it be non-discriminatory? And does the use of public funds or resources or involvement in government contracts transform private action into state action?

There is, I think, something Pilate-like in the state's washing its hands of responsibility for "private" action which its own actions support, sustain, and even make possible; it is difficult to acquiesce in the involvement of public resource and government power in discriminatory action. But it is also difficult to accept the extension of this line of argument to the point where it threatens to eclipse the very notion of private action and association.

We need here to remind ourselves that "private" as applied to actions and institutions has several relevant meanings. In one sense it signifies what is not an action of, or an institution which is a part of, the formal structure of authority—the "private" as the "non-governmental." In another sense, however, "private" signifies a domain which is distinct from the "social" or "public," a domain free from the demands of public authority because it is intimate, personal, and essentially without consequency—not inconsequential in the sense that it is unimportant to the individual, but rather that its momentum does not carry very far and that it has no disturbing or significant social consequences. The "private" in this sense is the purely "personal."

The defense of the "private" has taken two corresponding forms: private, or non-governmental power has been regarded as a necessary or desirable check on the power of government; and the autonomy of the individual in a private ("personal") sphere has been justified because such freedom is personally precious and does not harm or affect others. The difference is important. The claimed private right to act out one's prejudices when such action is largely inconsequential is one thing. It is quite another matter to claim the right to discriminate when "private" means not simply "personal" but rather "non-governmental." The ambiguity of "private" can hardly justify treating the exercise of non-governmental power as though it were a purely personal matter. "My own business," we have learned, is not only "my own business."

The private right to discriminate seems to be under attack from two directions. First, the concept of state action is not only being interpreted as withdrawing state sanctions from certain private agreements, but the logic of this situation suggests the extension of a "quasi-governmental" status to private institutions whose power is so dependent upon state-created arrangements as to justify the claim that the private power is, in fact, delegated public authority. (See *Steele v. L. and N.R.Co.,* for example.)

And, second, the growing complexity of modern life has made us increasingly aware of the social consequences of our "personal" decisions and weakened the appeal to personal privilege. More and more erstwhile private action is seen as "affected with a public interest" and brought within the control of public authority.

The first line of attack seems to be the path of judicial action, while the second would call more appropriately for legislative and administrative action.

But both lines of development would seem to threaten the freedom of private association organized on ethnic or racial lines. Do we really want, in the end, to make impossible an Armenian or Jewish Home for the Aged? Do we really wish to deny to the harassed ethnocentric commuter to the polyglot city the solace of spending the evenings of his life in the bosom of a monochromatic suburb? Must the Black Muslims admit White Christians? Must the Far Eastern Cafe hire blond waiters? Cannot the Cosmos Club be silly without losing its liquor license? Is there not some point to saying that much must wait on the slow process of education and maturation?

But if there is a point to all this, there is an even more urgent point to the flat assertion that the denial of effective franchise to a racial minority is an intolerable scandal, that racial discrimination in the access to the material, educational, and cultural resources of the community is a disgrace, that legally enforced segregation is a standing affront to human dignity. When it is necessary to fight these barbarisms it is understandable that men seize and use whatever weapons come to hand and press doctrines with some indifference as to their ultimate reach. But there is, I think, a growing uneasiness in the minds of many who genuinely oppose segregation and racial discrimination over the failure to adequately clarify the public-private distinction in a way which gives some assurance that not every associational use of ethnic categories will be treated as a public offense.

The Supreme Court has, it appears, borne much of the brunt of the forging of doctrine and public policy in this area. Whether it has, in fact, done too much and overstepped its bounds is a question which troubles many who, though pleased with the results, are nevertheless sensitive to the "undemocratic" aspects of judicial review and judicial policy-making.

This is an old and familiar theme, but I suggest that the place of that peculiar institution, the Supreme Court, in the governing of the United States needs to be re-examined in the light of the growing impotence of our legislative institutions. This is not the only area in which the legislature, deep in the throes of bargaining and compromising, has failed to grapple adequately with urgent problems. We are, perhaps, moving into a period in which the direction of American life will be increasingly determined by a combination of executive and judicial action.

To study the cases collected here is to see the judicial mind struggling, in the context of passionate controversy, toward the clarification of the meaning of equality in the concrete life of a changing society.

Part I

SEGREGATION IN EDUCATION

Cumming v. Board of Education

Berea College v. Kentucky

Gong Lum v. Rice

Missouri ex. rel. Gaines v. Canada

Sipuel v. Oklahoma

Sweatt v. Painter

McLaurin v. Oklahoma State Regents

Brown v. Board of Education

Bolling v. Sharpe

Brown v. Board of Education

Cooper v. Aaron

These cases deal with segregation in education before and after the crucial Brown case.

Cumming v. Board of Education
175 U. S. 528   1899

Mr. Justice Harlan delivered the opinion of the Court.

. . . The constitution of Georgia provides: "There shall be a thorough system of common schools for the education of children in the elementary branches of an English education only, as nearly uniform as practicable, the expenses of which shall be provided for by taxation or otherwise. The schools shall be free to all children of the State, but separate schools shall be provided for the white and colored races."

It was said at the argument that the vice in the common school system of Georgia was the requirement that the white and colored children of the State be educated in separate schools. But we need not consider that question in this case. No such issue was made in the pleadings. Indeed, the plaintiffs distinctly state that they have no objection to the tax in question so far as levied for the support of primary, intermediate and grammar schools, in the management of which the rule as to the separation of races is enforced. We must dispose of the case as it is presented by the record.

The plaintiffs in error complain that the Board of Education used the funds in its hands to assist in maintaining a high school for white children without providing a similar school for colored children. The substantial relief asked is an injunction that would either impair the efficiency of the high school provided for white children or compel the Board to close it. But if that were done, the result would only be to take from white children educational privileges enjoyed by them, without giving to colored children additional opportunities for the education furnished in high schools. The colored school children of the county would not be advanced in the matter of their education by a decree compelling the defendant Board to cease giving support to a high school for white children. The Board had before it the question whether it should maintain, under its control, a high school for about sixty colored children or withhold the benefits of education in primary schools from three hundred children of the same race. It was impossible, the Board believed, to give educational facilities to the three hundred colored children who were unprovided for, if it maintained a separate school for the sixty children who wished to have a high school education. Its decision was in the interest of the greater number of colored children, leaving the smaller number to obtain a high school education in existing private institutions at an expense not beyond that incurred in the high school discontinued by the Board.

We are not permitted by the evidence in the record to regard that decision as having been made with any desire or purpose on the part of the Board to discriminate against any of the colored school children of the county on account of their race. But if it be assumed that the Board erred in supposing that its duty was to provide educational facilities for the three hundred colored children who were without an opportunity in primary schools to learn the alphabet and to read and write, rather than to maintain a school for the benefit of the sixty colored children who wished to attend a high school, that was not an error which a court of equity should attempt to remedy by an injunction that would compel the Board to withhold all assistance from the high school maintained for white children. If, in some appropriate proceeding instituted directly for that purpose, the plaintiffs had sought to compel the Board of Education, out of the funds in its hands or under its control, to establish and maintain a high school for colored children, and if it appeared that the Board's refusal to maintain such a school was in fact an abuse of its discretion and in hostility to the colored population because of their race, different questions might have arisen in the state court.

The state court did not deem the action of the Board of Education in suspending temporarily and for economic reasons the high school for colored children a sufficient reason why the defendant should be restrained by injunction from maintaining an existing high school for white children. It rejected the suggestion that the Board proceeded in bad faith or had abused the discretion with which it was invested by the statute under which it proceeded or had acted in hostility to the colored race. Under the circumstances disclosed, we cannot say that this action of the state court was, within the meaning of the Fourteenth Amendment, a denial by the State to the plaintiffs and to those associated with them of the equal protection of the laws or of any privileges belonging to them as citizens of the United States. We may add that while all admit that the benefits and burdens of public taxation must be shared by citizens without discrimination against any class on account of their race, the education of the people in schools maintained by state taxation is a matter belonging to the respective States, and any interference on the part of Federal authority with the management of such schools cannot be justified except in the case of a clear and unmistakable disregard of rights secured by the supreme law of the land. We have here no such case to be determined; and as this view disposes of the only question which this court has jurisdiction to review and decide, the judgment is

Affirmed.

Berea College v. Kentucky
211 U. S. 45   1908

Mr. Justice Brewer delivered the opinion of the Court.

There is no dispute as to the facts. That the act does not violate the Constitution of Kentucky is settled by the decision of its highest court, and the single question for our consideration is whether it conflicts with the Federal Constitution. The court of appeals discussed at some length the general power of the state in respect to the separation of the two races. It also ruled that "the right to teach white and negro children in a private school at the same time and place is not a property right. Besides, appellant, as a corporation created by this state, has no natural right to teach at all. Its right to teach is such as the state sees fit to give to it. The state may withhold it altogether, or qualify it."

. . . While the terms of the present charter are not given in the record, yet it was admitted on the trial that the defendant was a corporation organized and incorporated under the general statutes of the state of Kentucky, and of course the state courts, as well as this court on appeal, take judicial notice of those statutes. Further, in the brief of counsel for the defendant is given a history of the incorporation proceedings, together with the charters. From that it appears that Berea

College was organized under the authority of an act for the incorporation of voluntary associations, approved March 9, 1854, which act was amended by an act of March 10, 1856, and which in terms reserved to the general assembly "the right to alter or repeal the charter of any associations formed under the provisions of this act, and the act to which this act is an amendment, at any time hereafter." After the Constitution of 1891 was adopted by the state of Kentucky, and on June 10, 1899, the college was reincorporated under the provisions of chap. 32, art. 8, Ky. Stat., the charter defining its business in these words: "Its object is the education of all persons who may attend its institution of learning at Berea, and, in the language of the original articles, 'to promote the cause of Christ.'" The Constitution of 1891 provided in § 3 of the Bill of Rights that "every grant of a franchise, privilege, or exemption shall remain, subject to revocation, alteration, or amendment." So that the full power of amendment was reserved to the legislature.

It is undoubtedly true that the reserved power to alter or amend is subject to some limitations, and that, under the guise of an amendment, a new contract may not always be enforceable upon the corporation or the stockholders; but it is settled "that a power reserved to the legislature to alter, amend, or repeal a charter authorizes it to make any alteration or amendment of a charter granted subject to it, which will not defeat or substantially impair the object of the grant, or any rights vested under it, and which the legislature may deem necessary to secure either that object or any public right."

Construing the statute, the court of appeals held that "if the same school taught the different races at different times, though at the same place, or at different times at the same place, it would not be unlawful." Now, an amendment to the original charter, which does not destroy the power of the college to furnish education to all persons, but which simply separates them by time or place of instruction, cannot be said to "defeat or substantially impair the object of the grant." The language of the statute is not in terms an amendment, yet its effect is an amendment, and it would be resting too much on mere form to hold that a statute which in effect works a change in the terms of the charter is not to be considered as an amendment, because not so designated. The act itself, being separable, is to be read as though it, in one section, prohibited any person, in another section any corporation, and, in a third, any association of persons to do the acts named. Reading the statute as containing a separate prohibition on all corporations, at least, all state corporations, it substantially declares that any authority given by previous charters to instruct the two races at the same time and in the same place is forbidden, and that prohibition, being a departure from the terms of the original charter in this case, may properly be adjudged an amendment.

Again, it is insisted that the court of appeals did not regard the legislation as making an amendment, because another prosecution instituted against the same corporation under the 4th section of the act, which makes it a misdemeanor to teach pupils of the two races in the same institution, even although one race is taught in one branch and another in another branch, provided the two branches are within 25 miles of each other, was held could not be sustained, the court saying: "This last section, we think, violates the limitations upon the police power: it is unreasonable and oppressive." But, while so ruling, it also held that this section could be ignored and that the remainder of the act was complete notwithstanding. Whether the reasoning of the court concerning the 4th section be satisfactory or not is immaterial, for no question of its validity is presented, and the court of appeals, while striking it down, sustained the balance of the act. We need concern ourselves only with the inquiry whether the 1st section can be upheld as coming within the power of a state over its own corporate creatures.

We are of opinion, for reasons stated, that it does come within that power, and, on this ground, the judgment of the Court of Appeals of Kentucky is affirmed.

Mr. Justice Holmes and Mr. Justice Moody concur in the judgment.

Mr. Justice Harlan, dissenting.

This prosecution arises under the 1st section of an act of the general assembly of Kentucky, approved March 22d, 1904. The purpose and scope of the act is clearly indicated by its title. It is "An Act to Prohibit White and Colored Persons from Attending the Same School."

It is well to give here the entire statute, as follows:

"Sec. 1. That it shall be unlawful for any person, corporation, or association of persons to maintain or operate any college, school, or institution where persons of the white and negro races are both received as pupils for instruction; and any person or corporation who shall operate or maintain any such college, school, or institution shall be fined $1,000, and any person or corporation who may be convicted of violating the provisions of this act shall be fined $100 for each day they may operate said school, college, or institution after such conviction.

"Sec. 2. That any instructor who shall teach in any school, college, or institution where members of said two races are received as pupils for instruction shall be guilty of operating and maintaining same and fined as provided in the 1st section hereof.

"Sec. 3. It shall be unlawful for any white person to attend any school or institution where negroes are received as pupils or receive instruction, and it shall be unlawful for any negro or colored person to attend any school or institution where white persons are received as pupils or receive instruction. Any person so offending shall be fined $50 for each day he attends such institution or school: Provided, That the provisions of this law shall not apply to any penal institution or house of reform.

"Sec. 4. Nothing in this act shall be construed to prevent any private school, college, or institution of learning from maintaining a separate and distinct branch thereof, in a different locality, not less than 25 miles distant, for the education exclusively of one race or color.

"Sec. 5. This act shall not take effect, or be in operation, before the 15th day of July, 1904."

. . . In my judgment the court should directly meet and decide the broad question presented by the statute. It should adjudge whether the statute, as a whole, is or is not unconstitutional, in that it makes it a crime against the state to maintain or operate a private institution of learning where white and black pupils are received, at the same time, for instruction. In the view which I have as to my duty I feel obliged to express my opinion as to the validity of the act as a whole. I am of opinion that, in its essential parts, the statute is an arbitrary invasion of the rights of liberty and property guaranteed by the 14th Amendment against hostile state action, and is, therefore, void.

The capacity to impart instruction to others is given by the Almighty for beneficent purposes; and its use may not be forbidden or interfered with by government—certainly not, unless such instruction is, in its nature, harmful to the public morals or imperils the public safety. The right to impart instruction, harmless in itself or beneficial to those who receive it, is a substantial right of property—especially, where the services are rendered for compensation. But even if such right be not strictly a property right, it is, beyond question, part of one's liberty as guaranteed against hostile state action by the Constitution of the United States. This court has more than once said that the liberty guaranteed by the 14th Amendment embraces "the right of the citizen to be free in the enjoyment of all his faculties," and "to be free to use them in all lawful ways." If pupils, of whatever race—certainly, if they be citizens—choose, with the consent of their parents, or voluntarily, to sit together in a private institution of learning while receiving instruction which is not in its nature harmful or dangerous to the public, no government, whether Federal or state, can legally forbid their coming together, or being together temporarily, for such an innocent purpose. If the commonwealth of Kentucky can make it a crime to teach white and colored children together at the same time, in a private institution of learning, it is difficult to perceive why it may not forbid the assembling of white and colored children in the same Sabbath school, for the purpose of being instructed in the Word of God, although such teaching may be done under the authority of the church to which the school is attached as well as with the consent of the parents of the children. So, if the state court be right, white and colored children may even be forbidden to sit together in a house of worship or at a communion table in the same Christian church. In the cases supposed there would be the same association of white and colored persons as would occur when pupils of the two races sit together in a private institution of learning for the purpose of receiving instruction in purely secular matters. Will it be said that the cases supposed and the case here in hand are different, in that no government, in this country, can lay unholy hands on the religious faith of the people? The answer to this suggestion is that, in the eye of the law, the right to enjoy one's religious belief, unmolested by any human power, is no more sacred nor more fully or distinctly recognized than is the right to impart and receive instruction not harmful to the public. The denial of either right would be an infringement of the liberty inherent in the freedom secured by the fundamental law. Again, if the views of the highest court of Kentucky be sound, that commonwealth may, without infringing the Constitution of the United States, forbid the association in the same private school of pupils of the Anglo-Saxon and Latin races respectively, or pupils of the Christian and Jewish faiths, respectively. Have we become so inoculated with prejudice of race than an American government, professedly based on the principles of freedom, and charged with the protection of all citizens alike, can make distinctions between such citizens in the matter of their voluntary meeting for innocent purposes, simply because of their respective races? Further, if the lower court be right, then a state may make it a crime for white and colored persons to frequent the same market places at the same time, or appear in an assemblage of citizens convened to consider questions of a public or political nature, in which all citizens, without regard to race, are equally interested. Many other illustrations might be given to show the mischievous, not to say cruel, character of the statute in question, and how inconsistent such legislation is with the great principle of the equality of citizens before the law.

Of course, what I have said has no reference to regulations prescribed for public schools, established at the pleasure of the state and maintained at the public expense. No such question is here presented and it need not be now discussed. My observations have reference to the case before the court, and only to the provision of the statute making it a crime for any person to impart harmless instruction to white and colored pupils together, at the same time, in the same private institution of learning. That provision is, in my opinion, made an essential element in the policy of the statute, and, if regard be had to the object and purpose of this legislation, it cannot be treated as separable nor intended to be separated from the provisions relating to corporations. The whole statute should therefore be held void; otherwise, it will be taken as the law of Kentucky, to be enforced by its courts, that the teaching of white and black pupils, at the same time, even in a *private* institution, is a crime against that commonwealth, punishable by fine and imprisonment.

In my opinion the judgment should be reversed upon the ground that the statute is in violation of the Constitution of the United States.

Mr. Justice Day also dissents.

Gong Lum v. Rice
275 U. S. 78   1927

Mr. Chief Justice Taft delivered the opinion of the Court.

This was a petition for mandamus filed in the state Circuit Court of Mississippi for the First Judicial District of Bolivar County.

Gong Lum is a resident of Mississippi, resides in the Rosedale Consolidated High School District, and is the father of Martha Lum. He is engaged in the mercantile business. Neither he nor she was connected with the consular service or any other service of the government of China, or any other government, at the time of her birth. She was nine years old when the petition was filed, having been born January 21, 1915, and she sued by her next friend, Chew How, who is a native born citizen of the United States and the State of Mississippi. The petition alleged that she was of good moral character and between the ages of five and twenty-one years, and that, as she was such a citizen and an educable child, it became her father's duty under the law to send her to school; that she desired to attend the Rosedale Consolidated High School; that at the opening of the school she appeared as a pupil, but at the noon recess she was notified by the superintendent that she would not be allowed to return to the school; that an order had been issued by the Board of Trustees, who are made defendants, excluding her from attending the school solely on the ground that she was of Chinese descent and not a member of the white or Caucasian race, and that their order had been made in pursuance to instructions from the State Superintendent of Education of Mississippi, who is also made a defendant.

The petitioners further show that there is no school maintained in the District for the education of children of Chinese descent, and none established in Bolivar County where she could attend.

The Constitution of Mississippi requires that there shall be a county common school fund, made up of poll taxes from the various counties, to be retained in the counties where the same is collected, and a state common school fund to be taken from the general fund in the state treasury, which together shall be sufficient to maintain a common school for a term of four months in each scholastic year, but that any county or separate school district may levy an additional tax to maintain schools for a longer time than a term of four months, and that the said common school fund shall be distributed among the several counties and separate school districts in proportion to the number of educable children in each, to be collected from the data in the office of the State Superintendent of Education in the manner prescribed by law; that the legislature encourage by all suitable means the promotion of intellectual, scientific, moral and agricultural improvement, by the establishment of a uniform system of free public schools by taxation or otherwise, for all children between the ages of five and twenty-one years, and, as soon as practicable, establish schools of higher grade.

The petition alleged that, in obedience to this mandate of the Constitution, the legislature has provided for the establishment and for the payment of the expenses of the Rosedale Consolidated High School, and that the plaintiff, Gong Lum, the petitioner's father, is a taxpayer and helps to support and maintain the school; that Martha Lum is an educable child, is entitled to attend the school as a pupil, and that this is the only school conducted in the District available for her as a pupil; that the right to attend it is a valuable right; that she is not a member of the colored race nor is she of mixed blood, but that she is pure Chinese; that she is by the action of the Board of Trustees and the State Superintendent discriminated against directly and denied her right to be a member of the Rosedale School; that the school authorities have no discretion under the law as to her admission as a pupil in the school, but that they continue without authority of law to deny her the right to attend it as a pupil. For these reasons the writ of mandamus is prayed for against the defendants commanding them and each of them to desist from discriminating against her on account of her race or ancestry and to give her the same rights and privileges that other educable children between the ages of five and twenty-one are granted in the Rosedale Consolidated High School.

The petition was demurred to by the defendants on the ground, among others, that the bill showed on its face that plaintiff is a member of the Mongolian or yellow race, and therefore not entitled to attend the schools provided by law in the State of Mississippi for children of the white or Caucasian race.

The trial court overruled the demurrer and ordered that a writ of mandamus issue to the defendants as prayed in the petition.

The defendants then appealed to the Supreme Court of Mississippi, which heard the case. In its opinion, it directed its attention to the proper construction of § 207 of the State Constitution of 1890, which provides:

"Separate schools shall be maintained for children of the white and colored races."

The Court held that this provision of the Constitution divided the educable children into those of the pure white or Caucasian race, on the one hand, and the brown, yellow and black races, on the other, and therefore that Martha Lum of the Mongolian or yellow race could not insist on being classed with the whites under this constitutional division. The Court said:

"The legislature is not compelled to provide separate schools for each of the colored races, and, unless and until it does provide such schools and provide for segregation of the other races, such races are entitled to have the benefit of the colored public schools. Under our statutes a colored public school exists in every county and in some convenient district in which every colored child is entitled to obtain an education. These schools are within the reach of all the children of the state, and the plaintiff does not show by her petition that she applied for admission to such schools. On the contrary the petitioner takes the position that because there are no separate public schools for Mongolians that she is entitled to enter the white public schools in preference to the colored public schools. A consolidated school in this state is simply a common school conducted as other common schools are conducted; the only distinction being that two or more school districts have been consolidated into one school. Such consolidation is entirely discretionary with the county school board having reference to the condition existing in the particular territory. Where a school district has an unusual amount of territory, with an unusual valuation of property therein, it may levy additional taxes. But the other common schools under similar statutes have the same power.

"If the plaintiff desires, she may attend the colored public schools of her district, or, if she does not so desire, she may go to a private school. The compulsory school law of this state does not require the attendance at a public school, and a parent under the decisions of the Supreme Court of the United States has a right to educate his child in a private school if he so desires. But plaintiff is not entitled to attend a white public school."

As we have seen, the plaintiffs aver that the Rosedale Consolidated High School is the only school conducted in that district available for

Martha Lum as a pupil. They also aver that there is no school maintained in the district of Bolivar County for the education of Chinese children and none in the county. How are these averments to be reconciled with the statement of the State Supreme Court that colored schools are maintained in every county by virtue of the Constitution? This seems to be explained, in the language of the State Supreme Court, as follows:

"By statute it is provided that all the territory of each county of the state shall be divided into school districts separately for the white and colored races; that is to say, the whole territory is to be divided into white school districts, and then a new division of the county for colored school districts. In other words, the statutory scheme is to make the districts outside of the separate school districts, districts for the particular race, white or colored, so that the territorial limits of the school districts need not be the same, but the territory embraced in a school district for the colored race may not be the same territory embraced in the school district for the white race, and *vice versa,* which system of creating the common school districts for the two races, white and colored, does not require schools for each race as such to be maintained in each district, but each child, no matter from what territory, is assigned to some school district, the school buildings being separately located and separately controlled, but each having the same curriculum, and each having the same number of months of school term, if the attendance is maintained for the said statutory period, which school district of the common or public schools has certain privileges, among which is to maintain a public school by local taxation for a longer period of time than the said term of four months under named conditions which apply alike to the common schools for the white and colored races."

We must assume then that there are school districts for colored children in Bolivar County, but that no colored school is within the limits of the Rosedale Consolidated High School District. This is not inconsistent with there being, at a place outside of that district and in a different district, a colored school which the plaintiff Martha Lum, may conveniently attend. If so, she is not denied, under the existing school system, the right to attend and enjoy the privileges of a common school education in a colored school. If it were otherwise, the petition should have contained an allegation showing it. Had the petition alleged specifically that there was no colored school in Martha Lum's neighborhood to which she could conveniently go, a different question would have been presented, and this, without regard to the State Supreme Court's construction of the State Constitution as limiting the white schools provided for the education of children of the white or Caucasian race. But we do not find the petition to present such a situation.

The case then reduces itself to the question whether a state can be said to afford to a child of Chinese ancestry born in this country, and a citizen of the United States, equal protection of the laws by giving her the opportunity for a common school education in a school which receives only colored children of the brown, yellow or black races.

The right and power of the state to regulate the method of providing for the education of its youth at public expense is clear. In *Cumming* v. *Richmond County Board of Education* persons of color sued the Board of Education to enjoin it from maintaining a high school for white children without providing a similar school for colored children which had existed and had been discontinued. Mr. Justice Harlan, in delivering the opinion of the Court, said:

"Under the circumstances disclosed, we cannot say that this action of the state court was, within the meaning of the Fourteenth Amendment, a denial by the State to the plaintiffs and to those associated with them of the equal protection of the laws, or of any privileges belonging to them as citizens of the United States. We may add that while all admit that the benefits and burdens of public taxation must be shared by citizens without discrimination against any class on account of their race, the education of the people in schools maintained by state taxation is a matter belonging to the respective States, and any interference on the part of Federal authority with the management of such schools can not be justified except in the case of a clear and unmistakable disregard of rights secured by the supreme law of the land."

The question here is whether a Chinese citizen of the United States is denied equal protection of the laws when he is classed among the colored races and furnished facilities for education equal to that offered to all, whether white, brown, yellow or black. Were this a new question, it would call for very full argument and consideration, but we think that it is the same question which has been many times decided to be within the constitutional power of the state legislature to settle without intervention of the federal courts under the Federal Constitution.

In *Plessy* v. *Ferguson,* in upholding the validity under the Fourteenth Amendment of a statute of Louisiana requiring the separation of the white and colored races in railway coaches, a more difficult question than this, this Court, speaking of permitted race separation, said:

"The most common instance of this is connected with the establishment of separate schools for white and colored children, which has been held to be a valid exercise of the legislative power even by courts of States where the political rights of the colored race have been longest and most earnestly enforced."

The case of *Roberts* v. *City of Boston* in which Chief Justice Shaw of the Supreme Judicial Court of Massachusetts, announced the opinion of that court upholding the separation of colored and white schools under a state constitutional injunction of equal protection, the same as the Fourteenth Amendment, was then referred to, and this Court continued:

"Similar laws have been enacted by Congress under its general power of legislation over the District of Columbia as well as by the legislatures of many of the States, and have been generally, if not uniformly, sustained by the Courts," citing many of the cases above named.

Most of the cases cited arose, it is true, over the establishment of separate schools as between white pupils and black pupils, but we can not think that the question is any different or that any different result can be reached, assuming the cases above cited to be rightly decided, where the issue is as between white pupils and the pupils of the yellow races. The decision is within the discretion of the state in regulating its public schools and does not conflict with the Fourteenth Amendment. The judgment of the Supreme Court of Mississippi is

Affirmed.

Missouri ex. rel. Gaines v. Canada
305 U. S. 337   1938

Mr. Chief Justice Hughes delivered the opinion of the Court.

Petitioner Lloyd Gaines, a negro, was refused admission to the School of Law at the State University of Missouri. Asserting that this refusal constituted a denial by the State of the equal protection of the laws in violation of the Fourteenth Amendment of the Federal Constitution, petitioner brought this action for mandamus to compel the curators of the University to admit him. On final hearing, an alternative writ was quashed and a peremptory writ was denied by the Circuit Court. The Supreme Court of the State affirmed the judgment. We granted certiorari, October 10, 1938.

Petitioner is a citizen of Missouri. In August, 1935, he was graduated with the degree of Bachelor of Arts at the Lincoln University, an institution maintained by the State of Missouri for the higher education of negroes. That University has no law school. Upon the filing of his application for admission to the law school of the University of Missouri, the registrar advised him to communicate with the president of Lincoln University and the latter directed petitioner's attention to § 9622 of the Revised Statutes of Missouri (1929), providing as follows:

"Sec. 9622. *May arrange for attendance at university of any adjacent state—Tuition fees.*—Pending the full development of the Lincoln university, the board of curators shall have the authority to arrange for the attendance of negro residents of the state of Missouri at the university of any adjacent state to take any course or to study any subjects provided for at the state university of Missouri, and which are not taught at the Lincoln university and to pay the reasonable tuition fees for such attendance; *provided* that whenever the board of curators deem it advisable they shall have the power to open any necessary school or department."

Petitioner was advised to apply to the State Superintendent of Schools for aid under that statute. It was admitted on the trial that petitioner's "work and credits at the Lincoln University would qualify him for admission to the School of Law of the University of Missouri if he were found otherwise eligible." He was refused admission upon the ground that it was "contrary to the constitution, laws and public policy of the State to admit a negro as a student in the University of Missouri." It appears that there are schools of law in connection with the state universities of four adjacent States, Kansas, Nebraska, Iowa and Illinois, where nonresident negroes are admitted.

The clear and definite conclusions of the state court in construing the pertinent state legislation narrow the issue. The action of the curators, who are representatives of the State in the management of the state university must be regarded as state action. The state constitution provides that separate free public schools shall be established for the education of children of African descent, and by statute separate high school facilities are supplied for colored students equal to those provided for white students. While there is no express constitutional provision requiring that the white and negro races be separated for the purpose of higher education, the state court on a comprehensive review of the state statutes held that it was intended to separate the white and negro races for that purpose also. Referring in particular to Lincoln University, the court deemed it to be clear "that the Legislature intended to bring the Lincoln University up to the standard of the University of Missouri, and give to the whites and negroes an equal opportunity for higher education—the whites at the University of Missouri, and the negroes at Lincoln University." Further, the court concluded that the provisions of § 9622 (above quoted) to the effect that negro residents "may attend the university of any adjacent State with their tuition paid, pending the full development of Lincoln University," made it evident "that the Legislature did not intend that negroes and whites should attend the same university in this State." In that view it necessarily followed that the curators of the University of Missouri acted in accordance with the policy of the State in denying petitioner admission to its School of Law upon the sole ground of his race.

In answering petitioner's contention that this discrimination constituted a denial of his constitutional right, the state court has fully recognized the obligation of the State to provide negroes with advantages for higher education substantially equal to the advantages afforded to white students. The State has sought to fulfill that obligation by furnishing equal facilities in separate schools, a method the validity of which has been sustained by our decisions. Respondents' counsel have appropriately emphasized the special solicitude of the State for the higher education of negroes as shown in the establishment of Lincoln University, a state institution well conducted on a plane with the University of Missouri so far as the offered courses are concerned. It is said that Missouri is a pioneer in that field and is the only State in the Union which has established a separate university for negroes on the same basis as the state university for white students. But, commendable as is that action, the fact remains that instruction in law for negroes is not now afforded by the State, either at Lincoln University or elsewhere within the State, and that the State excludes negroes from the advantages of the law school it has established at the University of Missouri.

It is manifest that this discrimination, if not relieved by the provisions we shall presently discuss, would constitute a denial of equal protection. That was the conclusion of the Court of Appeals of Maryland in circumstances substantially similar in that aspect. If there appeared that the State of Maryland had "undertaken the function of education in the law" but had "omitted students of one race from the only adequate provision made for it, and omitted them solely because of their color"; that if those students were to be offered "equal treatment in the performance of the function, they must, at present, be admitted to the one school provided." A provision for scholarships to enable negroes to attend colleges outside the State, mainly for the purpose of professional studies, was found to be inadequate and the question, "whether with aid in any amount it is sufficient to send the negroes outside the State for legal education," the Court of Appeals found it unnecessary to discuss. Accordingly, a writ of mandamus to admit the applicant was issued to the officers and regents of the University of Maryland as the agents of the State entrusted with the conduct of that institution.

The Supreme Court of Missouri in the instant case has distinguished the decision in Maryland upon the grounds—(1) that in Missouri, but not in Maryland, there is "a legislative declaration of a purpose to establish a law school for negroes at Lincoln University whenever necessary or practical"; and (2) that, "pending the establishment of such a school, adequate provision has been made for the legal education of negro students in recognized schools outside of this State."

As to the first ground, it appears that the policy of establishing a law school at Lincoln University has not yet ripened into an actual establishment, and it cannot be said that a mere declaration of purpose, still unfulfilled, is enough. The provision for legal education at Lincoln is at present entirely lacking. Respondents' counsel urge that if, on the date when petitioner applied for admission to the University of Missouri, he had instead applied to the curators of Lincoln University it would have been their duty to establish a law school; that this "agency of the State," to which he should have applied, was "specifically charged with the mandatory duty to furnish him what he seeks." We do not read the opinion of the Supreme Court as construing the state statute to impose such a "mandatory duty" as the argument seems to assert. The state court quoted the language of § 9618, R. S. Mo. 1929, making it the mandatory duty of the board of curators to establish a law school in Lincoln University "whenever necessary and practicable in their opinion." This qualification of their duty, explicitly stated in the statute, manifestly leaves it to the judgment of the curators to decide when it will be necessary and practicable to establish a law school, and the state court so construed the statute. Emphasizing the discretion of the curators, the court said:

"The statute was enacted in 1921. Since its enactment no negro, not even appellant, has applied to Lincoln University for a law education. This fact demonstrates the wisdom of the legislature in leaving it to the judgment of the board of curators to determine when it would be necessary or practicable to establish a law school for negroes at Lincoln University. Pending that time adequate provision is made for the legal education of negroes in the university of some adjacent State, as heretofore pointed out."

The state court has not held that it would have been the duty of the curators to establish a law school at Lincoln University for the petitioner on his application. Their duty, as the court defined it, would have been either to supply a law school at Lincoln University as provided in § 9618 or to furnish him the opportunity to obtain his legal training in another State as provided in § 9622. Thus the law left the curators free to adopt the latter course. The state court has not ruled or intimated that their failure or refusal to establish a law school for a very few students, still less for one student, would have been an abuse of the discretion with which the curators were entrusted. And, apparently, it was because of that discretion, and of the postponement which its exercise in accordance with the terms of the statute would entail until necessity and practicability appeared, that the state court considered and upheld as adequate the provision for the legal education of negroes, who were citizens of Missouri, in the universities of adjacent States. We may put on one side respondent's contention that there were funds available at Lincoln University for the creation of a law department and the suggestions with respect to the number of instructors who would be needed for that purpose and the cost of supplying them. The president of Lincoln University did not advert to the existence or prospective use of funds for that purpose when he advised petitioner to apply to the State Superintendent of Schools for aid under § 9622. At best, the evidence to which argument as to available funds is addressed admits of conflicting inferences, and the decision of the state court did not hinge on any such matter. In the light of its ruling we must regard the question whether the provision for the legal education in other States of negroes resident in Missouri is sufficient to satisfy the constitutional requirement of equal protection, as the pivot upon which this case turns.

The state court stresses the advantages that are afforded by the law schools of the adjacent States—Kansas, Nebraska, Iowa and Illinois,—which admit non-resident negroes. The court considered that these were schools of high standing where one desiring to practice law in Missouri can get "as sound, comprehensive, valuable legal education" as in the University of Missouri; that the system of education in the former is the same as that in the latter and is designed to give the students a basis for the practice of law in any State where the Anglo-American system of law obtains; that the law school of the University of Missouri does not specialize in Missouri law and that the course of study and the case books used in the five schools are substantially identical. Petitioner insists that for one intending to practice in Missouri there are special advantages in attending a law school there, both in relation to the opportunities for the particular study of Missouri law and for the observation of the local courts, and also in view of the prestige of the Missouri law school among the citizens of the State, his prospective clients. Proceeding with its examination of relative advantages, the state court found that the difference in distances to be traveled afforded no substantial ground of complaint and that there was an adequate appropriation to meet the full tuition fees which petitioner would have to pay.

We think that these matters are beside the point. The basic consideration is not as to what sort of opportunities other States provide, or whether they are as good as those in Missouri, but as to what opportunities Missouri itself furnishes to white students and denies to negroes solely upon the ground of color. The admissibility of laws separating the races in the enjoyment of privileges afforded by the State rests wholly upon the equality of the privileges which the laws give to the separated groups within the State. The question here is not of a duty of the State to supply legal training, or of the quality of the training which it does supply, but of its duty when it provides such training to furnish it to the residents of the State upon the basis of an equality of right. By the operation of the laws of Missouri a privilege has been created for white law students which is denied to negroes by reason of their race. The white resident is afforded legal education within the State; the negro resident having the same qualifications is refused it there and must go outside the State to obtain it. That is a denial of the equality of legal right to the enjoyment of the privilege which the State has set up, and the provision for the payment of tuition fees in another State does not remove the discrimination.

The equal protection of the laws is "a pledge of the protection of equal laws." Manifestly, the obligation of the State to give the protection of equal laws can be performed only where its laws operate, that is, within its own jurisdiction. It is there that the equality of legal right must be maintained. That obligation is imposed by the Constitution upon the States severally as governmental entities—each responsible for its own laws establishing the rights and duties of persons within its borders. It is an obligation the burden of which cannot be cast by one State upon another, and no State can be excused from performance by what another State may do or fail to do. That separate responsibility of each State within its own sphere is of the essence of statehood maintained under our dual system. It seems to be implicit in respondents' argument that if other States did not provide courses for legal education, it would nevertheless be the constitutional duty of Missouri when it supplied such courses for white students to make equivalent provision for negroes. But that plain duty would exist because it rested upon the State independently of the action of other States. We find it impossible to conclude that what otherwise would be an unconstitutional discrimination, with respect to the legal right to the enjoyment of opportunities within the State, can be justified by requiring resort to opportunities elsewhere. That resort may mitigate the inconvenience of the discrimination but cannot serve to validate it.

Nor can we regard the fact that there is but a limited demand in Missouri for the legal education of negroes as excusing the discrimination in favor of whites. We had occasion to consider a cognate question in the case of *McCabe* v. *Atchison, T. & S. F. Ry. Co.* There the argument was advanced, in relation to the provision by a carrier of sleeping cars, dining and chair cars, that the limited demand by negroes justified the State in permitting the furnishing of such accommodations exclusively for white persons. We found that argument to be without merit. It made, we said, the constitutional right "depend upon the number of persons who may be discriminated against, whereas the essence of the constitutional right is that it is a personal one. Whether or not particular facilities shall be provided may doubtless be conditioned upon there being a reasonable demand therefor, but, if facilities are provided, substantial equality of treatment of persons traveling under like conditions cannot be refused. It is the individual who is entitled to the equal protection of the laws, and if he is denied by a common carrier, acting in the matter under the authority of a state law, a facility or convenience in the course of his journey which under substantially the same circumstances is furnished to another traveler, he may properly complain that his constitutional privilege has been invaded."

Here, petitioner's right was a personal one. It was as an individual that he was entitled to the equal protection of the laws, and the State was bound to furnish him within its borders facilities for legal education substantially equal to those which the State there afforded for persons of the white race, whether or not other negroes sought the same opportunity.

It is urged, however, that the provision for tuition outside the State is a temporary one—that it is intended to operate merely pending the establishment of a law department for negroes at Lincoln University. While in that sense the discrimination may be termed temporary, it may nevertheless continue for an indefinite period by reason of the discretion given to the curators of Lincoln University and the alternative of arranging for tuition in other States, as permitted by the state law as construed by the state court, so long as the curators find it unnecessary and impracticable to provide facilities for the legal instruction of negroes within the State. In that view, we cannot regard the discrimination as excused by what is called its temporary character.

We do not find that the decision of the state court turns on any procedural question. The action was for mandamus, but it does not appear that the remedy would have been deemed inappropriate if the asserted federal right had been sustained. In that situation the remedy by mandamus was found to be a proper one in *University of Maryland* v. *Murray*. In the instant case, the state court did note that petitioner had not applied to the management of Lincoln University for legal training. But, as we have said, the state court did not rule that it would have been the duty of the curators to grant such an application, but on the contrary took the view, as we understand it, that the curators were entitled under the state law to refuse such an application and in its stead to provide for petitioner's tuition in an adjacent State. That conclusion presented the federal question as to the constitutional adequacy of such a provision while equal opportunity for legal training within the State was not furnished, and this federal question the state court entertained and passed upon. We must conclude that in so doing the court denied the federal right which petitioner set up and the question as to the correctness of that decision is before us. We are of the opinion that the ruling was error, and that petitioner was entitled to be admitted to the law school of the State University in the absence of other and proper provision for his legal training within the State.

The judgment of the Supreme Court of Missouri is reversed and the cause is remanded for further proceedings not inconsistent with this opinion.

Separate opinion of Mr. Justice McReynolds.

Considering the disclosures of the record, the Supreme Court of Missouri arrived at a tenable conclusion and its judgment should be affirmed. That court well understood the grave difficulties of the situation and rightly refused to upset the settled legislative policy of the State by directing a mandamus.

In *Cumming* v. *Richmond County Board of Education,* this Court through Mr. Justice Harlan declared—"The education of the people in schools maintained by state taxation is a matter belonging to the respective States, and any interference on the part of Federal authority with the management of such schools cannot be justified except in the case of a clear and unmistakable disregard of rights secured by the supreme law of the land." *Gong Lum* v. *Rice*—opinion by Mr. Chief Justice Taft— asserts: "The right and power of the state to regulate the method of providing for the education of its youth at public expense is clear."

For a long time Missouri has acted upon the view that the best interest of her people demands separation of whites and negroes in schools. Under the opinion just announced, I presume she may abandon her law school and thereby disadvantage her white citizens without improving petitioner's opportunities for legal instruction; or she may break down the settled practice concerning separate schools and thereby, as indicated by experience, damnify both races. Whether by some other course it may be possible for her to avoid condemnation is matter for conjecture.

The State has offered to provide the negro petitioner opportunity for study of the law–if perchance that is the thing really desired—by paying his tuition at some nearby school of good standing. This is far from unmistakable disregard of his rights and in the circumstances is enough to satisfy any reasonable demand for specialized training. It appears that never before has a negro applied for admission to the Law School and none has ever asked that Lincoln University provide legal instruction.

The problem presented obviously is a difficult and highly practical one. A fair effort to solve it has been made by offering adequate opportunity for study when sought in good faith. The State should not be unduly hampered through theorization inadequately restrained by experience.

This proceeding commenced in April, 1936. Petitioner then twenty-four years old asked mandamus to compel his admission to the University in September, 1936, notwithstanding plain legislative inhibition. Mandamus is not a writ of right but is granted only in the court's discretion upon consideration of all the circumstances.

The Supreme Court of Missouri did not consider the propriety of granting the writ under the theory of the law now accepted here. That, of course, will be matter open for its consideration upon return of the cause.

Mr. Justice Butler concurs in the above views.

Sipuel v. Oklahoma
332 U. S. 631   1948

Per Curiam.

On January 14, 1946, the petitioner, a Negro, concededly qualified to receive the professional legal education offered by the State, applied for admission to the School of Law of the University of Oklahoma, the only institution for legal education supported and maintained by the taxpayers of the State of Oklahoma. Petitioner's application for admission was denied, solely because of her color.

Petitioner then made application for a writ of mandamus in the District Court of Cleveland County, Oklahoma. The writ of mandamus was refused, and the Supreme Court of the State of Oklahoma affirmed the judgment of the District Court. We brought the case here for review.

The petitioner is entitled to secure legal education afforded by a state institution. To this time, it has been denied her although during the same period many white applicants have been afforded legal education by the State. The State must provide it for her in conformity with the equal protection clause of the Fourteenth Amendment and provide it as soon as it does for applicants of any other group.

The judgment of the Supreme Court of Oklahoma is reversed and the cause is remanded to that court for proceedings not inconsistent with this opinion.

The mandate shall issue forthwith.

Sweatt v. Painter

339 U. S. 629   1950

Mr. Chief Justice Vinson delivered the opinion of the Court.

This case and *McLaurin* v. *Oklahoma State Regents* present different aspects of this general question: To what extent does the Equal Protection Clause of the Fourteenth Amendment limit the power of a state to distinguish between students of different races in professional and graduate education in a state university? Broader issues have been urged for our consideration, but we adhere to the principle of deciding constitutional questions only in the context of the particular case before the Court. We have frequently reiterated that this Court will decide constitutional questions only when necessary to the disposition of the case at hand, and that such decisions will be drawn as narrowly as possible. Because of this traditional reluctance to extend constitutional interpretations to situations or facts which are not before the Court, much of the excellent research and detailed argument presented in these cases is unnecessary to their disposition.

In the instant case, petitioner filed an application for admission to the University of Texas Law School for the February, 1946 term. His application was rejected solely because he is a Negro. Petitioner thereupon brought this suit for mandamus against the appropriate school officials, respondents here, to compel his admission. At that time, there was no law school in Texas which admitted Negroes.

The state trial court recognized that the action of the State in denying petitioner the opportunity to gain a legal education while granting it to others deprived him of the equal protection of the laws guaranteed by the Fourteenth Amendment. The court did not grant the relief requested, however, but continued the case for six months to allow the State to supply substantially equal facilities. At the expiration of the six months, in December, 1946, the court denied the writ on the showing that the authorized university officials had adopted an order calling for the opening of a law school for Negroes the following February. While petitioner's appeal was pending, such a school was made available, but petitioner refused to register therein. The Texas Court of Civil Appeals set aside the trial court's judgment and ordered the cause "remanded generally to the trial court for further proceedings without prejudice to the rights of any party to this suit."

On remand, a hearing was held on the issue of the equality of the educational facilities at the newly established school as compared with the University of Texas Law School. Finding that the new school offered petitioner "privileges, advantages, and opportunities for the study of law substantially equivalent to those offered by the State to white students at the University of Texas," the trial court denied mandamus. The Court of Civil Appeals affirmed. Petitioner's application for a writ of error was denied by the Texas Supreme Court. We granted certiorari because of the manifest importance of the constitutional issues involved.

The University of Texas Law School, from which petitioner was excluded, was staffed by a faculty of sixteen full-time and three part-time professors, some of whom are nationally recognized authorities in their field. Its student body numbered 850. The library contained over 65,000 volumes. Among the other facilities available to the students were a law review, moot court facilities, scholarship funds, and Order of the Coif affiliation. The school's alumni occupy the most distinguished positions in the private practice of the law and in the public life of the State. It may properly be considered one of the nation's ranking law schools.

The law school for Negroes which was to have opened in February, 1947, would have had no independent faculty or library. The teaching was to be carried on by four members of the University of Texas Law School faculty, who were to maintain their offices at the University of Texas while teaching at both institutions. Few of the 10,000 volumes ordered for the library had arrived; nor was there any full-time librarian. The school lacked accreditation.

Since the trial of this case, respondents report the opening of a law school at the Texas State University for Negroes. It is apparently on the road to full accreditation. It has a faculty of five full-time professors; a student body of 23; a library of some 16,500 volumes serviced by a full-time staff; a practice court and legal aid association; and one alumnus who has become a member of the Texas Bar.

Whether the University of Texas Law School is compared with the original or the new law school for Negroes, we cannot find substantial equality in the educational opportunities offered white and Negro law students by the State. In terms of number of the faculty, variety of courses and opportunity for specialization, size of the student body, scope of the library, availability of law review and similar activities, the University of Texas Law School is superior. What is more important, the University of Texas Law School possesses to a far greater degree those qualities which are incapable of objective measurement but which make for greatness in a law school. Such qualities, to name but a few, include reputation of the faculty, experience of the administration, position and influence of the alumni, standing in the community, traditions and prestige. It is difficult to believe that one who had a free choice between these law schools would consider the question close.

Moreover, although the law is a highly learned profession, we are well aware that it is an intensely practical one. The law school, the proving ground for legal learning and practice, cannot be effective in isolation from the individuals and institutions with which the law interacts. Few students and no one who has practiced law would choose to study in an academic vacuum, removed from the interplay of ideas and the exchange of views with which the law is concerned. The law school to which Texas is willing to admit petitioner excludes from its student body members of the racial groups which number 85% of the population of the State and include most of the lawyers, witnesses, jurors, judges and other officials with whom petitioner will inevitably be dealing when he becomes a member of the Texas Bar. With such a substantial and significant segment of society excluded, we cannot conclude that the education offered petitioner is substantially equal to that which he would receive if admitted to the University of Texas Law School.

It may be argued that excluding petitioner from that school is no different from excluding white students from the new law school. This contention overlooks realities. It is unlikely that a member of a group so decisively in the majority, attending a school with rich traditions and prestige which only a history of consistently maintained excellence could command, would claim that the opportunities afforded him for legal education were unequal to those held open to petitioner. That such a claim, if made, would be dishonored by the State, is no answer. "Equal protection of the laws is not achieved through indiscriminate imposition of inequalities."

It is fundamental that these cases concern rights which are personal and present. This Court has stated unanimously that "The State must provide [legal education] for [petitioner] in conformity with the equal protection clause of the Fourteenth Amendment and provide it as soon as it does for applicants of any other group." That case "did not present the issue whether a state might not satisfy the equal protection clause of the Fourteenth Amendment by establishing a separate law school for Negroes." In *Missouri ex rel. Gaines* v. *Canada* the Court, speaking through Chief Justice Hughes, declared that "petitioner's right was a personal one. It was as an individual that he was entitled to the equal protection of the laws, and the State was bound to furnish him within its borders facilities for legal education substantially equal to those which the State there afforded for persons of the white race, whether or not other negroes sought the same opportunity." These are the only cases in this Court which present the issue of the constitutional validity of race distinctions in state-supported graduate and professional education.

In accordance with these cases, petitioner may claim his full constitutional right: legal education equivalent to that offered by the State to students of other races. Such education is not available to him in a separate law school as offered by the State. We cannot, therefore, agree with respondents that the doctrine of *Plessy* v. *Ferguson* requires affirmance of the judgment below. Nor need we reach petitioner's contention that *Plessy* v. *Ferguson* should be reexamined in the light of contemporary knowledge respecting the purposes of the Fourteenth Amendment and the effects of racial segregation.

We hold that the Equal Protection Clause of the Fourteenth Amendment requires that petitioner be admitted to the University of Texas Law School. The judgment is reversed and the cause is remanded for proceedings not inconsistent with this opinion.

McLaurin v. Oklahoma State Regents
339 U. S. 637   1950

Mr. Chief Justice Vinson delivered the opinion of the Court.

In this case, we are faced with the question whether a state may, after admitting a student to graduate instruction in its state university, afford him different treatment from other students solely because of his race. We decide only this issue.

Appellant is a Negro citizen of Oklahoma. Possessing a Master's Degree, he applied for admission to the University of Oklahoma in order to pursue studies and courses leading to a Doctorate in Education. At that time, his application was denied, solely because of his race. The school authorities were required to exclude him by the Oklahoma statutes which made it a misdemeanor to maintain or operate, teach or attend a school at which both whites and Negroes are enrolled or taught. Appellant filed a complaint requesting injunctive relief, alleging that the action of the school authorities and the statutes upon which their action was based were unconstitutional and deprived him of the equal protection of the laws. Citing our decisions in *Missouri ex rel. Gaines* v. *Canada* and *Sipuel* v. *Board of Regents* a statutory three-judge District Court held that the State had a Constitutional duty to provide him with the education he sought as soon as it provided that education for applicants of any other group. It further held that to the extent the Oklahoma statutes denied him admission they were unconstitutional and void. On the assumption, however, that the State would follow the constitutional mandate, the court refused to grant the injunction, retaining jurisdiction of the cause with full power to issue any necessary and proper orders to secure McLaurin the equal protection of the laws.

Following this decision, the Oklahoma legislature amended these statutes to permit the admission of Negroes to institutions of higher learning attended by white students, in cases where such institutions offered courses not available in the Negro schools. The amendment provided, however, that in such cases the program of instruction "shall be given at such colleges or institutions of higher education upon a segregated basis." Appellant was thereupon admitted to the University of Oklahoma Graduate School. In apparent conformity with the amendment, his admission was made subject to "such rules and regulations as to segregation as the President of the University shall consider to afford to Mr. G. W. McLaurin substantially equal educational opportunities as are afforded to other persons seeking the same education in the Graduate College," a condition which does not appear to have been withdrawn. Thus he was required to sit apart at a designated desk in an anteroom adjoining the classroom; to sit at a designated desk on the mezzanine floor of the library, but not to use the desks in the regular reading room; and to sit at a designated table and to eat at a different time from the other students in the school cafeteria.

To remove these conditions, appellant filed a motion to modify the order and judgment of the District Court. That court held that such treatment did not violate the provisions of the Fourteenth Amendment and denied the motion. This appeal followed.

In the interval between the decision of the court below and the hearing in this Court, the treatment afforded appellant was altered. For some time, the section of the classroom in which appellant sat was surrounded by a rail on which there was a sign stating, "Reserved For Colored," but these have been removed. He is now assigned to a seat in the classroom in a row specified for colored students; he is assigned to a table in the library on the main floor; and he is permitted to eat at the same time in the cafeteria as other students, although here again he is assigned to a special table.

It is said that the separations imposed by the State in this case are in form merely nominal. McLaurin uses the same classroom, library and cafeteria as students of other races; there is no indication that the seats to which he is assigned in these rooms have any disadvantage of location. He may wait in line in the cafeteria and there stand and talk with his fellow students, but while he eats he must remain apart.

These restrictions were obviously imposed in order to comply, as nearly as could be, with the statutory requirements of Oklahoma. But they signify that the State, in administering the facilities it affords for professional and graduate study, sets McLaurin apart from the other students. The result is that appellant is handicapped in his pursuit of effective graduate instruction. Such restrictions impair and inhibit his ability to study, to engage in discussions and exchange views with other students, and, in general, to learn his profession.

Our society grows increasingly complex, and our need for trained leaders increases correspondingly. Appellant's case represents, perhaps, the epitome of that need, for he is attempting to obtain an advanced degree in education, to become, by definition, a leader and trainer of others. Those who will come under his guidance and influence must be directly affected by the education he receives. Their own education and development will necessarily suffer to the extent that his training is unequal to that of his classmates. State-imposed restrictions which produce such inequalities cannot be sustained.

It may be argued that appellant will be in no better position when these restrictions are removed, for he may still be set apart by his fellow students. This we think irrelevant. There is a vast difference—a Constitutional difference—between restrictions imposed by the state which prohibit the intellectual commingling of students, and the refusal of individuals to commingle where the state presents no such bar. The removal of the state restrictions will not necessarily abate individual and group predilections, prejudices and choices. But at the very least, the state will not be depriving appellant of the opportunity to secure acceptance by his fellow students on his own merits.

We conclude that the conditions under which this appellant is required to receive his education deprive him of his personal and present right to the equal protection of the laws. We hold that under these circumstances the Fourteenth Amendment precludes differences in treatment by the state based upon race. Appellant, having been admitted to a state-supported graduate school, must receive the same treatment at the hands of the state as students of other races. The judgment is

Reversed.

Brown v. Board of Education
347 U. S. 483   1954

Mr. Chief Justice Warren delivered the opinion of the Court.

These cases come to us from the States of Kansas, South Carolina, Virginia, and Delaware. They are premised on different facts and different local conditions, but a common legal question justifies their consideration together in this consolidated opinion.

In each of the cases, minors of the Negro race, through their legal representatives, seek the aid of the courts in obtaining admission to the public schools of their community on a nonsegregated basis. In each instance, they had been denied admission to schools attended by white children under laws requiring or permitting segregation according to race. This segregation was alleged to deprive the plaintiffs of the equal protection of the laws under the Fourteenth Amendment. In each of the cases other than the Delaware case, a three-judge federal district court denied relief to the plaintiffs on the so-called "separate but equal" doctrine announced by this Court in *Plessy* v. *Ferguson*. Under that doctrine, equality of treatment is accorded when the races are provided substantially equal facilities, even though these facilities be separate. In the Delaware case, the Supreme Court of Delaware adhered to that doctrine, but ordered that the plaintiffs be admitted to the white schools because of their superiority to the Negro schools.

The plaintiffs contend that segregated public schools are not "equal" and cannot be made "equal," and that hence they are deprived of the equal protection of the laws. Because of the obvious importance of the question presented, the Court took jurisdiction. Argument was heard in the 1952 Term, and reargument was heard this Term on certain questions propounded by the Court.

Reargument was largely devoted to the circumstances surrounding the adoption of the Fourteenth Amendment in 1868. It covered exhaustively consideration of the Amendment in Congress, ratification by the states, then existing practices in racial segregation, and the views of proponents and opponents of the Amendment. This discussion and our own investigation convince us that, although these sources cast some light, it is not enough to resolve the problem with which we are faced. At best, they are inconclusive. The most avid proponents of the post-War Amendments undoubtedly intended them to remove all legal distinctions among "all persons born or naturalized in the United States." Their opponents, just as certainly, were antagonistic to both the letter and the spirit of the Amendments and wished them to have the most limited effect. What others in Congress and the state legislatures had in mind cannot be determined with any degree of certainty.

An additional reason for the inconclusive nature of the Amendment's history, with respect to segregated schools, is the status of public education at that time. In the South, the movement toward free common schools, supported by general taxation, had not yet taken hold. Education of white children was largely in the hands of private groups. Education of Negroes was almost non-existent, and practically all of the race were illiterate. In fact, any education of Negroes was forbidden by law in some states. Today, in contrast, many Negroes have achieved outstanding success in the arts and sciences as well as in the business and professional world. It is true that public school education at the time of the Amendment had advanced further in the North, but the effect of the Amendment on Northern States was generally ignored in the congressional debates. Even in the North, the conditions of public education did not approximate those existing today. The curriculum was usually rudimentary; ungraded schools were common in rural areas; the school term was but three months a year in many states; and compulsory school attendance was virtually unknown. As a consequence, it is not surprising that there should be so little in the history of the Fourteenth Amendment relating to its intended effect on public education.

In the first cases in this Court construing the Fourteenth Amendment, decided shortly after its adoption, the Court interpreted it as proscribing all state-imposed discriminations against the Negro race. The doctrine of "separate but equal" did not make its appearance in this Court until 1896 in the case of *Plessy* v. *Ferguson* involving not education but transportation. American courts have since labored with the doctrine for over half a century. In this Court, there have been six cases involving the "separate but equal" doctrine in the field of public education. In *Cumming* v. *County Board of Education* and *Gong Lum* v. *Rice* the validity of the doctrine itself was not challenged. In more recent cases, all on the graduate school level, inequality was found in that specific benefits enjoyed by white students were denied to Negro students of the same educational qualifications. In none of these cases was it necessary to re-examine the doctrine to grant relief to the Negro plaintiff. And in *Sweatt* v. *Painter* the Court expressly reserved decision on the question whether *Plessy* v. *Ferguson* should be held inapplicable to public education.

In the instant cases, that question is directly presented. Here, unlike *Sweatt* v. *Painter,* there are findings below that the Negro and white schools involved have been equalized, or are being equalized, with respect to buildings, curricula, qualifications and salaries of teachers, and other "tangible" factors. Our decision, therefore, cannot turn on merely a comparison of these tangible factors in the Negro and white schools involved in each of the cases. We must look instead to the effect of segregation itself on public education.

In approaching this problem, we cannot turn the clock back to 1868 when the Amendment was adopted, or even to 1896 when *Plessy* v. *Ferguson* was written. We must consider public education in the light of its full development and its present place in American life throughout the Nation. Only in this way can it be determined if segregation in public schools deprives these plaintiffs of the equal protection of the laws.

Today, education is perhaps the most important function of state and local governments. Compulsory school attendance laws and the great expenditures for education both demonstrate our recognition of the importance of education to our democratic society. It is required in the performance of our most basic public responsibilities, even service in the armed forces. It is the very foundation of good citizenship. Today it is a principal instrument in awakening the child to cultural values, in preparing him for later professional training, and in helping him to adjust normally to his environment. In these days, it is doubtful that any child may reasonably be expected to succeed in life if he is denied the opportunity of an education. Such an opportunity, where the state has undertaken to provide it, is a right which must be made available to all on equal terms.

We come then to the question presented: Does segregation of children in public schools solely on the basis of race, even though the physical facilities and other "tangible" factors may be equal, deprive the children of the minority group of equal educational opportunities? We believe that it does.

In *Sweatt* v. *Painter* in finding that a segregated law school for Negroes could not provide them equal educational opportunities, this Court relied in large part on "those qualities which are incapable of objective measurement but which make for greatness in a law school." In *McLaurin* v. *Oklahoma State Regents* the Court, in requiring that a Negro admitted to a white graduate school be treated like all other students, again resorted to intangible considerations: ". . . his ability to study, to engage in discussions and exchange views with other students, and, in general, to learn his profession." Such considerations apply with added force to children in grade and high schools. To separate them from others of similar age and qualifications solely because of their race generates a feeling of inferiority as to their status in the community that may affect their hearts and minds in a way unlikely ever to be undone. The effect of this separation on their educational opportunities was well stated by a finding in the Kansas case by a court which nevertheless felt compelled to rule against the Negro plaintiffs:

"Segregation of white and colored children in public schools has a detrimental effect upon the colored children. The impact is greater when it has the sanction of the law; for the policy of separating the races is usually interpreted as denoting the inferiority of the negro group. A sense of inferiority affects the motivation of a child to learn. Segregation with the sanction of law, therefore, has a tendency to [retard] the educational and mental development of negro children and to deprive them of some of the benefits they would receive in a racial[ly] integrated school system."

Whatever may have been the extent of psychological knowledge at the time of *Plessy* v. *Ferguson,* this finding is amply supported by modern authority. Any language in *Plessy* v. *Ferguson* contrary to this finding is rejected.

We conclude that in the field of public education the doctrine of "separate but equal" has no place. Separate educational facilities are inherently unequal. Therefore, we hold that the plaintiffs and others similarly situated for whom the actions have been brought are, by reason of the segregation complained of, deprived of the equal protection of the laws guaranteed by the Fourteenth Amendment. This disposition makes unnecessary any discussion whether such segregation also violates the Due Process Clause of the Fourteenth Amendment.

Because these are class actions, because of the wide applicability of this decision, and because of the great variety of local conditions, the formulation of decrees in these cases presents problems of considerable complexity. On reargument, the consideration of appropriate relief was necessarily subordinated to the primary question—the constitutionality of segregation in public education. We have now announced that such segregation is a denial of the equal protection of the laws. In order that we may have the full assistance of the parties in formulating decrees, the cases will be restored to the docket, and the parties are requested to present further argument on Questions 4 and 5 previously propounded by the Court for the reargument this Term. The Attorney General of the United States is again invited to participate. The Attorneys General of the states requiring or permitting segregation in public education will also be permitted to appear as *amici curiae* upon request to do so by September 15, 1954, and submission of briefs by October 1, 1954.

Bolling v. Sharpe
347 U. S. 497   1954

Mr. Chief Justice Warren delivered the opinion of the Court.

This case challenges the validity of segregation in the public schools of the District of Columbia. The petitioners, minors of the Negro race, allege that such segregation deprives them of due process of law under the Fifth Amendment. They were refused admission to a public school attended by white children solely because of their race. They sought the aid of the District Court for the District of Columbia in obtaining admission. That court dismissed their complaint. The Court granted a writ of certiorari before judgment in the Court of Appeals because of the importance of the constitutional question presented.

We have this day held that the Equal Protection Clause of the Fourteenth Amendment prohibits the states from maintaining racially segregated public schools. The legal problem in the District of Columbia is somewhat different, however. The Fifth Amendment, which is applicable in the District of Columbia, does not contain an equal protection clause as does the Fourteenth Amendment which applies only to the states. But the concepts of equal protection and due process, both stemming from our American ideal of fairness, are not mutually exclusive. The "equal protection of the laws" is a more explicit safeguard of prohibited unfairness than "due process of law," and, therefore, we do not imply that the two are always interchangeable phrases. But, as this Court has recognized, discrimination may be so unjustifiable as to be violative of due process.

Classifications based solely upon race must be scrutinized with particular care, since they are contrary to our traditions and hence constitutionally suspect. As long ago as 1896, this Court declared the principle "that the Constitution of the United States, in its present form, forbids, so far as civil and political rights are concerned, discrimination by the General Government, or by the States, against any citizen because of his race." And in *Buchanan* v. *Warley* the Court held that a statute which limited the right of a property owner to convey his property to a person of another race was, as an unreasonable discrimination, a denial of due process of law.

Although the Court has not assumed to define "liberty" with any great precision, that term is not confined to mere freedom from bodily restraint. Liberty under law extends to the full range of conduct which the individual is free to pursue, and it cannot be restricted except for a proper governmental objective. Segregation in public education is not reasonably related to any proper governmental objective, and thus it imposes on Negro children of the District of Columbia a burden that constitutes an arbitrary deprivation of their liberty in violation of the Due Process Clause.

In view of our decision that the Constitution prohibits the states from maintaining racially segregated public schools, it would be unthinkable that the same Constitution would impose a lesser duty on the Federal Government. We hold that racial segregation in the public schools of the District of Columbia is a denial of the due process of law guaranteed by the Fifth Amendment to the Constitution.

For the reasons set out in *Brown* v. *Board of Education,* this case will be restored to the docket for reargument on Questions 4 and 5 previously propounded by the Court.

Brown v. Board of Education
349 U. S. 294   1955

Mr. Chief Justice Warren delivered the opinion of the Court.

These cases were decided on May 17, 1954. The opinions of that date, declaring the fundamental principle that racial discrimination in public education is unconstitutional, are incorporated herein by reference. All provisions of federal, state, or local law requiring or permitting such discrimination must yield to this principle. There remains for consideration the manner in which relief is to be accorded.

Because these cases arose under different local conditions and their disposition will involve a variety of local problems, we requested further argument on the question of relief. In view of the nationwide importance of the decision, we invited the Attorney General of the United States and the Attorneys General of all states requiring or permitting racial discrimination in public education to present their views on that question. The parties, the United States, and the States of Florida, North Carolina, Arkansas, Oklahoma, Maryland, and Texas filed briefs and participated in the oral argument.

These presentations were informative and helpful to the Court in its consideration of the complexities arising from the transition to a system of public education freed of racial discrimination. The presentations also demonstrated that substantial steps to eliminate racial discrimination in public schools have already been taken, not only in some of the communities in which these cases arose, but in some of the states appearing as *amici curiae,* and in other states as well. Substantial progress has been made in the District of Columbia and in the communities in Kansas and Delaware involved in this litigation. The defendants in the cases coming to us from South Carolina and Virginia are awaiting the decision of this Court concerning relief.

Full implementation of these constitutional principles may require solution of varied local school problems. School authorities have the primary responsibility for elucidating, assessing, and solving these problems; courts will have to consider whether the action of school authorities constitutes good faith implementation of the governing constitutional principles. Because of their proximity to local conditions and the possible need for further hearings, the courts which originally heard these cases can best perform this judicial appraisal. Accordingly, we believe it appropriate to remand the cases to those courts.

In fashioning and effectuating the decrees, the courts will be guided by equitable principles. Traditionally, equity has been characterized by a practical flexibility in shaping its remedies and by a facility for adjusting and reconciling public and private needs. These cases call for the exercise of these traditional attributes of equity power. At stake is the personal interest of the plaintiffs in admission to public schools as soon as practicable on a nondiscriminatory basis. To effectuate this interest may call for elimination of a variety of obstacles in making the transition to school systems operated in accordance with the constitutional principles set forth in our May 17, 1954, decision. Courts of equity may properly take into account the public interest in the elimination of such obstacles in a systematic and effective manner. But it should go without saying that the vitality of these constitutional principles cannot be allowed to yield simply because of disagreement with them.

While giving weight to these public and private considerations, the courts will require that the defendants make a prompt and reasonable start toward full compliance with our May 17, 1954 ruling. Once such a start has been made, the courts may find that additional time is necessary to carry out the ruling in an effective manner. The burden rests upon the defendants to establish that such time is necessary in the public interest and is consistent with good faith compliance at the earliest practicable date. To that end, the courts may consider problems related to administration, arising from the physical condition of the school plant, the school transportation system, personnel, revision of school districts and attendance areas into compact units to achieve a system of determining admission to the public schools on a nonracial basis, and revision of local laws and regulations which may be necessary in solving the foregoing problems. They will also consider the adequacy of any plans the defendants may propose to meet these problems and to effectuate a transition to a racially nondiscriminatory school system. During this period of transition, the courts will retain jurisdiction of these cases.

The judgments below, except that in the Delaware case, are accordingly reversed and the cases are remanded to the District Courts to take such proceedings and enter such orders and decrees consistent with this opinion as are necessary and proper to admit to public schools on a racially nondiscriminatory basis with all deliberate speed the parties to these cases. The judgment in the Delaware case—ordering the immediate admission of the plaintiffs to schools previously attended only by white children—is affirmed on the basis of the principles stated in our May 17, 1954, opinion, but the case is remanded to the Supreme Court of Delaware for such further proceedings as that Court may deem necessary in light of this opinion.

Cooper v. Aaron
358 U. S. 1   1958

Opinion of the Court by the Chief Justice, Mr. Justice Black, Mr. Justice Frankfurter, Mr. Justice Douglas, Mr. Justice Burton, Mr. Justice Clark, Mr. Justice Harlan, Mr. Justice Brennan, and Mr. Justice Whittaker.

As this case reaches us it raises questions of the highest importance to the maintenance of our federal system of government. It necessarily involves a claim by the Governor and Legislature of a State that there is no duty on state officials to obey federal court orders resting on this Court's considered interpretation of the United States Constitution. Specifically it involves actions by the Governor and Legislature of Arkansas upon the premise that they are not bound by our holding in *Brown* v. *Board of Education*. That holding was that the Fourteenth Amendment forbids States to use their governmental powers to bar children on racial grounds from attending schools where there is state participation through any arrangement, management, funds or property. We are urged to uphold a suspension of the Little Rock School Board's plan to do away with segregated public schools in Little Rock until state laws and efforts to upset and nullify our holding in *Brown* v. *Board of Education* have been further challenged and tested in the courts. We reject these contentions.

The case was argued before us on September 11, 1958. On the following day we unanimously affirmed the judgment of the Court of Appeals for the Eighth Circuit which had reversed a judgment of the District Court for the Eastern District of Arkansas. The District Court had granted the application of the petitioners, the Little Rock School Board and School Superintendent, to suspend for two and one-half years the operation of the School Board's court-approved desegregation program. In order that the School Board might know, without doubt, its duty in this regard before the opening of school, which had been set for the following Monday, September 15, 1958, we immediately issued the judgment, reserving the expression of our supporting views to a later date. This opinion of all of the members of the Court embodies those views.

The following are the facts and circumstances so far as necessary to show how the legal questions are presented.

On May 17, 1954, this Court decided that enforced racial segregation in the public schools of a State is a denial of the equal protection of the laws enjoined by the Fourteenth Amendment. The Court postponed, pending further argument, formulation of a decree to effectuate this decision. That decree was rendered May 31, 1955. In the formulation of that decree the Court recognized that good faith compliance with the principles declared in *Brown* might in some situations "call for elimination of a variety of obstacles in making the transition to school systems operated in accordance with the constitutional principles set forth in our May 17, 1954, decision." The Court went on to state:

"Courts of equity may properly take into account the public interest in the elimination of such obstacles in a systematic and effective manner. But it should go without saying that the vitality of these constitutional principles cannot be allowed to yield simply because of disagreement with them.

"While giving weight to these public and private considerations, the courts will require that the defendants make a prompt and reasonable start toward full compliance with our May 17, 1954, ruling. Once such a start has been made, the courts may find that additional time is necessary to carry out the ruling in an effective manner. The burden rests upon the defendants to establish that such time is necessary in the public interest and is consistent with good faith compliance at the earliest practicable date. To that end, the courts may consider problems related to administration, arising from the physical condition of the school plant, the school transportation system, personnel, revision of school districts and attendance areas into compact units to achieve a system of determining admission to the public schools on a nonracial basis, and revision of local laws and regulations which may be necessary in solving the foregoing problems."

Under such circumstances, the District Courts were directed to require "a prompt and reasonable start toward full compliance," and to take such action as was necessary to bring about the end of racial segregation in the public schools "with all deliberate speed." Of course, in many locations, obedience to the duty of desegregation would require the immediate general admission of Negro children, otherwise qualified as students for their appropriate classes, at particular schools. On the other hand, a District Court, after analysis of the relevant factors (which, of course, excludes hostility to racial desegregation), might conclude that justification existed for not requiring the present nonsegregated admission of all qualified Negro children. In such circumstances, however, the courts should scrutinize the program of the school authorities to make sure that they had developed arrangements pointed toward the earliest practicable completion of desegregation, and had taken appropriate steps to put their program into effective operation. It was made plain that delay in any guise in order to deny the constitutional rights of Negro children could not be countenanced, and that only a prompt start, diligently and earnestly pursued, to eliminate racial segregation from the public schools could constitute good faith compliance. State authorities were thus duty bound to devote every effort toward initiating desegregation and bringing about the elimination of racial discrimination in the public school system.

On May 20, 1954, three days after the first *Brown* opinion, the Little Rock District School Board adopted, and on May 23, 1954, made public, a statement of policy entitled "Supreme Court Decision—Segregation in Public Schools." In this statement the Board recognized that

"It is our responsibility to comply with Federal Constitutional Requirements and we intend to do so when the Supreme Court of the United States outlines the method to be followed."

Thereafter the Board undertook studies of the administrative problems confronting the transition to a desegregated public school system at Little Rock. It instructed the Superintendent of Schools to prepare a plan for desegregation, and approved such a plan on May 24, 1955, seven days before the second *Brown* opinion. The plan provided for desegregation at the senior high school level (grades 10 through 12) as the first stage.

Desegregation at the junior high and elementary levels was to follow. It was contemplated that desegregation at the high school level would commence in the fall of 1957, and the expectation was that complete desegregation of the school system would be accomplished by 1963. Following the adoption of this plan, the Superintendent of Schools discussed it with a large number of citizen groups in the city. As a result of these discussions, the Board reached the conclusion that "a large majority of the residents" of Little Rock were of "the belief . . . that the Plan, although objectionable in principle," from the point of view of those supporting segregated schools, "was still the best for the interests of all pupils in the District."

Upon challenge by a group of Negro plaintiffs desiring more rapid completion of the desegregation process, the District Court upheld the School Board's plan. The Court of Appeals affirmed. Review of that judgment was not sought here.

While the School Board was thus going forward with its preparation for desegregating the Little Rock school system, other state authorities, in contrast, were actively pursuing a program designed to perpetuate in Arkansas the system of racial segregation which this Court had held violated the Fourteenth Amendment. First came, in November 1956, an amendment to the State Constitution flatly commanding the Arkansas General Assembly to oppose "in every Constitutional manner the Unconstitutional desegregation decisions of May 17, 1954 and May 31, 1955 of the United States Supreme Court," and, through the initiative, a pupil assignment law. Pursuant to this state constitutional command, a law relieving school children from compulsory attendance at racially mixed schools and a law establishing a State Sovereignty Commission were enacted by the General Assembly in February 1957.

The School Board and the Superintendent of Schools nevertheless continued with preparations to carry out the first stage of the desegregation program. Nine Negro children were scheduled for admission in September 1957 to Central High School, which has more than two thousand students. Various administrative measures, designed to assure the smooth transition of this first stage of desegregation, were undertaken.

On September 2, 1957, the day before these Negro students were to enter Central High, the school authorities were met with drastic opposing action on the part of the Governor of Arkansas who dispatched units of the Arkansas National Guard to the Central High School grounds and placed the school "off limits" to colored students. As found by the District Court in subsequent proceedings, the Governor's action had not been requested by the school authorities, and was entirely unheralded. The findings were these:

"Up to this time [September 2], no crowds had gathered about Central High School and no acts of violence or threats of violence in connection with the carrying out of the plan had occurred. Nevertheless, out of an abundance of caution, the school authorities had frequently conferred with the Mayor and Chief of Police of Little Rock about taking appropriate steps by the Little Rock police to prevent any possible disturbances or acts of violence in connection with the attendance of the 9 colored students at Central High School. The Mayor considered that the Little Rock police force could adequately cope with any incidents which might arise at the opening of school. The Mayor, the Chief of Police, and the school authorities made no request to the Governor or any representative of his for State assistance in maintaining peace and order at Central High School. Neither the Governor nor any other official of the State government consulted with the Little Rock authorities about whether the Little Rock police were prepared to cope with any incidents which might arise at the school, about any need for State assistance in maintaining peace and order, or about stationing the Arkansas National Guard at Central High School."

The Board's petition for postponement in this proceeding states: "The effect of that action [of the Governor] was to harden the core of opposition to the Plan and cause many persons who theretofore had reluctantly accepted the Plan to believe there was some power in the State of Arkansas which, when exerted, could nullify the Federal law and permit disobedience of the decree of this [District] Court, and from that date hostility to the Plan was increased and criticism of the officials of the [School] District has become more bitter and unrestrained." The Governor's action caused the School Board to request the Negro students on September 2 not to attend the high school "until the legal dilemma was solved." The next day, September 3, 1957, the Board petitioned the District Court for instructions, and the court, after a hearing, found that the Board's request of the Negro students to stay away from the high school had been made because of the stationing of the military guards by the state authorities. The court determined that this was not a reason for departing from the approved plan, and ordered the School Board and Superintendent to proceed with it.

On the morning of the next day, September 4, 1957, the Negro children attempted to enter the high school but, as the District Court later found, units of the Arkansas National Guard "acting pursuant to the

Governor's order, stood shoulder to shoulder at the school grounds and thereby forcibly prevented the 9 Negro students . . . from entering," as they continued to do every school day during the following three weeks.

That same day, September 4, 1957, the United States Attorney for the Eastern District of Arkansas was requested by the District Court to begin an immediate investigation in order to fix responsibility for the interference with the orderly implementation of the District Court's direction to carry out the desegregation program. Three days later, September 7, the District Court denied a petition of the School Board and the Superintendent of Schools for an order temporarily suspending continuance of the program.

Upon completion of the United States Attorney's investigation, he and the Attorney General of the United States, at the District Court's request, entered the proceedings and filed a petition on behalf of the United States, as *amicus curiae,* to enjoin the Governor of Arkansas and officers of the Arkansas National Guard from further attempts to prevent obedience to the court's order. After hearings on the petition, the District Court found that the School Board's plan had been obstructed by the Governor through the use of National Guard troops, and granted a preliminary injunction on September 20, 1957, enjoining the Governor and the officers of the Guard from preventing the attendance of Negro children at Central High School, and from otherwise obstructing or interfering with the orders of the court in connection with the plan. The National Guard was then withdrawn from the school.

The next school day was Monday, September 23, 1957. The Negro children entered the high school that morning under the protection of the Little Rock Police Department and members of the Arkansas State Police. But the officers caused the children to be removed from the school during the morning because they had difficulty controlling a large and demonstrating crowd which had gathered at the high school. On September 25, however, the President of the United States dispatched federal troops to Central High School and admission of the Negro students to the school was thereby effected. Regular army troops continued at the high school until November 27, 1957. They were then replaced by federalized National Guardsmen who remained throughout the balance of the school year. Eight of the Negro students remained in attendance at the school throughout the school year.

We come now to the aspect of the proceedings presently before us. On February 20, 1958, the School Board and the Superintendent of Schools filed a petition in the District Court seeking a postponement of their program for desegregation. Their position in essence was that because of extreme public hostility, which they stated had been engendered largely by the official attitudes and actions of the Governor and the Legislature, the maintenance of a sound educational program at Central High School, with the Negro students in attendance, would be impossible. The Board therefore proposed that the Negro students already admitted to the school be withdrawn and sent to segregated schools, and that all further steps to carry out the Board's desegregation program be postponed for a period later suggested by the Board to be two and one-half years.

After a hearing the District Court granted the relief requested by the Board. Among other things the court found that the past year at Central High School had been attended by conditions of "chaos, bedlam and turmoil"; that there were "repeated incidents of more or less serious violence directed against the Negro students and their property"; that there was "tension and unrest among the school administrators, the class-room teachers, the pupils, and the latters' parents, which inevitably had an adverse effect upon the educational program"; that a school official was threatened with violence; that a "serious financial burden" had been cast on the School District; that the education of the students had suffered "and under existing conditions will continue to suffer"; that the Board would continue to need "military assistance or its equivalent"; that the local police department would not be able "to detail enough men to afford the necessary protection"; and that the situation was "intolerable."

The District Court's judgment was dated June 20, 1958. The Negro respondents appealed to the Court of Appeals for the Eighth Circuit and also sought there a stay of the District Court's judgment. At the same time they filed a petition for certiorari in this Court asking us to review the District Court's judgment without awaiting the disposition of their appeal to the Court of Appeals, or of their petition to that court for a stay. That we declined to do. The Court of Appeals did not act on the petition for a stay, but, on August 18, 1958, after convening in special session on August 4 and hearing the appeal, reversed the District Court. On August 21, 1958, the Court of Appeals stayed its mandate to permit the School Board to petition this Court for certiorari. Pending the filing of the School Board's petition for certiorari, the Negro respondents, on August 23, 1958, applied to Mr. Justice Whittaker, as Circuit Justice for the Eighth Circuit, to stay the order of the Court of Appeals withholding its own mandate and also to stay the District Court's judgment. In view of the nature of the motions, he referred them to the entire Court. Recognizing the vital importance of a decision of the issues in time to permit arrangements to be made for the 1958–1959 school year we convened in Special Term on August 28, 1958, and heard oral argument on the respondents' motions, and also argument of the Solicitor General who, by invitation, appeared for the United States as *amicus curiae,* and asserted that the Court of Appeals' judgment was clearly correct on the merits, and urged that we vacate its stay forthwith. Finding that respondents' application necessarily involved consideration of the merits of the litigation, we entered an order which deferred decision upon the motions pending the disposition of the School Board's petition for certiorari, and fixed September 8, 1958, as the day on or before which such petition might be filed, and September 11, 1958, for oral argument upon the petition. The petition for certiorari, duly filed, was granted in open Court on September 11, 1958, and further arguments were had, the Solicitor General again urging the correctness of the judgment of the Court of Appeals. On September 12, 1958, as already mentioned, we unanimously affirmed the judgment of the Court of Appeals in the *per curiam* opinion set forth in the margin at the outset of this opinion.

In affirming the judgment of the Court of Appeals which reversed the District Court we have accepted without reservation the position of the School Board, the Superintendent of Schools, and their counsel that they displayed entire good faith in the conduct of these proceedings and in dealing with the unfortunate and distressing sequence of events which has been outlined. We likewise have accepted the findings of the District Court as to the conditions at Central High School during the 1957–1958 school year, and also the findings that the educational progress of all the students, white and colored, of that school has suffered and will continue to suffer if the conditions which prevailed last year are permitted to continue.

The significance of these findings, however, is to be considered in light of the fact, indisputably revealed by the record before us, that the conditions they depict are directly traceable to the actions of legislators and executive officials of the State of Arkansas, taken in their official capacities, which reflect their own determination to resist this Court's decision in the *Brown* case and which have brought about violent resistance to that decision in Arkansas. In its petition for certiorari filed in this Court, the

School Board itself describes the situation in this language: "The legislative, executive, and judicial departments of the state government opposed the desegregation of Little Rock schools by enacting laws, calling out troops, making statements villifying federal law and federal courts, and failing to utilize state law enforcement agencies and judicial processes to maintain public peace."

One may well sympathize with the position of the Board in the face of the frustrating conditions which have confronted it, but, regardless of the Board's good faith, the actions of the other state agencies responsible for those conditions compel us to reject the Board's legal position. Had Central High School been under the direct management of the State itself, it could hardly be suggested that those immediately in charge of the school should be heard to assert their own good faith as a legal excuse for delay in implementing the constitutional rights of these respondents, when vindication of those rights was rendered difficult or impossible by the actions of other state officials. The situation here is in no different posture because the members of the School Board and the Superintendent of Schools are local officials; from the point of view of the Fourteenth Amendment, they stand in this litigation as the agents of the State.

The constitutional rights of respondents are not to be sacrificed or yielded to the violence and disorder which have followed upon the actions of the Governor and Legislature. As this Court said some 41 years ago in a unanimous opinion in a case involving another aspect of racial segregation: "It is urged that this proposed segregation will promote the public peace by preventing race conflicts. Desirable as this is, and important as is the preservation of the public peace, this aim cannot be accomplished by laws or ordinances which deny rights created or protected by the Federal Constitution." Thus law and order are not here to be preserved by depriving the Negro children of their constitutional rights. The record before us clearly establishes that the growth of the Board's difficulties to a magnitude beyond its unaided power to control is the product of state action. Those difficulties, as counsel for the Board forthrightly conceded on the oral argument in this Court, can also be brought under control by state action.

The controlling legal principles are plain. The command of the Fourteenth Amendment is that no "State" shall deny to any person within its jurisdiction the equal protection of the laws. "A State acts by its legislative, its executive, or its judicial authorities. It can act in no other way.

The constitutional provision, therefore, must mean that no agency of the State, or of the officers or agents by whom its powers are exerted, shall deny to any person within its jurisdiction the equal protection of the laws. Whoever, by virtue of public position under a State government, . . . denies or takes away the equal protection of the laws, violates the constitutional inhibition; and as he acts in the name and for the State, and is clothed with the State's power, his act is that of the State. This must be so, or the constitutional prohibition has no meaning." Thus the prohibitions of the Fourteenth Amendment extend to all action of the State denying equal protection of the laws; whatever the agency of the State taking the action, or whatever the guise in which it is taken. In short, the constitutional rights of children not to be discriminated against in school admission on grounds of race or color declared by this Court in the *Brown* case can neither be nullified openly and directly by state legislators or state executive or judicial officers, nor nullified indirectly by them through evasive schemes for segregation whether attempted "ingeniously or ingenuously."

What has been said, in the light of the facts developed, is enough to dispose of the case. However, we should answer the premise of the actions of the Governor and Legislature that they are not bound by our holding in the *Brown* case. It is necessary only to recall some basic constitutional propositions which are settled doctrine.

Article VI of the Constitution makes the Constitution the "supreme Law of the Land." In 1803, Chief Justice Marshall, speaking for a unanimous Court, referring to the Constitution as "the fundamental and paramount law of the nation," declared in the notable case of *Marbury* v. *Madison* that "It is emphatically the province and duty of the judicial department to say what the law is." This decision declared the basic principle that the federal judiciary is supreme in the exposition of the law of the Constitution, and that principle has ever since been respected by this Court and the Country as a permanent and indispensable feature of our constitutional system. It follows that the interpretation of the Fourteenth Amendment enunciated by this Court in the *Brown* case is the supreme law of the land, and Art. VI of the Constitution makes it of binding effect on the States "any Thing in the Constitution or Laws of any State to the Contrary notwithstanding." Every state legislator and executive and judicial officer is solemnly committed by oath taken pursuant to Art. VI, cl. 3, "to support this Constitution." Chief Justice Taney, speaking for a unanimous Court in 1859, said that this requirement reflected the framers' "anxiety to preserve it [the Constitution] in full force, in all its powers, and to guard against resistance to or evasion of its authority, on the part of a State. . . ."

No state legislator or executive or judicial officer can war against the Constitution without violating his undertaking to support it. Chief Justice Marshall spoke for a unanimous Court in saying that: "If the legislatures of the several states may, at will, annul the judgments of the courts of the United States, and destroys the rights acquired under those judgments, the constitution itself becomes a solemn mockery. . . ." A Governor who asserts a power to nullify a federal court order is similarly restrained. If he had such power, said Chief Justice Hughes, in 1932, also for a unanimous Court, "it is manifest that the fiat of a state Governor, and not the Constitution of the United States, would be the supreme law of the land; that the restrictions of the Federal Constitution upon the exercise of state power would be but impotent phrases. . . ."

It is, of course, quite true that the responsibility for public education is primarily the concern of the States, but it is equally true that such responsibilities, like all other state activity, must be exercised consistently with federal constitutional requirements as they apply to state action. The Constitution created a government dedicated to equal justice under law. The Fourteenth Amendment embodied and emphasized that ideal. State support of segregated schools through any arrangement, management, funds, or property cannot be squared with the Amendment's command that no State shall deny to any person within its jurisdiction the equal protection of the laws. The right of a student not to be segregated on racial grounds in schools so maintained is indeed so fundamental and pervasive that it is embraced in the concept of due process of law. The basic decision in *Brown* was unanimously reached by this Court only after the case had been briefed and twice argued and the issues had been given the most serious consideration. Since the first *Brown* opinion three new Justices have come to the Court. They are at one with the Justices still on the Court who participated in that basic decision as to its correctness, and that decision is now unanimously reaffirmed. The principles announced in that decision and the obedience of the States to them, according to the command of the Constitution, are indispensable for the protection of the freedoms guaranteed by our fundamental charter for all of us. Our constitutional ideal of equal justice under law is thus made a living truth.

Concurring opinion of Mr. Justice Frankfurter.

While unreservedly participating with my brethren in our joint opinion, I deem it appropriate also to deal individually with the great issue here at stake.

By working together, by sharing in a common effort, men of different minds and tempers, even if they do not reach agreement, acquire understanding and thereby tolerance of their differences. This process was under way in Little Rock. The detailed plan formulated by the Little Rock School Board, in the light of local circumstances, had been approved by the United States District Court in Arkansas as satisfying the requirements of this Court's decree in *Brown* v. *Board of Education*. The Little Rock School Board had embarked on an educational effort "to obtain public acceptance" of its plan. Thus the process of the community's accommodation to new demands of law upon it, the development of habits of acceptance of the right of colored children to the equal protection of the laws guaranteed by the Constitution, had peacefully and promisingly begun. The condition in Little Rock before this process was forcibly impeded by those in control of the government of Arkansas was thus described by the District Court, and these findings of fact have not been controverted:

"14. Up to this time, no crowds had gathered about Central High School and no acts of violence or threats of violence in connection with the carrying out of the plan had occurred. Nevertheless, out of an abundance of caution, the school authorities had frequently conferred with the Mayor and Chief of Police of Little Rock about taking appropriate steps by the Little Rock police to prevent any possible disturbances or acts of violence in connection with the attendance of the 9 colored students at Central High School. The Mayor considered that the Little Rock police force could adequately cope with any incidents which might arise at the opening of school. The Mayor, the Chief of Police, and the school authorities made no request to the Governor or any representative of his for State assistance in maintaining peace and order at Central High School. Neither the Governor nor any other official of the State government consulted with the Little Rock authorities about whether the Little Rock police were prepared to cope with any incidents which might arise at the school, about any need for State assistance in maintaining peace and order, or about stationing the Arkansas National Guard at Central High School."

All this was disrupted by the introduction of the state militia and by other obstructive measures taken by the State. The illegality of these interferences with the constitutional right of Negro children qualified to enter the Central High School is unaffected by whatever action or non-action the Federal Government had seen fit to take. Nor is it neutralized by the undoubted good faith of the Little Rock School Board in endeavoring to discharge its constitutional duty.

The use of force to further obedience to law is in any event a last resort and one not congenial to the spirit of our Nation. But the tragic aspect of this disruptive tactic was that the power of the State was used not to sustain law but as an instrument for thwarting law. The State of Arkansas is thus responsible for disabling one of its subordinate agencies, the Little Rock School Board, from peacefully carrying out the Board's and the State's constitutional duty. Accordingly, while Arkansas is not a formal party in these proceedings and a decree cannot go against the State, it is legally and morally before the Court.

We are now asked to hold that the illegal, forcible interference by the State of Arkansas with the continuance of what the Constitution commands, and the consequences in disorder that it entrained, should be recognized as justification for undoing what the School Board had formulated, what the District Court in 1955 had directed to be carried out, and what was in process of obedience. No explanation that may be offered in support of such a request can obscure the inescapable meaning that law should bow to force. To yield to such a claim would be to enthrone official lawlessness, and lawlessness if not checked is the precursor of anarchy. On the few tragic occasions in the history of the Nation, North and South, when law was forcibly resisted or systematically evaded, it has signalled the breakdown of constitutional processes of government on which ultimately rest the liberties of all. Violent resistance to law cannot be made a legal reason for its suspension without loosening the fabric of our society. What could this mean but to acknowledge that disorder under the aegis of a State has moral superiority over the law of the Constitution? For those in authority thus to defy the law of the land is profoundly subversive not only of our constitutional system but of the presuppositions of a democratic society. The State "must . . . yield to an authority that is paramount to the State." This language of command to a State is Mr. Justice Holmes', speaking for the Court that comprised Mr. Justice Van Devanter, Mr. Justice McReynolds, Mr. Justice Brandeis, Mr. Justice Sutherland, Mr. Justice Butler, and Mr. Justice Stone.

When defiance of law judicially pronounced was last sought to be justified before this Court, views were expressed which are now especially relevant:

"The historic phrase 'a government of laws and not of men' epitomizes the distinguishing character of our political society. When John Adams put that phrase into the Massachusetts Declaration of Rights he was not indulging in a rhetorical flourish. He was expressing the aim of those who, with him, framed the Declaration of Independence and founded the Republic. 'A government of laws and not of men' was the rejection in positive terms of rule by fiat, whether by the fiat of governmental or private power. Every act of government may be challenged by an appeal to law, as finally pronounced by this Court. Even this Court has the last say only for a time. Being composed of fallible men, it may err. But revision of its errors must be by orderly process of law. The Court may be asked to reconsider its decisions, and this has been done successfully again and again throughout our history. Or, what this Court has deemed its duty to decide may be changed by legislation, as it often has been, and, on occasion, by constitutional amendment.

"But from their own experience and their deep reading in history, the Founders knew that Law alone saves a society from being rent by internecine strife or ruled by mere brute power however disguised. 'Civilization involves subjection of force to reason, and the agency of this subjection is law.' (Pound, *The Future of Law*). The conception of a government by laws dominated the thoughts of those who founded this Nation and designed its Constitution, although they knew as well as the belittlers of the conception that laws have to be made, interpreted and enforced by men. To that end, they set apart a body of men, who were to be the depositories of law, who by their disciplined training and character and by withdrawal from the usual temptations of private interest may reasonably be expected to be 'as free, impartial, and independent as the lot of humanity will admit.' So strongly were the framers of the Constitution bent on securing a reign of law that they endowed the judicial office with extraordinary safeguards and prestige. No one, no matter how exalted his public office or how righteous his private motive, can be judge in his own case. That is what courts are for." *United States* v. *United Mine Workers*.

The duty to abstain from resistance to "the supreme Law of the Land," U. S. Const., Art. VI, ¶ 2, as declared by the organ of our Government for ascertaining it, does not require immediate approval of it nor does it deny the right of dissent. Criticism need not be stilled. Active obstruction or defiance is barred. Our kind of society cannot endure if the controlling authority of the Law as derived from the Constitution is not to be the tribunal specially charged with the duty of ascertaining and declaring what is "the supreme Law of the Land." (See President Andrew Jackson's Message to Congress of January 16, 1833.) Particularly is this so where the declaration of what "the supreme Law" commands on an underlying moral issue is not the dubious pronouncement of a gravely divided Court but is the unanimous conclusion of a long-matured deliberative process. The Constitution is not the formulation of the merely personal views of the members of this Court, nor can its authority be reduced to the claim that state officials are its controlling interpreters. Local customs, however hardened by time, are not decreed in heaven. Habits and feelings they engender may be counteracted and moderated. Experience attests that such local habits and feelings will yield, gradually though this be, to law and education. And educational influences are exerted not only by explicit teaching. They vigorously flow from the fruitful exercise of the responsibility of those charged with political official power and from the almost unconsciously transforming actualities of living under law.

The process of ending unconstitutional exclusion of pupils from the common school system—"common" meaning shared alike—solely because of color is no doubt not an easy, overnight task in a few States where a drastic alteration in the ways of communities is involved. Deep emotions have, no doubt, been stirred. They will not be calmed by letting violence loose—violence and defiance employed and encouraged by those upon whom the duty of law observance should have the strongest claim—nor by submitting to it under whatever guise employed. Only the constructive use of time will achieve what an advanced civilization demands and the Constitution confirms.

For carrying out the decision that color alone cannot bar a child from a public school, this Court has recognized the diversity of circumstances in local school situations. But is it a reasonable hope that the necessary endeavors for such adjustment will be furthered, that racial frictions will be ameliorated, by a reversal of the process and interrupting effective measures toward the necessary goal? The progress that has been made in respecting the constitutional rights of the Negro children, according to the graduated plan sanctioned by the two lower courts, would have to be retraced, perhaps with even greater difficulty because of deference to forcible resistance. It would have to be retraced against the seemingly vindicated feeling of those who actively sought to block that progress. Is there not the strongest reason for concluding that to accede to the Board's request, on the basis of the circumstances that gave rise to it, for a suspension of the Board's non-segregation plan, would be but the beginning of a series of delays calculated to nullify this Court's adamant decisions in the *Brown* case that the Constitution precludes compulsory segregation based on color in state-supported schools?

That the responsibility of those who exercise power in a democratic government is not to reflect inflamed public feeling but to help form its understanding, is especially true when they are confronted with a problem like a racially discriminating public school system. This is the lesson to be drawn from the heartening experience in ending enforced racial segregation in the public schools in cities with Negro populations of large proportions. Compliance with decisions of this Court, as the constitutional organ of the supreme Law of the Land, has often, throughout our history, depended on active support by state and local authorities. It presupposes such support. To withhold it, and indeed to use political power to try to paralyze the supreme Law, precludes the maintenance of our federal system as we have known and cherished it for one hundred and seventy years.

Lincoln's appeal to "the better angels of our nature" failed to avert a fratricidal war. But the compassionate wisdom of Lincoln's First and Second Inaugurals bequeathed to the Union, cemented with blood, a moral heritage which, when drawn upon in times of stress and strife, is sure to find specific ways and means to surmount difficulties that may appear to be insurmountable.

Part II

SEGREGATION WHILE TRAVELING AND DINING

Plessy v. Ferguson

Boynton v. Virginia

Burton v. Wilmington Parking Authority

Garner v. Louisiana

Bailey v. Patterson

Turner v. Memphis

This group begins with the famous case of *Plessy v. Ferguson*. Because of considerations of space many earlier cases involving equal facilities in rail travel have been passed over, in order to present in full the recent cases dealing with the problem—including the case of "sit-in" demonstrations.

Plessy v. Ferguson
163 U. S. 537   1896

Mr. Justice Brown delivered the opinion of the Court.

This case turns upon the constitutionality of an act of the general assembly of the state of Louisiana, passed in 1890, providing for separate railway carriages for the white and colored races.

The 1st section of the statute enacts "that all railway companies carrying passengers in their coaches in this state shall provide equal but separate accommodations for the white and colored races, by providing two or more passenger coaches for each passenger train, or by dividing the passenger coaches by a partition so as to secure separate accommodations: *Provided,* That this section shall not be construed to apply to street railroads. No person or persons shall be permitted to occupy seats in coaches other than the ones assigned to them, on account of the race they belong to."

By the 2d section it was enacted "that the officers of such passenger trains shall have power and are hereby required to assign each passenger to the coach or compartment used for the race to which such passenger belongs; any passenger insisting on going into a coach or compartment to which by race he does not belong, shall be liable to a fine of $25 or in lieu thereof to imprisonment for a period of not more than twenty days in the parish prison, and any officer of any railroad insisting on assigning a passenger to a coach or compartment other than the one set aside for the race to which said passenger belongs, shall be liable to a fine of $25, or in lieu thereof to imprisonment for a period of not more than twenty days in the parish prison; and should any passenger refuse to occupy the coach or compartment to which he or she is assigned by the officer of such railway, said officer shall have power to refuse to carry such passenger on his train, and for such refusal neither he nor the railway company which he represents shall be liable for damages in any of the courts of this state."

The 3d section provides penalties for the refusal or neglect of the officers, directors, conductors, and employees of railway companies to comply with the act, with a proviso that "nothing in this act shall be construed as applying to nurses attending children of the other race." The 4th section is immaterial.

The information filed in the criminal district court charged in substance that Plessy, being a passenger between two stations within the state of Louisiana, was assigned by officers of the company to the coach used for the race to which he belonged, but he insisted upon going into a coach used by the race to which he did not belong. Neither in the information nor plea was his particular race or color averred.

The petition for the writ of prohibition averred that petitioner was seven eighths Caucasian and one eighth African blood; that the mixture of colored blood was not discernible in him, and that he was entitled to every right, privilege, and immunity secured to citizens of the United States of the white race; and that, upon such theory, he took possession of a vacant seat in a coach where passengers of the white race were accommodated, and was ordered by the conductor to vacate said coach and take a seat in another assigned to persons of the colored race, and having refused to comply with such demand he was forcibly ejected with the aid of a police officer, and imprisoned in the parish jail to answer a charge of having violated the above act.

The constitutionality of this act is attacked upon the ground that it conflicts both with the 13th Amendment of the Constitution, abolishing slavery, and the 14th Amendment, which prohibits certain restrictive legislation on the part of the states.

1. That it does not conflict with the 13th Amendment, which abolished slavery and involuntary servitude, except as a punishment for crime, is too clear for argument. Slavery implies involuntary servitude —a state of bondage; the ownership of mankind as a chattel, or at least the control of the labor and services of one man for the benefit of another, and the absence of a legal right to the disposal of his own person, property, and services. This amendment was said in *Butcher's Benev. Asso.* v. *Crescent City L. S. L. & S. H. Co.* (*"Slaughter-House Cases"*) to have been intended primarily to abolish slavery, as it had been previously known in this country, and that it equally forbade Mexican peonage or the Chinese coolie trade when they amounted to slavery or involuntary servitude, and that the use of the word "servitude" was intended to prohibit the use of all forms of involuntary slav-

ery, of whatever class or name. It was intimated, however, in that case, that this amendment was regarded by the statesmen of that day as insufficient to protect the colored race from certain laws which had been enacted in the southern states, imposing upon the colored race onerous disabilities and burdens, and curtailing their rights in the pursuit of life, liberty, and property to such an extent that their freedom was of little value; and that the 14th Amendment was devised to meet this exigency.

So, too, in *United States* v. *Stanley ("Civil Rights Cases")*, it was said that the act of a mere individual, the owner of an inn, a public conveyance, or place of amusement, refusing accommodations to colored people, cannot be justly regarded as imposing any badge of slavery or servitude upon the applicant, but only as involving an ordinary civil injury, properly cognizable by the laws of the state, and presumably subject to redress by those laws until the contrary appears. "It would be running the slavery argument into the ground," said Mr. Justice Bradley, "to make it apply to every act of discrimination which a person may see fit to make as to the guests he will entertain, or as to the people he will take into his coach or cab or car, or admit to his concert or theater, or deal with in other matters of intercourse or business."

A statute which implies merely a legal distinction between the white and colored races—a distinction which is founded in the color of the two races, and which must always exist so long as white men are distinguished from the other race by color—has no tendency to destroy the legal equality of the two races, or re-establish a state of involuntary servitude. Indeed, we do not understand that the 13th Amendment is strenuously relied upon by the plaintiff in error in this connection.

2. By the 14th Amendment, all persons born or naturalized in the United States, and subject to the jurisdiction thereof, are made citizens of the United States and of the state wherein they reside; and the states are forbidden from making or enforcing any law which shall abridge the privileges or immunities of citizens of the United States, or shall deprive any person of life, liberty, or property without due process of law, or deny to any person within their jurisdiction the equal protection of the laws.

The proper construction of this amendment was first called to the attention of this court in *Butchers' Benev. Asso.* v. *Crescent City L. S. L. & S. H. Co. ("Slaughter-House Cases")* which involved, however, not a question of race, but one of exclusive privileges. The case did not call for any expression of opinion as to the exact rights it was intended to secure to the colored race, but it was said generally that its main purpose was to establish the citizenship of the negro; to give definitions of citizenship of the United States and of the states, and to protect from the hostile legislation of the states the privileges and immunities of citizens of the United States, as distinguished from those of citizens of the states.

The object of the amendment was undoubtedly to enforce the absolute equality of the two races before the law, but in the nature of things it could not have been intended to abolish distinctions based upon color, or to enforce social, as distinguished from political, equality, or a commingling of the two races upon terms unsatisfactory to either. Laws permitting, and even requiring their separation in places where they are liable to be brought into contact do not necessarily imply the inferiority of either race to the other, and have been generally, if not universally, recognized as within the competency of the state legislatures in the exercise of their police power. The most common instance of this is connected with the establishment of separate schools for white and colored children, which have been held to be a valid exercise of the legislative power even by courts of states where the political rights of the colored race have been longest and most earnestly enforced.

One of the earliest of these cases is that of *Roberts* v. *Boston* in which the supreme judicial court of Massachusetts held that the general school committee of Boston had power to make provision for the instruction of colored children in separate schools established exclusively for them, and to prohibit their attendance upon the other schools. "The great principle," said Chief Justice Shaw, "advanced by the learned and eloquent advocate of the plaintiff [Mr. Charles Sumner] is, that by the Constitution and laws of Massachusetts, all persons without distinction of age or sex, birth or color, origin or condition, are equal before the law. . . . But, when this great principle comes to be applied to the actual and various conditions of persons in society, it will not warrant the assertion that men and women are legally clothed with the same civil and political powers, and that children and adults are legally to have the same functions and be subject to the same treatment; but only that the rights of all, as they are settled and regulated by law, are equally entitled to the paternal consideration and protection of the law for their maintenance and security." It was held that the powers of the committee extended to the establishment of separate schools for children of different ages, sexes, and colors, and that they might also establish special schools for poor and neglected children, who have become too old to attend the primary school, and yet have not acquired the rudiments of learning, to enable them to enter the ordinary schools. Similar laws have been enacted by Congress under its general power of legislation over the District of Columbia as well as by the legislatures of many of the states, and have been generally, if not uniformly, sustained by the courts.

Laws forbidding the intermarriage of the two races may be said in a technical sense to interfere with the freedom of contract, and yet have been universally recognized as within the police power of the state.

The distinction between laws interfering with the political equality of the negro and those requiring the separation of the two races in schools, theaters, and railway carriages, has been frequently drawn by this court. Thus, in *Strauder* v. *West Virginia* it was held that a law of West Virginia limiting to white male persons, twenty-one years of age and citizens of the state, the right to sit upon juries, was a discrimination which implied a legal inferiorty in civil society, which lessened the security of the right of the colored race, and was a step towards reducing them to a condition of servility. Indeed, the right of a colored man that, in the selection of jurors to pass upon his life, liberty, and property, there shall be no exclusion of his race and no discrimination against them because of color, has been asserted in a number of cases. So, where the laws of a particular locality or the charter of a particular railway corporation has provided that no person shall be excluded from the cars on account of color, we have held that this meant that persons of color should travel in the same car as white ones, and that the enactment was not satisfied by the company providing cars assigned exclusively to people of color, though they were as good as those which they assigned exclusively to white persons.

Upon the other hand, where a statute of Louisiana required those engaged in the transportation of passengers among the states to give to all persons traveling within that state, upon vessels employed in that business, equal rights and privileges on account of race or color, and subjected to an action for damages, the owner of such a vessel, who excluded colored passengers on account of their color from the cabin set aside by him for the use of whites, it was held to be, so far as it applied to interstate commerce, unconstitutional and void. The court in this case, however, expressly disclaimed that it had anything whatever to do with the statute as a regulation of internal commerce, or affecting anything else than commerce among the states.

In *United States* v. *Stanley* (*"Civil Rights Cases"*) it was held that an act of Congress, entitling all persons within the jurisdiction of the United States to the full and equal enjoyment of the accommodations, advantages, facilities, and privileges of inns, public conveyances on land or water, theaters, and other places of public amusement, and made applicable to citizens of every race and color, regardless of any previous condition of servitude, was unconstitutional and void upon the ground that the 14th Amendment was prohibitory upon the states only, and the legislation authorized to be adopted by Congress for enforcing it was not direct legislation on matters respecting which the states were prohibited from making or enforcing certain laws or doing certain acts, but was corrective legislation such as might be necessary or proper for counteracting and redressing the effect of such laws or acts. In delivering the opinion of the court Mr. Justice Bradley observed that the 14th Amendment "does not invest Congress with power to legislate upon subjects that are within the domain of state legislation; but to provide modes of relief against state legislation or state action, of the kind referred to. It does not authorize Congress to create a code of municipal law for the regulation of private rights; but to provide modes of redress against the operation of state laws, and the action of state officers, executive or judicial, when these are subversive of the fundamental rights specified in the amendment. Positive rights and privileges are undoubtedly secured by the 14th Amendment; but they are secured by way of prohibition against state laws and state proceedings affecting those rights and privileges, and by power given to Congress to legislate for the purpose of carrying such prohibition into effect; and such legislation must necessarily be predicated upon such supposed state laws or state proceedings, and be directed to the correction of their operation and effect."

Much nearer, and, indeed, almost directly in point, is the case of the *Louisville, N. O. & T. R. Co.* v. *Mississippi,* wherein the railway company was indicted for a violation of a statute of Mississippi, enacting that all railroads carrying passengers should provide equal, but separate, accommodations for the white and colored races, by providing two or more passenger cars for each passenger train, or by dividing the passenger cars by a partition, so as to secure separate accommodations. The case was presented in a different aspect from the one under consideration, inasmuch as it was an indictment against the railway company for failing to provide the separate accommodations, but the question considered was the constitutionality of the law. In that case, the supreme court of Mississippi had held that the statute applied solely to commerce within the state, and, that being the construction of the state statute by its highest court, was accepted as conclusive. "If it be a matter," said the court, "respecting commerce wholly within a state, and not interfering with commerce between the states, then, obviously, there is no violation of the commerce clause of the Federal Constitution. . . . No question arises under this section as to the power of the state to separate in different compartments interstate passengers, or to affect in any manner, the privileges and rights of such passengers. All that we can consider is, whether the state has the power to require that railroad trains within her limits shall have separate accommodations for the two races; that affecting only commerce within the state is no invasion of the powers given to Congress by the commerce clause."

A like course of reasoning applies to the case under consideration, since the supreme court of Louisiana in the case of *State, Abbott,* v. *Hicks* held that the statute in question did not apply to interstate passengers, but was confined in its application to passengers traveling exclusively within the borders of the state. The case was decided largely upon the authority of *Louisville, N. O. & T. R. Co.* v. *State* and affirmed by this court in 133 U. S. 587. In the present case no question of interference with interstate commerce can possibly arise, since the East Louisiana Railway appears to have been purely a local line with both its termini within the state of Louisiana. Similar statutes for the separation of the two races upon public conveyances were held to be constitutional in *West Chester & P. R. Co.* v. *Miles, Day* v. *Owen, Chicago & N. W. R. Co.* v. *Williams, Chesapeake, O. & S. R. Co.* v. *Wells, Memphis & C. R. Co.* v. *Benson, The Sue, Logwood* v. *Memphis & C. R. Co., McGuinn* v. *Forbes, People* v. *King, Houck* v. *Southern P. R. Co., Heard* v. *Georgia R. Co.*

While we think the enforced separation of the races, as applied to the internal commerce of the state, neither abridges the privileges or immunities of the colored man, deprives him of his property without due process of law, nor denies him the equal protection of the laws, within the meaning of the 14th Amendment, we are not prepared to say that the conductor, in assigning passengers to the coaches according to their race, does not act at his peril, or that the provision of the 2d section of the act that denies to the passenger compensation in damages for a refusal to receive him into the coach in which he properly belongs, is a valid exercise of the legislative power. Indeed, we understand it to be conceded by the state's attorney that such part of the act that exempts from liability the railway company and its officers is unconstitutional. The power to assign to a particular coach obviously implies the power to determine to which race the passenger belongs, as well as the power to determine who under the laws of the particular state, is to be deemed a white and who a colored person. This question, though indicated in the brief of the plaintiff in error, does not properly arise in the record of this case, since the only issue made is as to the unconstitutionality of the act, so far as it requires the railway to provide separate accommodations, and the conductor to assign passengers according to their race.

It is claimed by the plaintiff in error that, in any mixed community, the reputation of belonging to the dominant race, in this instance the white race, is *property,* in the same sense that a right of action or of inheritance, is property. Conceding this to be so, for the purposes of this case, we are unable to see how this statute deprives him of, or in any way affects his right to, such property. If he be a white man and assigned to a colored coach, he may have his action for damages against the company for being deprived of his so-called property. Upon the other hand, if he be a colored man and be so assigned, he has been deprived of no property, since he is not lawfully entitled to the reputation of being a white man.

In this connection it is also suggested by the learned counsel for the plaintiff in error that the same argument that will justify the state legislature in requiring railways to provide separate accommodations for the two races will also authorize them to require separate cars to be provided for people whose hair is of a certain color, or who are aliens, or who belong to certain nationalities, or to enact laws requiring colored people to walk upon one side of the street, and white people upon the other, or requiring white men's houses to be painted white, and colored men's black, or their vehicles or business signs to be of different colors, upon the theory that one side of the street is as good as the other, or that a house or vehicle of one color is as good as one of another color. The reply to all this is that every exercise of the police power must be reasonable, and extend only to such laws as are enacted in good faith for the promotion of the public good, and not for the annoyance or oppression of a particular class. Thus in *Yick Wo* v. *Hopkins* it was held by this court that a municipal ordinance of the city of San Francisco to regulate the carrying on of public laundries within the limits of the municipality violated the provisions of the Constitution of the United States if it conferred upon the municipal authorities arbitrary power, at their own will, and without regard to discretion, in the legal sense of the term, to give or withhold consent as to persons or places, without regard to the competency of the persons applying, or the propriety of the places selected for the carrying on of the business. It was held to be a covert attempt on the part of the municipality to make an arbitrary and unjust discrimination against the Chinese race. While this was the case of a municipal ordinance a like principle has been held to apply to acts of a state legislature passed in the exercise of the police power.

So far, then, as a conflict with the 14th Amendment is concerned, the case reduces itself to the question whether the statute of Louisiana is a reasonable regulation, and with respect to this there must necessarily be a large discretion on the part of the legislature. In determining the question of reasonableness it is at liberty to act with reference to the established usages, customs, and traditions of the people, and with a view to the promotion of their comfort, and the preservation of the public peace and good order. Gauged by this standard, we cannot say that a law which authorizes or even requires the separation of the two races in public conveyances is unreasonable or more obnoxious to the 14th Amendment than the acts of Congress requiring separate schools for colored children in the District of Columbia, the constitutionality of which does not seem to have been questioned, or the corresponding acts of state legislatures.

We consider the underlying fallacy of the plaintiff's argument to consist in the assumption that the enforced separation of the two races stamps the colored race with a badge of inferiority. If this be so, it is not by reason of anything found in the act, but solely because the colored race choses to put that construction upon it. The argument necessarily assumes that if, as has been more than once the case, and is not unlikely to be so again, the colored race should become the dominant power in the state legislature, and should enact a law in precisely similar terms, it would thereby relegate the white race to an inferior position. We imagine that the white race, at least, would not acquiesce in this assumption. The argument also assumes that social prejudices may be overcome by legislation, and that equal rights cannot be secured to the negro except by an enforced commingling of the two races. We cannot accept this proposition. If the two races are to meet on terms of social equality, it must be the result of natural affinity, a mutual appreciation of each other's merits and a voluntary consent of individuals. As was said by the court of appeals of New York in *People* v. *Gallagher,* "this end can neither be accomplished nor promoted by laws which conflict with the general sentiment of the community upon whom they are designed to operate. When the government, therefore, has secured to each of its citizens equal rights before the law and equal opportunities for improvement and progress, it has accomplished the end for which it is organized and performed all of the functions respecting social advantages with which it is endowed." Legislation is powerless to eradicate racial instincts or to abolish distinctions based upon physical differences, and the attempt to do so can only result in accentuating the difficulties of the present situation. If the civil and political rights of both races be equal, one cannot be inferior to the other civilly or politically. If one race be inferior to the other socially, the Constitution of the United States cannot put them upon the same plane.

It is true that the question of the proportion of colored blood necessary to constitute a colored person, as distinguished from a white person, is one upon which there is a difference of opinion in the different states, some holding that any visible admixture of black blood stamps the person as belonging to the colored race; others that it depends upon the preponderance of blood; and still others that the predominance of white blood must only be in the proportion of three fourths. But these are questions to be determined under the laws of each state and are not properly put in issue in this case. Under the allegation of his petition it may undoubtedly become a question of importance whether, under the laws of Louisiana, the petitioner belongs to the white or colored race.

The judgment of the Court below is therefore affirmed.

Mr. Justice Brewer did not hear the argument or participate in the decision of this case.

Mr. Justice Harlan dissenting.

By the Louisiana statute, the validity of which is here involved, all railway companies (other than street railway companies) carrying passengers in that state are required to have separate but equal accommodations for white and colored persons, "by providing two or more passenger coaches for each passenger train, *or* by dividing the passenger coaches by *partition* so as to secure separate accommodations." Under this statute, no colored person is permitted to occupy a seat in a coach assigned to white persons; nor any white person to occupy a seat in the coach assigned to colored persons. The managers of the railroad are not allowed to exercise any discretion in the premises, but are required to assign each passenger to some coach or compartment set apart for the exclusive use of his race. If a passenger insists upon going into a coach or compartment not set apart for persons of his race, he is subject to be fined, or to be imprisoned in the parish jail. Penalties are prescribed for the refusal or neglect of the officers, directors, conductors, and employees of railroad companies to comply with the provisions of the act.

Only "nurses attending children of the other race" are excepted from the operation of the statute. No exception is made of colored attendants traveling with adults. A white man is not permitted to have his colored servant with him in the same coach, even if his condition of health requires the constant personal assistance of such servant. If a colored maid insists upon riding in the same coach with a white woman whom she has been employed to serve, and who may need her personal attention while traveling, she is subject to be fined or imprisoned for such an exhibition of zeal in the discharge of duty.

While there may be in Louisiana persons of different races who are not citizens of the United States, the words in the act, "white and colored races" necessarily include all citizens of the United States of both races residing in that state. So that we have before us a state enactment that compels, under penalties, the separation of the two races in railroad passenger coaches, and makes it a crime for a citizen of either race to enter a coach that has been assigned to citizens of the other race.

Thus the state regulates the use of a public highway by citizens of the United States solely upon the basis of race.

However apparent the injustice of such legislation may be, we have only to consider whether it is consistent with the Constitution of the United States.

That a railroad is a public highway, and that the corporation which owns or operates it is in the exercise of public functions, is not, at this day, to be disputed. Mr. Justice Nelson, speaking for this court in *New Jersey Steam Nav. Co.* v. *Merchants' Bank* said that a common carrier was in the exercise "of a sort of public office, and has public duties to perform, from which he should not be permitted to exonerate himself without the assent of the parties concerned." Mr. Justice Strong, delivering the judgment of this court in *Olcott* v. *Fond du Lac County Supers.* said: "That railroads, though constructed by private corporations and owned by them, are public highways, has been the doctrine of nearly all the courts ever since such conveyances for passage and transportation have had any existence. Very early the question arose whether a state's right of eminent domain could be exercised by a private corporation created for the purpose of constructing a railroad. Clearly it could not, unless taking land for such a purpose by such an agency is taking land for public use. The right of eminent domain nowhere justifies taking property for a private use. Yet it is a doctrine universally accepted that the state legislature may authorize a private corporation to take land for the construction of such a road, making compensation to the owner. What else does this doctrine mean if not that building a railroad, though it be built by a private corporation, is an act done for a public use?" So, in *Pine Grove Twp*. v. *Talcott*: "Though the corporation [a railroad company] was private, its work was public, as much so as if it were to be constructed by the state." So, in *Worcester* v. *Western R. Corp.*: "The establishment of that great thoroughfare is regarded as a public work, established by public authority, intended for the public use and benefit, the use of which is secured to the whole community, and constitutes therefore, like a canal, turnpike, or highway, a public easement. . . . It is true that the real and personal property necessary to the establishment and management of the railroad is vested in the corporation; but it is in trust for the public."

In respect of civil rights, common to all citizens, the Constitution of the United States does not, I think, permit any public authority to know the race of those entitled to be protected in the enjoyment of such rights. Every true man has pride of race, and under appropriate circumstances, when the rights of others, his equals before the law, are not to be affected, it is his privilege to express such pride and to take such action based upon it as to him seems proper. But I deny that any legislative body or judicial tribunal may have regard to the race of citizens when the civil rights of those citizens are involved. Indeed such legislation as that here in question is inconsistent, not only with that equality of rights which pertains to citizenship, national and state, but with the personal liberty enjoyed by every one within the United States.

The 13th Amendment does not permit the withholding or the deprivation of any right necessarily inhering in freedom. It not only struck down the institution of slavery as previously existing in the United States, but it prevents the imposition of any burdens or disabilities that constitute badges of slavery or servitude. It decreed universal civil freedom in this country. This court has so adjudged. But that amendment having been found inadequate to the protection of the rights of those who had been in slavery, it was followed by the 14th Amendment, which added greatly to the dignity and glory of American citizenship, and to the security of personal liberty, by declaring that "all persons born or naturalized in the United States, and subject to the jurisdiction thereof, are citizens of the United States and of the state wherein they reside," and that "no state shall make or enforce any law which shall abridge the privileges or immunities of citizens of the United States; nor shall any state deprive any person of life, liberty, or property without due process of law, nor deny to any person within its jurisdiction the equal protection of the laws." These two amendments, if enforced according to their true intent and meaning, will protect all the civil rights that pertain to freedom and citizenship. Finally, and to the end that no citizen should be denied, on account of his race, the privilege of participating in the political control of his country, it was declared by the 15th Amendment that "the right of citizens of the United States to vote shall not be denied or abridged by the United States or by any state on account of race, color, or previous condition of servitude."

These notable additions to the fundamental law were welcomed by the friends of liberty throughout the world. They removed the race line from our governmental systems. They had, as this court has said, a common purpose, namely, to secure "to a race recently emanicipated, a race that through many generations have been held in slavery, all the civil rights that the superior race enjoy." They declared, in legal effect, this court has further said, "that the law in the states shall be the same for the black as for the white; that all persons, whether colored or white, shall stand equal before the laws of the states, and, in regard to the colored race, for whose protection the amendment was primarily designed, that no discrimination shall be made against them by law because of their color." We also said: "The words of the amendment, it is true, are prohibitory, but they contain a necessary implication of a positive immunity, or right, most valuable to the colored race—the right to exemption from unfriendly legislation against them distinctively as colored—exemption from legal discriminations, implying inferiority in civil society, lessening the security of their enjoyment of the rights which others enjoy, and discriminations which are steps towards reducing them to the condition of a subject race." It was consequently adjudged that a state law that excluded citizens of the colored race from juries because of their race and however well qualified in other respects to discharge the duties of jurymen was repugnant to the 14th Amendment. At the present term, referring to the previous adjudications, this court declared that "underlying all of those decisions is the principle that the Constitution of the United States, in its present form, forbids, so far as civil and political rights are concerned, discrimination by the general government or the states against any citizen because of his race. All citizens are equal before the law."

The decisions referred to show the scope of the recent amendments of the Constitution. They also show that it is not within the power of a state to prohibit colored citizens, because of their race, from participating as jurors in the administration of justice.

It was said in argument that the statute of Louisiana does not discriminate against either race, but prescribes a rule applicable alike to white and colored citizens. But this argument does not meet the difficulty. Everyone knows that the statute in question had its origin in the purpose, not so much to exclude white persons from railroad cars occupied by blacks, as to exclude colored people from coaches occupied by or assigned to white persons. Railroad corporations of Louisiana did not make discrimination among whites in the matter of accommodation for travelers. The thing to accomplish was, under the guise of giving equal accommodation for whites and blacks to compel the latter to keep to themselves while traveling in railroad passenger coaches. No one would be so wanting in candor as to assert the contrary. The fundamental objection, therefore, to the statute, is that it interferes with the personal freedom of citizens. "Personal liberty," it has been well said, "consists in the power of locomotion, of changing situation, or removing one's person to whatsoever places one's own inclination may direct, without imprisonment or restraint, unless by due course of law." If a white man and a black man choose to occupy the same public conveyance on a public highway, it is their right to do so, and no government, proceeding alone on grounds of race, can prevent it without infringing the personal liberty of each.

It is one thing for railroad carriers to furnish, or to be required by law to furnish, equal accommodations for all whom they are under a legal duty to carry. It is quite another thing for government to forbid citizens of the white and black races from traveling in the same public conveyance, and to punish officers of railroad companies for permitting persons of the two races to occupy the same passenger coach. If a state can prescribe as a rule of civil conduct, that whites and blacks shall not travel as passengers in the same railroad coach, why may it not so regulate the use of the streets of its cities, and towns as to compel white citizens to keep on one side of the street and black citizens to keep on the other? Why may it not, upon like grounds, punish whites and blacks who ride together in street cars or in open vehicles on a public road or street? Why may it not require sheriffs to assign whites to one side of a court-room and blacks to the other? And why may it not also prohibit the commingling of the two races in the galleries of legislative halls or in public assemblages convened for the political questions of the day? Further, if this statute of Louisiana is consistent with the personal liberty of citizens, why may not the state require the separation in railroad coaches of native and naturalized citizens of the United States, or of Protestants and Roman Catholics?

The answer given at the argument to these questions was that regulations of the kind they suggest would be unreasonable, and could not, therefore, stand before the law. Is it meant that the determination of questions of legislative power depends upon the inquiry whether the statute whose validity is questioned is, in the judgment of the courts, a reasonable one, taking all the circumstances into consideration? A statute may be unreasonable merely because a sound public policy forbade its enactment. But I do not understand that the courts have anything to do with the policy or expediency of legislation. A statute may be valid, and yet upon grounds of public policy may well be characterized as unreasonable. Mr. Sedgwick correctly states the rule when he says that the legislative intention being clearly ascertained, "the courts have no other duty to perform than to execute the legislative will, without any regard to their views as to the wisdom or justice of the particular enactment." There is a dangerous tendency in these latter days to enlarge the functions of the courts, by means of judicial interference with the will of the people as expressed by the legislature. Our institutions have the distinguishing characteristic that the three departments of government are co-ordinate and separate. Each must keep within the limits defined by the Constitution. And the courts best discharge their duty by executing the will of the lawmaking power, constitutionally expressed, leaving the results of legislation to be dealt with by the people through their representatives. Statutes must always have a reasonable construction. Sometimes they are to be construed strictly; sometimes literally, in order to carry out the legislative will. But however construed, the intent of the legislature is to be respected, if the particular statute in question is valid, although the courts, looking at the public interests, may conceive the statute to be both unreasonable and impolitic. If the power exists to enact a statute, that ends the matters so far as the courts are concerned. The adjudged cases in which statutes have been held to be void, because unreasonable, are those in which the means employed by the legislature were not at all germane to the end to which the legislature was competent.

The white race deems itself to be the dominant race in this country. And so it is, in prestige, in achievements, in education, in wealth, and in power. So, I doubt not that it will continue to be for all time, if it remains true to its great heritage and holds fast to the principles of constitutional liberty. But in view of the Constitution, in the eye of the law, there is in this country no superior, dominant, ruling class of citizens. There is no caste here. Our Constitution is color-blind, and neither knows nor tolerates classes among citizens. In respect of civil rights, all citizens are equal before the law. The humblest is the peer of the most powerful. The law regards man as man, and takes no account of his surroundings or of his color when his civil rights as guaranteed by the supreme law of the land are involved. It is therefore to be regretted that this high tribunal, the final expositor of the fundamental law of the land, has reached the conclusion that it is competent for a state to regulate the enjoyment by citizens of their civil rights solely upon the basis of race.

In my opinion, the judgment this day rendered will, in time, prove to be quite as pernicious as the decision made by this tribunal in the *Dred Scott Case*. It was adjudged in that case that the descendants of Africans who were imported into this country and sold as slaves were not included nor intended to be included under the word "citizens" in the Constitution, and could not claim any of the rights and privileges which that instrument provided for and secured to citizens of the United States; that at the time of the adoption of the Constitution they were "considered as a subordinate and inferior class of beings, who had been subjugated by the dominant race, and, whether emancipated or not, yet remained subject to their authority, and had no rights or privileges but such as those who held the power and the government might choose to grant them." The recent amendments of the Constitution, it was supposed, had eradicated these principles from our institutions. But it seems that we have yet, in some of the states, a dominant race, a superior class of citizens, which assumes to regulate the enjoyment of civil rights, common to all citizens, upon the basis of race. The present decision, it may well be apprehended, will not stimulate aggressions, more or less brutal and irritating, upon the admitted rights of colored citizens, but will encourage the belief that it is possible, by means of state enactments, to defeat the beneficent purposes which the people of the United States had in view when they adopted the recent amendments of the Constitution, by one of which the blacks of this country were made citizens of the United States and of the states in which they respectively reside and whose privileges and immunities, as citizens, the states are forbidden to abridge. Sixty millions of whites are in no danger from the presence here of eight millions of blacks. The destinies of the two races in this country are indissolubly linked together, and the interests of both require that the common government of all shall not permit the seeds of race hate to be planted under the sanction of law. What can more certainly arouse race hate, what more certainly create and perpetuate a feeling of distrust between these races, than state enactments which in fact proceed on the ground that colored citizens are so inferior and degraded that they cannot be allowed to sit in public coaches occupied by white citizens? That, as all will admit, is the real meaning of such legislation as was enacted in Louisiana.

The sure guaranty of the peace and security of each race is the clear, distinct, unconditional recognition by our governments, national and state, of every right that inheres in civil freedom, and of the equality before the law of all citizens of the United States without regard to race. State enactments, regulating the enjoyment of civil rights, upon the basis of race, and cunningly devised to defeat legitimate results of the war, under the pretense of recognizing equality of rights, can have no other result than to render permanent peace impossible and to keep alive a conflict of races, the continuance of which must do harm to all concerned. This question is not met by the suggestion that social equality cannot exist between the white and black races in this country. That argument, if it can be properly regarded as one, is scarcely worthy of consideration, for social equality no more exists between two races when traveling in a passenger coach or a public highway than when members of the same races sit by each other in a street car or in the jury box, or stand or sit with each other in a political assembly, or when they use in common the streets of a city or town, or when they are in the same room for the purpose of having their names placed on the registry of voters, or when they approach the ballot-box in order to exercise the high privilege of voting.

There is a race so different from our own that we do not permit those belonging to it to become citizens of the United States. Persons belonging to it are, with few exceptions, absolutely excluded from our country. I allude to the Chinese race. But by the statute in question a Chinaman can ride in the same passenger coach with white citizens of the United States, while citizens of the black race in Louisiana, many of whom, perhaps, risked their lives for the preservation of the Union, who are entitled by law to participate in the political control of the state and nation, who are not excluded, by law or by reason of their race, from public stations of any kind, and who have all the legal rights that belong to white citizens, are yet declared to be criminals, liable to imprisonment, if they ride in a public coach occupied by citizens of the white race. It is scarcely just to say that a colored citizen should not object to occupying a public coach assigned to his own race. He does not object, nor, perhaps, would he object to separate coaches for his race, if his rights under the law were recognized. But he does object, and he ought never to cease objecting, that citizens of the white and black races can be adjudged criminals because they sit, or claim the right to sit, in the same public coach on a public highway.

The arbitrary separation of citizens, on the basis of race, while they are on a public highway, is a badge of servitude wholly inconsistent with the civil freedom and the equality before the law established by the Constitution. It cannot be justified upon any legal grounds.

If evils will result from the commingling of the two races upon public highways established for the benefit of all, they will be infinitely less than those that will surely come from state legislation regulating the enjoyment of civil rights upon the basis of race. We boast of the freedom enjoyed by our people above all other peoples. But it is difficult to reconcile that boast with a state of the law which, practically, puts the brand of servitude and degradation upon a large class of our fellow citizens, our equals before the law. The thin disguise of "equal" accommodations for passengers in railroad coaches will not mislead anyone, or atone for the wrong this day done.

The result of the whole matter is that while this court has frequently adjudged, and at the present term has recognized the doctrine, that a state cannot, consistently with the Constitution of the United States, prevent white and black citizens, having the required qualifications for jury service, from sitting in the same jury box, it is now solemnly held that a state may prohibit white and black citizens from sitting in the same passenger coach on a public highway, or may require that they be separated by a "partition," when in the same passenger coach. May it not now be reasonably expected that astute men of the dominant race, who affect to be disturbed at the possibility that the integrity of the white race may be corrupted, or that its supremacy will be imperiled, by contact on public highways with black people, will endeavor to procure statutes requiring white and black jurors to be separated in the jury box by a "partition," and that, upon retiring from the court room to consult as to their verdict, such partition, if it be a movable one, shall be taken to their consultation room, and set up in such way as to prevent black jurors from coming too close to their brother jurors of the white race. If the "partition" used in the court room happens to be stationary, provision could be made for screens with openings through which jurors of the two races could confer as to their verdict without coming into personal contact with each other. I cannot see but that, according to the principles this day announced, such state legislation, although conceived in hostility to, and enacted for the purpose of humiliating, citizens of the United States of a particular race, would be held to be consistent with the Constitution.

I do not deem it necessary to review the decisions of state courts to which reference was made in argument. Some, and the most important, of them are wholly inapplicable, because rendered prior to the adoption of the last amendments of the Constitution, when colored people had very few rights which the dominant race felt obliged to respect. Others were made at a time when public opinion, in many localities, was dominated by the institution of slavery; when it would not have been safe to do justice to the black man: and when, so far as the rights of blacks were concerned, race prejudice was, practically, the supreme law of the land. Those decisions cannot be guides in the era introduced by the recent amendments of the supreme law, which established universal civil freedom, gave citizenship to all born or naturalized in the United States and residing here, obliterated the race line from our systems of governments, national and state, and placed our free institutions upon the broad and sure foundation of the equality of all men before the law.

I am of opinion that the statute of Louisiana is inconsistent with the personal liberty of citizens, white and black, in that state, and hostile to both the spirit and letter of the Constitution of the United States. If laws of like character should be enacted in the several states of the Union, the effect would be in the highest degree mischievous. Slavery as an institution tolerated by law would, it is true, have disappeared from our country, but there would remain a power in the states, by sinister legislation, to interfere with the full enjoyment of the blessings of freedom; to regulate civil rights, common to all citizens, upon the basis of race; and to place in a condition of legal inferiority a large body of American citizens, now constituting a part of the political community, called the people of the United States, for whom and by whom, through representatives, our government is administered. Such a system is inconsistent with the guarantee given by the Constitution to each state of a republican form of government, and may be stricken down by congressional action, or by the courts in the discharge of their solemn duty to maintain the supreme law of the land, anything in the Constitution or laws of any state to the contrary notwithstanding.

For the reasons stated, I am constrained to withhold my assent from the opinion and judgment of the majority.

Boynton v. Virginia
364 U. S. 454   1960

Mr. Justice Black delivered the opinion of the Court.

The basic question presented in this case is whether an interstate bus passenger is denied a federal statutory or constitutional right when a restaurant in a bus terminal used by the carrier along its route discriminates in serving food to the passenger solely because of his color.

Petitioner, a Negro law student, bought a Trailways bus ticket from Washington, D. C., to Montgomery, Alabama. He boarded a bus at

8 P.M. which arrived at Richmond, Virginia, about 10:40 P.M. When the bus pulled up at the Richmond "Trailways Bus Terminal" the bus driver announced a forty-minute stopover there. Petitioner got off the bus and went into the bus terminal to get something to eat. In the station he found a restaurant in which one part was used to serve white people and one to serve Negroes. Disregarding this division, petitioner sat down on a stool in the white section. A waitress asked him to move over to the other section where there were "facilities" to serve colored people. Petitioner told her he was an interstate bus passenger, refused to move and ordered a sandwich and tea. The waitress then brought the Assistant Manager, who "instructed" petitioner to "leave the white portion of the restaurant and advised him he could be served in the colored portion." Upon petitioner's refusal to leave an officer was called and petitioner was arrested and later tried, convicted and fined ten dollars in the Police Justice's Court of Richmond on a charge that he *"Unlawfully* did remain on the premises of the Bus Terminal Restaurant of Richmond, Inc. after having been forbidden to do so" by the Assistant Manager. (Emphasis supplied.) The charge was based on § 18–225 of the Code of Virginia of 1950, as amended (1958), which provides in part:

"If any person shall *without authority of law* go upon or remain upon the lands or premises of another, after having been forbidden to do so by the owner, lessee, custodian or other person lawfully in charge of such land, . . . he shall be deemed guilty of a misdemeanor, and upon conviction thereof shall be punished by a fine by not more than one hundred dollars or by confinement in jail not exceeding thirty days, or by both such fine and imprisonment." (Emphasis supplied.)

Petitioner appealed his conviction to the Hustings Court of Richmond, where, as in the Police Court, he admitted that he had remained in the white portion of the Terminal Restaurant although ordered not to do so. His defense in both courts was that he had a federal right as an interstate passenger of Trailways to be served without discrimination by this restaurant used by the bus carrier for the accommodation of its interstate passengers. On this basis petitioner claimed he was on the restaurant premises lawfully, not "unlawfully" as charged, and that he remained there with, not "without authority of law." His federal claim to this effect was spelled out in a motion to dismiss the warrant in Hustings Court, which was overruled both before and after the evidence was heard. Pointing out that the restaurant was an integral part of the bus service for interstate passengers such as petitioner, and asserting that refusal to serve him was a discrimination based on color, the motion to dismiss charged that application of the Virginia law to petitioner violated the Interstate Commerce Act and the Equal Protection, Due Process and Commerce Clauses of the Federal Constitution. On appeal the Virginia Supreme Court held that the conviction was "plainly right" and affirmed without opinion, thereby rejecting petitioner's assignments of error based on the same grounds of discrimination set out in his motion to dismiss in Hustings Court but not specifically charging that the discrimination violated the Interstate Commerce Act. We think, however, that the claims of discrimination previously made under the Act are sufficiently closely related to the assignments that were made to be considered within the scope of the issues presented to the State Supreme Court. We granted certiorari because of the serious federal questions raised concerning discrimination based on color.

The petition for certiorari we granted presented only two questions: first, whether the conviction of petitioner is invalid as a burden on commerce in violation of Art. I, § 8, cl. 3 of the Constitution; and second, whether the conviction violates the Due Process and Equal Protection Clauses of the Fourteenth Amendment. Ordinarily we limit our review to the questions presented in an application for certiorari. We think there are persuasive reasons, however, why this case should be decided, if it can, on the Interstate Commerce Act contention raised in the Virginia courts. Discrimination because of color as the core of the two broad constitutional questions presented to us by petitioner, just as it is the core of the Interstate Commerce Act question presented to the Virginia courts. Under these circumstances we think it appropriate not to reach the constitutional questions but to proceed at once to the statutory issue.

The Interstate Commerce Act, as we have said, uses language of the broadest type to bar discriminations of all kinds. We have held that the Act forbids railroad dining cars to discriminate in service to passengers on account of their color. *Henderson* v. *United States;* see also *Mitchell* v. *United States.*

Section 216 (d) of Part II of the Interstate Commerce Act, 49 U. S. C. § 316 (d), which applies to motor carriers, provides in part:

"It shall be unlawful for any common carrier by motor vehicle engaged in interstate or foreign commerce to make, give, or cause any undue or unreasonable preference or advantage to any particular person . . . in any respect whatsoever; or to subject any particular person . . . to any unjust discrimination or any unjust or unreasonable prejudice or disadvantage in any respect whatsoever . . . ."

So far as relevant to our problem, the provisions of § 216 (d) quoted are the same as those in § 3 (1) of the Act, 49 U. S. C. § 3 (1), except that the latter refers to railroads as defined in Part I of the Act instead of motor carriers as defined in Part II. Section 3 (1) was the basis for this Court's holding in *Henderson* v. *United States* that it was an "undue or unreasonable prejudice" under that section for a railroad to divide its dining car by curtains, partitions and signs in order to separate passengers according to race. The Court said that under § 3 (1) "[w]here a dining car is available to passengers holding tickets entitling them to use it, each such passenger is equally entitled to its facilities in accordance with reasonable regulations." The *Henderson* case largely rested on *Mitchell* v. *United States* which pointed out that while the railroads might not be required by law to furnish dining car facilities, yet if they did, substantial equality of treatment of persons traveling under like conditions could not be refused consistently with § 3(1). It is also of relevance that both cases upset Interstate Commerce Commission holdings, the Court stating in *Mitchell* that since the "discrimination shown was palpably unjust and forbidden by the Act" no room was left for administrative or expert judgment with reference to practical difficulties.

It follows from the *Mitchell* and *Henderson* cases as a matter of course that should buses in transit decide to supply dining service, discrimination of the kind shown here would violate § 216 (d). Although this Court has not decided whether the same result would follow from a similar discrimination in service by a restaurant in a railroad or bus terminal, we have no doubt that the reasoning underlying the *Mitchell* and *Henderson* cases would compel the same decision as to the unlawfulness of discrimination in transportation services against interstate passengers in terminals and terminal restaurants owned or operated or controlled by interstate carriers. This is true as to railroad terminals because they are expressly made carriers by § 1 (3) (a) of the Act, 49 U. S. C. § 1 (3) (a), and as to bus terminals because § 203 (a) (19) of the Act, 49 U. S. C. § 303 (a) (19), specifically includes interstate transportation facilities and property operated or controlled by a motor carrier within the definition of the "services" and "transportation" to which the motor carrier provisions of the Act apply.

Respondent correctly points out, however, that, whatever may be the facts, the evidence in this record does not show that the bus company owns or actively operates or directly controls the bus terminal or the restaurant in it. But the fact that § 203 (a) (19) says that the protections of the motor carrier provisions of the Act extend to "include" facilities so operated or controlled by no means should be interpreted to exempt motor carriers from their statutory duty under § 216 (d) not to discriminate should they choose to provide their interstate passengers with services that are an integral part of transportation through the use of facilities they neither own, control nor operate. The protections afforded by the Act against discriminatory transportation services are not so narrowly limited. We have held that a railroad cannot escape its statutory duty to treat its shippers alike either by use of facilities it does not own or by contractual arrangement with the owner of those facilities. And so here, without regard to contracts, if the bus carrier has volunteered to make terminal and restaurant facilities and services available to its interstate passengers as a regular part of their transportation, and the terminal and restaurant have acquiesced and cooperated in this undertaking, the terminal and restaurant must perform these services without discriminations prohibited by the Act. In the performance of these services under such conditions the terminal and restaurant stand in the place of the bus company in the performance of its transportation obligations. Although the courts below made no findings of fact, we think the evidence in this case shows such a relationship and situation here.

The manager of the restaurant testified that it was not affiliated in any way with the Trailways Bus Company and that the bus company had no control over the operation of the restaurant, but that while the restaurant had "quite a bit of business" from local people, it was primarily or partly for the service of the passengers on the Trailways bus. This last statement was perhaps much of an understatement, as shown by the lease agreement executed in writing and signed both by the "Trailways Bus Terminal, Inc.," as lessor, and the "Bus Terminal Restaurant of Richmond, Inc.," as lessee. The first part of the document showed that Trailways Terminal was then constructing a "bus station" with built-in facilities "for the operation of a restaurant, soda fountain, and news stand." Terminal covenanted to lease this space to Restaurant for its use; to grant Restaurant the exclusive right to sell foods and other things usually sold in restaurants, newsstands, soda fountains and lunch counters; to keep the terminal building in good repair and to furnish certain utilities. Restaurant on its part agreed to use its space for the sale of commodities agreed on at prices that are "just and reasonable"; to sell no commodities not usually sold or installed in a bus terminal concession without Terminal's permission; to discontinue the sale of any commodity objectionable to Terminal; to buy, maintain, and replace equipment subject to Terminal's approval in writing as to its quality; to make alterations and additions only after Terminal's written consent and approval; to make no "sales on buses operating in and out said bus station" but only "through the windows of said buses"; to keep its employees neat and clean; to perform no terminal service other than that pertaining to the operation of its restaurant as agreed on; and that neither Restaurant nor its employees were to "sell transportation of any kind or give information pertaining to schedules, rates or transportation matters, but shall refer all such inquiries to the proper agents of" Terminal. In short, as Terminal and Restaurant agreed, "the operation of the restaurant and the said stands shall be in keeping with the character of service maintained in an up-to-date, modern bus terminal."

All of these things show that this terminal building, with its grounds, constituted one project for a single purpose, and that was to serve passengers of one or more bus companies—certainly Trailways' passengers. The restaurant area was specifically designed and built into the structure from the beginning to fill the needs of bus passengers in this "up-to-date, modern bus terminal." Whoever may have had technical title or immediate control of the details of the various activities in the terminal, such as waiting-room seating, furnishing of schedule information, ticket sales, and restaurant service, they were all geared to the service of bus companies and their passengers, even though local people who might happen to come into the terminal or its restaurant might also be accommodated. Thus we have a well-coordinated and smoothly functioning plan for continuous cooperative transportation services between the terminal, the restaurant and buses like Trailways that made stopovers there. All of this evidence plus Trailways' use on this occasion shows that Trailways was not utilizing the terminal and restaurant services merely on a sporadic or occasional basis. This bus terminal plainly was just as essential and necessary, and as available for that matter, to passengers and carriers like Trailways that used it, as though such carriers had legal title and complete control over all of its activities. Interstate passengers have to eat, and the very terms of the lease of the built-in restaurant space in this terminal constitute a recognition of the essential need of interstate passengers to be able to get food conveniently on their journey and an undertaking by the restaurant to fulfill that need. Such passengers in transit on a paid interstate Trailways journey had a right to expect that this essential transportation food service voluntarily provided for them under such circumstances would be rendered without discrimination prohibited by the Interstate Commerce Act. Under the circumstances of this case, therefore, petitioner had a federal right to remain in the white portion of the restaurant. He was there under "authority of law"—the Interstate Commerce Act—and it was error for the Supreme Court of Virginia to affirm his conviction.

Because of some of the arguments made here it is necessary to say a word about what we are not deciding. We are not holding that every time a bus stops at a wholly independent roadside restaurant the Interstate Commerce Act requires that restaurant service be supplied in harmony with the provisions of that Act. We decide only this case, on its facts, where circumstances show that the terminal and restaurant operate as an integral part of the bus carrier's transportation service for interstate passengers. Under such circumstances, an interstate passenger need not inquire into documents of title or contractual arrangements in order to determine whether he has a right to be served without discrimination.

The judgment of the Supreme Court of Virginia is reversed and the cause is remanded to that Court for proceedings not inconsistent with this opinion.

Mr. Justice Whittaker, with whom Mr. Justice Clark joins, dissenting.

Neither in the Supreme Court of Appeals of Virginia nor in his petition for certiorari or in his brief on the merits in this Court did petitioner challenge the judgment on the ground that it was obtained in violation of the Interstate Commerce Act. I therefore respectfully submit that, under our rules and decisions, no such question is presented or open for consideration here. But even if the Court properly may proceed, as it has proceeded, to decide the case under that Act, and not at all on the constitutional grounds solely relied on by petitioner, I must say, with all deference, that the facts in this record do not show that petitioner was convicted of trespass in violation of that Act.

For me, the decisive question in this case is whether petitioner had a legal right to remain in the restaurant involved after being ordered to leave it by the proprietor. If he did not have that legal right, however arising, he was guilty of trespass and, unless proscribed by some federal law, his conviction therefor was legally adjudged under § 18–225 of the Code of Virginia.

If the facts in this record could fairly be said to show that the restaurant was a facility "operated or controlled by any [motor] carrier or carriers, and used in the transportation of passengers or property in interstate or foreign commerce," I would agree that petitioner had a legal right to remain in and to insist on service by that restaurant and, hence, was not guilty of trespass in so remaining and insisting though in defiance of the manager's order to leave, for § 216 (d) of the Act, 49 U. S. C. § 316 (d), makes it unlawful for a motor carrier while engaged in interstate commerce "to subject any particular person . . . to any unjust discrimination," and this Court has held that any discrimination by a carrier against its interstate passenger on account of his color in the use of its dining facilities is an unjust discrimination.

But I respectfully submit that those are not the facts shown by this record. As I read it, there is no evidence in this record even tending to show that the restaurant was "operated or controlled by any such carrier," directly or indirectly. Instead, all of the relevant evidence, none of which was contradicted, shows that the restaurant was owned and controlled by a noncarrier who alone operated it as a local and private enterprise. The evidence was very brief, consisting only of an exhibit (a lease) and the testimony of the assistant manager of the restaurant, of a police officer and of petitioner—all, except the exhibit, being contained on 10 pages of the printed record. The lease is in the usual and common form and terms. By it, the owner of the building, Trailways Bus Terminal, Inc., a Virginia corporation, as lessor, demised to the restaurant company, Bus Terminal Restaurant of Richmond, Inc., a Virginia corporation, as lessee, certain described "space" in the lessor's bus station building in Richmond, Virginia, "for use by Lessee as a restaurant, lunchroom, soda fountain and news stand," for a term of five years from December 2, 1953 (with an option in the lessee to renew, on the same terms, for an additional five-year term), at an annual rental of $30,000 (payable in equal monthly installments) plus 12% of lessee's gross receipts from the demised premises in excess of $275,000 (payable at the end of each year).

There is not a word of evidence that any carrier had any interest in or control over the lessee or its restaurant. Nor is there any suggestion in the record that the lease or the lessee's restaurant operations under it were anything other than bona fide and for a legitimate and private business purpose. Indeed, there is not a word of evidence in the record tending to show that any carrier even had any interest in or control over the lessor corporation that owned the building. In truth, the record does not even show the name of the carrier on which petitioner was traveling or identify it other than as "Trailways." On the other hand, the assistant manager of the restaurant testified, without suggestion of contradiction, that "[t]he company that operates the restaurant is not affiliated in any way with the bus company," and that "[t]he bus company has no control over the operation of the restaurant." There was simply no evidence to the contrary.

The Court seems to agree that "[r]espondent correctly points out [that] . . . the evidence in this record does not show that the bus company owns or actively operates or directly controls the bus terminal or the restaurant in it." But it seems to hold, as I read its opinion, that a motor carrier's regular "use" of a restaurant, though it be "neither own[ed], control[led] nor operate[d]" by the motor carrier, makes the restaurant a facility "operated or controlled by [the motor] carrier or carriers" within the meaning of § 203 (a)(19) of the Interstate Commerce Act. I must respectfully disagree. To me, it seems rather plain that when Congress, in § 203 (a)(19), said that the " 'services' and 'transportation' " to which Part II of the Act applies shall include "all vehicles . . . together with all facilities and property operated or controlled by any such carrier or carriers, and used in the transportation of passengers or property in interstate or foreign commerce or in the performance of any service in connection therewith," it hardly meant to include a private restaurant, "neither owned, operated nor controlled" by a carrier. Surely such "use" of a private restaurant by a motor carrier as results from stopping and opening its buses in front of or near a restaurant does not make the restaurant a facility "operated or controlled by" the carrier, within the meaning of § 203 (a)(19) or in any true sense. This simple, and I think obvious, principle was recognized and correctly applied by the Commission as recently as November 1955 in *N. A. A. C. P.* v. *St. Louis, S. F. R. Co.* There, the railroad terminal or station building in Richmond, Virginia, was owned by Richmond Terminal Railway Company—itself a carrier under § 3 (1) of Part I of the Act—which had leased space in that building to Union News Company for a term of 10 years, but subject to termination at the option of either party on 90 days' notice, for use as a restaurant. In rejecting the contention that the Union News Company's operation of the restaurant on a racially segregated basis violated § 3 (1) of Part I of the Act, the Commission said:

> *"Unless the operation of the lunchrooms can be found to be that of a common carrier* subject to part I of the act, it cannot be regulated under section 3 (1), and we are unable so to find on the facts before us." (Emphasis added.)

and the Commission concluded:

> "We further find that the operation *by a lessee (noncarrier)* of separate lunchroom facilities for white and colored persons in the railway station at Richmond, constitutes a function or service which is not within the jurisdiction of this Commission." (Emphasis added.)

I would agree with the Court that "if the bus carrier [had] volunteered to make . . . restaurant facilities and services available to its interstate passengers as a regular part of their transportation, and the . . . restaurant [had] acquiesced . . . in this undertaking," the restaurant would then have been bound to serve the carrier's interstate passengers without discrimination. For, in that case, the restaurant would have been made a facility of the carrier, within the meaning of § 203 (a)(19), and § 216 (d) would inhibit both the carrier and the restaurant from discriminating against the carrier's interstate passengers on account of their color, or on any other account, in the use of the restaurant facilities thus provided. *Henderson* v. *United States.* But that is not this case. As we have shown, there is no evidence in this record that the carrier on which petitioner was traveling, whatever may have been its name, had "volunteered to make . . . restaurant facilities and services available to its interstate passengers" *at this restaurant* "as a regular part of their transportation," or that the proprietor of this restaurant ever "acquiesced" in any such "undertaking." There is no evidence of any agreement, express or implied, between the proprietor of this restaurant and any bus carrier. Instead, the undisputed evidence is that the restaurant was not in any way affiliated with or controlled by any bus carrier. On this evidence, I am unable to find any basis to support a conclusion that this restaurant was in some way made a facility of the bus carrier, or subject to Part II of the Interstate Commerce Act.

For these reasons, I cannot agree on this record that petitioner's conviction of trespass under § 18–225 of the Code of Virginia was had in violation of the Interstate Commerce Act. Since the Court's opinion does not explore the constitutional grounds relied on by petitioner, I refrain from intimating any views on those subjects.

Burton v. Wilmington Parking Authority
365 U. S. 715   1960

Mr. Justice Clark delivered the opinion of the Court.

In this action for declaratory and injunctive relief it is admitted that the Eagle Coffee Shoppe, Inc., a restaurant located within an off-street automobile parking building in Wilmington, Delaware, has refused to serve appellant food or drink solely because he is a Negro. The parking building is owned and operated by the Wilmington Parking Authority, an agency of the State of Delaware, and the restaurant is the Authority's lessee. Appellant claims that such refusal abridges his rights under the Equal Protection Clause of the Fourteenth Amendment to the United States Constitution. The Supreme Court of Delaware has held that Eagle was acting in "a purely private capacity" under its lease; that its action was not that of the Authority and was not, therefore, state action within the contemplation of the prohibitions contained in that Amendment. It also held that under 24 Del. Cole, § 1501, Eagle was a restaurant, not an inn, and that as such it "is not required [under Delaware law] to serve any and all persons entering its place of business." On appeal here from the judgment as having been based upon a statute construed unconstitutionally, we postponed consideration of the question of jurisdiction under 28 U. S. C. § 1257 (2) to the hearing on the merits. We agree with the respondents that the appeal should be dismissed and accordingly the motion to dismiss is granted. However, since the action of Eagle in excluding appellant raises an important constitutional question, the papers whereon the appeal was taken are treated as a petition for a writ of certiorari and the writ is granted. On the merits we have concluded that the exclusion of appellant under the circumstances shown to be present here was discriminatory state action in violation of the Equal Protection Clause of the Fourteenth Amendment.

The Authority was created by the City of Wilmington pursuant to 22 Del. Code, §§ 501–515. It is "a public body corporate and politic, exercising public powers of the State as an agency thereof." Its statutory purpose is to provide adequate parking facilities for the convenience of the public and thereby relieve the "parking crisis, which threatens the welfare of the community . . . ." To this end the Authority is granted wide powers including that of constructing or acquiring by lease, purchase or condemnation, lands and facilities, and that of leasing "portions of any of its garage buildings or structures for commercial use by the lessee, where, in the opinion of the Authority, such leasing is necessary and feasible for the financing and operation of such facilities." The Act provides that the rates and charges for its facilities must be reasonable and are to be determined exclusively by the Authority "for the purposes of providing for the payment of the expenses of the Authority, the construction, improvement, repair, maintenance, and operation of its facilities and properties, the payment of the principal of and interest on its obligations, and to fulfill the terms and provisions of any agreements made with the purchasers or holders of any such obligations or with the city." The Authority has no power to pledge the credit of the State of Delaware but may issue its own revenue bonds which are tax exempt. Any and all property owned or used by the Authority is likewise exempt from state taxation.

The first project undertaken by the Authority was the erection of a parking facility on Ninth Street in downtown Wilmington. The tract consisted of four parcels, all of which were acquired by negotiated purchases from private owners. Three were paid for in cash, borrowed from Equitable Security Trust Company, and the fourth, purchased from Diamond Ice and Coal Company, was paid for "partly in Revenue Bonds of the Authority and partly in cash [$934,000] donated by the City of Wilmington, pursuant to 22 Del. C. c. 5 . . . . Subsequently, the City of Wilmington gave the Authority $1,822,827.69 which sum the Authority applied to the redemption of the Revenue Bonds delivered to Diamond Ice & Coal Co. and to the repayment of the Equitable Security Trust Company loan."

Before it began actual construction of the facility, the Authority was advised by its retained experts that the anticipated revenue from the parking of cars and proceeds from sale of its bonds would not be sufficient to finance the construction costs of the facility. Moreover, the bonds were not expected to be marketable if payable solely out of parking revenues. To secure additional capital needed for its "debt-service" requirements, and thereby to make bond financing practicable, the Authority decided it was necessary to enter long-term leases with responsible tenants for commercial use of some of the space available in the projected "garage building." The public was invited to bid for these leases.

In April 1957 such a private lease, for 20 years and renewable for another 10 years, was made with Eagle Coffee Shoppe, Inc., for use as a "restaurant, dining room, banquet hall, cocktail lounge and bar and for no other use and purpose." The multi-level space of the building which was let to Eagle, although "within the exterior walls of the structure, has no marked public entrance leading from the parking portion of the facility into the restaurant proper . . . [whose main entrance] is located on Ninth Street." In its lease the Authority covenanted to complete construction expeditiously, including completion of "the decorative finishing of the leased premises and utilities therefor, without cost to Lessee," including necessary utility connections, toilets, hung acoustical tile and plaster ceilings; vinyl asbestos, ceramic tile and concrete floors; connecting stairs and wrought iron railings; and wood-floored show windows. Eagle spent some $220,000 to make the space suitable for its operation and, to the extent such improvements were so attached to realty as to become part thereof, Eagle to the same extent enjoys the Authority's tax exemption.

The Authority further agreed to furnish heat for Eagle's premises, gas service for the boiler room, and to make, at its own expense, all necessary structural repairs, all repairs to exterior surfaces except store fronts and any repairs caused by lessee's own act or neglect. The Authority retained the right to place any directional signs on the exterior of the let space which would not interfere with or obscure Eagle's display signs. Agreeing to pay an annual rental of $28,700, Eagle covenanted to "occupy and use the leased premises in accordance with all applicable laws, statutes, ordinances and rules and regulations of any federal, state or municipal authority." Its lease, however, contains no requirement that its restaurant services be made available to the general public on a nondiscriminatory basis, in spite of the fact that the Authority has power to adopt rules and regulations respecting the use of its facilities except any as would impair the security of its bondholders.

Other portions of the structure were leased to other tenants, including a bookstore, a retail jeweler, and a food store. Upon completion of the building, the Authority located at appropriate places thereon official signs indicating the public character of the building, and flew from mastheads on the roof both the state and national flags.

In August 1958 appellant parked his car in the building and walked around to enter the restaurant by its front door on Ninth Street. Having entered and sought service, he was refused it. Thereafter he filed this declaratory judgment action in the Court of Chancery. On motions for summary judgment, based on the pleadings and affidavits, the Chancellor concluded, contrary to the contentions of respondents, that whether in fact the lease was a "device" or was executed in good faith, it would not "serve to insulate the public authority from the force and effect of the Fourteenth Amendment." He found it not necessary, therefore, to pass upon the rights of private restaurateurs under state common and statutory law, including 24 Del. Code § 1501. The Supreme Court of Delaware reversed, as we mentioned above, holding that Eagle "in the conduct of its business, is acting in a purely private capacity." It, therefore, denied appellant's claim under the Fourteenth Amendment. Upon reaching the application of state law, it held, contrary to appellant's assertion that Eagle maintained an inn, that Eagle's operation was "primarily a restaurant and thus subject to the provisions of 24 Del. C. § 1501, which does not compel the operator of a restaurant to give service to all persons seeking such." Delaware's highest court has thus denied the equal protection claim of the appellant as well as his state-law contention concerning the applicability of § 1501.

On the jurisdictional question, we agree that the judgment of Delaware's court does not depend for its ultimate support upon a determination of the constitutional validity of a state statute, but rather upon the holding that on the facts Eagle's racially discriminatory action was exercised in "a purely private capacity" and that it was, therefore, beyond the prohibitive scope of the Fourteenth Amendment.

The *Civil Rights Cases* "embedded in our constitutional law" the principle "that the action inhibited by the first section [Equal Protection Clause] of the Fourteenth Amendment is only such action as may fairly be said to be that of the States. That Amendment erects no shield against merely private conduct, however discriminatory or wrongful." Chief Justice Vinson in *Shelley* v. *Kraemer*. It was language in the opinion in the *Civil Rights Cases* that phrased the broad test of state responsibility under the Fourteenth Amendment, predicting its consequence upon

"State action of every kind . . . which denies . . . the equal protection of the laws." And only two Terms ago, some 75 years later, the same concept of state responsibility was interpreted as necessarily following upon "state participation through any arrangement, management, funds or property." *Cooper* v. *Aaron*. It is clear, as it always has been since the *Civil Rights Cases* that "Individual invasion of individual rights is not the subject-matter of the amendment," and that private conduct abridging individual rights does no violence to the Equal Protection Clause unless to some significant extent the State in any of its manifestations has been found to have become involved in it. Because the virtue of the right to equal protection of the laws could lie only in the breadth of its application, its constitutional assurance was reserved in terms whose imprecision was necessary if the right were to be enjoyed in the variety of individual-state relationships which the Amendment was designed to embrace. For the same reason, to fashion and apply a precise formula for recognition of state responsibility under the Equal Protection Clause is an "impossible task" which "This Court has never attempted." Only by sifting facts and weighing circumstances can the nonobvious involvement of the State in private conduct be attributed its true significance.

The trial court's disposal of the issues on summary judgment has resulted in a rather incomplete record, but the opinion of the Supreme Court as well as that of the Chancellor presents the facts in sufficient detail for us to determine the degree of state participation in Eagle's refusal to serve petitioner. In this connection the Delaware Supreme Court seems to have placed controlling emphasis on its conclusion, as to the accuracy of which there is doubt, that only some 15% of the total cost of the facility was "advanced" from public funds; that the cost of the entire facility was allocated three-fifths to the space for commercial leasing and two-fifths to parking space; that anticipated revenue from parking was only some 30.5% of the total income, the balance of which was expected to be earned by the leasing; that the Authority had no original intent to place a restaurant in the building, it being only a happenstance resulting from the bidding; that Eagle expended considerable moneys on furnishings; that the restaurant's main and marked public entrance is on Ninth Street without any public entrance direct from the parking area; and that "the only connection Eagle has with the public facility . . . is the furnishing of the sum of $28,700 annually in the form of rent which is used by the Authority to defray a portion of the operating expense of an otherwise unprofitable enterprise." While these factual considerations are indeed validly accountable aspects of the enterprise upon which the State has embarked, we cannot say that they lead inescapably to the conclusion that state action is not present. Their persuasiveness is diminished when evaluated in the context of other factors which must be acknowledged.

The land and building were publicly owned. As an entity, the building was dedicated to "public uses" in performance of the Authority's "essential governmental functions." The costs of land acquisition, construction, and maintenance are defrayed entirely from donations by the City of Wilmington, from loans and revenue bonds and from the proceeds of rentals and parking services out of which the loans and bonds were payable. Assuming that the distinction would be significant, the commercially leased areas were not surplus state property, but constituted a physically and financially integral and, indeed, indispensable part of the State's plan to operate its project as a self-sustaining unit. Upkeep and maintenance of the building, including necessary repairs, were responsibilities of the Authority and were payable out of public funds. It cannot be doubted that the peculiar relationship of the restaurant to the parking facility in which it is located confers on each an incidental variety of mutual benefits. Guests of the restaurant are afforded a convenient place to park their automobiles, even if they cannot enter the restaurant directly from the parking area. Similarly, its convenience for diners may well provide additional demand for the Authority's parking facilities. Should any improvements effected in the leasehold by Eagle become part of the realty, there is no possibility of increased taxes being passed on to it since the fee is held by a tax-exempt government agency. Neither can it be ignored, especially in view of Eagle's affirmative allegation that for it to serve Negroes would injure its business, that profits earned by discrimination not only contribute to, but also are indispensable elements in, the financial success of a governmental agency.

Addition of all these activities, obligations and responsibilities of the Authority, the benefits mutually conferred, together with the obvious fact that the restaurant is operated as an integral part of a public building devoted to a public parking service, indicates that degree of state participation and involvement in discriminatory action which it was the design of the Fourteenth Amendment to condemn. It is irony amounting to grave injustice that in one part of a single building, erected and maintained with public funds by an agency of the State to serve a public purpose, all persons have equal rights, while in another portion, also serving the public, a Negro is a second-class citizen, offensive because of his race, without rights and unentitled to service, but at the same time fully enjoys equal access to nearby restaurants in wholly privately owned buildings. As the Chancellor pointed out, in its lease with Eagle the Authority could have affirmatively required Eagle to discharge the responsibilities under the Fourteenth Amendment imposed upon the private enterprise as a consequence of state participation. But no State may effectively abdicate its responsibilities by either ignoring them or by merely failing to discharge them whatever the motive may be. It is of no consolation to an individual denied the equal protection of the laws that it was done in good faith. Certainly the conclusions drawn in similar cases by the various Courts of Appeals do not depend upon such a distinction. By its inaction, the Authority, and through it the State, has not only made itself a party to the refusal of service, but has elected to place its power, property and prestige behind the admitted discrimination. The State has so far insinuated itself into a position of interdependence with Eagle that it must be recognized as a joint participant in the challenged activity, which, on that account, cannot be considered to have been so "purely private" as to fall without the scope of the Fourteenth Amendment.

Because readily applicable formulae may not be fashioned, the conclusions drawn from the facts and circumstances of this record are by no means declared as universal truths on the basis of which every state leasing agreement is to be tested. Owing to the very "largeness" of government, a multitude of relationships might appear to some to fall within the Amendment's embrace, but that, it must be remembered, can be determined only in the framework of the peculiar facts or circumstances present. Therefore respondents' prophecy of nigh universal application of a constitutional precept so peculiarly dependent for its invocation upon appropriate facts fails to take into account "Differences in circumstances [which] beget appropriate differences in law." Specifically defining the limits of our inquiry, what we hold today is that when a State leases public property in the manner and for the purpose shown to have been the case here, the proscriptions of the Fourteenth Amendment must be complied with by the lessee as certainly as though they were binding covenants written into the agreement itself.

The judgment of the Supreme Court of Delaware is reversed and the cause remanded for further proceedings consistent with this opinion.

Mr. Justice Stewart, concurring.

I agree that the judgment must be reversed, but I reach that conclusion by a route much more direct than the one traveled by the Court. In upholding Eagle's right to deny service to the appellant solely because of his race, the Supreme Court of Delaware relied upon a statute of that State which permits the proprietor of a restaurant to refuse to serve "persons whose reception or entertainment by him would be offensive to the major part of his customers . . . ." There is no suggestion in the record that the appellant as an individual was such a person. The highest court of Delaware has thus construed this legislative enactment as authorizing discriminatory classification based exclusively on color. Such a law seems to me clearly violative of the Fourteenth Amendment. I think, therefore, that the appeal was properly taken, and that the statute, as authoritatively construed by the Supreme Court of Delaware, is constitutionally invalid.

Mr. Justice Frankfurter, dissenting.

According to my brother Stewart, the Supreme Court of Delaware has held that one of its statutes sanctions a restaurateur denying service to a person solely because of his color. If my brother is correct in so reading the decision of the Delaware Supreme Court, his conclusion inevitably follows. For a State to place its authority behind discriminatory treatment based solely on color is indubitably a denial by a State of the equal protection of the laws, in violation of the Fourteenth Amendment. My brother Harlan also would find the claim of invalidity of the statute decisive if he could read the state court's construction of it as our brother Stewart reads it. But for him the state court's view of its statute is so ambiguous that he deems it necessary to secure a clarification from the state court of how in fact it did construe the statute.

I certainly do not find the clarity that my brother Stewart finds in the views expressed by the Supreme Court of Delaware regarding 24 Del. Code, § 1501. If I were forced to construe that court's construction, I should find the balance of considerations leading to the opposite conclusion from his, namely, that it was merely declaratory of the common law and did not give state sanction to refusing service to a person merely because he is colored. The Court takes no position regarding the statutory meaning which divides my brothers Harlan and Stewart. Clearly it does not take Mr. Justice Stewart's view of what the Supreme Court of Delaware decided. If it did, it would undoubtedly take his easy route to decision and not reach the same result by its much more circuitous route.

Since the pronouncement of the Supreme Court of Delaware thus lends itself to three views, none of which is patently irrational, why is not my brother Harlan's suggestion for solving this conflict the most appropriate solution? Were we to be duly advised by the Supreme Court of Delaware that Mr. Justice Stewart is correct in his reading of what it said, there would be an easy end to our problem. There would be no need for resolving the problems in state-federal relations with which the Court's opinion deals. If, on the other hand, the Delaware court did not mean to give such an invalidating construction to its statute, we would be confronted with the problems which the Court now entertains for decision, unembarrassed by disregard of a simpler issue. This would involve some delay in adjudication. But the time would be well spent, because the Court would not be deciding serious questions of constitutional law any earlier than due regard for the appropriate process of constitutional adjudication requires.

Accordingly, I join in Mr. Justice Harlan's proposed disposition of the case without intimating any view regarding the question, prematurely considered by the Court, as to what constitutes state action.

Mr. Justice Harlan, whom Mr. Justice Whittaker joins, dissenting.

The Court's opinion, by a process of first undiscriminatingly throwing together various factual bits and pieces and then undermining the resulting structure by an equally vague disclaimer, seems to me to leave completely at sea just what it is in this record that satisfies the requirement of "state action."

I find it unnecessary, however, to inquire into the matter at this stage, for it seems to me apparent that before passing on the far-reaching constitutional questions that may, or may not, be lurking in this judgment, the case should first be sent back to the state court for clarification as to the precise basis of its decision. In deciding this case the Delaware Supreme Court, among other things, said:

"It [Eagle] acts as a restaurant keeper and, as such, is not required to serve any and all persons entering its place of business, any more than the operator of a bookstore, barber shop, or other retail business is required to sell its product to every one. This is the common law, and the law of Delaware as restated in 24 Del. C. § 1501 with respect to restaurant keepers. We, accordingly, hold that the operation of its restaurant by Eagle does not fall within the scope of the prohibitions of the Fourteenth Amendment."

If in the context of this record this means, as my brother Stewart suggests, that the Delaware court construed this state statute "as authorizing discriminatory classification based exclusively on color," I would certainly agree, without more, that the enactment is offensive to the Fourteenth Amendment. It would then be quite unnecessary to reach the much broader questions dealt with in the Court's opinion. If, on the other hand, the state court meant no more than that under the statute, as at common law, Eagle was free to serve only those whom it pleased, then, and only then, would the question of "state action" be presented in full-blown form.

I think that sound principles of constitutional adjudication dictate that we should first ascertain the exact basis of this state judgment, and for that purpose I would either remand the case to the Delaware Supreme Court or hold the case pending application to the state court for clarification. It seems to me both unnecessary and unwise to reach issues of such broad constitutional significance as those now decided by the Court, before the necessity for deciding them has become apparent.

Garner v. Louisiana
368 U.S. 157   1961

Mr. Chief Justice Warren delivered the opinion of the Court.

These cases come to us from the Supreme Court of Louisiana and draw in question the constitutionality of the petitioners' convictions in the 19th Judicial District Court, Parish of East Baton Rouge, Louisiana, for the crime of disturbing the peace. The petitioners were brought to trial and convicted on informations charging them with violating Article 103, Section 7, of the Louisiana Criminal Code, in that "they refused to move from a cafe counter seat . . . after having been ordered to do so by the agent [of the establishment]; said conduct being in such manner as to unreasonably and foreseeably disturb the public . . . ." In accordance with state procedure, petitioners sought post-conviction review in the Supreme Court of Louisiana through writs of certiorari, mandamus and prohibition. They contended that the state had presented no evidence to support the findings of statutory violation, and that their convictions were invalid on other constitutional grounds, both state and federal. Relief was denied. Federal questions were properly raised and preserved throughout the proceedings, and timely petitions for certiorari filed in this Court were granted. The United States Government appeared as *amicus curiae* urging, on various grounds, that the convictions be reversed. An *amicus* brief also urging reversal was filed by the Committee on the Bill of Rights of the Association of the Bar of the City of New York.

In our view of these cases and for our disposition of them, the slight variance in the facts of the three cases is immaterial. Although the alleged offenses did not occur on the same day or in the same establishment, the petitioners were all arrested by the same officers, charged with commission of the same acts, represented by the same counsel, tried and convicted by the same judge, and given identical sentences. Because of this factual similarity and the identical nature of the problems involved, in granting certiorari, we ordered the cases consolidated for argument and now deem it sufficient to file one opinion. In addition, as the facts are simple, we think it sufficient to recite but one of the cases in detail, noting whatever slight variations exist in the others.

In No. 28, *Hoston et al*. v. *Louisiana,* Jeannette Hoston, a student at Southern University, and six of her colleagues, took seats at a lunch counter in Kress' Department Store in Baton Rouge, Louisiana, on March 29, 1960. In Kress', as in Sitman's Drug Store in No. 26 where Negroes are considered "very good customers," a segregation policy is maintained only with regard to the service of food. Hence, although both stores solicit business from white and Negro patrons, and the latter as well as the former may make purchases in the general merchandise sections without discrimination, the stores do not provide integrated service at their lunch counters.

The manager at Kress' store, who was also seated at the lunch counter, told the waitress to advise the students that they could be served at the counter across the aisle, which she did. The petitioners made no response and remained quietly in their seats. After the manager had finished his lunch, he telephoned the police and told them that "[some Negroes] were sitting at the counter reserved for whites." The police arrived at the store and ordered the students to leave. The arresting officer testified that the petitioners did and said nothing except that one of them stated that she would like a glass of iced tea, but that he believed they were disturbing the peace "by sitting there." When none of the petitioners showed signs of leaving their seats, they were placed under arrest and taken to the police station. They then were charged with violating Article 103, Section 7, of the Louisiana Criminal Code, a section of the Louisiana disturbance of the peace statute.

Before trial, the petitioners moved for a bill of particulars as to the details of their allegedly disruptive behavior and to quash the informations for failure to state any unlawful acts of which they could be constitutionally convicted. The motions were denied, and the petitioners applied to the Supreme Court of Louisiana for writs of certiorari, prohibition and mandamus to review the rulings. The Supreme Court denied the writs on the ground that an adequate remedy was available through resort to its supervisory jurisdiction in the event of a conviction. The petitioners were then tried and convicted, and sentenced to imprisonment for four months, three months of which would be suspended upon the payment of a fine of $100. Subsequent to their convictions, the Supreme Court, in denying relief on appeal, issued the following oral opinion in each case.

"Writs refused.
"This court is without jurisdiction to review facts in criminal cases.
"The rulings of the district judge on matters of law are not erroneous."

Before this Court, petitioners and the *amici* have presented a number of questions claiming deprivation of rights guaranteed to them by the First and Fourteenth Amendments to the United States Constitution. The petitioners contend:

(a) The decision below affirms a criminal conviction based upon no evidence of guilt and, therefore, deprives them of due process of law as defined in *Thompson* v. *City of Louisville*.

(b) The petitioners were convicted of a crime under the provisions of a state statute which, as applied to their acts, is so vague, indefinite and uncertain as to offend the Due Process Clause of the Fourteenth Amendment.

(c) The decisions below conflict with the Fourteenth Amendment's guarantee of freedom of expression.

(d) The decision below conflicts with prior decisions of this Court which condemn racially discriminatory administration of State criminal laws in contravention of the Equal Protection Clause of the Fourteenth Amendment.

With regard to argument (d), the petitioners and the New York Committee on the Bill of Rights contend that the participation of the police and the judiciary to enforce a state custom of segregation resulted in the use of "state action" and was therefore plainly violative of the Fourteenth Amendment. The petitioners also urge that even if these cases contain a relevant component of "private action," that action is substantially infected with state power and thereby remains state action for purposes of the Fourteenth Amendment.

In the view we take of the cases we find it unnecessary to reach the broader constitutional questions presented, and in accordance with our practice not to formulate a rule of constitutional law broader than is required by the precise facts presented in the record, for the reasons hereinafter stated, we hold that the convictions in these cases are so totally devoid of evidentiary support as to render them unconstitutional under the Due Process Clause of the Fourteenth Amendment. As in *Thompson* v. *City of Louisville,* our inquiry does not turn on a question of sufficiency of evidence to support a conviction, but on whether these convictions rest upon any evidence which would support a finding that the petitioners' acts caused a disturbance of the peace. In addition, we cannot be concerned with whether the evidence proves the commission of some other crime, for it is as much a denial of due process to send an accused to prison following conviction for a charge that was never made as it is to convict him upon a charge for which there is no evidence to support that conviction.

The respondent, both in its brief and its argument to this Court, implied that the evidence proves the elements of a criminal trespass. In oral argument it contended that the real question here "is whether or not a private property owner and proprietor of a private establishment has the right to serve only those whom he chooses and to refuse to serve those whom he desires not to serve for whatever reason he may determine." That this is not a question presented by the records in these cases seems too apparent for debate. Even assuming it were the question, however, which it clearly is not, these convictions could not stand for the reason stated in *Cole* v. *Arkansas.*

Under our view of these cases, our task is to determine whether there is any evidence in the records to show that the petitioners, by their actions at the lunch counters in the business establishments involved, violated Article 103, Section 7, of the Louisiana Criminal Code. At the time of petitioners' acts, Article 103 provided:

Disturbing the peace is the doing of any of the following in such a manner as would foreseeably disturb or alarm the public:

(1) Engaging in a fistic encounter; or
(2) Using of any unnecessarily loud, offensive or insulting language; or
(3) Appearing in an intoxicated condition; or
(4) Engaging in any act in a violent and tumultuous manner by any three or more persons; or
(5) Holding of an unlawful assembly, or
(6) Interruption of any lawful assembly of people; or
(7) Commission of any other act in such a manner as to unreasonably disturb or alarm the public.

I

Our initial inquiry is necessary to determine the type of conduct proscribed by this statute and the elements of guilt which the evidence must prove to support a criminal conviction thereunder. First, it is evident from a reading of the statute that the accused must conduct himself in a manner that would "foreseeably disturb or alarm the public." In addition, when a person is charged with a violation of Section 7, an earlier version of which was aptly described by the Supreme Court of Louisiana as "the general portion of the statute which does not define the 'conduct or acts' the members of the legislature had in mind," it would also seem apparent from the words of the statute that the acts, whatever they might be, be done "in such a manner as to [actually] unreasonably disturb or alarm the public." However, because we find the records barren of any evidence that would support a finding that the petitioners' conduct would even "foreseeably" have disturbed the public, we need not consider whether the statute also requires the acts to be done in a manner as actually to disturb the peace.

We of course are bound by a state's interpretation of its own statute and will not substitute our judgment for that of the state's when it becomes necessary to analyze the evidence for the purpose of determining whether that evidence supports the findings of a state court. Hence, we must look to Louisiana for guidance in the meaning of the phrase "foreseeably disturb or alarm the public" in order to determine the type of conduct proscribed by L. S. A.-R. S. 14:103 (7).

The Supreme Court of Louisiana has had occasion in the past, in interpreting the predecessor of Article 103, to give content to these words, and it is evident from the court's prior treatment of them that they were not intended to embrace peaceful conduct. On the contrary, it is plain that under the court's application of the statute these words encompass only conduct which is violent or boisterous in itself, or which is provocative in the sense that it induces a foreseeable physical disturbance. In *State* v. *Sanford* the evidence showed that thirty Jehovah's Witnesses approached a Louisiana town for the purpose of distributing religious tracts and persuading the public to make contributions to their cause. The Witnesses were warned by the mayor and police officers that "their presence and activities would cause trouble among the population and asked them to stay away from the town. . . ." The Witnesses failed to yield to the warning and proceeded on their mission. The trial court found that the acts of the Witnesses in entering the town and stopping passers-by in the crowded street "might or would tend to incite rioting and disorderly conduct." The Supreme Court of Louisiana set aside convictions for breach of the peace, holding that the defendants did not commit any unlawful act or pursue any disorderly course of conduct which would tend to disturb the peace, thus, in effect, that peaceful conduct, even though conceivably offensive to another class of the public, is not conduct which may be proscribed by Louisiana's disturbance of the peace statute without evidence that the actor conducted himself in some outwardly unruly manner.

The conclusion of the highest Louisiana court that the breach of the peace statute does not reach peaceful and orderly conduct is substantiated by the conclusion drawn from reading the statute as a whole. The catch-all provision under which the petitioners were tried and convicted follows an enumeration of six specific offenses, each of which describes overtly tumultuous or disruptive behavior. It would therefore normally be interpreted in the light of the preceding sections as an effort to cover other forms of violence or loud and boisterous conduct not already listed. We do not mean to imply that an *ejusdem generis* reading of the statute is constitutionally compelled to the exclusion of other reasonable interpretations, but we do note that here such a reading is consistent with the Louisiana Supreme Court's application in Sanford.

Further evidence that Article 103 (7) was not designed to encompass the petitioners' conduct in these cases has been supplied by the Louisiana legislature. Shortly after the events for which the petitioners were arrested took place, the legislature amended its disturbance of the peace statute in an obvious attempt to reach the type of activity involved in these cases. The contrast between the language of the present statute and the one under which the petitioners were convicted confirms the interpretation given the general term of the latter by the Supreme Court in *State* v. *Sanford* and the natural meaning of the words used in Article 103.

We are aware that the Louisiana courts have the final authority to interpret and, where they see fit, to reinterpret that state's legislation. However, we have seen no indication that the Louisiana Supreme Court has changed its *Sanford* interpretation of L. S. A.-R. S. 14:103 (7), and we will not infer that an inferior Louisiana court intended to overrule a long-standing and reasonable interpretation of a state statute by that state's highest court. Our reluctance so to infer is supported, moreover, by the fact that *State* v. *Sanford* was argued by the petitioners to both the trial court and to the Supreme Court, and that neither court mentioned in their opinions that *Sanford* was no longer to be the law in Louisiana.

We think that the above discussion would give ample support to a conclusion that Louisiana law requires a finding of outwardly boisterous or unruly conduct in order to charge a defendant with "foreseeably" disturbing or alarming the public. However, because this case comes to us from a state court and necessitates a delicate involvement in federal-state relations, we are willing to assume with the respondent that the Louisiana courts might construe the statute more broadly to encompass the traditional common-law concept of disturbing the peace. Thus construed, it might permit the police to prevent an imminent public commotion even though caused by peaceful and orderly conduct on the part of the accused. We therefore treat these cases as though evidence of such imminent danger, as well as evidence of a defendant's active conduct which is outwardly provocative, could support a finding that the acts might "foreseeably disturb or alarm the public" under the Louisiana statute.

II

Having determined what evidence is necessary to support a finding of disturbing the peace under Louisiana law, the ultimate question, as in *Thompson* v. *City of Louisville* is whether the records in these cases contain any such evidence. With appropriate notations to the slight differences in testimony in the other two cases, we again turn to the record in No. 28. The manager of the department store in which the lunch counter was located testified that after the students had taken their seats at the "white lunch counter" where he was also occupying a seat, he advised the waitress on duty to offer the petitioners service at the counter across the aisle which served Negroes. The petitioners, however, after being "advised that they would be served at the other counter," remained in their seats, and the manager continued eating his lunch at the same counter. In No. 26, where there were no facilities to serve colored persons, the petitioners were merely told that they couldn't be served, but were never even asked to move. In No. 27, a waitress testified that the petitioners were merely told that they would have to go "to the other side to be served." The petitioners not only made no speeches, they did not even speak to anyone except to order food; they carried no placards, and did nothing, beyond their mere presence at the lunch counter, to attract attention to themselves or to others. In none of the cases was there any testimony that the petitioners were told that their mere presence was causing, or was likely to cause, a disturbance of the peace, not that the petitioners were ever asked to leave the counters or the establishments by anyone connected with the stores.

The manager in No. 28 testified that after finishing his meal he went to the telephone and called the police department, advising them that Negroes were in his store sitting at the lunch counter reserved for whites. This is the only case in which "the owner or his agent" notified the police of the petitioners' presence at the lunch counter, and even here the manager gave no indication to the officers that he feared any disturbance or that he had received any complaint concerning the petitioners' presence. In No. 27, a waitress testified that a bus driver sitting in the restaurant notified the police that "there were several colored people sitting at the lunch counter." In No. 26, the arresting officers were not summoned to the drug store by anyone even remotely connected with Sitman's but, rather, by a call from an officer on his "beat" who had observed the petitioners sitting quietly at the lunch counter.

Although the manager of Kress' Department Store testified that the only conduct which he considered disruptive was the petitioners' mere presence at the counter, he did state that he called the police because "he feared that some disturbance might occur." However, his fear is completely unsubstantiated by the record. The manager continued eating his lunch in an apparently leisurely manner at the same counter at which the petitioners were sitting before calling the police. Moreover, not only did he fail to give the petitioners any warning of his alleged "fear," but he specifically testified to the fact that the petitioners were never asked to move or to leave the store. Nor did the witness elaborate on the basis of his fear except to state that "it isn't customary for the two races to sit together and eat together." In addition, there is no evidence that this alleged fear was ever communicated to the arresting officers, either at the time the manager made the initial call to police headquarters or when the police arrived at the store. Under these circumstances, the manager's general statement gives no support for the convictions within the meaning of *Thompson* v. *City of Louisville.*

Subsequent to the manager's notification, the police arrived at the store and, without consulting the manager or anyone else on the premises, went directly to confront the petitioners. An officer asked the petitioners to leave the counter because "they were disturbing the peace by sitting there." One of the students stated that she wished to get a glass of iced tea, but she and her friends were told, again by the police, that they were disturbing the peace by sitting at a counter reserved for whites and that they would have to leave. When the petitioners continued to occupy the seats, they were arrested, as the officer testified, for disturbing the peace "[b]y sitting there" "because that place was reserved for white people." The same officer testified that the petitioners had done nothing other than take seats at that particular lunch counter which he considered to be a breach of the peace.

The respondent discusses at length the history of race relations and the high degree of racial segregation which exists throughout the South. Although there is no reference to such facts in the records, the respondent argues that the trial court took judicial notice of the general situation, as he may do under Louisiana law, and that it therefore became apparent to the court that the petitioners' presence at the lunch counters might cause a disturbance which it was the duty of the police to prevent. There is nothing in the records to indicate that the trial judge did in fact take judicial notice of anything. To extend the doctrine of judicial notice to the length pressed by the respondent would require us to allow the prosecution to do through argument to this Court what it is required by due process to do at the trial, and would be "to turn the doctrine into a pretext for dispensing with a trial." Furthermore, unless an accused is informed at the trial of the facts of which the court is taking judicial notice, not only does he not know upon what evidence he is being convicted, but, in addition, he is deprived of any opportunity to challenge the deductions drawn from such notice or to dispute the notoriety or truth of the facts allegedly relied upon. Moreover, there is no way by which an appellate court may review the facts and law of a case and intelligently decide whether the findings of the lower court are supported by the evidence where that evidence is unknown. Such an assumption would be a denial of due process.

Thus having shown that these records contain no evidence to support a finding that petitioners disturbed the peace, either by outwardly boisterous conduct or by passive conduct likely to cause a public disturbance, we hold that these convictions violated petitioners' rights to due process of law guaranteed them by the Fourteenth Amendment to the United States Constitution. The undisputed evidence shows that the police who arrested the petitioners were left with nothing to support their actions except their own opinions that it was a breach of the peace for the petitioners to sit peacefully in a place where custom decreed they should not sit. Such activity, in the circumstances of these cases, is not evidence of any crime and cannot be so considered either by the police or the courts.

The judgments are reversed.

Mr. Justice Frankfurter, concurring in the judgment.

Whether state statutes are to be construed one way or another is a question of state law, final decision of which rests, of course, with the courts of the State. When as here those courts have not spelled out the meaning of a statute, this Court must extrapolate its allowable meaning and attribute that to the highest court of the State. We must do so in a manner that affords the widest latitude to state legislative power consistent with the United States Constitution.

Since La. Rev. Stat. § 14:103 is concededly a statute aimed at "disturbing the peace," we begin with the breadth of meaning derived from that phrase in *Town of Ponchatoula* v. *Bates*. To be sure, that amounted to an abstract discussion and in the limited circumstances considered by the Louisiana Supreme Court in *State* v. *Sanford* the allowable scope of the statutory prohibition was not fully explored. But construction of the statute to prohibit non-violent, non-religious behavior in a private shop when that behavior has a tendency to disturb or alarm the public is fairly derivable from a reading of the *Sanford* opinion.

The action of the Louisiana legislature in amending its statutes after the events now under review took place is not a safe or even relevant guide to the scope of the prior statute. Legislatures not uncommonly seek to make prior law more explicit or reiterate a prohibition by more emphatic concreteness. The rule of evidence that excludes proof of post-injury repairs offers a useful analogy here. It is not our province to limit the meaning of a state statute beyond its confinement by reasonably read state-court rulings.

Assuming for present purposes the constitutionality of a statute prohibiting non-violent activity that tends to provoke public alarm or disturbance, such a tendency, as a crucial element of a criminal offense, must be established by evidence disclosed in the record to sustain a conviction. A judge's private knowledge, or even "knowledge by notoriety," to use Dean Wigmore's phrase, not presented as part of the prosecution's case capable of being met by a defendant, is not an adequate basis, as a matter of due process, to establish an essential element of what is punished as crime.

It may be unnecessary to require formal proof, even as to an issue crucial in determining guilt in a criminal prosecution, of what is incontestably obvious. But some showing cannot be dispensed with when an inference is at all doubtful. And it begs the whole question on the answer to which the validity of these convictions turns to assume that the "public" tended to be alarmed by the conduct of the petitioners here disclosed. Conviction under this Louisiana statute cannot be sustained by reliance merely upon likely consequences in the generality of cases. Since particular persons are being sent to jail for conduct allegedly having a particular effect on a particular occasion under particular circumstances, it becomes necessary to appraise that conduct and effect by the particularity of evidence adduced.

The records in these cases, whatever variance in unimportant details they may show, contain no evidence of disturbance or alarm in the behavior of the cafe employees or customers or even passers-by, the relevant "public" fairly in contemplation of these charges. What they do show was aptly summarized both in the testimony of the arresting police and in the recitation of the trial judge as the "mere presence" of the petitioners.

Silent persistence in sitting after service is refused could no doubt conceivably exacerbate feelings to the boiling point. It is not fanciful speculation, however, that a proprietor who invites trade in most parts of his establishment and restricts it in another may change his policy when non-violently challenged. With records as barren as these of evidence from which a tendency to disturb or alarm the public immediately involved can be drawn, there is nothing before us on which to sustain such an inference from what may be hypothetically lodged in the unopened bosom of the local court.

Since the "mere presence" that these records prove has, in any event, not been made a crime by the Louisiana statute under which these petitioners were charged, their convictions must be reversed.

Mr. Justice Douglas, concurring.

If these cases had arisen in the Pacific northwest—the area I know best—I could agree with the opinion of the Court. For while many communities north and south, east and west, at times have racial problems, those areas which have never known segregation would not be inflamed or aroused by the presence of a member of a minority race in a restaurant. But in Louisiana racial problems have agitated the people since the days of slavery. The landmark case of *Plessy* v. *Ferguson*—the decision that announced in 1896 the now-repudiated doctrine of "separate but equal" facilities for whites and blacks—came from Louisiana which had enacted in 1890 a statute requiring segregation of the races on railroad trains. In the environment of a segregated community I can understand how the mere presence of a Negro at a white lunch counter might inflame some people as much as fisticuffs would in other places. For the reasons stated by Mr. Justice Harlan in these cases, I read the Louisiana opinions as meaning that this law includes "peaceful conduct of a kind that foreseeably may lead to public disturbance"—a kind of "generally known condition" that may be "judicially noticed" even in a criminal case.

This does not mean that the police were justified in making these arrests. For the police are supposed to be on the side of the Constitution, not on the side of discrimination. Yet if all constitutional questions are to be put aside and the problem treated merely in terms of disturbing the peace, I would have difficulty in reversing these judgments. I think, however, the constitutional questions must be reached and that they make reversal necessary.

Restaurants, whether in a drug store, department store, or bus terminal, are a part of the public life of most of our communities. Though they are private enterprises, they are public facilities in which the states may not enforce a policy of racial segregation.

I

It is, of course, state action that is prohibited by the Fourteenth Amendment, not the actions of individuals. So far as the Fourteenth Amendment is concerned, individuals can be as prejudiced and intolerant as they like. They may as a consequence subject themselves to suits for assault, battery, or trespass. But those actions have no footing in the Federal Constitution. The line of forbidden conduct marked by the Equal Protection Clause of the Fourteenth Amendment is crossed only when a State makes prejudice or intolerance its policy and enforces it as held in the *Civil Rights Cases*. Mr. Justice Bradley, speaking for the Court, said: ". : . civil rights, such as are guaranteed by the Constitution against State aggression, cannot be impaired by the wrongful acts of individuals, unsupported by State authority in the shape of laws, *customs,* or judicial or executive proceedings." (Italics added.)

State policy violative of the Fourteenth Amendment may be expressed in *legislative* enactments that permit or require segregation of the races in public places or public facilities or in residential areas.

It may be expressed through *executive* action, as where the police or other law enforcement officials act pursuant to, or under the color of, state law.

It may be expressed through the *administrative* action of state agencies in leasing public facilities.

It may result from *judicial action,* as where members of a race are systematically excluded from juries, or where restrictive covenants based on race are enforced by the judiciary, or where a state court fines or imprisons a person for asserting his federal right to use the facilities of an interstate bus terminal.

As noted, Mr. Justice Bradley suggested in the *Civil Rights Cases* that state policy may be as effectively expressed in *customs* as in formal legislative, executive, or judicial action.

It was indeed held in *Baldwin* v. *Morgan* that the "custom, practice and usage" of a city and its police in arresting four Negroes for using "white" waiting rooms was state action in violation of the Fourteenth Amendment, even though no ordinance was promulgated and no order issued. In the instant cases such an inference can be drawn from the totality of circumstances permeating the environment where the arrests were made—not an isolated arrest but three arrests; not arrests on account of fisticuffs but arrests because the defendants were Negroes seeking restaurant service at counters and tables reserved for "whites."

There is a deep-seated pattern of segregation of the races in Louisiana, going back at least to *Plessy* v. *Ferguson*. It was restated in 1960—

the year in which petitioners were arrested and charged for sitting in white restaurants—by Act No. 630, which in its preamble states:

"Whereas, Louisiana has always maintained a policy of segregation of the races, and
"Whereas, it is the intention of the citizens of this sovereign state that such a policy be continued."

Louisiana requires that all circuses, shows, and tent exhibitions to which the public is invited have one entrance for whites and one for Negroes. No dancing, social functions, entertainment, athletic training, games, sports, contests "and other such activities involving personal and social contacts" may be open to both races. Any public entertainment or athletic contest must provide separate seating arrangements and separate sanitary drinking water and "any other facilities" for the two races. Marriage between members of the two races is banned. Segregation by race is required in prisons. The blind must be segregated. Teachers in public schools are barred from advocating desegregation of the races in the public school system. So are other state employees. Segregation on trains is required. Common carriers of passengers must provide separate waiting rooms and reception room facilities for the two races and separate toilets and separate facilities for drinking water as well. Employers must provide separate sanitary facilities for the two races. Employers must also provide separate eating places in separate rooms and separate eating and drinking utensils for members of the two races. Persons of one race may not establish their residence in a community of another race without approval of the majority of the other race. Court dockets must reveal the race of the parties in divorce actions. And all public parks, recreation centers, playgrounds, community centers and "other such facilities at which swimming, dancing, golfing, skating or other recreational activities are conducted" must be segregated.

Though there may have been no state law or municipal ordinance that *in terms* required segregation of the races in restaurants, it is plain that the proprietors in the instant cases were segregating blacks from whites pursuant to Louisiana's custom. Segregation is basic to the structure of Louisiana as a community; the custom that maintains it is at least as powerful as any law. If these proprietors also choose segregation, their preference does not make the action "private," rather than "state," action. If it did, a miniscule of private prejudice would convert state into private action. Moreover, where the segregation policy is the policy of a state, it matters not that the agency to enforce it is a private enterprise.

II

It is my view that a State may not constitutionally enforce a policy of segregation in restaurant facilities. Some of the argument assumed that restaurants are "private" property in the sense that one's home is "private" property. They are, of course, "private" property for many purposes of the Constitution. Yet so are street railways, power plants, warehouses, and other types of enterprises which have long been held to be affected with a public interest. Where constitutional rights are involved, the proprietary interests of individuals must give way. Towns, though wholly owned by private interests, perform municipal functions and are held to the same constitutional requirements as ordinary municipalities. State regulation of private enterprise falls when it discriminates against interstate commerce. State regulation of private enterprise that results in impairment of other constitutional rights should stand on no firmer footing, at least in the area where facilities of a public nature are involved.

Long before Chief Justice Waite wrote the opinion in *Munn* v. *Illinois* holding that the prices charged by grain warehouses could be regulated by the state, a long list of businesses had been held to be "affected with a public interest." Among these were ferries, common carriers, hackmen, bakers, millers, wharfingers, and innkeepers. The test used in *Munn* v. *Illinois* was stated as follows: "Property does become clothed with a public interest when used in a manner to make it of public consequence, and affect the community at large." In reply to the charge that price regulation deprived the warehouses of property, Chief Justice Waite stated, "There is no attempt to compel these owners to grant the public an interest in their property, but to declare their obligations, if they use it in this particular manner."

There was a long span between *Munn* v. *Illinois* and *Nebbia* v. *New York* which upheld the power of a State to fix the price of milk. A business may have a "public interest" even though it is not a "public utility" in the accepted sense, even though it enjoys no franchise from the state, and even though it enjoys no monopoly. The examples cover a wide range from price control to prohibition of certain types of business. Various systems or devices designed by States or municipalities to protect the wholesomeness of food in the interests of health are deep-seated as any exercise of the police power.

Years ago Lord Chief Justice Hale stated in *De Portibus Maris* ". . . if a man set out a street in new building on his own land, it is now no longer bare private interest, but is affected by a public interest." Those who run a retail establishment under permit from a municipality operate in my view a public facility in which there can be no more discrimination based on race than is constitutionally permissible in the more customary types of public facility.

Under Louisiana law, restaurants are a form of private property affected with a public interest. Local Boards of Health are given broad powers. The City of Baton Rouge in its City Code requires all restaurants to have a permit. The Director of Public Health is given broad powers of inspection and permits issued can be suspended. Permits are not transferable. One who operates without a permit commits a separate offense each day a violation occurs. Moreover, detailed provisions are made concerning the equipment that restaurants must have, the protection of ready-to-eat foods and drink, and the storage of food.

Restaurants, though a species of private property, are in the public domain. Or to paraphrase the opinion in *Nebbia* v. *New York,* restaurants in Louisiana have a "public consequence" and "affect the community at large."

While the concept of a business "affected with a public interest" normally is used as a measure of a State's police power over it, it also has other consequences. A state may not require segregation of the races on conventional public utilities any more than it can segregate them in ordinary public facilities. As stated by the court in *Boman* v. *Birmingham Transit Co.* a public utility "is doing something the state deems useful for the public necessity or convenience." It was this idea that the first Mr. Justice Harlan, dissenting in *Plessy* v. *Ferguson* advanced. Though a common carrier is private enterprise, "its work" he maintained is public. And there can be no difference, in my view, between one kind of business that is regulated in the public interest and another kind so far as the problem of racial segregation is concerned. I do not believe that a State that licenses a business can license it to serve only whites or only blacks or only yellows or only browns. Race is an impermissible classification when it comes to parks or other municipal facilities by reason of the Equal Protection Clause of the Fourteenth Amendment. By the same token, I do not see how a State can constitutionally exercise its licensing power over business either in terms or in effect to segregate the races in the licensed premises. The authority to license a business for public use is derived from the public. Negroes are as much a part of that public as are whites. A municipality granting a license to operate a business for the public represents Negroes as well as all other races who live there. A license to establish a restaurant is a license to establish a public facility and necessarily imports, in law, equality of use for all members of the public. I see no way whereby licenses issued by a State to serve the public can be distinguished from leases of public facilities for that end.

One can close the doors of his home to anyone he desires. But one who operates an enterprise under a license from the government enjoys a privilege that derives from the people. Whether retail stores, not licensed by the municipality, stand on a different footing is not presented here. But the necessity of a license shows that the public has rights in respect to those premises. Those who license enterprises for public use should not have under our Constitution the power to license it for the use of only one race. For there is the overriding constitutional requirement that all state power be exercised so as not to deny equal protection to any group. As the first Mr. Justice Harlan stated in dissent in *Plessy* v. *Ferguson* ". . . in view of the Constitution, in the eye of the law, there is in this country no superior, dominant, ruling class of citizens. There is no caste here. Our Constitution is color blind . . . ."

Mr. Justice Harlan, concurring in the judgment.

I agree that these convictions are unconstitutional, but not for the reasons given by the Court. Relying on *Thompson* v. *City of Louisville* the Court strikes down the convictions on the ground that there is no evidence whatever to support them. In my opinion the *Thompson* doctrine does not fit these cases. However, I believe the convictions are vulnerable under the Fourteenth Amendment on other grounds: (1) the kind of conduct revealed in *Garner*, No. 26, and in *Hoston*, No. 28, could not be punished under a generalized breach of the peace provision, such as § (7) of Art. 103, La. Crim. Code; (2) Art. 103 (7) as applied in *Briscoe*, No. 27 (as well as in the *Garner* and *Hoston* cases) is unconstitutionally vague and uncertain.

The Court's reversal for lack of evidence rests on two different views of Art. 103 (7). First, it is said that the statute, as construed by the

Louisiana courts, reaches at most only "violent," "boisterous," or "outwardly provocative" conduct that may foreseeably induce a public disturbance. On this view, these cases are found evidentially wanting because the petitioners' conduct, being entirely peaceful, was not of the character proscribed by the statute so construed. Alternatively, it is recognized that the statute is susceptible of a construction that would embrace as well other kinds of conduct having the above effect. On that view, the convictions are also found evidentially deficient, in that petitioners' conduct, so it is said, could not properly be taken as having any tendency to cause a public disturbance. In my opinion, the first of these holdings cannot withstand analysis with appropriate regard for the limitations upon our powers of review over state criminal cases; the second holding rests on untenable postulates as to the law of evidence.

I

Turning to the first holding, it goes without saying that we are not at liberty to determine for ourselves the scope of this Louisiana statute. That was a function belonging exclusively to the state courts, and their interpretation is binding on us. For me, the Court's view that the statute covers only nonpeaceful conduct, is unacceptable, since I believe that the Louisiana Supreme Court decided the opposite in these very cases. I think the State Supreme Court's refusal to review these convictions, taken in light of its assertion that the "rulings of the district judge on matters of law are not erroneous," must be accepted as an authoritative and binding state determination that the petitioners' activities, as revealed in these records, did violate the statute; in other words that, contrary to what this Court now says in Part I of its opinion, the enactment *does* cover peaceful conduct of a kind that foreseeably may lead to public disturbance.

This Court's view of the statute rests primarily, if not entirely, on an earlier Louisiana case, *State* v. *Sanford,* involving a different, but comparable, breach of the peace statute. That case is regarded as establishing that breaches of the peace under Louisiana law are confined to nonpeaceful conduct. While I do not find the *Sanford* case as "plain" as the Court does, that earlier holding cannot in any event be deemed controlling on the significance to be attributed to the action of the State Supreme Court in *these* cases. There can be no doubt but that Louisiana had to follow the principles of *Sanford* only to the extent that it felt bound by *stare decisis*. A departure from precedent may have been wrong, unwise, or even unjust, but it was not unconstitutional.

More basically, established principles of constitutional adjudication require us to consider that the Louisiana Supreme Court's refusal to review these cases signifies a holding that the breach of the peace statute which controls these cases does embrace the conduct of the petitioners, peaceful though it was.

These state judgments come to us armored with a presumption that they are not founded "otherwise than is required by the fundamental law of the land," comparable to the presumption which has always attached to state legislative enactments. That presumption should render impermissible an interpretation of these judgments as resting on the view that the relevant breach of the peace statute reaches only unruly behaviour. For, on the Court's premise that there is no evidence of that kind of behaviour, such an interpretation in effect attributes to the Louisiana Supreme Court a deliberately unconstitutional decision, under principles established by *Thompson* v. *City of Louisville* which had already been decided at the time these cases came before the Louisiana courts.

Moreover, the kind of speculation in which the Court has indulged as to the meaning of the Louisiana statute is surely out of keeping with the principle that federal courts should abstain from constitutional decision involving doubtful state law questions until a clarifying adjudication on them has first been obtained from the state courts. If there be doubt as to how the statute was construed in this respect, the cases should be returned to the Louisiana Supreme Court for clarification of its judgments.

Our recent decision in *Thompson* v. *City of Louisville* cannot well be taken as justification for considering the judgments under review as other than a holding by Louisiana's highest court that breach of the peace under then existing state law may include conduct that in itself is peaceful. In *Thompson,* the petitioner was convicted of two offenses defined by ordinances of the City of Louisville. One of these ordinances, prohibiting loitering, expressly enumerated three elements of the offense. The prosecution introduced no evidence to establish any of these definitely prescribed components, which were not suggested to have, by virtue of state judicial interpretation, any other than their plain meaning. We held that "under the words of the ordinance itself," there was no evidence to support the conviction.

The other offense of which the petitioner in *Thompson* was convicted was "disorderly conduct," not at all defined in the ordinance. The only evidence in the record relating to conduct which might conceivably have come within the prohibited scope indicated was that the petitioner was "argumentative" with the arresting officers. We said of this conviction: "We assume, for we are justified in assuming that merely 'arguing' with a policeman is not, because it could not be, 'disorderly conduct' as a matter of the substantive law of Kentucky." In other words, we held that the ordinance could not, for want of adequate notice, *constitutionally* be construed by the Kentucky courts to cover the activity for which the City sought to punish the petitioner.

Where, as was true of the disorderly conduct charge in *Thompson,* application of a generally drawn state statute or municipal ordinance to the conduct of a defendant would require a constitutionally impermissible construction of the enactment, we are not bound by the state court's finding that the conduct was criminal. In the cases now before us, however, the Court does not suggest that Louisiana's disturbance of the peace statute was too vague to be constitutionally applied to the conduct of the petitioners. I think we are obliged, because of the state courts' dispositions of these cases, to hold that there was presented at petitioners' trials evidence of criminal conduct under Louisiana law.

Thompson v. *Louisville* should be recognized for what it is, a case involving a situation which, I think it fair to say, was unique in the annals of the Court. The case is bound to lead us into treacherous territory, unless we apply its teaching with the utmost circumspection, and with due sense of the limitations upon our reviewing authority.

The Court's holding on this phase of the matter also suffers from additional infirmities. I do not think that *State* v. *Sanford,* the cornerstone of this branch of the Court's opinion, is as revealing upon the meaning of breach of the peace under Louisiana law as the Court would make it seem. In that case the Louisiana Supreme Court reversed the convictions, under the then breach of the peace statute, of four Jehovah's Witnesses who had solicited contributions and distributed pamphlets in a Louisiana town, with an opinion which cited, *inter alia, Cantwell* v. *Connecticut and Martin* v. *Struthers.* Reference was made to "the provisions of the Constitution of the United States guaranteeing freedom of religion, of the press and of speech." The court said, most clearly, "The application of the statute by the trial judge to the facts of this case and his construction thereof would render it unconstitutional under the above Federal authorities." In addition, the opinion noted, conviction under the statute might violate the Louisiana Constitution "because it is well-settled that no act or conduct, however reprehensible, is a crime in Louisiana, unless it is defined and made a crime clearly and unmistakably by statute." In the concluding part of its opinion the Louisiana Supreme Court also said what this Court now considers to be the sole ground of its decision: "It is our opinion that the statute is inapplicable to this case because it appears that the defendants did not commit any unlawful act or pursue an unlawful or disorderly course of conduct which would tend to disturb the peace."

Thus, a full reading of *Sanford* will disclose that there were at least three considerations which led to the result: (1) the likelihood that a contrary holding would violate provisions of the Federal Constitution relating to religion, speech, and press under the principles declared in then-recent Supreme Court decisions; (2) the possibility that the statute was too vague and unclear under the Louisiana Constitution adequately to define the bounds of the conduct being declared criminal; (3) the unfairness of convicting under a general breach of the peace statute persons engaged in such peaceable religious activity.

The Court now isolates out this last factor from this multifaceted opinion, and, using it as an immutable measure of what Louisiana law requires, declares that the present convictions must fall because the standard so unclearly set out in *Sanford* has not been met. Apart from other considerations already discussed, I am not prepared to rest a constitutional decision on so insecure a foundation.

It is further significant that the State Supreme Court's order refusing to review the present cases does not cite *State* v. *Sanford,* but rather relies on another earlier case, *Town of Ponchatoula* v. *Bates.* The *Bates* decision, upholding the constitutionality of an ordinance making it a crime "to engage in a fight or in any manner disturb the peace," defined disturbance of the peace as "any act or conduct of a person which molests the inhabitants in the enjoyment of that peace and quiet to which they are entitled, or which throws into confusion things settled, or which causes excitement, unrest, disquietude, or fear among persons of ordinary normal temperament." Such a definition would of course bring within the compass of the statute even peaceful activity, so long as it threw "into confusion things settled," or caused disquietude among ordinary members of the community. I think it was that construction which the Louisiana Supreme Court placed upon the breach of the peace statute involved in the cases now before us.

II

The alternative holding of the Court in Part II of its opinion also stands on unsolid foundations. Conceding that this breach of the peace statute "might" be construed to cover peaceful conduct carried on "in such a manner as would foreseeably disturb or alarm the public," the Court holds that there was no evidence that petitioners' conduct tended to disturb or alarm those who witnessed their activity.

There is, however, more to these cases than what physically appears in the record. It is an undisputed fact that the "sit-in" program, of which petitioners' demonstrations were a part, had caused considerable racial tension in various States, including Louisiana. Under Louisiana law Louisiana courts may take judicial notice of "the political social and racial conditions prevailing in this state." This Court holds, nonetheless, that the Louisiana courts could not, consistently with the procedural guarantees of the Fourteenth Amendment, judicially notice the undisputed fact that there was racial tension in and around Baton Rouge on March 28 and 29, 1960 (the dates of these "sit-ins"), without informing the parties that such notice was being taken, and without spreading the source of the information on the record.

Support for this constitutional proposition is found in *Ohio Bell Telephone Co.* v. *Public Utilities Commission.* The Court there held that it was repugnant to the Fourteenth Amendment for a state agency to deprive the telephone company of property on the basis of rates set by a precise mathematical computation derived from undisclosed statistics. This was because the procedure afforded no opportunity for rebuttal with respect to the underlying data, and for possible demonstration that the figures should not be judicially noticed, since their source was unknown and the statistics were not disclosed to any reviewing court.

The situation we have here is quite different. The existence of racial tensions, of which the Louisiana courts must have taken judicial notice in order to find that petitioners' conduct alarmed or disturbed the public, was notorious throughout the community and, indeed, throughout that part of the United States. The truth of that proposition is not challenged, nor is any particular authority required to confirm it. This kind of generally known condition may be judicially noticed by trial and appellate courts without prior warning to the parties, since it does not require any foundation establishing the accuracy of a specific source of information. I perceive no reason why that principle should be considered as applying only in civil cases, and I am not aware of any American authority which so holds.

Indeed, the fact of which I think we must consider judicial notice was taken in this instance was so notorious throughout the country that far from its being unconstitutional for a court to take it into consideration, it would be quite amiss for us not to deem that the Louisiana courts did so on their own initiative. It might have been procedurally preferable had the trial judge announced to the parties that he was taking judicial notice, as is suggested in Model Code of Evidence, Rule 804. But we would be exalting the sheerest of technicalities were we to hold that a conviction is constitutionally void because of a judge's failure to declare that he has noticed a common proposition when, at no stage in the proceeding, is it suggested that the proposition may be untrue. Whether a trial judge need notify the parties of his intention to take judicial notice of "routine matters of common knowledge which . . . [he] would notice as a matter of course" is best left to his "reasonable discretion." Appellate courts have always reserved the authority to notice such commonly known propositions as are needed to support the judgment of a lower court, even if no express reference has been made below.

Moreover, in this instance, the fact that the trial court had taken judicial notice of the impact of petitioners' conduct, which indeed had obviously been engaged in for the very purpose of producing an impact on others in this field of racial relations, albeit, I shall assume, with the best of motives, could hardly have failed to cross the minds of petitioners' counsel before the trial had ended. They however neither sought to introduce countervailing evidence on that issue, nor have they undertaken at any stage of these proceedings, including that in this Court, to question the availability of judicial notice on this aspect of the State's case.

Were we to follow the reasoning of the majority opinion where it would logically lead, this Court would be violating due process every time it noticed a generally known fact without first calling in the parties to apprise them of its intention. Yet without any such notification this Court has many times taken judicial notice of well-known economic and social facts, and even of the tendency of particular epithets to cause a breach of the peace.

It is no answer to say in these cases that while it was permissible for the Louisiana courts to take judicial notice of racial conditions generally, they could not take notice of the particular conditions on the premises involved in these prosecutions. In the absence of contrary evidence, it was certainly not constitutionally impermissible for the Louisiana courts to consider that the racial conditions in Baton Rouge and in the establishments where petitioners sat were not dissimilar to those existing throughout the State. Judicial notice of racial conditions in a State has sufficient probative value in determining what were the racial conditions at a particular location within the State to withstand constitutional attack. Reversing these convictions for want of evidence of racial tension would in effect be putting this Court into the realm of reviewing the *sufficiency* of the evidence to support these convictions, something which both *Thompson* v. *City of Louisville* and the Court's opinion in the present cases recognize is not properly within our purview.

In my opinion, skimpy though these records are, the convictions do not fall for want of evidence, in the constitutional sense.

III

Were there no more to these cases, I should have to vote to affirm. But in light of principles established by *Cantwell* v. *Connecticut* and consistently since recognized, I think the convictions are subject to other constitutional infirmities.

At the outset it is important to focus on the precise factual situation in each of these cases. Common to all three are the circumstances that petitioners were given the invitation extended to the public at large to patronize these establishments; that they were told that they could be served food only at the Negro lunch counters; that their conduct was not unruly or offensive; and that none of them was ever asked by the owners or their agents to leave the establishments. While in *Briscoe*, No. 27, there was some very slight, but in my view constitutionally adequate, evidence that those petitioners were expressly asked "to move" from the "white" lunch counter, and undisputed evidence that they did not do so, in *Garner*, No. 26, and *Hoston*, No. 28, there was no evidence whatever of any express request to the petitioners in those cases that they move from the "white" lunch counters where they were sitting.

Nor do I think that any such request is fairly to be implied from the fact that petitioners were told by the management that they could not be served with food at such counters. The premises in both instances housed merchandising establishments, a drug store in *Garner*, a department store in *Hoston,* which solicited business from all-comers to the stores. I think the reasonable inference is that the management did not want to risk losing Negro patronage in the stores by requesting these petitioners to leave the "white" lunch counters, preferring to rely on the hope that the irritations of white customers or the force of custom would drive them away from the counters. This view seems the more probable in circumstances when, as here, the "sitters'" behaviour was entirely quiet and courteous, and, for all we know, the counters may have been only sparsely, if to any extent, occupied by white persons.

In short, I believe that in the *Garner* and *Hoston* cases the records should be taken as indicating that the petitioners remained at the "white" lunch counters with the implied consent of the management, even though a similar conclusion may not be warranted in the *Briscoe* case. Under these circumstances, applying principles announced in *Cantwell,* I would hold all these convictions offensive to the Fourteenth Amendment, in that: (1) in *Garner* and *Hoston* petitioners' conduct, occurring with the managements' implied consent, was a form of expression within the range of protections afforded by the Fourteenth Amendment which could in no event be punished by the State under a *general* breach of the peace statute; and (2) in *Briscoe,* while petitioners' "sitting," over the management's objection, cannot be deemed to be within the reach of such protections, their convictions must nonetheless fall because the Louisiana statute, as there applied (and *a fortiori* as applied in the other two cases), was unconstitutionally vague and uncertain.

In the *Cantwell* case a Jehovah's Witness had been convicted for breach of the peace under a Connecticut statute embracing what was considered to be the common-law concept of that offense. "The facts which were held to support the conviction . . . were that he stopped two men in the street, asked, and received, permission to play a phonograph record, and played the record 'Enemies,' which attacked the religion and church of the two men, who were Catholics. Both were incensed by the contents of the record and were tempted to strike Cantwell [the defendant] unless he went away. On being told to be on his way he left their presence. There was no evidence that he was personally offensive or entered into any argument with those he interviewed."

Accepting the determination of the state courts that although the defendant himself had not been disorderly or provocative, his conduct under Connecticut law nonetheless constituted a breach of the peace because of its tendency to inflame others, this Court reversed. Starting from the premise that the "fundamental concept of liberty embodied in the [Fourteenth] Amendment embraces the liberties guaranteed by the First Amendment," the Court found that the defendant's activities fell within the protection granted to the "free exercise" of religion. Then recognizing the danger to such liberties of "leaving to the executive and judicial branches too wide a discretion" in the application of a statute "sweeping in a great variety of conduct under a general and indefinite characterization," the Court held that the defendant's activities could not constitutionally be reached under a general breach of the peace statute, but only under one specifically and narrowly aimed at such conduct. The Court stated:

"Although the contents of the [phonograph] record not unnaturally aroused animosity, we think that, in the absence of a statute narrowly drawn to define and punish specific conduct as constituting a clear and present danger to a substantial interest of the State, the petitioner's communication, considered in the light of the constitutional guaranties, raised no such clear and present danger to public peace and order as to render him liable to conviction of the common law offense in question."

I think these principles control the *Garner* and *Hoston* cases. There was more to the conduct of those petitioners than a bare desire to remain at the "white" lunch counter and their refusal of a police request to move from the counter. We would surely have to be blind not to recognize that petitioners were sitting at these counters, where they knew they would not be served, in order to demonstrate that their race was being segregated in dining facilities in this part of the country.

Such a demonstration, in the circumstances of these two cases, is as much a part of the "free trade in ideas" as is verbal expression, more commonly thought of as "speech." It, like speech, appeals to good sense and to "the power of reason as applied through public discussion" just as much as, if not more than, a public oration delivered from a soapbox at a street corner. This Court has never limited the right to speak, a protected "liberty" under the Fourteenth Amendment, to mere verbal expression. If the act of displaying a red flag as a symbol of opposition to organized government is a liberty encompassed within free speech as protected by the Fourteenth Amendment, the act of sitting at a privately owned lunch counter with the consent of the owner, as a demonstration of opposition to enforced segregation, is surely within the same range of protections. This is not to say, of course, that the Fourteenth Amendment reaches to demonstrations conducted on private property over the objection of the owner (as in *Briscoe*), just as it would surely not encompass verbal expression in a private home if the owner has not consented.

No one can deny the interest that a State has in preserving peace and harmony within its borders. Pursuant to this interest, a state legislature may enact a trespass statute, or a disturbance of the peace statute which either lists in detail the acts condemned by legitimate state policy or proscribes breaches of the peace generally, thus relating the offense to the already developed body of common law defining that crime. Or it may, as Louisiana has done, append to a specific enumeration in a breach of the peace statute a "catch-all" clause to provide for unforeseen but obviously disruptive and offensive behavior which cannot be justified, and which is not within the range of constitutional protection.

But when a State seeks to subject to criminal sanctions conduct which, except for a demonstrated paramount state interest, would be within the range of freedom of expression as assured by the Fourteenth Amendment, it cannot do so by means of a general and all-inclusive breach of the peace prohibition. It must bring the activity sought to be proscribed within the ambit of a statute or clause "narrowly drawn to define and punish specific conduct as constituting a clear and present danger to a substantial interest of the State." And of course that interest must be a legitimate one. A State may not "suppress free communication of views, religious or other under the guise of conserving desirable conditions."

These limitations exist not because control of such activity is beyond the power of the State, but because sound constitutional principles demand of the state legislature that it focus on the nature of the otherwise "protected" conduct it is prohibiting, and that it then make a legislative judgment as to whether that conduct presents so clear and present a danger to the welfare of the community that it may legitimately be criminally proscribed.

The Louisiana Legislature made no such judgment before the petitioners in *Garner* and *Hoston* engaged in their "sit-in" activity. In light of the *Cantwell* case, whose reasoning of course cannot be deemed limited to "expression" taking place on the public streets, Louisiana could not, in my opinion, constitutionally reach those petitioners' conduct under subsection (7)—the "catch-all clause"—of its then existing disturbance of the peace statute. In so concluding, I intimate no view as to whether Louisiana could by a specifically drawn statute constitutionally proscribe conduct of the kind evinced in these two cases, or upon the constitutionality of the statute which the State has recently passed. I deal here only with these two cases, and the statute that is before us now.

IV

Finally, I believe that the principles of *Cantwell* lead to the conclusion that this general breach of the peace provision must also be deemed unconstitutional for vagueness and uncertainty, *as applied* in the circumstances of all these cases. As to *Garner* and *Hoston* this affords an alternative ground for reversal. As to *Briscoe,* where the evidence falls short of establishing that those petitioners remained at the "white" lunch counter with the express or implied consent of the owner, I would rest reversal solely on this ground.

While *Cantwell* was not explicitly founded on that premise, it seems to me implicit in the opinion that a statute which leaves the courts in uncertainty as to whether it was intended to reach otherwise constitutionally protected conduct must by the same token be deemed inadequate warning to a defendant that his conduct has been condemned by the State. Such warning is, of course, a requirement of the Fourteenth Amendment.

This conclusion finds added support in the cases requiring of state legislatures more specificity in statutes impinging on freedom of expression than might suffice for other criminal enactments. To the extent that this Louisiana statute is explicit on the subject of expression it prohibits only that which is "unnecessarily loud, offensive, or insulting" or activity carried on "in a violent or tumultuous manner by three or more persons." No charge was made or proved that petitioners' conduct met any of those criteria. Nor has the statute been elucidated in this respect before, or since, petitioners' conviction, by any decision of the Louisiana courts of which we have been advised. Lastly, it is worth observing that in *State* v. *Sanford* the Louisiana Supreme Court seriously questioned on the score of vagueness the validity of that earlier breach of the peace statute under the State Constitution, as there applied to conduct within the same range of constitutional protection.

In the absence of any Louisiana statute purporting to express the State's overriding interest in prohibiting petitioners' conduct as a clear and present danger to the welfare of the community, peaceful demonstration on public streets, and on private property with the consent of the owner, was constitutionally protected as a form of expression. Louisiana's breach of the peace statute drew no distinct line between presumably constitutionally protected activity and the conduct of the petitioners in *Briscoe,* as a criminal trespass statute might have done. The fact that in *Briscoe,* unlike *Garner* and *Hoston,* the management did not consent to the petitioners' remaining at the "white" lunch counter does not serve to permit the application of this general breach of the peace statute to the conduct shown in that case. For the statute by its terms appears to be as applicable to "incidents fairly within the protection of the guarantee of free speech," as to that which is not within the range of such protection. Hence such a law gives no warning as to what may fairly be deemed to be within its compass.

For the foregoing reasons I dissent from the opinion of the Court, but join in the judgment.

Bailey v. Patterson
369 U.S. 31 1962

Per Curiam.

Appellants, Negroes living in Jackson, Mississippi, brought this civil rights action, in the United States District Court for the Southern District of Mississippi, on behalf of themselves and others similarly situated, seeking temporary and permanent injunctions to enforce their constitutional rights to nonsegregated service in interstate and intrastate transportation, alleging that such rights had been denied them under color of state statutes, municipal ordinances, and state custom and usage. A three-judge District Court was convened and, Circuit Judge Rives dissenting, abstained from further proceedings pending construction of the challenged laws by the state courts. Plaintiffs have appealed. We denied a motion to stay the prosecution of a number of criminal cases pending disposition of this appeal.

Appellants lack standing to enjoin criminal prosecutions under Mississippi's breach of peace statutes, since they do not allege that they have been prosecuted or threatened with prosecution under them. They cannot represent a class of whom they are not a part. But as passengers using the segregated transportation facilities they are aggrieved parties and have standing to enforce their rights to nonsegregated treatment.

We have settled beyond question that no State may require racial segregation of interstate or intrastate transportation facilities. The question is no longer open; it is foreclosed as a litigable issue. Section 2281 does not require a three-judge court when the claim that a statute is unconstitutional is wholly insubstantial, legally speaking non-existent. We hold that three judges are similarly not required when, as here, prior decisions make frivolous any claim that a state statute on its face is not unconstitutional. We denied leave to file petitions for mandamus in *Bush* and from a similar ruling in *Booker* v. *Tennessee Board of Education*. The reasons for convening an extraordinary court are inapplicable in such cases, for the policy behind the three-judge requirement—that a single judge ought not to be empowered to invalidate a state statute under a federal claim—does not apply. The three-judge requirement is a technical one to be narrowly construed. The statute comes into play only when an injunction is sought "on the ground of the unconstitutionality" of a statute. There is no such ground when the constitutional issue presented is essentially fictitious.

This case is therefore not one "required . . . to be heard and determined by a district court of three judges" and therefore cannot be brought here on direct appeal. However, we have jurisdiction to determine the authority of the court below and "to make such corrective order as may be appropriate to the enforcement of the limitations which that section imposes." Accordingly, we vacate the judgment and remand the case to the District Court for expeditious disposition, in light of this opinion, of the appellants' claims of right to unsegregated transportation service.

Turner v. Memphis
369 U.S. 350   1962

Per Curiam.

Appellant, a Negro, refused nonsegregated service in a Memphis Municipal Airport restaurant operated by appellee, Dobbs Houses, Inc., under a lease from appellee City of Memphis, instituted this action on behalf of himself and other Negroes similarly situated seeking an injunction against such discrimination. He rested jurisdiction upon 28 U. S. C. § 1343 (3) and premised the cause of action upon 42 U. S. C. § 1983. Although the complaint alleged that appellees acted under color of state law, it did not identify any particular state statutes or regulations being challenged. But appellees' answers, in addition to asserting that the restaurant was a private enterprise to which the Fourteenth Amendment did not apply, invoked Tenn. Code Ann. §§ 53–2120, 53–2121, and Regulation No. R–18 (L). The statutes authorize the Division of Hotel and Restaurant Inspection of the State Department of Conservation to issue "such rules and regulations . . . as may be necessary pertaining to the safety and/or sanitation of hotels and restaurants . . ." and make violations of such regulations a misdemeanor. The regulation, promulgated by the Division, provides that "restaurants catering to both white and negro patrons should be arranged so that each race is properly segregated." The answers also set up the lease agreement which provides, *inter alia,* that the leased premises are to be used "only and exclusively for lawful purposes, and no part of the premises shall be used in any manner whatsoever for any purpose in violation of the laws of . . . the State of Tennessee . . . ." The City of Memphis alleged further that unless and until the regulation was declared unconstitutional, the city would be bound to object to desegregation of the restaurant by Dobbs Houses as a violation of Tennessee law and of the lease. Dobbs Houses alleged that desegregation by it of the restaurant would therefore subject it to forfeiture of the lease. Dobbs Houses later amended its answer to include a defense based on Tenn. Code Ann. § 62–710. That statute "abrogates" Tennessee's common-law cause of action for exclusion from hotels or other public places, and declares that the operators of such establishments are free to exclude persons "for any reason whatever."

When the appellant moved for summary judgment before a single district judge, the appellees opposed the motion on the ground that the relief sought necessarily challenged the constitutionality of the state statutes and regulation so that under 28 U. S. C. §§ 2281, 2284, a three-judge court was required. The single judge thereupon convened a three-judge court. Upon renewal by the appellant before that court of his motion for summary judgment the appellees urged, and the three-judge court ordered, that appellant's suit should be held in abeyance pending a "Declaratory Judgment suit to be brought by plaintiffs in the Tennessee Courts seeking an interpretation of the State statutes under consideration." Appellant, being in doubt whether the case was one "required . . . to be heard and determined by a district court of three judges," in addition to appealing from the abstention order directly to this Court under 28 U. S. C. § 1253, also perfected a timely appeal to the Court of Appeals for the Sixth Circuit. We postponed consideration of the question of our jurisdiction of the direct appeal to the hearing on the merits.

Whether or not it may be said that appellant's complaint is to be read as seeking, under 28 U. S. C. § 2281, an "injunction restraining the enforcement, operation or execution of [a] . . . State statute by restraining the action of any officer of such State in the enforcement or execution of such statute," a question which we need not decide, it is clear for other reasons that a three-judge court was not required for the disposition of this case. Since, as was conceded by Dobbs Houses at the bar of this Court, the Dobbs Houses restaurant was subject to the strictures of the Fourteenth Amendment under *Burton* v. *Wilmington Parking Authority,* the statutes and regulation invoked by appellees could have furnished a defense to the action only insofar as they expressed an affirmative state policy fostering segregation in publicly operated facilities. But our decisions have foreclosed any possible contention that such a statute or regulation may stand consistently with the Fourteenth Amendment. It follows under our recent decision in *Bailey* v. *Patterson* that a three-judge court was not required and that jurisdiction of this appeal is invested in the Court of Appeals.

But we see no reason why disposition of the case should await decision of the appeal by the Court of Appeals. On the merits, no issue remains to be resolved. This is clear under prior decisions and the undisputed facts of the case. Accordingly no occasion is presented for abstention, and the litigation should be disposed of as expeditiously as is consistent with proper judicial administration. In light of the perfected appeal to the Sixth Circuit Court of Appeals, it is appropriate that we treat, and we do treat, appellant's jurisdictional statement as a petition for writ of certiorari prior to judgment in the Court of Appeals. The petition is granted, the District Court's abstention order is vacated and the case is remanded to the District Court with directions to enter a decree granting appropriate injunctive relief against the discrimination complained of.

Mr. Justice Whittaker did not participate in the decision of this case.

Part III

RACE AND FREEDOM OF SPEECH

Beauharnais v. Illinois

N.A.A.C.P. v. Alabama

Bates v. Little Rock

Louisiana v. N.A.A.C.P.

These cases concern attempts by state governments to control, limit, or harass individuals or organizations advocating action in the area of race relations. In the Beauharnais case, a divided Court upholds the validity of a "group-libel" law used to curb the distribution of literature by the White Circle League. In the other cases, the Court strikes down attempts to curb the activities of the N.A.A.C.P.

Beauharnais v. Illinois

343 U. S. 250 1952

Mr. Justice Frankfurter delivered the opinion of the Court.

The petitioner was convicted upon information in the Municipal Court of Chicago of violating § 224a of the Illinois Criminal Code. He was fined $200. The section provides:

"It shall be unlawful for any person, firm or corporation to manufacture, sell, or offer for sale, advertise or publish, present or exhibit in any public place in this state any lithograph, moving picture, play, drama or sketch, which publication or exhibition portrays depravity, criminality, unchastity, or lack of virtue of a class of citizens, of any race, color, creed or religion which said publication or exhibition exposes the citizens of any race, color, creed or religion to contempt, derision, or obloquy or which is productive of breach of the peace or riots. . . ."

Beauharnais challenged the statute as violating the liberty of speech and of the press guaranteed as against the States by the Due Process Clause of the Fourteenth Amendment, and as too vague, under the restrictions implicit in the same Clause, to support conviction for crime. The Illinois courts rejected these contentions and sustained defendant's conviction. We granted certiorari in view of the serious questions raised concerning the limitations imposed by the Fourteenth Amendment on the power of a State to punish utterances promoting friction among racial and religious groups.

The information, cast generally in the terms of the statute, charged that Beauharnais "did unlawfully . . . exhibit in public places lithographs, which publications portray depravity, criminality, unchastity or lack of virtue of citizens of Negro race and color and which exposes [sic] citizens of Illinois of the Negro race and color to contempt, derision, or obloquy . . . ." The lithograph complained of was a leaflet setting forth a petition calling on the Mayor and City Council of Chicago "to halt the further encroachment, harassment and invasion of white people, their property, neighborhoods and persons, by the Negro . . . ." Below was a call for "One million self respecting white people in Chicago to unite . . . ." with the statement added that "if persuasion and the need to prevent the white race from becoming mongrelized by the negro will not unite us, then the aggressions . . . rapes, robberies, knives, guns and marijuana of the negro, surely will." This, with more language, similar if not so violent, concluded with an attached application for membership in the White Circle League of America, Inc.

The testimony at the trial was substantially undisputed. From it the jury could find that Beauharnais was president of the White Circle League; that, at a meeting on January 6, 1950, he passed out bundles of the lithographs in question, together with other literature, to volunteers for distribution on downtown Chicago street corners the following day; that he carefully organized that distribution, giving detailed instructions for it; and that the leaflets were in fact distributed on January 7 in accordance with his plan and instructions. The court, together with other charges on burden of proof and the like, told the jury "if you find . . . that the defendant, Joseph Beauharnais, did . . . manufacture, sell, or offer for sale, advertise or publish, present or exhibit in any public place the lithograph . . . then you are to find the defendant guilty . . . ." He refused to charge the jury, as requested by the defendant, that in order to convict they must find "that the article complained of was likely to produce a clear and present danger of a serious substantive evil that rises far above public inconvenience, annoyance or unrest." Upon this evidence and these instructions, the jury brought in the conviction here for review.

The statute before us is not a catchall enactment left at large by the State court which applied it. It is a law specifically directed at a defined evil, its language drawing from history and practice in Illinois and in more than a score of other jurisdictions a meaning confirmed by the Supreme Court of that State in upholding this conviction. We do not, therefore, parse the statute as grammarians or treat it as an abstract exercise in lexicography. We read it in the animating context of well-defined usage and State court construction which determines its meaning for us.

The Illinois Supreme Court tells us that § 224a "is a form of criminal libel law." The defendant, the trial court and the Supreme Court consistently treated it as such. The defendant offered evidence tending to prove the truth of parts of the utterance, and the courts below considered and disposed of this offer in terms of ordinary criminal libel precedents. Section 224a does not deal with the defense of truth, but by the Illinois Constitution "in all trials for libel, both civil and criminal, the truth, when published with good motives and for justifiable ends, shall be a sufficient defense." Similarly, the action of the trial court in deciding as a matter of law the libelous character of the utterance, leaving to the jury only the question of publication, follows the settled rule in prosecutions for libel in Illinois and other States. Moreover, the Supreme Court's characterization of the words prohibited by the statute as those "liable to cause violence and disorder" paraphrases the traditional justification for punishing libels criminally, namely their "tendency to cause breach of the peace."

Libel of an individual was a common-law crime, and thus criminal in the colonies. Indeed, at common law, truth or good motives was no defense. In the first decades after the adoption of the Constitution, this was changed by judicial decision, statute or constitution in most States, but nowhere was there any suggestion that the crime of libel be abolished. Today, every American jurisdiction—the forty-eight States, the District of Columbia, Alaska, Hawaii and Puerto Rico—punish libels directed at individuals. "There are certain well-defined and narrowly limited classes of speech, the prevention and punishment of which have never been thought to raise any Constitutional problem. These include the lewd and obscene, the profane, the libelous, and the insulting or 'fighting' words—those which by their very utterance inflict injury or tend to incite an immediate breach of the peace. It has been well observed that such utterances are no essential part of any exposition of ideas, and are of such slight social value as a step to truth that any benefit that may be derived from them is clearly outweighed by the social interest in order and morality. 'Resort to epithets or personal abuse is not in any proper sense communication of information or opinion safeguarded by the Constitution, and its punishment as a criminal act would raise no question under that instrument.'" Such were the views of a unanimous Court in *Chaplinsky* v. *New Hampshire*.

No one will gainsay that it is libelous falsely to charge another with being a rapist, robber, carrier of knives and guns, and user of marijuana. The precise question before us, then, is whether the protection of "liberty" in the Due Process Clause of the Fourteenth Amendment prevents a State from punishing such libels—as criminal libel has been defined, limited and constitutionally recognized time out of mind—

directed at designated collectivities and flagrantly disseminated. There is even authority, however dubious, that such utterances were also crimes at common law. It is certainly clear that some American jurisdictions have sanctioned their punishment under ordinary criminal libel statutes. We cannot say, however, that the question is concluded by history and practice. But if an utterance directed at an individual may be the object of criminal sanctions, we cannot deny to a State power to punish the same utterance directed at a defined group, unless we can say that this is a wilful and purposeless restriction unrelated to the peace and well-being of the State.

Illinois did not have to look beyond her own borders or await the tragic experience of the last three decades to conclude that wilful purveyors of falsehood concerning racial and religious groups promote strife and tend powerfully to obstruct the manifold adjustments required for free, ordered life in a metropolitan, polyglot community. From the murder of the abolitionist Lovejoy in 1837 to the Cicero riots of 1951, Illinois has been the scene of exacerbated tension between races, often flaring into violence and destruction. In many of these outbreaks, utterances of the character here in question, so the Illinois legislature could conclude, played a significant part. The law was passed on June 29, 1917, at a time when the State was struggling to assimilate vast numbers of new inhabitants, as yet concentrated in discrete racial or national or religious groups—foreign-born brought to it by the crest of the great wave of immigration, and Negroes attracted by jobs in war plants and the allurements of northern claims. Nine years earlier, in the very city where the legislature sat, what is said to be the first northern race riot had cost the lives of six people, left hundreds of Negroes homeless and shocked citizens into action far beyond the borders of the State. Less than a month before the bill was enacted, East St. Louis had seen a day's rioting, prelude to an outbreak, only four days after the bill became law, so bloody that it led to Congressional investigation. A series of bombings had begun which was to culminate two years later in the awful race riot which held Chicago in its grip for seven days in the summer of 1919. Nor has tension and violence between the groups defined in the statute been limited in Illinois to clashes between whites and Negroes.

In the face of this history and its frequent obligato of extreme racial and religious propaganda, we would deny experience to say that the Illinois legislature was without reason in seeking ways to curb false or malicious defamation of racial and religious groups, made in public places and by means calculated to have a powerful emotional impact on those to whom it was presented. "There are limits to the exercise of these liberties [of speech and of the press]. The danger in these times from the coercive activities of those who in the delusion of racial or religious conceit would incite violence and breaches of the peace in order to deprive others of their equal right to the exercise of their liberties, is emphasized by events familiar to all. These and other transgressions of those limits the States appropriately may punish." This was the conclusion, again of a unanimous Court, in 1940.

It may be argued, and weightily, that this legislation will not help matters; that tension and on occasion violence between racial and religious groups must be traced to causes more deeply embedded in our society than the rantings of modern Know-Nothings. Only those lacking responsible humility will have a confident solution for problems as intractable as the frictions attributable to differences of race, color or religion. This being so, it would be out of bounds for the judiciary to deny the legislature a choice of policy, provided it is not unrelated to the problem and not forbidden by some explicit limitation on the State's power. That the legislative remedy might not in practice mitigate the evil, or might itself raise new problems, would only manifest once more the paradox of reform. It is the price to be paid for the trial-and-error inherent in legislative efforts to deal with obstinate social issues. "The science of government is the most abstruse of all sciences; if, indeed, that can be called a science which has but few fixed principles, and practically consists in little more than the exercise of a sound discretion, applied to the exigencies of the state as they arise. It is the science of experiment." Certainly the Due Process Clause does not require the legislature to be in the vanguard of science—especially sciences as young as human ecology and cultural anthropology.

Long ago this Court recognized that the economic rights of an individual may depend for the effectiveness of their enforcement on rights in the group, even though not formally corporate, to which he belongs. Such group-protection on behalf of the individual may, for all we know, be a need not confined to the part that a trade union plays in effectuating rights abstractly recognized as belonging to its members. It is not within our competence to confirm or deny claims of social scientists as to the dependence of the individual on the position of his racial or religious group in the community. It would, however, be arrant dog-

143

matism, quite outside the scope of our authority in passing on the powers of a State, for us to deny that the Illinois legislature may warrantably believe that a man's job and his educational opportunities and the dignity accorded him may depend as much on the reputation of the racial and religious group to which he willy-nilly belongs, as on his own merits. This being so, we are precluded from saying that speech concededly punishable when immediately directed at individuals cannot be outlawed if directed at groups with whose position and esteem in society the affiliated individual may be inextricably involved.

We are warned that the choice open to the Illinois legislature here may be abused, that the law may be discriminatorily enforced; prohibiting libel of a creed or of a racial group, we are told, is but a step from prohibiting libel of a political party. Every power may be abused, but the possibility of abuse is a poor reason for denying Illinois the power to adopt measures against criminal libels sanctioned by centuries of Anglo-American law. "While this Court sits" it retains and exercises authority to nullify action which encroaches on freedom of utterance under the guise of punishing libel. Of course discussion cannot be denied and the right, as well as the duty, of criticism must not be stifled.

The scope of the statute before us, as construed by the Illinois court, disposes of the contention that the conduct prohibited by the law is so ill-defined that judges and juries in applying the statute and men in acting cannot draw from it adequate standards to guide them. The clarifying construction and fixed usage which govern the meaning of the enactment before us were not present, so the Court found, in the New York law held invalid in *Winters* v. *New York*. Nor, thus construed and limited, is the act so broad that the general verdict of guilty on an indictment drawn in the statutory language might have been predicated on constitutionally protected conduct. On this score, the conviction here reviewed differs from those upset in *Stromberg* v. *California, Thornhill* v. *Alabama,* and *Terminiello* v. *Chicago.* Even the latter case did not hold that the unconstitutionality of a statute is established *because* the speech prohibited by it raises a ruckus.

It is suggested that while it was clearly within the constitutional power of Illinois to punish this utterance if the proceeding were properly safeguarded, in this particular case Illinois denied the defendant rights which the Due Process Clause commands. Specifically, it is argued that the defendant was not permitted to raise at the trial defenses constitutionally guaranteed in a criminal libel prosecution: (1) the defense of truth; (2) justification of the utterance as "fair comment"; and (3) its privilege as a means for redressing grievances.

Neither by proffer of evidence, requests for instructions, nor motion before or after verdict did the defendant seek to justify his utterance as "fair comment" or as privileged. Nor has the defendant urged as a ground for reversing his conviction in this Court that his opportunity to make those defenses was denied below. And so, whether a prosecution for libel of a racial or religious group is unconstitutionally invalid where the State did deny the defendant such opportunities is not before us. Certainly the State may cast the burden of justifying what is patent defamation upon the defamer. The benefits of hypothetical defenses, never raised below or pressed upon us, are not to be invoked in the abstract.

As to the defense of truth, Illinois in common with many States requires a showing not only that the utterance state the facts, but also that the publication be made "with good motives and for justifiable ends." Both elements are necessary if the defense is to prevail. What has been called "the common sense of American criminal law," as formulated, with regard to necessary safeguards in criminal libel prosecutions, in the New York Constitution of 1821 has been adopted in terms by Illinois. The teaching of a century and a half of criminal libel prosecutions in this country would go by the board if we were to hold that Illinois was not within her rights in making this combined requirement. Assuming that defendant's offer of proof directed to a part of the defense was adequate, it did not satisfy the entire requirement which Illinois could exact.

Libelous utterances not being within the area of constitutionally protected speech, it is unnecessary, either for us or for the State courts, to consider the issues behind the phrase "clear and present danger." Certainly no one would contend that obscene speech, for example, may be punished only upon a showing of such circumstances. Libel, as we have seen, is in the same class.

We find no warrant in the Constitution for denying to Illinois the power to pass the law here under attack. But it bears repeating—although it should not—that our finding that the law is not constitutionally objectionable carries no implication of approval of the wisdom of the legislation or of its efficacy. These questions may raise doubts in our minds as well as in others. It is not for us, however, to make the legislative judgment. We are not at liberty to erect those doubts into fundamental law.

Affirmed.

Mr. Justice Black, with whom Mr. Justice Douglas concurs, dissenting.

This case is here because Illinois inflicted criminal punishment on Beauharnais for causing the distribution of leaflets in the city of Chicago. The conviction rests on the leaflet's contents, not on the time, manner or place of distribution. Beauharnais is head of an organization that opposes amalgamation and favors segregation of white and colored people. After discussion, an assembly of his group decided to petition the mayor and council of Chicago to pass laws for segregation. Volunteer members of the group agreed to stand on street corners, solicit signers to petitions addressed to the city authorities, and distribute leaflets giving information about the group, its beliefs and its plans. In carrying out this program a solicitor handed out a leaflet which was the basis of this prosecution. Since the Court opinion quotes only parts of the leaflet, I am including all of it as an appendix to this dissent.

I

That Beauharnais and his group were making a genuine effort to petition their elected representatives is not disputed. Even as far back as 1689, the Bill of Rights exacted of William & Mary said: "It is the Right of the Subjects to petition the King, and all Commitments and Prosecutions for such petitioning are illegal." And 178 years ago the Declaration of Rights of the Continental Congress proclaimed to the monarch of that day that his American subjects had "a right peaceably to assemble, consider of their grievances, and petition the King; and that all prosecutions, prohibitory proclamations, and commitments for the same, are illegal." After independence was won, Americans stated as the first unequivocal command of their Bill of Rights: "Congress shall make no law . . . abridging the freedom of speech, or of the press; or the right of the people peaceably to assemble, and to petition the Government for a redress of grievances." Without distortion, this First Amendment could not possibly be read so as to hold that Congress has power to punish Beauharnais and others for petitioning Congress as they have here sought to petition the Chicago authorities. And we have held in a number of prior cases that the Fourteenth Amendment makes the specific prohibitions of the First Amendment equally applicable to the states.

In view of these prior holdings, how does the Court justify its holding today that states can punish people for exercising the vital freedoms intended to be safeguarded from suppression by the First Amendment? The prior holdings are not referred to; the Court simply acts on the bland assumption that the First Amendment is wholly irrelevant. It is not even accorded the respect of a passing mention. This follows logically, I suppose, from recent constitutional doctrine which appears to measure state laws solely by this Court's notions of civilized "canons of decency," reasonableness, etc. Under this "reasonableness" test, state laws abridging First Amendment freedoms are sustained if found to have a "rational basis." But in *Board of Education* v. *Barnette,* we said:

"In weighing arguments of the parties it is important to distinguish between the due process clause of the Fourteenth Amendment as an instrument for transmitting the principles of the First Amendment and those cases in which it is applied for its own sake. The test of legislation which collides with the Fourteenth Amendment, because it also collides with the principles of the First, is much more definite than the test when only the Fourteenth is involved. Much of the vagueness of the due process clause disappears when the specific prohibitions of the First become its standard. The right of a State to regulate, for example, a public utility may well include, so far as the due process test is concerned, power to impose all of the restrictions which a legislature may have a 'rational basis' for adopting. But freedoms of speech and of press, of assembly, and of worship may not be infringed on such slender grounds."

Today's case degrades First Amendment freedoms to the "rational basis" level. It is now a certainty that the new "due process" coverall offers far less protection to liberty than would adherence to our former cases compelling states to abide by the unequivocal First Amendment command that its defined freedoms shall not be abridged.

The Court's holding here and the constitutional doctrine behind it leave the rights of assembly, petition, speech and press almost completely at the mercy of state legislative, executive, and judicial agencies. I say "almost" because state curtailment of these freedoms may still be invalidated if a majority of this Court conclude that a particular infringement is "without reason," or is "a wilful and purposeless restriction unrelated to the peace and well being of the State." But lest this encouragement should give too much hope as to how and when this Court might protect these basic freedoms from state invasion, we are cautioned that state legislatures must be left free to "experiment" and to make "legislative" judgments. We are told that mistakes may be made during the legislative process of curbing public opinion. In such event the Court fortunately does not leave those mistakenly curbed, or any of us for that matter, unadvised. Consolation can be sought and must be found in the philosophical reflection that state legislative error in stifling speech and press "is the price to be paid for the trial-and-error inherent in legislative efforts to deal with obstinate social issues." My own belief is that no legislature is charged with the duty or vested with the power to decide what public issues Americans can discuss. In a free country that is the individual's choice, not the state's. State experimentation in curbing freedom of expression is startling and frightening doctrine in a country dedicated to self-government by its people. I reject the holding that either state or nation can punish people for having their say in matters of public concern.

II

The Illinois statute upheld by the Court makes it a crime:

1. for "any person, firm or corporation,"
2. to "manufacture, sell, or offer for sale, advertise or publish, present or exhibit in any public place,"
3. any "lithograph [construed to include any printed matter], moving picture, play, drama or sketch,"
4. which portrays "depravity, criminality, unchastity, or lack of virtue,"
5. of "a class of citizens, of any race, color, creed or religion,"
6. and exposes such a class to "contempt, derision, or obloquy,"
7. *or* "is productive of breach of the peace or riots."

This statute imposes state censorship over the theater, moving pictures, radio, television, leaflets, magazines, books and newspapers. No doubt the statute is broad enough to make criminal the "publication, sale, presentation or exhibition" of many of the world's great classics, both secular and religious.

The Court condones this expansive state censorship by painstakingly analogizing it to the law of criminal libel. As a result of this refined analysis, the Illinois statute emerges labeled a "group libel law." This label may make the Court's holding more palatable for those who sustain it, but the sugar-coating does not make the censorship less deadly.

148

However tagged, the Illinois law is not that criminal libel which has been "defined, limited and constitutionally recognized time out of mind." For as "constitutionally recognized" that crime has provided for punishment of false, malicious, scurrilous charges against individuals, not against huge groups. This limited scope of the law of criminal libel is of no small importance. It has confined state punishment of speech and expression to the narrowest of areas involving nothing more than purely private feuds. Every expansion of the law of criminal libel so as to punish discussions of matters of public concern means a corresponding invasion of the area dedicated to free expression by the First Amendment.

Prior efforts to expand the scope of criminal libel beyond its traditional boundaries have not usually met with widespread popular acclaim. "Seditious libel" was such an expansion and it did have its day, particularly in the English Court of Star Chamber. But the First Amendment repudiated seditious libel for this country. And one need only glance through the parliamentary discussion of Fox's Libel Law passed in England in 1792, to sense the bad odor of criminal libel in that country even when confined to charges against individuals only.

The Court's reliance on *Chaplinsky* v. *New Hampshire* is also misplaced. New Hampshire had a state law making it an offense to direct insulting words at an *individual* on a public street. Chaplinsky had violated that law by calling a man vile names "face-to-face." We pointed out in that context that the use of such "fighting" words was not an essential part of exposition of ideas. Whether the words used in their context here are "fighting" words in the same sense is doubtful, but whether so or not they are not addressed to or about *individuals*. Moreover, the leaflet used here was also the means adopted by an assembled group to enlist interest in their efforts to have legislation enacted. And the fighting words were but a part of arguments on questions of wide public interest and importance. Freedom of petition, assembly, speech and press could be greatly abridged by a practice of meticulously scrutinizing every editorial, speech, sermon or other printed matter to extract two or three naughty words on which to hang charges of "group libel." The *Chaplinsky* case makes no such broad inroads on First Amendment freedoms. Nothing Mr. Justice Murphy wrote for the Court in that case or in any other case justifies any such inference.

Unless I misread history the majority is giving libel a more expansive scope and more respectable status than it was ever accorded even in the

Star Chamber. For here it is held to be punishable to give publicity to any picture, moving picture, play, drama or sketch, or any printed matter which a judge may find unduly offensive to any race, color, creed or religion. In other words, in arguing for or against the enactment of laws that may differently affect huge groups, it is now very dangerous indeed to say something critical of one of the groups. And any "person, firm or corporation" can be tried for this crime. "Person, firm or corporation" certainly includes a book publisher, newspaper, radio or television station, candidate or even a preacher.

It is easy enough to say that none of this latter group have been proceeded against under the Illinois Act. And they have not—yet. But emotions bubble and tempers flare in racial and religious controversies, the kind here involved. It would not be easy for any court, in good conscience, to narrow this Act so as to exclude from it any of those I have mentioned. Furthermore, persons tried under the Act could not even get a jury trial except as to the bare fact of publication. Here, the court simply charged the jury that Beauharnais was guilty if he had caused distribution of the leaflet. Such trial by judge rather than by jury was outlawed in England in 1792 by Fox's Libel Law.

This Act sets up a system of state censorship which is at war with the kind of free government envisioned by those who forced adoption of our Bill of Rights. The motives behind the state law may have been to do good. But the same can be said about most laws making opinions punishable as crimes. History indicates that urges to do good have led to the burning of books and even to the burning of "witches."

No rationalization on a purely legal level can conceal the fact that state laws like this one present a constant overhanging threat to freedom of speech, press and religion. Today Beauharnais is punished for publicly expressing strong views in favor of segregation. Ironically enough, Beauharnais, convicted of crime in Chicago, would probably be given a hero's reception in many other localities, if not in some parts of Chicago itself. Moreover, the same kind of state law that makes Beauharnais a criminal for advocating segregation in Illinois can be utilized to send people to jail in other states for advocating equality and nonsegregation. What Beauharnais said in his leaflet is mild compared with usual arguments on both sides of racial controversies.

We are told that freedom of petition and discussion are in no danger "while this Court sits." This case raises considerable doubt. Since those who peacefully petition for changes in the law are not to be protected "while this Court sits," who is? I do not agree that the Constitution leaves freedom of petition, assembly, speech, press or worship at the mercy of a case-by-case, day-by-day majority of this Court. I had supposed that our people could rely for their freedom on the Constitution's commands, rather than on the grace of this Court on an individual case basis. To say that a legislative body can, with this Court's approval, make it a crime to petition for and publicly discuss proposed legislation seems as farfetched to me as it would be to say that a valid law could be enacted to punish a candidate for President for telling the people his views. I think the First Amendment, with the Fourteenth, "absolutely" forbids such laws without any "ifs" or "buts" or "whereases." Whatever the danger, if any, in such public discussions, it is a danger the Founders deemed outweighed by the danger incident to the stifling of thought and speech. The Court does not act on this view of the Founders. It calculates what it deems to be the danger of public discussion, holds the scales are tipped on the side of state suppression, and upholds state censorship. This method of decision offers little protection to First Amendment liberties "while this Court sits."

If there be minority groups who hail this holding as their victory, they might consider the possible relevancy of this ancient remark:

"Another such victory and I am undone."

Mr. Justice Reed, with whom Mr. Justice Douglas joins, dissenting.

. . . The Court speaks at length of the constitutional power of a state to pass group libel laws to protect the public peace. This dissent assumes that power. What is under discussion is whether the conviction of Beauharnais on a general charge of violation of the statute can stand when the statute contains without statutory or judicial definition words of such ambiguous meaning and uncertain connotation as "virtue," "derision," or "obloquy." The Court does not attempt to speak specifically as to that contention.

The importance of a definite ruling on that point is manifest. Racial, religious, and political biases and prejudices lead to charge and counter-charge, acrimony and bitterness. If words are to be punished criminally, the Constitution at least requires that only words or expressions or statements that can be reasonably well defined, or that have through long usage an accepted meaning, shall furnish a basis for conviction.

These words—"virtue," "derision," and "obloquy"—have neither general nor special meanings well enough known to apprise those within their reach as to limitations on speech. Philosophers and poets, thinkers of high and low degree from every age and race have sought to expound the meaning of virtue, but each teaches his own conception of the moral excellence that satisfies standards of good conduct. Are the tests of the Puritan or the Cavalier to be applied, those of the city or the farm, the Christian or non-Christian, the old or the young? Does the Bill of Rights permit Illinois to forbid any reflection on the virtue of racial or religious classes which a jury or a judge may think exposes them to derision or obloquy, words themselves of quite uncertain meaning as used in the statute? I think not. A general and equal enforcement of this law would restrain the mildest expressions of opinion in all those areas where "virtue" may be thought to have a role. Since this judgment may rest upon these vague and undefined words, which permit within their scope the punishment of incidents secured by the guarantee of free speech, the conviction should be reversed.

Mr. Justice Douglas, dissenting.

Hitler and his Nazis showed how evil a conspiracy could be which was aimed at destroying a race by exposing it to contempt, derision, and obloquy. I would be willing to concede that such conduct directed at a race or group in this country could be made an indictable offense. For such a project would be more than the exercise of free speech. Like picketing, it would be free speech plus.

I would also be willing to concede that even without the element of conspiracy there might be times and occasions when the legislative or executive branch might call a halt to inflammatory talk, such as the shouting of "fire" in a school or a theatre.

My view is that if in any case other public interests are to override the plain command of the First Amendment, the peril of speech must be clear and present, leaving no room for argument, raising no doubts as to the necessity of curbing speech in order to prevent disaster.

The First Amendment is couched in absolute terms—freedom of speech shall not be abridged. Speech has therefore a preferred position as contrasted to some other civil rights. For example, privacy, equally sacred to some, is protected by the Fourth Amendment only against unreasonable searches and seizures. There is room for regulation of the ways and means of invading privacy. No such leeway is granted the invasion of the right of free speech guaranteed by the First Amendment. Until recent years that had been the course and direction of constitutional law. Yet recently the Court in this and in other cases has engrafted the right of regulation onto the First Amendment by placing in the hands of the legislative branch the right to regulate "within reasonable limits" the right of free speech. This to me is an ominous and alarming trend. The free trade in ideas which the Framers of the Constitution visualized disappears. In its place there is substituted a new orthodoxy—an orthodoxy that changes with the whims of the age or the day, an orthodoxy which the majority by solemn judgment proclaims to be essential to the safety, welfare, security, morality, or health of society. Free speech in the constitutional sense disappears. Limits are drawn—limits dictated by expediency, political opinion, prejudices or some other desideratum of legislative action.

An historic aspect of the issue of judicial supremacy was the extent to which legislative judgment would be supreme in the field of social legislation. The vague contours of the Due Process Clause were used to strike down laws deemed by the Court to be unwise and improvident. That trend has been reversed. In matters relating to business, finance, industrial and labor conditions, health and the public welfare, great leeway is now granted the legislature; for there is no guarantee in the Constitution that the *status quo* will be preserved against regulation by government. Freedom of speech, however, rests on a different constitutional basis. The First Amendment says that freedom of speech, freedom of press, and the free exercise of religion shall not be abridged. That is a negation of power on the part of each and every department of government. Free speech, free press, free exercise of religion are placed separate and apart; they are above and beyond the police power; they are not subject to regulation in the manner of factories, slums, apartment houses, production of oil, and the like.

The Court in this and in other cases places speech under an expanding legislative control. Today a white man stands convicted for protesting in unseemly language against our decisions invalidating restrictive covenants. Tomorrow a Negro will be haled before a court for denouncing lynch law in heated terms. Farm laborers in the West who compete with field hands drifting up from Mexico; whites who feel the pressure of orientals; a minority which finds employment going to members of the dominant religious group—all of these are caught in the mesh of today's decision. Debate and argument even in the court-

153

room are not always calm and dispassionate. Emotions sway speakers and audiences alike. Intemperate speech is a distinctive characteristic of man. Hotheads blow off and release destructive energy in the process. They shout and rave, exaggerating weaknesses, magnifying error, viewing with alarm. So it has been from the beginning; and so it will be throughout time. The Framers of the Constitution knew human nature as well as we do. They too had lived in dangerous days; they too knew the suffocating influence of orthodoxy and standardized thought. They weighed the compulsions for restrained speech and thought against the abuses of liberty. They chose liberty. That should be our choice today no matter how distasteful to us the pamphlet of Beauharnais may be. It is true that this is only one decision which may later be distinguished or confined to narrow limits. But it represents a philosophy at war with the First Amendment—a constitutional interpretation which puts free speech under the legislative thumb. It reflects an influence moving ever deeper into our society. It is notice to the legislatures that they have the power to control unpopular blocs. It is a warning to every minority that when the Constitution guarantees free speech it does not mean what it says.

Mr. Justice Jackson, dissenting.

. . . I agree with the Court that a State has power to bring classes "of any race, color, creed, or religion" within the protection of its libel laws, if indeed traditional forms do not already accomplish it. But I am equally clear that in doing so it is essential to our concept of ordered liberty that the State also protect the accused by those safeguards the necessity for which is verified by legal history.

III

The Illinois statute, as applied in this case, seems to me to have dispensed with accepted safeguards for the accused. Trial of this case ominously parallels the trial of *People* v. *Croswell* in that the Illinois court here instructed the jury, in substance, that if it found that defendant published this leaflet he must be found guilty of criminal libel. Rulings of the trial court precluded the effort to justify statements of fact by proving their truth. The majority opinion concedes the unvarying recognition by the States that truth plus good motives is a defense in a prosecution for criminal libel. But here the trial court repeatedly refused defendant's offer of proof as to the truth of the matter published. Where an offer to prove the dominant element of a defense is rejected as immaterial, we can hardly refuse to consider defendant's constitutional question because he did not go through the useless ceremony of offering proof of a subsidiary element of the defense. If the court would not let him try to prove he spoke truth, how could he show that he spoke truth for good ends? Furthermore, the record indicates that defendant was asked to state what he had meant by the use of certain phrases, and the reason for forming the White Circle League—statements which apparently bore on the issue of motive and ends. But the trial court sustained a sweeping objection "to this whole line of examination." The Supreme Court of Illinois noted the offer of proof of truth and its exclusion, and apparently went on to rule as a matter of law that the statement was not published for justifiable ends. At all events, it is clear that the defense was ruled out as matter of law and defendant was never allowed to present it for decision by either court or jury upon the facts, a practice which I think is contrary to the overwhelming verdict of Anglo-Saxon history and practice. I do not intimate that this defendant stood even a remote chance of justifying what impresses me, as it did the trial court, as reckless and vicious libel. But the point is that his evidence, proffered for that purpose, was excluded instead of being received and evaluated. Society has an interest in preserving truth as a justification, however obnoxious the effort may be. A publication which diffuses its attack over unnamed and impersonal multitudes is likely to be harder to justify than one which concentrates its attack on named individuals, but the burden may properly be cast on an accused and punishment follow failure to carry it.

The same may be said of the right to comment upon matters of public interest insofar as the statement includes matters of opinion, a point, however, which the defense may have inadequately raised. When any naturally cohesive or artificially organized group possesses a racial or sectarian solidarity which is or may be exploited to influence public affairs, that group becomes a legitimate subject for public comment. Of course, one can only deplore the habitual intemperance and bitter disparagement which characterizes most such comment. While I support the right of a State to place decent bounds upon it, I am not ready to hold that group purposes, characteristics and histories are to be immunized from comment or may be discussed only at the risk of prosecution free of all usual safeguards.

Another defense almost universally recognized, which it seems the jury were not allowed to consider here, is that of privilege. Petition for redress of grievances is specifically privileged by many State Constitutions. I do not think we should hold this whole document to be constitutionally privileged just because, in part, it stimulates a petition for redress of grievances. A court or jury could have found that its primary purpose was not to petition but to appeal for members and contributions to the White Circle League. If some part of it were privileged, that, so it has been held, does not extend constitutional protection to unprivileged matter. But the question of privilege seems not to have been specifically passed on by the court and certainly was not submitted for the jury's consideration.

In this case, neither the court nor jury found or were required to find any injury to any person, or group, or to the public peace, nor to find any probability, let alone any clear and present danger, of injury to any of these. Even though no individuals were named or described as targets of this pamphlet, if it resulted in a riot or caused injury to any individual Negro, such as being refused living quarters in a particular section, house or apartment, or being refused employment, certainly there would be no constitutional obstacle to imposing civil or criminal liability for actual results. But in this case no actual violence and no specific injury was charged or proved.

The leaflet was simply held punishable as criminal libel *per se* irrespective of its actual or probable consequences. No charge of conspiracy complicates this case. The words themselves do not advocate the commission of any crime. The conviction rests on judicial attribution of a likelihood of evil results. The trial court, however, refused to charge the jury that it must find some "clear and present danger," and the Supreme Court of Illinois sustained conviction because, in its opinion, the words used had a tendency to cause a breach of the peace.

Referring to the clear and present danger doctrine in *Dennis* v. *United States,* I said:

"I would save it, unmodified, for application as a 'rule of reason' in the kind of case for which it was devised. When the issue is criminality of a hot-headed speech on a street corner, or circulation of a few incendiary pamphlets, or parading by some zealots behind a red flag, or refusal of a handful of school children to salute our flag, it is not beyond the capacity of the judicial process to gather, comprehend, and weigh the necessary materials for decision whether it is a clear and present danger of substantive evil or a harmless letting off of steam. It is not a prophecy, for the danger in such cases has matured by the time of trial or it was never present. The test applies and has meaning where a conviction is sought to be based on a speech or writing which does not directly or explicitly advocate a crime but to which such tendency is sought to be attributed by construction or by implication from external circumstances. The formula in such cases favors freedoms that are vital to our society, and, even if sometimes applied too generously, the consequences cannot be grave. . . ."

Not the least of the virtues of this formula in such tendency cases is that it compels the prosecution to make up its mind what particular evil it sought or is seeking to prevent. It must relate its interference with speech or press to some identifiable evil to be prevented. Words on their own account are not to be punished in such cases but are reachable only as the root of punishable evils.

Punishment of printed words, based on their *tendency* either to cause breach of the peace or injury to persons or groups, in my opinion, is justifiable only if the prosecution survives the "clear and present danger" test. It is the most just and workable standard yet evolved for determining criminality of words whose injurious or inciting tendencies are not demonstrated by the event but are ascribed to them on the basis of probabilities.

Its application is important in this case because it takes account of the particular form, time, place, and manner of communication in question. "The moving picture screen, the radio, the newspaper, the handbill, the sound truck and the street corner orator have differing natures, values, abuses and dangers. Each, in my view, is a law unto itself . . . ." It would consider whether a leaflet is so emotionally exciting to immediate action as the spoken word, especially the incendiary street or public speech. It will inquire whether this publication was obviously so foul and extreme as to defeat its own ends, whether its appeals for money—which has a cooling effect on many persons—would not negative its inflammatory effect, whether it would not impress the passer-by as the work of an irresponsible who needed mental examination.

One of the merits of the clear and present danger test is that the triers of fact would take into account the realities of race relations and any smouldering fires to be fanned into holacausts. Such consideration might well warrant a conviction here when it would not in another and different environment.

Group libel statutes represent a commendable desire to reduce sinister abuses of our freedoms of expression—abuses which I have had occasion to learn can tear apart a society, brutalize its dominant elements, and persecute, even to extermination, its minorities. While laws or prosecutions might not alleviate racial or sectarian hatreds and may even invest scoundrels with a specious martyrdom, I should be loath to foreclose the States from a considerable latitude of experimentation in this field. Such efforts, if properly applied, do not justify frenetic forebodings of crushed liberty. But these acts present most difficult policy and technical problems, as thoughtful writers who have canvassed the problem more comprehensively than is appropriate in a judicial opinion have well pointed out.

No group interest in any particular prosecution should forget that the shoe may be on the other foot in some prosecution tomorrow. In these, as in other matters, our guiding spirit should be that each freedom is balanced with a responsibility, and every power of the State must be checked with safeguards. Such is the spirit of our American law of criminal libel, which concedes the power to the State, but only as a power restrained by recognition of individual rights. I cannot escape the conclusion that as the Act has been applied in this case it lost sight of the rights.

N.A.A.C.P. v. Alabama
357 U. S. 449   1957

Mr. Justice Harlan delivered the opinion of the Court.

We review from the standpoint of its validity under the Federal Constitution a judgment of civil contempt entered against petitioner, the National Association for the Advancement of Colored People, in the courts of Alabama. The question presented is whether Alabama, consistently with the Due Process Clause of the Fourteenth Amendment, can compel petitioner to reveal to the State's Attorney General the names and addresses of all its Alabama members and agents, without regard to their positions or functions in the Association. The judgment of contempt was based upon petitioner's refusal to comply fully with a court order requiring in part the production of membership lists. Petitioner's claim is that the order, in the circumstances shown by this record, violated rights assured to petitioner and its members under the Constitution.

Alabama has a statute similar to those of many other States which requires a foreign corporation, except as exempted, to qualify before doing business by filing its corporate charter with the Secretary of State and designating a place of business and an agent to receive service of process. The statute imposes a fine on a corporation transacting intrastate business before qualifying and provides for criminal prosecution of officers of such a corporation. The National Association for the Advancement of Colored People is a nonprofit membership corporation organized under the laws of New York. Its purposes, fostered on a nation-wide basis, are those indicated by its name, and it operates through chartered affiliates which are independent unincorporated associations, with membership therein equivalent to membership in petitioner. The first Alabama affiliates were chartered in 1918. Since that time the aims of the Association have been advanced through activities of its affiliates, and in 1951 the Association itself opened a regional office in Alabama, at which it employed two supervisory persons and one clerical worker. The Association has never complied with the qualification statute, from which it considered itself exempt.

In 1956 the Attorney General of Alabama brought an equity suit in the State Circuit Court, Montgomery County, to enjoin the Association from conducting further activities within, and to oust it from, the State. Among other things the bill in equity alleged that the Association had opened a regional office and had organized various affiliates in Alabama; had recruited members and solicited contributions within the State; had given financial support and furnished legal assistance to Negro students seeking admission to the state university; and had supported a Negro boycott of the bus lines in Montgomery to compel the seating of passengers without regard to race. The bill recited that the Association, by continuing to do business in Alabama without complying with the qualification statute, was ". . . causing irreparable injury to the property and civil rights of the residents and citizens of the State of Alabama for which criminal prosecution and civil actions at law afford no adequate relief . . . ." On the day the complaint was filed, the Circuit Court issued *ex parte* an order restraining the Association, *pendente lite*, from engaging in further activities within the State and forbidding it to take any steps to qualify itself to do business therein.

Petitioner demurred to the allegations of the bill and moved to dissolve the restraining order. It contended that its activities did not subject it to the qualification requirements of the statute and that in any event what the State sought to accomplish by its suit would violate rights to freedom of speech and assembly guaranteed under the Fourteenth Amendment to the Constitution of the United States. Before the date set for a hearing on this motion, the State moved for the production of a large number of the Association's records and papers, including bank statements, leases, deeds, and records containing the names and addresses of all Alabama "members" and "agents" of the Association. It alleged that all such documents were necessary for adequate preparation for the hearing, in view of petitioner's denial of the conduct of intrastate business within the meaning of the qualification statute. Over petitioner's objections, the court ordered the production of a substantial part of the requested records, including the membership lists, and postponed the hearing on the restraining order to a date later than the time ordered for production.

Thereafter petitioner filed its answer to the bill in equity. It admitted its Alabama activities substantially as alleged in the complaint and that it had not qualified to do business in the State. Although still disclaiming the statute's application to it, petitioner offered to qualify if the bar from qualification made part of the restraining order were lifted, and it submitted with the answer an executed set of the forms required by the statute. However petitioner did not comply with the production order, and for this failure was adjudged in civil contempt and fined $10,000. The contempt judgment provided that the fine would be subject to reduction or remission if compliance were forthcoming within five days but otherwise would be increased to $100,000.

At the end of the five-day period petitioner produced substantially all the data called for by the production order except its membership lists, as to which it contended that Alabama could not constitutionally compel disclosure, and moved to modify or vacate the contempt judgment, or stay its execution pending appellate review. This motion was denied. While a similar stay application, which was later denied, was pending before the Supreme Court of Alabama, the Circuit Court made a further order adjudging petitioner in continuing contempt and increasing the fine already imposed to $100,000. Under Alabama law the effect of the contempt adjudication was to foreclose petitioner from obtaining a hearing on the merits of the underlying ouster action, or from taking any steps to dissolve the temporary restraining order which had been issued *ex parte*, until it purged itself of contempt.

The State Supreme Court thereafter twice dismissed petitions for certiorari to review this final contempt judgment, the first time for insufficiency of the petition's allegations and the second time on procedural grounds. We granted certiorari because of the importance of the constitutional questions presented.

II

. . . The Association both urges that it is constitutionally entitled to resist official inquiry into its membership lists, and that it may assert, on behalf of its members, a right personal to them to be protected from compelled disclosure by the State of their affiliation with the Association as revealed by the membership lists. We think that petitioner argues more appropriately the rights of its members, and that its nexus with them is sufficient to permit that it act as their representative before this Court. In so concluding, we reject respondent's argument that the Association lacks standing to assert here constitutional rights pertaining to the members, who are not of course parties to the litigation.

To limit the breadth of issues which must be dealt with in particular litigation, this Court has generally insisted that parties rely only on constitutional rights which are personal to themselves. This rule is related to the broader doctrine that constitutional adjudication should where possible be avoided. The principle is not disrespected where constitutional rights of persons who are not immediately before the Court could not be effectively vindicated except through an appropriate representative before the Court.

If petitioner's rank-and-file members are constitutionally entitled to withhold their connection with the Association despite the production order, it is manifest that this right is properly assertable by the Association. To require that it be claimed by the members themselves would result in nullification of the right at the very moment of its assertion. Petitioner is the appropriate party to assert these rights, because it and its members are in every practical sense identical. The Association, which provides in its constitution that "[a]ny person who is in accordance with [its] principles and policies . . ." may become a member, is but the medium through which its individual members seek to make more effective the expression of their own views. The reasonable likelihood

161

that the Association itself through diminished financial support and membership may be adversely affected if production is compelled is a further factor pointing towards our holding that petitioner has standing to complain of the production order on behalf of its members.

III

We thus reach petitioner's claim that the production order in the state litigation trespasses upon fundamental freedoms protected by the Due Process Clause of the Fourteenth Amendment. Petitioner argues that in view of the facts and circumstances shown in the record, the effect of compelled disclosure of the membership lists will be to abridge the rights of its rank-and-file members to engage in lawful association in support of their common beliefs. It contends that governmental action which, although not directly suppressing association, nevertheless carries this consequence, can be justified only upon some overriding valid interest of the State.

Effective advocacy of both public and private points of view, particularly controversial ones, is undeniably enhanced by group association, as this Court has more than once recognized by remarking upon the close nexus between the freedoms of speech and assembly. It is beyond debate that freedom to engage in association for the advancement of beliefs and ideas is an inseparable aspect of the "liberty" assured by the Due Process Clause of the Fourteenth Amendment, which embraces freedom of speech. Of course, it is immaterial whether the beliefs sought to be advanced by association pertain to political, economic, religious or cultural matters, and state action which may have the effect of curtailing the freedom to associate is subject to the closest scrutiny.

The fact that Alabama, so far as is relevant to the validity of the contempt judgment presently under review, has taken no direct action to restrict the right of petitioner's members to associate freely, does not end inquiry into the effect of the production order. In the domain of these indispensable liberties, whether of speech, press, or association, the decisions of this Court recognize that abridgement of such rights, even though unintended, may inevitably follow from varied forms of governmental action. Thus in *Douds,* the Court stressed that the legislation there challenged, which on its face sought to regulate labor unions and to secure stability in interstate commerce, would have the practical effect "of discouraging" the exercise of constitutionally protected political rights and it upheld the statute only after concluding that the reasons advanced for its enactment were constitutionally sufficient to justify its possible deterrent effect upon such freedoms. Similar recognition of possible unconstitutional intimidation of the free exercise of the right to advocate underlay this Court's narrow construction of the authority of a congressional committee investigating lobbying and of an Act regulating lobbying, although in neither case was there an effort to suppress speech. The governmental action challenged may appear to be totally unrelated to protected liberties. Statutes imposing taxes upon rather than prohibiting particular activity have been struck down when perceived to have the consequence of unduly curtailing the liberty of freedom of press assured under the Fourteenth Amendment.

It is hardly a novel perception that compelled disclosure of affiliation with groups engaged in advocacy may constitute as effective a restraint on freedom of association as the forms of governmental action in the cases above were thought likely to produce upon the particular constitutional rights there involved. This Court has recognized the vital relationship between freedom to associate and privacy in one's associations. When referring to the varied forms of governmental action which might interfere with freedom of assembly, it said in *American Communications Assn. v. Douds:* "A requirement that adherents of particular religious faiths or political parties wear identifying arm-bands, for example, is obviously of this nature." Compelled disclosure of membership in an organization engaged in advocacy of particular beliefs is of the same order. Inviolability of privacy in group association may in many circumstances be indispensable to preservation of freedom of association, particularly where a group espouses dissident beliefs.

We think that the production order, in the respects here drawn in question, must be regarded as entailing the likelihood of a substantial restraint upon the exercise by petitioner's members of their right to freedom of association. Petitioner has made an uncontroverted showing that on past occasions revelation of the identity of its rank-and-file members has exposed these members to economic reprisal, loss of employment, threat of physical coercion, and other manifestations of public hostility. Under these circumstances, we think it apparent that compelled disclosure of petitioner's Alabama membership is likely to affect adversely the ability of petitioner and its members to pursue their collective effort to foster beliefs which they admittedly have the right to advocate, in that it may induce members to withdraw from the Association and dissuade others from joining it because of fear of exposure of their beliefs shown through their associations and of the consequences of this exposure.

It is not sufficient to answer, as the State does here, that whatever repressive effect compulsory disclosure of names of petitioner's members may have upon participation by Alabama citizens in petitioner's activities follows not from *state* action but from *private* community pressures. The crucial factor is the interplay of governmental and private action, for it is only after the initial exertion of state power represented by the production order that private action takes hold.

We turn to the final question whether Alabama has demonstrated an interest in obtaining the disclosures it seeks from petitioner which is sufficient to justify the deterrent effect which we have concluded these disclosures may well have on the free exercise by petitioner's members of their constitutionally protected right of association. Such a ". . . subordinating interest of the State must be compelling." It is not of moment that the State has here acted solely through its judicial branch, for whether legislative or judicial, it is still the application of state power which we are asked to scrutinize.

It is important to bear in mind that petitioner asserts no right to absolute immunity from state investigation, and no right to disregard Alabama's laws. As shown by its substantial compliance with the production order, petitioner does not deny Alabama's right to obtain from it such information as the State desires concerning the purposes of the Association and its activities within the State. Petitioner has not objected to divulging the identity of its members who are employed by or hold official positions with it. It has urged the rights solely of its ordinary rank-and-file members. This is therefore not analogous to a case involving the interest of a State in protecting its citizens in their dealings with paid solicitors or agents of foreign corporations by requiring identification.

Whether there was "justification" in this instance turns solely on the substantiality of Alabama's interest in obtaining the membership lists. During the course of a hearing before the Alabama Circuit Court on a motion of petitioner to set aside the production order, the State Attorney General presented at length, under examination by petitioner, the State's reason for requesting the membership lists. The exclusive purpose was to determine whether petitioner was conducting intrastate business in violation of the Alabama foreign corporation registration statute, and the membership lists were expected to help resolve this question. The issues in the litigation commenced by Alabama by its bill in equity were whether the character of petitioner and its activities in Alabama had been such as to make petitioner subject to the registration statute, and whether the extent of petitioner's activities without qualifying suggested its permanent ouster from the State. Without intimating the slightest view upon the merits of these issues, we are unable to perceive that the disclosure of the names of petitioner's rank-and-file members has a substantial bearing on either of them. As matters stand in the state court, petitioner (1) has admitted its presence and conduct of activities in Alabama since 1918; (2) has offered to comply in all respects with the state qualification statute, although preserving its contention that the statute does not apply to it; and (3) has apparently complied satisfactorily with the production order, except for the membership lists, by furnishing the Attorney General with varied business records, its charter and statement of purposes, the names of all of its directors and officers, and with the total number of its Alabama members and the amount of their dues. These last items would not on this record appear subject to constitutional challenge and have been furnished, but whatever interest the State may have in obtaining names of ordinary members has not been shown to be sufficient to overcome petitioner's constitutional objections to the production order.

From what has already been said, we think it apparent that *Bryant* v. *Zimmerman* cannot be relied on in support of the State's position, for that case involved markedly different considerations in terms of the interest of the State in obtaining disclosure. There, this Court upheld, as applied to a member of a local chapter of the Ku Klux Klan, a New York statute requiring any unincorporated association which demanded an oath as a condition to membership to file with state officials copies of its ". . . constitution, by-laws, rules, regulations and oath of membership, together with a roster of its membership and a list of its officers for the current year." In its opinion, the Court took care to emphasize the nature of the organization which New York sought to regulate. The decision was based on the particular character of the Klan's activities, involving acts of unlawful intimidation and violence, which the Court assumed was before the state legislature when it enacted the statute, and of which the Court itself took judicial notice. Furthermore, the situation before us is significantly different from that in *Bryant,* because the organization there had made no effort to comply with any of the require-ments of New York's statute but rather had refused to furnish the State with *any* information as to its local activities.

We hold that the immunity from state scrutiny of membership lists which the Association claims on behalf of its members is here so related to the right of the members to pursue their lawful private interests privately and to associate freely with others in so doing as to come within the protection of the Fourteenth Amendment. And we conclude that Alabama has fallen short of showing a controlling justification for the deterrent effect on the free enjoyment of the right to associate which disclosure of membership lists is likely to have. Accordingly, the judg-ment of civil contempt and the $100,000 fine which resulted from peti-tioner's refusal to comply with the production order in this respect must fall.

IV

Petitioner joins with its attack upon the production order a challenge to the constitutionality of the State's *ex parte* temporary restraining order preventing it from soliciting support in Alabama, and it asserts that the Fourteenth Amendment precludes such state action. But as noted above, petitioner has never received a hearing on the merits of the ouster suit, and we do not consider these questions properly here. The Supreme Court of Alabama noted in its denial of the petition for certiorari that such petition raised solely a question pertinent to the contempt adjudica-tion. "The ultimate aim and purpose of the litigation is to determine the right of the state to enjoin petitioners from doing business in Ala-bama. That question, however, is not before us in this proceeding." The proper method for raising questions in the state appellate courts pertinent to the underlying suit for an injunction appears to be by appeal, after a hearing on the merits and final judgment by the lower state court. Only from the disposition of such an appeal can review be sought here.

For the reasons stated, the judgment of the Supreme Court of Ala-bama must be reversed and the case remanded for proceedings not in-consistent with this opinion.

Bates v. Little Rock
361 U. S. 516 1959

Mr. Justice Stewart delivered the opinion of the Court.

Each of the petitioners has been convicted of violating an identical ordinance of an Arkansas municipality by refusing a demand to furnish city officials with a list of the names of the members of a local branch of the National Association for the Advancement of Colored People. The question for decision is whether these convictions can stand under the Due Process Clause of the Fourteenth Amendment to the United States Constitution.

Municipalities in Arkansas are authorized by the State to levy a license tax on any person, firm, individual, or corporation engaging in any "trade, business, profession, vocation or calling" within their corporate limits. Pursuant to this authority, the City of Little Rock and the City of North Little Rock have for some years imposed annual license taxes on a broad variety of businesses, occupations, and professions. Charitable organizations which engage in the activities affected are relieved from paying the taxes.

In 1957 the two cities added identical amendments to their occupation license tax ordinances. These amendments require that any organization operating within the municipality in question must supply to the City Clerk, upon request and within a specified time, (1) the official name of the organization; (2) its headquarters or regular meeting place; (3) the names of the officers, agents, servants, employees, or representatives, and their salaries; (4) the purpose of the organization; (5) a statement as to dues, assessments, and contributions paid, by whom and when paid, together with a statement reflecting the disposition of the funds and the total net income; (6) an affidavit stating whether the organization is subordinate to a parent organization, and if so, the latter's name. The ordinances expressly provide that all information furnished shall be public and subject to the inspection of any interested party at all reasonable business hours.

Petitioner Bates was the custodian of the records of the local branch of the National Association for the Advancement of Colored People in Little Rock, and petitioner Williams was the custodian of the records of the North Little Rock branch. These local organizations supplied the two municipalities with all the information required by the ordinances, except that demanded under § 2E of each ordinance which would have required disclosure of the names of the organizations' members and contributors. Instead of furnishing the detailed breakdown required by this section of the North Little Rock ordinance, the petitioner Williams wrote to the City Clerk as follows:

"E. The financial statement is as follows:
January 1, 1957 to December 4, 1957.
Total receipts from membership and
contributors $252.00.

Total expenditures	$183.60
(to National Office)	
Secretarial help	5.00
Stationery, stamps, etc.	3.00
Total	$191.60
On Hand	60.40

"F. I am attaching my affidavit as president indicating that we are a Branch of the National Association for the Advancement of Colored People, a New York Corporation.

"We cannot give you any information with respect to the names and addresses of our members and contributors or any information which may lead to the ascertainment of such information. We base this refusal on the anti-NAACP climate in this state. It is our good faith and belief that the public disclosure of the names of our members and contributors might lead to their harassment, economic reprisals, and even bodily harm. Moreover, even aside from that possibility, we have been advised by our counsel, and we do so believe that the city has no right under the Constitution and laws of the United States, and under the Constitution and laws of the State of Arkansas to demand the names and addresses of our members and contributors. We assert on behalf of the organization and its members the right to contribute to the NAACP and to seek under its aegis to accomplish the aims and purposes herein described free from any restraints or interference from city or state officials. In addition we assert the right of our members and contributors to participate in the activities of the NAACP, anonymously, a right which has been recognized as the basic right of every American citizen since the founding of this country. . . ."

A substantially identical written statement was submitted on behalf of the Little Rock branch of the Association to the Clerk of that city.

After refusing upon further demand to submit the names of the members of her organization, each petitioner was tried, convicted, and fined for a violation of the ordinance of her respective municipality. At the Bates trial evidence was offered to show that many former members of the local organization had declined to renew their membership because of the existence of the ordinance in question. Similar evidence was received in the Williams trial, as well as evidence that those who had been publicly identified in the community as members of the National Association for the Advancement of Colored People had been subjected to harassment and threats of bodily harm.

On appeal the cases were consolidated in the Supreme Court of Arkansas, and, with two justices dissenting, the convictions were upheld. The court concluded that compulsory disclosure of the membership lists under the circumstances was "not an unconstitutional invasion of the freedoms guaranteed . . ." but "a mere incident to a permissible legal result." Because of the significant constitutional question involved, we granted certiorari.

Like freedom of speech and a free press, the right of peaceable assembly was considered by the Framers of our Constitution to lie at the foundation of a government based upon the consent of an informed citizenry—a government dedicated to the establishment of justice and the preservation of liberty. And it is now beyond dispute that freedom of association for the purpose of advancing ideas and airing grievances is protected by the Due Process Clause of the Fourteenth Amendment from invasion by the States.

Freedoms such as these are protected not only against heavy-handed frontal attack, but also from being stifled by more subtle governmental interference. "It is hardly a novel perception that compelled disclosure of affiliation with groups engaged in advocacy may constitute [an] effective . . . restraint on freedom of association. . . . This Court has recognized the vital relationship between freedom to associate and privacy in one's associations. . . . Inviolability of privacy in group association may in many circumstances be indispensable to preservation of freedom of association, particularly where a group espouses dissident beliefs."

On this record it sufficiently appears that compulsory disclosure of the membership lists of the local branches of the National Association for the Advancement of Colored People would work a significant interference with the freedom of association of their members. There was substantial uncontroverted evidence that public identification of persons in the community as members of the organizations had been followed by harassment and threats of bodily harm. There was also evidence that fear of community hostility and economic reprisals that would follow public disclosure of the membership lists had discouraged new members from joining the organizations and induced former members to withdraw. This repressive effect, while in part the result of private attitudes and pressures, was brought to bear only after the exercise of governmental power had threatened to force disclosure of the members' names. Thus, the threat of substantial government encroachment upon important and traditional aspects of individual freedom is neither speculative nor remote.

Decision in this case must finally turn, therefore, on whether the cities as instrumentalities of the State have demonstrated so cogent an interest in obtaining and making public the membership lists of these organizations as to justify the substantial abridgment of associational freedom which such disclosures will effect. Where there is a significant encroachment upon personal liberty, the State may prevail only upon showing a subordinating interest which is compelling.

It cannot be questioned that the governmental purpose upon which the municipalities rely is a fundamental one. No power is more basic to the ultimate purpose and function of government than is the power to tax. Nor can it be doubted that the proper and efficient exercise of this essential governmental power may sometimes entail the possibility of encroachment upon individual freedom.

It was as an adjunct of their power to impose occupational license taxes that the cities enacted the legislation here in question. But governmental action does not automatically become reasonably related to the achievement of a legitimate and substantial governmental purpose by mere assertion in the preamble of an ordinance. When it is shown that state action threatens significantly to impinge upon constitutionally protected freedom it becomes the duty of this Court to determine whether the action bears a reasonable relationship to the achievement of the governmental purpose asserted as its justification.

In this record we can find no relevant correlation between the power of the municipalities to impose occupational license taxes and the compulsory disclosure and publication of the membership lists of the local branches of the National Association for the Advancement of Colored People. The occupational license tax ordinances of the municipalities are squarely aimed at reaching all the commercial, professional, and business occupations within the communities. The taxes are not, and as a matter of state law cannot be, based on earnings or income, but upon the nature of the occupation or enterprise conducted.

Inquiry of organizations within the communities as to the purpose and nature of their activities would thus appear to be entirely relevant to enforcement of the ordinances. Such an inquiry was addressed to these organizations and was answered as follows:

"We are an affiliate of a national organization seeking to secure for American Negroes their rights as guaranteed by the Constitution of the United States. Our purposes may best be described by quoting from the Articles of Incorporation of our National Organization where these purposes are set forth as:

" '. . . voluntarily to promote equality of rights and eradicate caste or race prejudice among the citizens of the United States; to advance the interest of colored citizens; to secure for them impartial suffrage; and to increase their opportunities for securing justice in the courts, education for their children, employment according to their ability, and complete equality before the law. To ascertain and publish all facts bearing upon these subjects and to take any lawful action thereon; together with any kind and all things which may lawfully be done by a membership corporation organized under the laws of the State of New York for the further advancement of these objects.'

"The Articles of Incorporation hereinabove referred to are on file in the office of the Secretary of State of the State of Arkansas. In accord with these purposes and aims, [this] . . . Branch, NAACP was chartered and organized, and we are seeking to effectuate these principles within [this municipality]."

The municipalities have not suggested that an activity so described, even if conducted for profit, would fall within any of the occupational classifications for which a license is required or a tax payable. On oral argument counsel for the City of Little Rock was unable to relate any activity of these organizations to which a license tax might attach. And there is nothing in the record to indicate that a tax claim has ever been asserted against either organization. If the organizations were to claim the exemption which the ordinance grants to charitable endeavors, information as to the specific sources and expenditures of their funds might well be a subject of relevant inquiry. But there is nothing to show that any exemption has ever been sought, claimed, or granted—and positive evidence in the record to the contrary.

In sum, there is a complete failure in this record to show (1) that the organizations were engaged in any occupation for which a license would be required, even if the occupation were conducted for a profit; (2) that the cities have ever asserted a claim against the organizations for payment of an occupational license tax; (3) that the organizations have ever asserted exemption from a tax imposed by the municipalities, either because of their alleged nonprofit character or for any other reason.

We conclude that the municipalities have failed to demonstrate a controlling justification for the deterrence of free association which compulsory disclosure of the membership lists would cause. The petitioners cannot be punished for refusing to produce information which the municipalities could not constitutionally require. The judgments cannot stand.

Mr. Justice Black and Mr. Justice Douglas, concurring.

We concur in the judgment and substantially with the opinion because we think the facts show that the ordinances as here applied violate freedom of speech and assembly guaranteed by the First Amendment which this Court has many times held was made applicable to the States by the Fourteenth Amendment.

Moreover, we believe, as we indicated in *United States* v. *Rumely,* that First Amendment rights are beyond abridgment either by legislation that directly restrains their exercise or by suppression or impairment through harassment, humiliation, or exposure by government. One of those rights, freedom of assembly, includes of course freedom of association; and it is entitled to no less protection than any other First Amendment right as *N. A. A. C. P.* v. *Alabama* and *De Jonge* v. *Oregon* hold. These are principles applicable to all people under our Constitution irrespective of their race, color, politics, or religion. That is, for us, the essence of the present opinion of the Court.

Louisiana v. N.A.A.C.P.

366 U. S. 293   1960

Mr. Justice Douglas delivered the opinion of the Court.

One of the suits that is consolidated in this appeal was instituted in 1956 by the then Attorney General of Louisiana against appellee, the National Association for the Advancement of Colored People, in a Louisiana court and sought to enjoin it from doing business in the State. It was removed to the federal court. Thereafter NAACP sued appellants in the federal court asking for a declaratory judgment that two laws of Louisiana were unconstitutional. A three-judge court was convened and the cases were consolidated. After a hearing (on affidavits) and oral argument, the court entered a *temporary* injunction that denied relief to appellants and enjoined them from enforcing the two laws in question. The case is here on appeal. We noted probable jurisdiction.

One of the two statutes of Louisiana in question prohibits any "nontrading" association from doing business in Louisiana if it is affiliated with any "foreign or out of state non-trading" association "any of the officers or members of the board of directors of which are members of Communist, Communist-front or subversive organizations, as cited by the House of Congress [*sic*] un-American Activities Committee, or the United States Attorney." Every nontrading association affiliated with an out-of-state association must file annually with Louisiana's Secretary of State an affidavit that "none of the officers" of the affiliate is "a member" of any such organization. Penalties against the officers and members are provided for failure to file the affidavit and for false filings.

The NAACP is a New York corporation with some forty-eight directors, twenty vice-presidents, and ten chief executive officers. Only a few reside or work in Louisiana. The District Court commented that the statute "would require the impossible" of the Louisiana residents or workers. We have received no serious reply to that criticism. Such a requirement in a law compounds the vices present in statutes struck down on account of vagueness. It is not consonant with due process to require a person to swear to a fact that he cannot be expected to know or alternatively to refrain from a wholly lawful activity.

The other statute requires the principal officer of "each fraternal, patriotic, charitable, benevolent, literary, scientific, athletic, military, or social organization, or organization created for similar purposes" and operating in Louisiana to file with the Secretary of State annually "a full, complete and true list of the names and addresses of all of the members and officers" in the State. Members of organizations whose lists have not been filed are prohibited from holding or attending any meeting of the organization. Criminal penalties are attached both to officers and to members.

We are told that this law was passed in 1924 to curb the Ku Klux Klan, but that it was never enforced against any other organization until this litigation started; that when the State brought its suit some affiliates of NAACP in Louisiana filed membership lists; and that after those filings, members were subjected to economic reprisals. The State denies that this law is presently being enforced only against NAACP; it also challenges the assertions that disclosure of membership in the NAACP results in reprisals. While hearings were held before the temporary injunction issued, the case is in a preliminary stage and we do not know what facts further hearings before the injunction becomes final may disclose. It is clear from our decisions that NAACP has standing to assert the constitutional rights of its members. We deal with a constitutional right, since freedom of association is included in the bundle of First Amendment rights made applicable to the States by the Due Process Clause of the Fourteenth Amendment. And where it is shown, as it was in *N. A. A. C. P.* v. *Alabama,* that disclosure of membership lists results in reprisals against and hostility to the members, disclosure is not required.

We are in an area where, as *Shelton* v. *Tucker* emphasized, any regulation must be highly selective in order to survive challenge under the First Amendment. As we there stated: ". . . even though the governmental purpose be legitimate and substantial, that purpose cannot be pursued by means that broadly stifle fundamental personal liberties when the end can be more narrowly achieved."

The most frequent expressions of that view have been made in cases dealing with local ordinances regulating the distribution of literature. Broad comprehensive regulations of those First Amendment rights have been repeatedly struck down, though the power to regulate the time, manner, and place of distribution was never doubted. As stated in *Schneider* v. *State* the municipal authorities have the right to "regulate the conduct of those using the streets," to provide traffic regulations, to prevent "throwing literature broadcast in the streets," and the like. Yet, while public safety, peace, comfort, or convenience can be safeguarded by regulating the time and manner of solicitation, those regulations need to be "narrowly drawn to prevent the supposed evil."

Our latest application of this principle was in *Shelton* v. *Tucker* where we held that, while a State has the undoubted right to inquire into the fitness and competency of its teachers, a detailed disclosure of every conceivable kind of associational tie a teacher has had probed into relationships that "could have no possible bearing upon the teacher's occupational competence or fitness."

At one extreme is criminal conduct which cannot have shelter in the First Amendment. At the other extreme are regulatory measures which, no matter how sophisticated, cannot be employed in purpose or in effect to stifle, penalize, or curb the exercise of First Amendment rights. These lines mark the area in which the present controversy lies, as the District Court rightly observed.

Affirmed.

Mr. Justice Harlan and Mr. Justice Stewart concur in the result.

Mr. Justice Frankfurter, whom Mr. Justice Clark joins, concurring in the judgment . . .

Part IV

THE JAPANESE EVACUATION

Hirabayashi v. United States

Korematsu v. United States

These cases concern the curfew and evacuation orders applied to American citizens of Japanese ancestry during World War II. The Court, which sustained the curfew order with uneasy unanimity, divided bitterly but upheld the constitutionality of the evacuation order.

Hirabayashi v. United States

320 U. S. 81   1943

Mr. Chief Justice Stone delivered the opinion of the Court.

Appellant, an American citizen of Japanese ancestry, was convicted in the district court of violating the Act of Congress of March 21, 1942, which makes it a misdemeanor knowingly to disregard restrictions made applicable by a military commander to persons in a military area prescribed by him as such, all as authorized by an Executive Order of the President.

The questions for our decision are whether the particular restriction violated, namely that all persons of Japanese ancestry residing in such an area be within their place of residence daily between the hours of 8:00 P.M. and 6:00 A.M., was adopted by the military commander in the exercise of an unconstitutional delegation by Congress of its legislative power, and whether the restriction unconstitutionally discriminated between citizens of Japanese ancestry and those of other ancestries in violation of the Fifth Amendment.

The indictment is in two counts. The second charges that appellant, being a person of Japanese ancestry, had on a specified date, contrary to a restriction promulgated by the military commander of the Western Defense Command, Fourth Army, failed to remain in his place of residence in the designated military area between the hours of 8:00 o'clock P.M. and 6:00 A.M. The first count charges that appellant, on May 11 and 12, 1942, had, contrary to a Civilian Exclusion Order issued by the military commander, failed to report to the Civil Control Station within the designated area, it appearing that appellant's required presence there was a preliminary step to the exclusion from that area of persons of Japanese ancestry.

By demurrer and plea in abatement, which the court overruled, appellant asserted that the indictment should be dismissed because he was an

American citizen who had never been a subject of and had never borne allegiance to the Empire of Japan, and also because the Act of March 21, 1942, was an unconstitutional delegation of Congressional power. On the trial to a jury it appeared that appellant was born in Seattle in 1918, of Japanese parents who had come from Japan to the United States, and who had never afterward returned to Japan; that he was educated in the Washington public schools and at the time of his arrest was a senior in the University of Washington; that he had never been in Japan or had any association with Japanese residing there.

The evidence showed that appellant had failed to report to the Civil Control Station on May 11 or May 12, 1942, as directed, to register for evacuation from the military area. He admitted failure to do so, and stated it had at all times been his belief that he would be waiving his rights as an American citizen by so doing. The evidence also showed that for like reason he was away from his place of residence after 8:00 P.M. on May 9, 1942. The jury returned a verdict of guilty on both counts and appellant was sentenced to imprisonment for a term of three months on each, the sentences to run concurrently.

On appeal the Court of Appeals for the Ninth Circuit certified to us questions of law upon which it desired instructions for the decision of the case. Acting under the authority conferred upon us by that section we ordered that the entire record be certified to this Court so that we might proceed to a decision of the matter in controversy in the same manner as if it had been brought here by appeal. Since the sentences of three months each imposed by the district court on the two counts were ordered to run concurrently, it will be unnecessary to consider questions raised with respect to the first count if we find that the conviction on the second count, for violation of the curfew order, must be sustained.

The curfew order which appellant violated, and to which the sanction prescribed by the Act of Congress has been deemed to attach, purported to be issued pursuant to an Executive Order of the President. In passing upon the authority of the military commander to make and execute the order, it becomes necessary to consider in some detail the official action which preceded or accompanied the order and from which it derives its purported authority.

On December 8, 1941, one day after the bombing of Pearl Harbor by a Japanese air force, Congress declared war against Japan. On February

19, 1942, the President promulgated Executive Order No. 9066. The Order recited that "the successful prosecution of the war requires every possible protection against espionage and against sabotage to national-defense material, national-defense premises, and national-defense utilities as defined in Section 4, Act of April 20, 1918, as amended by the Act of November 30, 1940, and the Act of August 21, 1941." By virtue of the authority vested in him as President and as Commander in Chief of the Army and Navy, the President purported to "authorize and direct the Secretary of War, and the Military Commanders whom he may from time to time designate, whenever he or any designated Commander deems such action necessary or desirable, to prescribe military areas in such places and of such extent as he or the appropriate Military Commander may determine, from which any or all persons may be excluded, and with respect to which, the right of any person to enter, remain in, or leave shall be subject to whatever restrictions the Secretary of War or the appropriate Military Commander may impose in his discretion."

On February 20, 1942, the Secretary of War designated Lt. General J. L. DeWitt as Military Commander of the Western Defense Command, comprising the Pacific Coast states and some others, to carry out there the duties prescribed by Executive Order No. 9066. On March 2, 1942, General DeWitt promulgated Public Proclamation No. 1. The proclamation recited that the entire Pacific Coast "by its geographical location is particularly subject to attack, to attempted invasion by the armed forces of nations with which the United States is now at war, and, in connection therewith, is subject to espionage and acts of sabotage, thereby requiring the adoption of military measures necessary to establish safeguards against such enemy operations." It stated that "the present situation requires as matter of military necessity the establishment in the territory embraced by the Western Defense Command of Military Areas and Zones thereof"; it specified and designated as military areas certain areas within the Western Defense Command; and it declared that "such persons or classes of persons as the situation may require" would, by subsequent proclamation, be excluded from certain of these areas, but might be permitted to enter or remain in certain others, under regulations and restrictions to be later prescribed. Among the military areas so designated by Public Proclamation No. 1 was Military Area No. 1, which embraced, besides the southern part of Arizona, all the coastal region of the three Pacific Coast states, including the City of Seattle,

Washington, where appellant resided. Military Area No. 2, designated by the same proclamation, included those parts of the coastal states and of Arizona not placed within Military Area No. 1.

Public Proclamation No. 2 of March 16, 1942, issued by General DeWitt, made like recitals and designated further military areas and zones. It contained like provisions concerning the exclusion, by subsequent proclamation, of certain persons or classes of persons from these areas, and the future promulgation of regulations and restrictions applicable to persons remaining within them.

An Executive Order of the President, No. 9102, of March 18, 1942, established the War Relocation Authority, in the Office for Emergency Management of the Executive Office of the President; it authorized the Director of War Relocation Authority to formulate and effectuate a program for the removal, relocation, maintenance and supervision of persons designated under Executive Order No. 9066, already referred to; and it conferred on the Director authority to prescribe regulations necessary or desirable to promote the effective execution of the program.

Congress, by the Act of March 21, 1942, provided: "That whoever shall enter, remain in, leave, or commit any act in any military area or military zone prescribed, under the authority of an Executive order of the President, by the Secretary of War, or by any military commander designated by the Secretary of War, contrary to the restrictions applicable to any such area or zone or contrary to the order of the Secretary of War or any such military commander, shall, if it appears that he knew or should have known of the existence and extent of the restrictions or order and that his act was in violation thereof, be guilty of a misdemeanor and upon conviction shall be liable" to fine or imprisonment, or both.

Three days later, on March 24, 1942, General DeWitt issued Public Proclamation No. 3. After referring to the previous designation of military areas by Public Proclamations No. 1 and 2, it recited that "* * * the present situation within these Military Areas and Zones requires as a matter of military necessity the establishment of certain regulations pertaining to all enemy aliens and all persons of Japanese ancestry within said Military Areas and Zones * * *." It accordingly declared and established that from and after March 27, 1942, "all alien Japanese, all alien Germans, all alien Italians, and all persons of Japanese ancestry residing or being within the geographical limits of Military Area No. 1 * * * shall be within their place of residence between the hours of

8:00 p.m. and 6:00 a.m., which period is hereinafter referred to as the hours of curfew". It also imposed certain other restrictions on persons of Japanese ancestry, and provided that any person violating the regulations would be subject to the criminal penalties provided by the Act of Congress of March 21, 1942.

Beginning on March 24, 1942, the military commander issued a series of Civilian Exclusion Orders pursuant to the provisions of Public Proclamation No. 1. Each such order related to a specified area within the territory of his command. The order applicable to appellant was Civilian Exclusion Order No. 57 of May 10, 1942. It directed that from and after 12:00 noon, May 16, 1942, all persons of Japanese ancestry, both alien and non-alien, be excluded from a specified portion of Military Area No. 1 in Seattle, including appellant's place of residence, and it required a member of each family, and each individual living alone, affected by the order to report on May 11 or May 12 to a designated Civil Control Station in Seattle. Meanwhile the military commander had issued Public Proclamation No. 4 of March 27, 1942, which recited the necessity of providing for the orderly evacuation and resettlement of Japanese within the area, and prohibited all alien Japanese and all persons of Japanese ancestry from leaving the military area until future orders should permit.

Appellant does not deny that he knowingly failed to obey the curfew order as charged in the second count of the indictment, or that the order was authorized by the terms of Executive Order No. 9066, or that the challenged Act of Congress purports to punish with criminal penalties disobedience of such an order. His contentions are only that Congress unconstitutionally delegated its legislative power to the military commander by authorizing him to impose the challenged regulation, and that, even if the regulation were in other respects lawfully authorized, the Fifth Amendment prohibits the discrimination made between citizens of Japanese descent and those of other ancestry.

It will be evident from the legislative history that the Act of March 21, 1942, contemplated and authorized the curfew order which we have before us. The bill which became the Act of March 21, 1942, was introduced in the Senate on March 9th and in the House on March 10th at the request of the Secretary of War who, in letters to the Chairman of the Senate Committee on Military Affairs and to the Speaker of the House, stated explicitly that its purpose was to provide means for the enforcement of orders issued under Executive Order No. 9066. This appears in the committee reports on the bill, which set out in full the Executive Order and the Secretary's letter. And each of the committee reports expressly mentions curfew orders as one of the types of restrictions which it was deemed desirable to enforce by criminal sanctions.

When the bill was under consideration, General DeWitt had published his Proclamation No. 1 of March 2, 1942, establishing Military Areas Nos. 1 and 2, and that Proclamation was before Congress. A letter of the Secretary to the Chairman of the House Military Affairs Committee, of March 14, 1942, informed Congress that "General DeWitt is strongly of the opinion that the bill, when enacted, should be broad enough to enable the Secretary of War or the appropriate military commander to enforce curfews and other restrictions within military areas and zones"; and that General DeWitt had "indicated that he was prepared to enforce certain restrictions at once for the purpose of protecting certain vital national defense interests but did not desire to proceed until enforcement machinery had been set up."

The Chairman of the Senate Military Affairs Committee explained on the floor of the Senate that the purpose of the proposed legislation was to provide means of enforcement of curfew orders and other military orders made pursuant to Executive Order No. 9066. He read General DeWitt's Public Proclamation No. 1, and statements from newspaper reports that "evacuation of the first Japanese aliens and American-born Japanese" was about to begin. He also stated to the Senate that "reasons for suspected widespread fifth-column activity among Japanese" were to be found in the system of dual citizenship which Japan deemed applicable to American-born Japanese, and in the propaganda disseminated by Japanese consuls, Buddhist priests and other leaders, among American-born children of Japanese. Such was stated to be the explanation of the contemplated evacuation from the Pacific Coast area of persons of Japanese ancestry, citizens as well as aliens. Congress also had before it the Preliminary Report of a House Committee investigating national defense migration, of March 19, 1942, which approved the provisions of Executive Order No. 9066, and which recommended the evacuation, from military areas established under the Order, of all persons of Japanese ancestry, including citizens. The proposed legislation provided criminal sanctions for violation of orders, in terms broad enough to include the curfew order now before us, and the legislative history demonstrates that Congress was advised that curfew orders were among those intended, and was advised also that regulation of citizen and alien Japanese alike was contemplated.

The conclusion is inescapable that Congress, by the Act of March 21, 1942, ratified and confirmed Executive Order No. 9066. And so far as it lawfully could, Congress authorized and implemented such curfew orders as the commanding officer should promulgate pursuant to the Executive Order of the President. The question then is not one of Congressional power to delegate to the President the promulgation of the Executive Order, but whether, acting in cooperation, Congress and the Executive have constitutional authority to impose the curfew restriction here complained of. We must consider also whether, acting together, Congress and the Executive could leave it to the designated military commander to appraise the relevant conditions and on the basis of that appraisal to say whether, under the circumstances, the time and place were appropriate for the promulgation of the curfew order and whether the order itself was an appropriate means of carrying out the Executive Order for the "protection against espionage and against sabotage" to national defense materials, premises and utilities. For reasons presently to be stated, we conclude that it was within the constitutional power of Congress and the executive arm of the Government to prescribe this curfew order for the period under consideration and that its promulgation by the military commander involved no unlawful delegation of legislative power.

Executive Order No. 9066, promulgated in time of war for the declared purpose of prosecuting the war by protecting national defense resources from sabotage and espionage, and the Act of March 21, 1942, ratifying and confirming the Executive Order, were each an exercise of the power to wage war conferred on the Congress and on the President, as Commander in Chief of the armed forces, by Articles I and II of the Constitution. We have no occasion to consider whether the President, acting alone, could lawfully have made the curfew order in question, or have authorized others to make it. For the President's action has the support of the Act of Congress, and we are immediately concerned with the question whether it is within the constitutional power of the national government, through the joint action of Congress and the Executive, to impose this restriction as an emergency war measure. The exercise of that power here involves no question of martial law or trial by military tribunal. Appellant has been tried and convicted in the civil courts and has been subjected to penalties prescribed by Congress for the acts committed.

The war power of the national government is "the power to wage war successfully." It extends to every matter and activity so related to war as substantially to affect its conduct and progress. The power is not restricted to the winning of victories in the field and the repulse of enemy forces. It embraces every phase of the national defense, including the protection of war materials and the members of the armed forces from injury and from the dangers which attend the rise, prosecution and progress of war. Since the Constitution commits to the Executive and to Congress the exercise of the war power in all the vicissitudes and conditions of warfare, it has necessarily given them wide scope for the exercise of judgment and discretion in determining the nature and extent of the threatened injury or danger and in the selection of the means for resisting it. Where, as they did here, the conditions call for the exercise of judgment and discretion and for the choice of means by those branches of the Government on which the Constitution has placed the responsibility of war-making, it is not for any court to sit in review of the wisdom of their action or substitute its judgment for theirs.

The actions taken must be appraised in the light of the conditions with which the President and Congress were confronted in the early months of 1942, many of which, since disclosed, were then peculiarly within the knowledge of the military authorities. On December 7, 1941, the Japanese air forces had attacked the United States Naval Base at Pearl Harbor without warning, at the very hour when Japanese diplomatic representatives were conducting negotiations with our State Department ostensibly for the peaceful settlement of differences between the two countries. Simultaneously or nearly so, the Japanese attacked Malaysia, Hong Kong, the Philippines, and Wake and Midway Islands. On the following day their army invaded Thailand. Shortly afterwards they sank two British battleships. On December 13th, Guam was taken. On December 24th and 25th they captured Wake Island and occupied Hong Kong. On January 2, 1942, Manila fell, and on February 10th Singapore, Britain's great naval base in the East, was taken. On February 27th the battle of the Java Sea resulted in a disastrous naval defeat to the United Nations. By the 9th of March Japanese forces had established control over the Netherlands East Indies; Rangoon and Burma were occupied; Bataan and Corregidor were under attack.

Although the results of the attack on Pearl Harbor were not fully disclosed until much later, it was known that the damage was extensive, and that the Japanese by their successes had gained a naval superiority over our forces in the Pacific which might enable them to seize Pearl Harbor, our largest naval base and the last stronghold of defense lying between Japan and the west coast. That reasonably prudent men charged with the responsibility of our national defense had ample ground for concluding that they must face the danger of invasion, take measures against it, and in making the choice of measures consider our internal situation, cannot be doubted.

The challenged orders were defense measures for the avowed purpose of safeguarding the military area in question, at a time of threatened air raids and invasion by the Japanese forces, from the danger of sabotage and espionage. As the curfew was made applicable to citizens residing in the area only if they were of Japanese ancestry, our inquiry must be whether in the light of all the facts and circumstances there was any substantial basis for the conclusion, in which Congress and the military commander united, that the curfew as applied was a protective measure necessary to meet the threat of sabotage and espionage which would substantially affect the war effort and which might reasonably be expected to aid a threatened enemy invasion. The alternative which appellant insists must be accepted is for the military authorities to impose the curfew on all citizens within the military area, or on none. In a case of threatened danger requiring prompt action, it is a choice between inflicting obviously needless hardship on the many, or sitting passive and unresisting in the presence of the threat. We think that constitutional government, in time of war, is not so powerless and does not compel so hard a choice if those charged with the responsibility of our national defense have reasonable ground for believing that the threat is real.

When the orders were promulgated there was a vast concentration, within Military Areas No. 1 and 2, of installations and facilities for the production of military equipment, especially ships and airplanes. Important Army and Navy bases were located in California and Washington. Approximately one-fourth of the total value of the major aircraft contracts then let by Government procurement officers were to be performed in the State of California. California ranked second, and Washington fifth, of all the states of the Union with respect to the value of ship-building contracts to be performed.

In the critical days of March, 1942, the danger to our war production by sabotage and espionage in this area seems obvious. The German invasion of the Western European countries had given ample warning to the world of the menace of the "fifth column." Espionage by persons in sympathy with the Japanese Government had been found to have been particularly effective in the surprise attack on Pearl Harbor. At a time of threatened Japanese attack upon this country, the nature of our inhabitants' attachments to the Japanese enemy was consequently a matter of grave concern. Of the 126,000 persons of Japanese descent in the United States, citizens and non-citizens, approximately 112,000 resided in California, Oregon and Washington at the time of the adoption of the military regulations. Of these approximately two-thirds are citizens because born in the United States. Not only did the great majority of such persons reside within the Pacific Coast states but they were concentrated in or near three of the large cities, Seattle, Portland and Los Angeles, all in Military Area No. 1.

There is support for the view that social, economic and political conditions which have prevailed since the close of the last century, when the Japanese began to come to this country in substantial numbers, have intensified their solidarity and have in large measure prevented their assimilation as an integral part of the white population. In addition, large numbers of children of Japanese parentage are sent to Japanese language schools outside the regular hours of public schools in the locality. Some of these schools are generally believed to be sources of Japanese nationalistic propaganda, cultivating allegiance to Japan. Considerable numbers, estimated to be approximately 10,000, of American-born children of Japanese parentage have been sent to Japan for all or a part of their education.

Congress and the Executive, including the military commander, could have attributed special significance, in its bearing on the loyalties of persons of Japanese descent, to the maintenance by Japan of its system of dual citizenship. Children born in the United States of Japanese alien parents, and especially those children born before December 1, 1924, are under many circumstances deemed, by Japanese law, to be citizens of Japan. No official census of those whom Japan regards as having thus retained Japanese citizenship is available, but there is ground for the belief that the number is large.

The large number of resident alien Japanese, approximately one-third of all Japanese inhabitants of the country, are of mature years and occupy positions of influence in Japanese communities. The association of influential Japanese residents with Japanese Consulates has been deemed a ready means for the dissemination of propaganda and for the maintenance of the influence of the Japanese Government with the Japanese population in this country.

As a result of all these conditions affecting the life of the Japanese, both aliens and citizens, in the Pacific Coast area, there has been relatively little social intercourse between them and the white population. The restrictions, both practical and legal, affecting the privileges and opportunities afforded to persons of Japanese extraction residing in the United States, have been sources of irritation and may well have tended to increase their isolation, and in many instances their attachments to Japan and its institutions.

Viewing these data in all their aspects, Congress and the Executive could reasonably have concluded that these conditions have encouraged the continued attachment of members of this group to Japan and Japanese institutions. These are only some of the many considerations which those charged with the responsibility for the national defense could take into account in determining the nature and extent of the danger of espionage and sabotage, in the event of invasion or air raid attack. The extent of that danger could be definitely known only after the event and after it was too late to meet it. Whatever views we may entertain regarding the loyalty to this country of the citizens of Japanese ancestry, we cannot reject as unfounded the judgment of the military authorities and of Congress that there were disloyal members of that population, whose number and strength could not be precisely and quickly ascertained. We cannot say that the war-making branches of the Government did not have ground for believing that in a critical hour such persons could not readily be isolated and separately dealt with, and constituted a menace to the national defense and safety, which demanded that prompt and adequate measures be taken to guard against it.

Appellant does not deny that, given the danger, a curfew was an appropriate measure against sabotage. It is an obvious protection against the perpetration of sabotage most readily committed during the hours of darkness. If it was an appropriate exercise of the war power its validity is not impaired because it has restricted the citizen's liberty. Like every military control of the population of a dangerous zone in war time, it necessarily involves some infringement of individual liberty, just as does the police establishment of fire lines during a fire, or the confinement of people to their houses during an air raid alarm—neither of which could be thought to be an infringement of constitutional right.

Like them, the validity of the restraints of the curfew order depends on all the conditions which obtain at the time the curfew is imposed and which support the order imposing it.

But appellant insists that the exercise of the power is inappropriate and unconstitutional because it discriminates against citizens of Japanese ancestry, in violation of the Fifth Amendment. The Fifth Amendment contains no equal protection clause and it restrains only such discriminatory legislation by Congress as amounts to a denial of due process. Congress may hit at a particular danger where it is seen, without providing for others which are not so evident or so urgent.

Distinctions between citizens solely because of their ancestry are by their very nature odious to a free people whose institutions are founded upon the doctrine of equality. For that reason, legislative classification or discrimination based on race alone has often been held to be a denial of equal protection. We may assume that these considerations would be controlling here were it not for the fact that the danger of espionage and sabotage, in time of war and of threatened invasion, calls upon the military authorities to scrutinize every relevant fact bearing on the loyalty of populations in the danger areas. Because racial discriminations are in most circumstances irrelevant and therefore prohibited, it by no means follows that, in dealing with the perils of war, Congress and the Executive are wholly precluded from taking into account those facts and circumstances which are relevant to measures for our national defense and for the successful prosecution of the war, and which may in fact place citizens of one ancestry in a different category from others. "We must never forget, that it is a constitution we are expounding," "a constitution intended to endure for ages to come, and, consequently, to be adapted to the various crises of human affairs." The adoption by Government, in the crisis of war and of threatened invasion, of measures for the public safety, based upon the recognition of facts and circumstances which indicate that a group of one national extraction may menace that safety more than others, is not wholly beyond the limits of the Constitution and is not to be condemned merely because in other and in most circumstances racial distinctions are irrelevant.

Here the aim of Congress and the Executive was the protection against sabotage of war materials and utilities in areas thought to be in danger of Japanese invasion and air attack. We have stated in detail facts and circumstances with respect to the American citizens of Japanese ancestry residing on the Pacific Coast which support the judgment of the war-waging branches of the Government that some restrictive measure was urgent. We cannot say that these facts and circumstances, considered in the particular war setting, could afford no ground for differentiating citizens of Japanese ancestry from other groups in the United States. The fact alone that attack on our shores was threatened by Japan rather than another enemy power set these citizens apart from others who have no particular associations with Japan.

Our investigation here does not go beyond the inquiry whether, in the light of all the relevant circumstances preceding and attending their promulgation, the challenged orders and statute afforded a reasonable basis for the action taken in imposing the curfew. We cannot close our eyes to the fact, demonstrated by experience, that in time of war residents having ethnic affiliations with an invading enemy may be a greater source of danger than those of a different ancestry. Nor can we deny that Congress, and the military authorities acting with its authorization, have constitutional power to appraise the danger in the light of facts of public notoriety. We need not now attempt to define the ultimate boundaries of the war power. We decide only the issue as we have defined it—we decide only that the curfew order as applied, and at the time it was applied, was within the boundaries of the war power. In this case it is enough that circumstances within the knowledge of those charged with the responsibility for maintaining the national defense afforded a rational basis for the decision which they made. Whether we would have made it is irrelevant.

What we have said also disposes of the contention that the curfew order involved an unlawful delegation by Congress of its legislative power. The mandate of the Constitution that all legislative power granted "shall be vested in a Congress" has never been thought, even in the administration of civil affairs, to preclude Congress from resorting to the aid of executive or administrative officers in determining by findings whether the facts are such as to call for the application of previously adopted legislative standards or definitions of Congressional policy.

The purpose of Executive Order No. 9066, and the standard which the President approved for the orders authorized to be promulgated by the military commander—as disclosed by the preamble of the Executive Order—was the protection of our war resources against espionage and sabotage. Public Proclamations No. 1 and 2, by General DeWitt, contain findings that the military areas created and the measures to be prescribed for them were required to establish safeguards against espionage and sabotage. Both the Executive Order and the Proclamations were before Congress when the Act of March 21, 1942, was under consideration. To the extent that the Executive Order authorized orders to be promulgated by the military commander to accomplish the declared purpose of the Order, and to the extent that the findings in the Proclamations establish that such was their purpose, both have been approved by Congress.

It is true that the Act does not in terms establish a particular standard to which orders of the military commander are to conform, or require findings to be made as a prerequisite to any order. But the Executive Order, the Proclamations and the statute are not to be read in isolation from each other. They were parts of a single program and must be judged as such. The Act of March 21, 1942, was an adoption by Congress of the Executive Order and of the Proclamations. The Proclamations themselves followed a standard authorized by the Executive Order —the necessity of protecting military resources in the designated areas against espionage and sabotage. And by the Act, Congress gave its approval to that standard. We have no need to consider now the validity of action if taken by the military commander without conforming to this standard approved by Congress, or the validity of orders made without the support of findings showing that they do so conform. Here the findings of danger from espionage and sabotage, and of the necessity of the curfew order to protect against them, have been duly made. General DeWitt's Public Proclamation No. 3, which established the curfew, merely prescribed regulations of the type and in the manner which Public Proclamations No. 1 and 2 had announced would be prescribed at a future date, and was thus founded on the findings of Proclamations No. 1 and 2.

The military commander's appraisal of facts in the light of the authorized standard, and the inferences which he drew from those facts, involved the exercise of his informed judgment. But as we have seen, those facts, and the inferences which could be rationally drawn from them, support the judgment of the military commander, that the danger of espionage and sabotage to our military resources was imminent, and that the curfew order was an appropriate measure to meet it.

Where, as in the present case, the standard set up for the guidance of the military commander, and the action taken and the reasons for it, are in fact recorded in the military orders, so that Congress, the courts and the public are assured that the orders, in the judgment of the commander, conform to the standards approved by the President and Congress, there is no failure in the performance of the legislative function. The essentials of that function are the determination by Congress of the legislative policy and its approval of a rule of conduct to carry that policy into execution. The very necessities which attend the conduct of military operations in time of war in this instance as in many others preclude Congress from holding committee meetings to determine whether there is danger, before it enacts legislation to combat the danger.

The Constitution as a continuously operating charter of government does not demand the impossible or the impractical. The essentials of the legislative function are preserved when Congress authorizes a statutory command to become operative, upon ascertainment of a basic conclusion of fact by a designated representative of the Government. The present statute, which authorized curfew orders to be made pursuant to Executive Order No. 9066 for the protection of war resources from espionage and sabotage, satisfies those requirements. Under the Executive Order the basic facts, determined by the military commander in the light of knowledge then available, were whether that danger existed and whether a curfew order was an appropriate means of minimizing the danger. Since his findings to that effect were, as we have said, not without adequate support, the legislative function was performed and the sanction of the statute attached to violations of the curfew order. It is unnecessary to consider whether or to what extent such findings would support orders differing from the curfew order.

The conviction under the second count is without constitutional infirmity. Hence we have no occasion to review the conviction on the first count since, as already stated, the sentences on the two counts are to run concurrently and conviction on the second is sufficient to sustain the sentence. For this reason also it is unnecessary to consider the Government's argument that compliance with the order to report at the Civilian Control Station did not necessarily entail confinement in a relocation center.

Affirmed.

Mr. Justice Douglas concurring.

While I concur in the result and agree substantially with the opinion of the Court, I wish to add a few words to indicate what for me is the narrow ground of decision.

After the disastrous bombing of Pearl Harbor the military had a grave problem on its hands. The threat of Japanese invasion of the west coast was not fanciful but real. The presence of many thousands of aliens and citizens of Japanese ancestry in or near to the key points along that coast line aroused special concern in those charged with the defense of the country. They believed that not only among aliens but also among citizens of Japanese ancestry there were those who would give aid and comfort to the Japanese invader and act as a fifth column before and during an invasion. If the military were right in their belief that among citizens of Japanese ancestry there was an actual or incipient fifth column, we were indeed faced with the imminent threat of a dire emergency. We must credit the military with as much good faith in that belief as we would any other public official acting pursuant to his duties. We cannot possibly know all the facts which lay behind that decision. Some of them may have been as intangible and as imponderable as the factors which influence personal or business decisions in daily life. The point is that we cannot sit in judgment on the military requirements of that hour. Where the orders under the present Act have some relation to "protection against espionage and against sabotage," our task is at an end.

Much of the argument assumes that as a matter of policy it might have been wiser for the military to have dealt with these people on an individual basis and through the process of investigation and hearings separated those who were loyal from those who were not. But the wisdom or expediency of the decision which was made is not for us to review. Nor are we warranted where national survival is at stake in insisting that those orders should not have been applied to anyone without some evidence of his disloyalty. The orders as applied to the petitioner are not to be tested by the substantial evidence rule. Peacetime procedures do not necessarily fit wartime needs. It is said that if citizens of Japanese ancestry were generally disloyal, treatment on a group basis might be justified. But there is no difference in power when the number of those who are finally shown to be disloyal or suspect is reduced to a small per cent. The sorting process might indeed be as time-consuming whether those who were disloyal or suspect constituted nine or ninety-nine per cent. And the pinch of the order on the loyal citizens would be as great in any case. But where the peril is great and the time is short, temporary treatment on a group basis may be the only practicable expedient whatever the ultimate percentage of those who are detained for cause. Nor should the military be required to wait until espionage or sabotage becomes effective before it moves.

It is true that we might now say that there was ample time to handle the problem on the individual rather than the group basis. But military decisions must be made without the benefit of hindsight. The orders must be judged as of the date when the decision to issue them was made. To say that the military in such cases should take the time to weed out the loyal from the others would be to assume that the nation could afford to have them take the time to do it. But as the opinion of the Court makes clear, speed and dispatch may be of the essence. Certainly we cannot say that those charged with the defense of the nation should have procrastinated until investigations and hearings were completed. At that time further delay might indeed have seemed to be wholly incompatible with military responsibilities.

Since we cannot override the military judgment which lay behind these orders, it seems to me necessary to concede that the army had the power to deal temporarily with these people on a group basis. Petitioner therefore was not justified in disobeying the orders.

But I think it important to emphasize that we are dealing here with a problem of loyalty not assimilation. Loyalty is a matter of mind and of heart not of race. That indeed is the history of America. Moreover, guilt is personal under our constitutional system. Detention for reasonable cause is one thing. Detention on account of ancestry is another.

In this case the petitioner tendered by a plea in abatement the question of his loyalty to the United States. I think that plea was properly stricken; military measures of defense might be paralyzed if it were necessary to try out that issue preliminarily. But a denial of that opportunity in this case does not necessarily mean that petitioner could not have had a hearing on that issue in some appropriate proceeding. Obedience to the military orders is one thing. Whether an individual member of a group must be afforded at some stage an opportunity to show that, being loyal, he should be reclassified is a wholly different question.

There are other instances in the law where one must obey an order before he can attack as erroneous the classification in which he has been placed. Thus it is commonly held that one who is a conscientious objector has no privilege to defy the Selective Service Act and to refuse or fail to be inducted. He must submit to the law. But that line of authority holds that after induction he may obtain through habeas corpus a hearing on the legality of his classification by the draft board. Whether in the present situation that remedy would be available is one of the large and important issues reserved by the present decision. It has been suggested that an administrative procedure has been established to relieve against unwarranted applications of these orders. Whether in that event the administrative remedy would be the only one available or would have to be first exhausted is also reserved. The scope of any relief which might be afforded—whether the liberties of an applicant could be restored only outside the areas in question—is likewise a distinct issue. But if it were plain that no machinery was available whereby the individual could demonstrate his loyalty as a citizen in order to be reclassified, questions of a more serious character would be presented. The United States, however, takes no such position. We need go no further here than to deny the individual the right to defy the law. It is sufficient to say that he cannot test in that way the validity of the orders as applied to him.

Mr. Justice Murphy, concurring.

It is not to be doubted that the action taken by the military commander in pursuance of the authority conferred upon him was taken in complete good faith and in the firm conviction that it was required by considerations of public safety and military security. Neither is it doubted that the Congress and the Executive working together may generally employ such measures as are necessary and appropriate to provide for the common defense and to wage war "with all the force necessary to make it effective." This includes authority to exercise measures of control over persons and property which would not in all cases be permissible in normal times.

It does not follow, however, that the broad guaranties of the Bill of Rights and other provisions of the Constitution protecting essential liberties are suspended by the mere existence of a state of war. It has been frequently stated and recognized by this Court that the war power, like the other great substantive powers of government, is subject to the limitations of the Constitution. We give great deference to the judgment of the Congress and of the military authorities as to what is necessary in the effective prosecution of the war, but we can never forget that there are constitutional boundaries which it is our duty to uphold. It would not be supposed, for instance, that public elections could be suspended or that the prerogatives of the courts could be set aside, or that persons not charged with offenses against the law of war could be deprived of due process of law and the benefits of trial by jury, in the absence of a valid declaration of martial law.

Distinctions based on color and ancestry are utterly inconsistent with our traditions and ideals. They are at variance with the principles for which we are now waging war. We cannot close our eyes to the fact that for centuries the Old World has been torn by racial and religious conflicts and has suffered the worst kind of anguish because of inequality of treatment for different groups. There was one law for one and a different law for another. Nothing is written more firmly into our law than the compact of the Plymouth voyagers to have just and equal laws. To say that any group cannot be assimilated is to admit that the great American experiment has failed, that our way of life has failed when confronted with the normal attachment of certain groups to the lands of their forefathers. As a nation we embrace many groups, some of them among the oldest settlements in our midst, which have isolated themselves for religious and cultural reasons.

Today is the first time, so far as I am aware, that we have sustained a substantial restriction of the personal liberty of citizens of the United States based upon the accident of race or ancestry. Under the curfew order here challenged no less than 70,000 American citizens have been placed under a special ban and deprived of their liberty because of their particular racial inheritance. In this sense it bears a melancholy resemblance to the treatment accorded to members of the Jewish race in Germany and in other parts of Europe. The result is the creation in this country of two classes of citizens for the purposes of a critical and perilous hour—to sanction discrimination between groups of United States citizens on the basis of ancestry. In my opinion this goes to the very brink of constitutional power.

Except under conditions of great emergency a regulation of this kind applicable solely to citizens of a particular racial extraction would not be regarded as in accord with the requirement of due process of law contained in the Fifth Amendment. We have consistently held that attempts to apply regulatory action to particular groups solely on the basis of racial distinction or classification is not in accordance with due process of law as prescribed by the Fifth and Fourteenth Amendments.

It is true that the Fifth Amendment, unlike the Fourteenth, contains no guarantee of equal protection of the laws. It is also true that even the guaranty of equal protection of the laws allows a measure of reasonable classification. It by no means follows, however, that there may not be discrimination of such an injurious character in the application of laws as to amount to a denial of due process of law as that term is used in the Fifth Amendment. I think that point is dangerously approached when we have one law for the majority of our citizens and another for those of a particular racial heritage.

In view, however, of the critical military situation which prevailed on the Pacific Coast area in the spring of 1942, and the urgent necessity of taking prompt and effective action to secure defense installations and military operations against the risk of sabotage and espionage, the military authorities should not be required to conform to standards of regulatory action appropriate to normal times. Because of the damage wrought by the Japanese at Pearl Harbor and the availability of new weapons and new techniques with greater capacity for speed and deception in offensive operations, the immediate possibility of an attempt at invasion somewhere along the Pacific Coast had to be reckoned with. However desirable such a procedure might have been, the military authorities could have reasonably concluded at the time that determinations as to the loyalty and dependability of individual members of the large and widely scattered group of persons of Japanese extraction on the West Coast could not be made without delay that might have had tragic consequences. Modern war does not always wait for the observance of procedural requirements that are considered essential and appropriate under normal conditions. Accordingly I think that the military arm, confronted with the peril of imminent enemy attack and acting under the authority conferred by the Congress, made an allowable judgment at the time the curfew restriction was imposed. Whether such a restriction is valid today is another matter.

In voting for affirmance of the judgment I do not wish to be understood as intimating that the military authorities in time of war are subject to no restraints whatsoever, or that they are free to impose any restrictions they may choose on the rights and liberties of individual citizens or groups of citizens in those places which may be designated as "military areas." While this Court sits, it has the inescapable duty of seeing that the mandates of the Constitution are obeyed. That duty exists in time of war as well as in time of peace, and in its performance we must not forget that few indeed have been the invasions upon essential liberties which have not been accompanied by pleas of urgent necessity advanced in good faith by responsible men.

Nor do I mean to intimate that citizens of a particular racial group whose freedom may be curtailed within an area threatened with attack should be generally prevented from leaving the area and going at large in other areas that are not in danger of attack and where special precautions are not needed. Their status as citizens, though subject to requirements of national security and military necessity, should at all times be accorded the fullest consideration and respect. When the danger is past, the restrictions imposed on them should be promptly removed and their freedom of action fully restored.

Mr. Justice Rutledge, concurring.

I concur in the Court's opinion, except for the suggestion, if that is intended (as to which I make no assertion), that the courts have no power to review any action a military officer may "in his discretion" find it necessary to take with respect to civilian citizens in military areas or zones, once it is found that an emergency has created the conditions requiring or justifying the creation of the area or zone and the institution of some degree of military control short of suspending habeas corpus. Given the generating conditions for exercise of military authority and recognizing the wide latitude for particular applications that ordinarily creates, I do not think it is necessary in this case to decide that there is no action a person in the position of General DeWitt here may take, and which he may regard as necessary to the region's or the country's safety, which will call judicial power into play. The officer of course must have wide discretion and room for its operation. But it does not follow there may not be bounds beyond which he cannot go and, if he oversteps them, that the courts may not have power to protect the civilian citizen. But in this case that question need not be faced and I merely add my reservation without indication of opinion concerning it.

Korematsu v. United States

323 U. S. 214   1944

Mr. Justice Black delivered the opinion of the Court.

The petitioner, an American citizen of Japanese descent, was convicted in a federal district court for remaining in San Leandro, California, a "Military Area," contrary to Civilian Exclusion Order No. 34 of the Commanding General of the Western Command, U. S. Army, which directed that after May 9, 1942, all persons of Japanese ancestry should be excluded from that area. No question was raised as to petitioner's loyalty to the United States. The Circuit Court of Appeals affirmed, and the importance of the constitutional question involved caused us to grant certiorari.

It should be noted, to begin with, that all legal restrictions which curtail the civil rights of a single racial group are immediately suspect. That is not to say that all such restrictions are unconstitutional. It is to say that courts must subject them to the most rigid scrutiny. Pressing public necessity may sometimes justify the existence of such restrictions; racial antagonism never can.

In the instant case prosecution of the petitioner was begun by information charging violation of an Act of Congress, of March 21, 1942, which provides that

". . . whoever shall enter, remain in, leave, or commit any act in any military area or military zone prescribed, under the authority of an Executive order of the President, by the Secretary of War, or by any military commander designated by the Secretary of War, contrary to the restrictions applicable to any such area or zone or contrary to the order of the Secretary of War or any such military commander, shall, if it appears that he knew or should have known of the existence and extent of the restrictions or order and that his act was in violation thereof, be guilty of a misdemeanor and upon conviction shall be liable to a fine of not to exceed $5,000 or to imprisonment for not more than one year, or both, for each offense."

Exclusion Order No. 34, which the petitioner knowingly and admittedly violated, was one of a number of military orders and proclamations, all of which were substantially based upon Executive Order No. 9066. That order, issued after we were at war with Japan, declared that "the successful prosecution of the war requires every possible protection against espionage and against sabotage to national-defense material, national-defense premises, and national-defense utilities. . . ."

One of the series of orders and proclamations, a curfew order, which like the exclusion order here was promulgated pursuant to Executive Order 9066, subjected all persons of Japanese ancestry in prescribed West Coast military areas to remain in their residences from 8 P.M. to 6 A.M. As is the case with the exclusion order here, that prior curfew order was designed as a "protection against espionage and against sabotage." In *Hirabayashi* v. *United States,* we sustained a conviction obtained for violation of the curfew order. The *Hirabayashi* conviction and this one thus rest on the same 1942 Congressional Act and the same basic executive and military orders, all of which orders were aimed at the twin dangers of espionage and sabotage.

The 1942 Act was attacked in the *Hirabayashi* case as an unconstitutional delegation of power; it was contended that the curfew order and other orders on which it rested were beyond the war powers of the Congress, the military authorities and of the President, as Commander in Chief of the Army; and finally that to apply the curfew order against none but citizens of Japanese ancestry amounted to a constitutionally prohibited discrimination solely on account of race. To these questions, we gave the serious consideration which their importance justified. We upheld the curfew order as an exercise of the power of the government to take steps necessary to prevent espionage and sabotage in an area threatened by Japanese attack.

In the light of the principles we announced in the *Hirabayashi* case, we are unable to conclude that it was beyond the war power of Congress and the Executive to exclude those of Japanese ancestry from the West Coast war area at the time they did. True, exclusion from the area in which one's home is located is a far greater deprivation than constant confinement to the home from 8 P.M. to 6 A.M. Nothing short of apprehension by the proper military authorities of the gravest imminent danger to the public safety can constitutionally justify either. But exclusion from a threatened area, no less than curfew, has a definite and close relationship to the prevention of espionage and sabotage. The military authorities, charged with the primary responsibility of defending our shores, concluded that curfew provided inadequate protection and ordered exclusion. They did so, as pointed out in our *Hirabayashi* opinion, in accordance with Congressional authority to the military to say who should, and who should not, remain in the threatened areas.

In this case the petitioner challenges the assumptions upon which we rested our conclusions in the *Hirabayashi* case. He also urges that by May 1942, when Order No. 34 was promulgated, all danger of Japanese invasion of the West Coast had disappeared. After careful consideration of these contentions we are compelled to reject them.

Here, as in the *Hirabayashi* case, ". . . we cannot reject as unfounded the judgment of the military authorities and of Congress that there were disloyal members of that population, whose number and strength could not be precisely and quickly ascertained. We cannot say that the war-making branches of the Government did not have ground for believing that in a critical hour such persons could not readily be isolated and separately dealt with, and constituted a menace to the national defense and safety, which demanded that prompt and adequate measures be taken to guard against it."

Like curfew, exclusion of those of Japanese origin was deemed necessary because of the presence of an unascertained number of disloyal members of the group, most of whom we have no doubt were loyal to this country. It was because we could not reject the finding of the military authorities that it was impossible to bring about an immediate segregation of the disloyal from the loyal that we sustained the validity of the curfew order as applying to the whole group. In the instant case, temporary exclusion of the entire group was rested by the military on the same ground. The judgment that exclusion of the whole group was for the same reason a military imperative answers the contention that the exclusion was in the nature of group punishment based on antagonism to those of Japanese origin. That there were members of the group who retained loyalties to Japan has been confirmed by investigations made subsequent to the exclusion. Approximately five thousand American citizens of Japanese ancestry refused to swear unqualified allegiance to the United States and to renounce allegiance to the Japanese Emperor, and several thousand evacuees requested repatriation to Japan.

We uphold the exclusion order as of the time it was made and when the petitioner violated it. In doing so, we are not unmindful of the hardships imposed by it upon a large group of American citizens. But hardships are part of war, and war is an aggregation of hardships. All citizens alike, both in and out of uniform, feel the impact of war in greater or lesser measure. Citizenship has its responsibilities as well as its privileges, and in time of war the burden is always heavier. Compulsory exclusion of large groups of citizens from their homes, except under circumstances of direst emergency and peril, is inconsistent with our basic governmental institutions. But when under conditions of modern warfare our shores are threatened by hostile forces, the power to protect must be commensurate with the threatened danger.

It is argued that on May 30, 1942, the date the petitioner was charged with remaining in the prohibited area, there were conflicting orders outstanding, forbidding him both to leave the area and to remain there. Of course, a person cannot be convicted for doing the very thing which it is a crime to fail to do. But the outstanding orders here contained no such contradictory commands.

There was an order issued March 27, 1942, which prohibited petitioner and others of Japanese ancestry from leaving the area, but its effect was specifically limited in time "until and to the extent that a future proclamation or order should so permit or direct." That "future order," the one for violation of which petitioner was convicted, was issued May 3, 1942, and it did "direct" exclusion from the area of all persons of Japanese ancestry, before 12 o'clock noon, May 9; furthermore it contained a warning that all such persons found in the prohibited area would be liable to punishment under the March 21, 1942 Act of Congress. Consequently, the only order in effect touching the petitioner's being in the area on May 30, 1942, the date specified in the information against him, was the May 3 order which prohibited his remaining there, and it was that same order, which he stipulated in his trial that he had violated, knowing of its existence. There is therefore no basis for the argument that on May 30, 1942, he was subject to punishment, under the March 27 and May 3 orders, whether he remained in or left the area.

It does appear, however, that on May 9, the effective date of the exclusion order, the military authorities had already determined that the evacuation should be effected by assembling together and placing under guard all those of Japanese ancestry, at central points, designated as "assembly centers," in order "to insure the orderly evacuation and resettlement of Japanese voluntarily migrating from Military Area No. 1, to restrict and regulate such migration." And on May 19, 1942, eleven days before the time petitioner was charged with unlawfully remaining in the area, Civilian Restrictive Order No. 1 provided for detention of those of Japanese ancestry in assembly or relocation centers. It is now argued that the validity of the exclusion order cannot be considered apart from the orders requiring him, after departure from the area, to report and to remain in an assembly or relocation center. The contention is that we must treat these separate orders as one and inseparable; that, for this reason, if detention in the assembly or relocation center would have illegally deprived the petitioner of his liberty, the exclusion order and his conviction under it cannot stand.

We are thus being asked to pass at this time upon the whole subsequent detention program in both assembly and relocation centers, although the only issues framed at the trial related to petitioner's remaining in the prohibited area in violation of the exclusion order. Had petitioner here left the prohibited area and gone to an assembly center we cannot say either as a matter of fact or law that his presence in that center would have resulted in his detention in a relocation center. Some who did report to the assembly center were not sent to relocation centers, but were released upon condition that they remain outside the prohibited zone until the military orders were modified or lifted. This illustrates that they pose different problems and may be governed by different principles. The lawfulness of one does not necessarily determine the lawfulness of the others. This is made clear when we analyze the requirements of the separate provisions of the separate orders. These separate requirements were that those of Japanese ancestry (1) depart from the area; (2) report to and temporarily remain in an assembly center; (3) go under military control to a relocation center there to remain for an indeterminate period until released conditionally or unconditionally by the military authorities. Each of these requirements, it will be noted, imposed distinct duties in connection with the separate steps in a complete evacuation program. Had Congress directly incorporated into one Act the language of these separate orders, and provided sanctions for their violations, disobedience of any one would have constituted a separate offense. There is no reason why violations of these orders, insofar as they were promulgated pursuant to Congressional enactment, should not be treated as separate offenses.

The *Endo* case graphically illustrates the difference between the validity of an order to exclude and the validity of a detention order after exclusion has been effected.

Since the petitioner has not been convicted of failing to report or to remain in an assembly or relocation center, we cannot in this case determine the validity of those separate provisions of the order. It is sufficient here for us to pass upon the order which petitioner violated. To do more would be to go beyond the issues raised, and to decide momentous questions not contained within the framework of the pleadings or the evidence in this case. It will be time enough to decide the serious constitutional issues which petitioner seeks to raise when an assembly or relocation order is applied or is certain to be applied to him, and we have its terms before us.

Some of the members of the Court are of the view that evacuation and detention in an Assembly Center were inseparable. After May 3, 1942, the date of Exclusion Order No. 34, Korematsu was under compulsion to leave the area not as he would choose but via an Assembly Center. The Assembly Center was conceived as a part of the machinery for group evacuation. The power to exclude includes the power to do it by force if necessary. And any forcible measure must necessarily entail some degree of detention or restraint whatever method of removal is selected. But whichever view is taken, it results in holding that the order under which petitioner was convicted was valid.

It is said that we are dealing here with the case of imprisonment of a citizen in a concentration camp solely because of his ancestry, without evidence or inquiry concerning his loyalty and good disposition towards the United States. Our task would be simple, our duty clear, were this a case involving the imprisonment of a loyal citizen in a concentration camp because of racial prejudice. Regardless of the true nature of the assembly and relocation centers—and we deem it unjustifiable to call them concentration camps with all the ugly connotations that term implies—we are dealing specifically with nothing but an exclusion order. To cast this case into outlines of racial prejudice, without reference to the real military dangers which were presented, merely confuses the issue. Korematsu was not excluded from the Military Area because of hostility to him or his race. He *was* excluded because we are at war with the Japanese Empire, because the properly constituted military authorities feared an invasion of our West Coast and felt constrained to take proper security measures, because they decided that the military urgency of the situation demanded that all citizens of Japanese ancestry be segregated from the West Coast temporarily, and finally, because Congress, reposing its confidence in this time of war in our military leaders—as inevitably it must—determined that they should have the power to do just this. There was evidence of disloyalty on the part of some, the military authorities considered that the need for action was great, and time was short. We cannot—by availing ourselves of the calm perspective of hindsight—now say that at that time these actions were unjustified.

Affirmed.

Mr. Justice Frankfurter, concurring.

According to my reading of Civilian Exclusion Order No. 34, it was an offense for Korematsu to be found in Military Area No. 1, the territory wherein he was previously living, except within the bounds of the established Assembly Center of that area. Even though the various orders issued by General DeWitt be deemed a comprehensive code of instructions, their tenor is clear and not contradictory. They put upon Korematsu the obligation to leave Military Area No. 1, but only by the method prescribed in the instructions, *i. e.,* by reporting to the Assembly Center. I am unable to see how the legal considerations that led to the decision in *Hirabayashi* v. *United States* fail to sustain the military order which made the conduct now in controversy a crime. And so I join in the opinion of the Court, but should like to add a few words of my own.

The provisions of the Constitution which confer on the Congress and the President powers to enable this country to wage war are as much part of the Constitution as provisions looking to a nation at peace. And we have had recent occasion to quote approvingly the statement of former Chief Justice Hughes that the war power of the Government is "the power to wage war successfully." Therefore, the validity of action under the war power must be judged wholly in the context of war. That action is not to be stigmatized as lawless because like action in times of peace would be lawless. To talk about a military order that expresses an allowable judgment of war needs by those entrusted with the duty of conducting war as "an unconstitutional order" is to suffuse a part of the Constitution with an atmosphere of unconstitutionality. The respective spheres of action of military authorities and of judges are of course very different. But within their sphere, military authorities are no more outside the bounds of obedience to the Constitution than are judges within theirs. "The war power of the United States, like its other powers . . . is subject to applicable constitutional limitations." To recognize that military orders are "reasonably expedient military precautions" in time of war and yet to deny them constitutional legitimacy makes of the Constitution an instrument for dialectic subtleties not reasonably to be attributed to the hard-headed Framers, of whom a majority had had actual participation in war. If a military order such as that under review does not transcend the means appropriate for conducting war, such action by the military is as constitutional as would be any authorized action by the Interstate Commerce Commission within the limits of the constitutional power to regulate commerce. And being an exercise of the war power explicitly granted by the Constitution for safeguarding the national life by prosecuting war effectively, I find nothing in the Constitution which denies to Congress the power to enforce such a valid military order by making its violation an offense triable in the civil courts. To find that the Constitution does not forbid the military measures now complained of does not carry with it approval of that which Congress and the Executive did. That is their business, not ours.

Mr. Justice Roberts.

I dissent, because I think the indisputable facts exhibit a clear violation of Constitutional rights.

This is not a case of keeping people off the streets at night as was *Hirabayashi* v. *United States,* nor a case of temporary exclusion of a citizen from an area for his own safety or that of the community, nor a case of offering him an opportunity to go temporarily out of an area where his presence might cause danger to himself or to his fellows. On the contrary, it is the case of convicting a citizen as a punishment for not submitting to imprisonment in a concentration camp, based on his ancestry, and solely because of his ancestry, without evidence or inquiry concerning his loyalty and good disposition towards the United States. If this be a correct statement of the facts disclosed by this record, and facts of which we take judicial notice, I need hardly labor the conclusion that Constitutional rights have been violated.

The Government's argument, and the opinion of the court, in my judgment, erroneously divide that which is single and indivisible and thus make the case appear as if the petitioner violated a Military Order, sanctioned by Act of Congress, which excluded him from his home, by refusing voluntarily to leave and, so, knowingly and intentionally, defying the order and the Act of Congress.

The petitioner, a resident of San Leandro, Alameda County, California, is a native of the United States of Japanese ancestry who, according to the uncontradicted evidence, is a loyal citizen of the nation.

A chronological recitation of events will make it plain that the petitioner's supposed offense did not, in truth, consist in his refusal voluntarily to leave the area which included his home in obedience to the order excluding him therefrom. Critical attention must be given to the dates and sequence of events.

December 8, 1941, the United States declared war on Japan.

February 19, 1942, the President issued Executive Order No. 9066, which, after stating the reason for issuing the order as "protection against espionage and against sabotage to national-defense material, national-defense premises, and national-defense utilities," provided that certain Military Commanders might, in their discretion, "prescribe military areas" and define their extent, "from which any or all persons may be excluded, and with respect to which the right of any person to enter, remain in, or leave shall be subject to whatever restrictions" the "Military Commander may impose in his discretion."

February 20, 1942, Lieutenant General DeWitt was designated Military Commander of the Western Defense Command embracing the westernmost states of the Union,—about one-fourth of the total area of the nation.

March 2, 1942, General DeWitt promulgated Public Proclamation No. 1, which recites that the entire Pacific Coast is "particularly subject to attack, to attempted invasion . . . and, in connection therewith, is subject to espionage and acts of sabotage." It states that "as a matter of military necessity" certain military areas and zones are established known as Military Areas Nos. 1 and 2. It adds that "Such persons or classes of persons as the situation may require" will, by subsequent orders, "be excluded from all of Military Area No. 1" and from certain zones in Military Area No. 2. Subsequent proclamations were made which, together with Proclamation No. 1, included in such areas and zones all of California, Washington, Oregon, Idaho, Montana, Nevada and Utah, and the southern portion of Arizona. The orders required that if any person of Japanese, German or Italian ancestry residing in Area No. 1 desired to change his habitual residence he must execute and deliver to the authorities a Change of Residence Notice.

San Leandro, the city of petitioner's residence, lies in Military Area No. 1.

On March 2, 1942, the petitioner, therefore, had notice that, by Executive Order, the President, to prevent espionage and sabotage, had authorized the Military to exclude him from certain areas and to prevent his entering or leaving certain areas without permission. He was on notice that his home city had been included, by Military Order, in Area No. 1, and he was on notice further that, at sometime in the future, the Military Commander would make an order for the exclusion of certain persons, not described or classified, from various zones including that in which he lived.

March 21, 1942, Congress enacted that anyone who knowingly "shall enter, remain in, leave, or commit any act in any military area or military zone prescribed . . . by any military commander . . . contrary to the restrictions applicable to any such area or zone or contrary to the order of . . . any such military commander" shall be guilty of a misdemeanor. This is the Act under which the petitioner was charged.

March 24, 1942, General DeWitt instituted the curfew for certain areas within his command, by an order the validity of which was sustained in *Hirabayashi* v. *United States*.

March 24, 1942, General DeWitt began to issue a series of exclusion orders relating to specified areas.

March 27, 1942, by Proclamation No. 4, the General recited that "it is necessary, in order to provide for the welfare and to insure the orderly evacuation and resettlement of Japanese *voluntarily migrating* from Military Area No. 1, to restrict and regulate such migration"; and ordered that, as of March 29, 1942, "all alien Japanese and persons of Japanese ancestry who are within the limits of Military Area No. 1, be and they are hereby prohibited from leaving that area for any purpose until and to the extent that a future proclamation or order of this headquarters shall so permit or direct."

No order had been made excluding the petitioner from the area in which he lived. By Proclamation No. 4 he was, after March 29, 1942, confined to the limits of Area No. 1. If the Executive Order No. 9066 and the Act of Congress meant what they said, to leave that area, in the face of Proclamation No. 4, would be to commit a misdemeanor.

May 3, 1942, General DeWitt issued Civilian Exclusion Order No. 34 providing that, after 12 o'clock May 8, 1942, all persons of Japanese ancestry, both alien and non-alien, were to be excluded from a described portion of Military Area No. 1, which included the County of Alameda, California. The order required a responsible member of each family and each individual living alone to report, at a time set, at a Civil

Control Station for instructions to go to an Assembly Center, and added that any person failing to comply with the provisions of the order who was found in the described area after the date set would be liable to prosecution under the Act of March 21, 1942. It is important to note that the order, by its express terms, had no application to persons within the bounds "of an established Assembly Center pursuant to instructions from this Headquarters . . ." The obvious purpose of the orders made, taken together, was to drive all citizens of Japaneses ancestry into Assembly Centers within the zones of their residence, under pain of criminal prosecution.

The predicament in which the petitioner thus found himself was this: He was forbidden, by Military Order, to leave the zone in which he lived; he was forbidden, by Military Order, after a date fixed, to be found within that zone unless he were in an Assembly Center located in that zone. General DeWitt's report to the Secretary of War concerning the programme of evacuation and relocation of Japanese makes it entirely clear, if it were necessary to refer to that document—and, in the light of the above recitation, I think it is not—that an Assembly Center was a euphemism for a prison. No person within such a center was permitted to leave except by Military Order.

In the dilemma that he dare not remain in his home, or voluntarily leave the area, without incurring criminal penalties, and that the only way he could avoid punishment was to go to an Assembly Center and submit himself to military imprisonment, the petitioner did nothing.

June 12, 1942, an Information was filed in the District Court for Northern California charging a violation of the Act of March 21, 1942, in that petitioner had knowingly remained within the area covered by Exclusion Order No. 34. A demurrer to the information having been overruled, the petitioner was tried under a plea of not guilty and convicted. Sentence was suspended and he was placed on probation for five years. We know, however, in the light of the foregoing recitation, that he was at once taken into military custody and lodged in an Assembly Center. We further know that, on March 18, 1942, the President had promulgated Executive Order No. 9102 establishing the War Relocation Authority under which so-called Relocation Centers, a euphemism for concentration camps, were established pursuant to cooperation between the military authorities of the Western Defense Command and the Relocation Authority, and that the petitioner has been confined either in an Assembly Center, within the zone in which he had lived or has been removed to a Relocation Center where, as the facts disclosed in *Ex parte Endo* demonstrate, he was illegally held in custody.

The Government has argued this case as if the only order outstanding at the time the petitioner was arrested and informed against was Exclusion Order No. 34 ordering him to leave the area in which he resided, which was the basis of the information against him. That argument has evidently been effective. The opinion refers to the *Hirabayashi* case, to show that this court has sustained the validity of a curfew order in an emergency. The argument then is that exclusion from a given area of danger, while somewhat more sweeping than a curfew regulation, is of the same nature—a temporary expedient made necessary by a sudden emergency. This, I think, is a substitution of an hypothetical case for the case actually before the court. I might agree with the court's disposition of the hypothetical case. The liberty of every American citizen freely to come and to go must frequently, in the face of sudden danger, be temporarily limited or suspended. The civil authorities must often resort to the expedient of excluding citizens temporarily from a locality. The drawing of fire lines in the case of a conflagration, the removal of persons from the area where a pestilence has broken out, are familiar examples. If the exclusion worked by Exclusion Order No. 34 were of that nature the *Hirabayashi* case would be authority for sustaining it. But the facts above recited, and those set forth in *Ex parte Endo,* show that the exclusion was but a part of an over-all plan for forceable detention. This case cannot, therefore, be decided on any such narrow ground as the possible validity of a Temporary Exclusion Order under which the residents of an area are given an opportunity to leave and go elsewhere in their native land outside the boundaries of a military area. To make the case turn on any such assumption is to shut our eyes to reality.

As I have said above, the petitioner, prior to his arrest, was faced with two diametrically contradictory orders given sanction by the Act of Congress of March 21, 1942. The earlier of those orders made him a criminal if he left the zone in which he resided; the later made him a criminal if he did not leave.

I had supposed that if a citizen was constrained by two laws, or two orders having the force of law, and obedience to one would violate the other, to punish him for violation of either would deny him due process of law. And I had supposed that under these circumstances a conviction for violating one of the orders could not stand.

We cannot shut our eyes to the fact that had the petitioner attempted to violate Proclamation No. 4 and leave the military area in which he lived he would have been arrested and tried and convicted for violation of Proclamation No. 4. The two conflicting orders, one which commanded him to stay and the other which commanded him to go, were nothing but a cleverly devised trap to accomplish the real purpose of the military authority, which was to lock him up in a concentration camp. The only course by which the petitioner could avoid arrest and prosecution was to go to that camp according to instructions to be given him when he reported at a Civil Control Center. We know that is the fact. Why should we set up a figmentary and artificial situation instead of addressing ourselves to the actualities of the case?

These stark realities are met by the suggestion that it is lawful to compel an American citizen to submit to illegal imprisonment on the assumption that he might, after going to the Assembly Center, apply for his discharge by suing out a writ of habeas corpus, as was done in the *Endo* case. The answer, of course, is that where he was subject to two conflicting laws he was not bound, in order to escape violation of one or the other, to surrender his liberty for any period. Nor will it do to say that the detention was a necessary part of the process of evacuation, and so we are here concerned only with the validity of the latter.

Again it is a new doctrine of constitutional law that one indicted for disobedience to an unconstitutional statute may not defend on the ground of the invalidity of the statute but must obey it though he knows it is no law and, after he has suffered the disgrace of conviction and lost his liberty by sentence, then, and not before, seek, from within prison walls, to test the validity of the law.

Moreover, it is beside the point to rest decision in part on the fact that the petitioner, for his own reasons, wished to remain in his home. If, as is the fact, he was constrained so to do, it is indeed a narrow application of constitutional rights to ignore the order which constrained him, in order to sustain his conviction for violation of another contradictory order.

I would reverse the judgment of conviction.

Mr. Justice Murphy, dissenting.

This exclusion of "all persons of Japanese ancestry, both alien and non-alien," from the Pacific Coast area on a plea of military necessity in the absence of martial law ought not to be approved. Such exclusion goes over "the very brink of constitutional power" and falls into the ugly abyss of racism.

In dealing with matters relating to the prosecution and progress of a war, we must accord great respect and consideration to the judgments of the military authorities who are on the scene and who have full knowledge of the military facts. The scope of their discretion must, as a matter of necessity and common sense, be wide. And their judgments ought not to be overruled lightly by those whose training and duties ill-equip them to deal intelligently with matters so vital to the physical security of the nation.

At the same time, however, it is essential that there be definite limits to military discretion, especially where martial law has not been declared. Individuals must not be left impoverished of their constitutional rights on a plea of military necessity that has neither substance nor support. Thus, like other claims conflicting with the asserted constitutional rights of the individual, the military claim must subject itself to the judicial process of having its reasonableness determined and its conflicts with other interests reconciled. "What are the allowable limits of military discretion, and whether or not they have been overstepped in a particular case, are judicial questions."

The judicial test of whether the Government, on a plea of military necessity, can validly deprive an individual of any of his constitutional rights is whether the deprivation is reasonably related to a public danger that is so "immediate, imminent, and impending" as not to admit of delay and not to permit the intervention of ordinary constitutional processes to alleviate the danger. Civilian Exclusion Order No. 34, banishing from a prescribed area of the Pacific Coast "all persons of Japanese ancestry, both alien and non-alien," clearly does not meet that test. Being an obvious racial discrimination, the order deprives all those within its scope of the equal protection of the laws as guaranteed by the Fifth Amendment. It further deprives these individuals of their constitutional rights to live and work where they will, to establish a home where they choose and to move about freely. In excommunicating them without benefit of hearings, this order also deprives them of all their constitutional rights to procedural due process. Yet no reasonable relation to an "immediate, imminent, and impending" public danger is evident to support this racial restriction which is one of the most sweeping and complete deprivations of constitutional rights in the history of this nation in the absence of martial law.

It must be conceded that the military and naval situation in the spring of 1942 was such as to generate a very real fear of invasion of the Pacific Coast, accompanied by fears of sabotage and espionage in that area. The military command was therefore justified in adopting all reasonable means necessary to combat these dangers. In adjudging the military action taken in light of the then apparent dangers, we must not erect too high or too meticulous standards; it is necessary only that the action have some reasonable relation to the removal of the dangers of invasion, sabotage and espionage. But the exclusion, either temporarily or permanently, of all persons with Japanese blood in their veins has no such reasonable relation. And that relation is lacking because the exclusion order necessarily must rely for its reasonableness upon the assumption that *all* persons of Japanese ancestry may have a dangerous tendency to commit sabotage and espionage and to aid our Japanese enemy in other ways. It is difficult to believe that reason, logic or experience could be marshalled in support of such an assumption.

That this forced exclusion was the result in good measure of this erroneous assumption of racial guilt rather than bona fide military necessity is evidenced by the Commanding General's Final Report on the evacuation from the Pacific Coast area. In it he refers to all individuals of Japanese descent as "subversive," as belonging to "an enemy race" whose "racial strains are undiluted," and as constituting "over 112,000 potential enemies . . . at large today" along the Pacific Coast. In support of this blanket condemnation of all persons of Japanese descent, however, no reliable evidence is cited to show that such individuals were generally disloyal, or had generally so conducted themselves in this area as to constitute a special menace to defense installations or war industries, or had otherwise by their behavior furnished reasonable ground for their exclusion as a group.

Justification for the exclusion is sought, instead, mainly upon questionable racial and sociological grounds not ordinarily within the realm of expert military judgment, supplemented by certain semi-military conclusions drawn from an unwarranted use of circumstantial evidence. Individuals of Japanese ancestry are condemned because they are said to be "a large, unassimilated, tightly knit racial group, bound to an enemy nation by strong ties of race, culture, custom and religion." They are claimed to be given to "emperor worshipping ceremonies" and to "dual citizenship." Japanese language schools and allegedly pro-Japanese organizations are cited as evidence of possible group disloyalty, together with facts as to certain persons being educated and residing at length in Japan. It is intimated that many of these individuals deliberately resided "adjacent to strategic points," thus enabling them "to carry into execution a tremendous program of sabotage on a mass scale should any considerable number of them have been inclined to do so." The need for protective custody is also asserted. The report refers without identity to "numerous incidents of violence" as well as to other admittedly unverified or cumulative incidents. From this, plus certain other events not shown to have been connected with the Japanese Americans, it is concluded that the "situation was fraught with danger to the Japanese population itself" and that the general public "was ready to take matters into its own hands." Finally, it is intimated, though not directly charged or proved, that persons of Japanese ancestry were responsible for three minor isolated shellings and bombings of the Pacific Coast area, as well as for unidentified radio transmissions and night signalling.

The main reasons relied upon by those responsible for the forced evacuation, therefore, do not prove a reasonable relation between the group characteristics of Japanese Americans and the dangers of invasion, sabotage and espionage. The reasons appear, instead, to be largely an accumulation of much of the misinformation, half-truths and insinuations that for years have been directed against Japanese Americans by people with racial and economic prejudices—the same people who have been among the foremost advocates of the evacuation. A military judgment based upon such racial and sociological considerations is not entitled to the great weight ordinarily given the judgments based upon strictly military considerations. Especially is this so when every charge relative to race, religion, culture, geographical location, and legal and economic status has been substantially discredited by independent studies made by experts in these matters.

The military necessity which is essential to the validity of the evacuation order thus resolves itself into a few intimations that certain individuals actively aided the enemy, from which it is inferred that the entire group of Japanese Americans could not be trusted to be or remain loyal to the United States. No one denies, of course, that there were some disloyal persons of Japanese descent on the Pacific Coast who did all in their power to aid their ancestral land. Similar disloyal activities have been engaged in by many persons of German, Italian and even more pioneer stock in our country. But to infer that examples of individual disloyalty prove group disloyalty and justify discriminatory action against the entire group is to deny that under our system of law individual guilt is the sole basis for deprivation of rights. Moreover, this inference, which is at the very heart of the evacuation orders, has been used in support of the abhorrent and despicable treatment of minority groups by the dictatorial tyrannies which this nation is now pledged to destroy. To give constitutional sanction to that inference in this case, however well-intentioned may have been the military command on the Pacific Coast, is to adopt one of the cruelest of the rationales used by our enemies to destroy the dignity of the individual and to encourage and open the door to discriminatory actions against other minority groups in the passions of tomorrow.

No adequate reason is given for the failure to treat these Japanese Americans on an individual basis by holding investigations and hearings to separate the loyal from the disloyal, as was done in the case of persons of German and Italian ancestry. It is asserted merely that the loyalties of this group "were unknown and time was of the essence." Yet nearly four months elapsed after Pearl Harbor before the first exclusion order was issued; nearly eight months went by until the last order was issued; and the last of these "subversive" persons was not actually removed until almost eleven months had elapsed. Leisure and deliberation seem to have been more of the essence than speed. And the fact that conditions were not such as to warrant a declaration of martial law adds strength to the belief that the factors of time and military necessity were not as urgent as they have been represented to be.

Moreover, there was no adequate proof that the Federal Bureau of Investigation and the military and naval intelligence services did not have the espionage and sabotage situation well in hand during this long period. Nor is there any denial of the fact that not one person of Japanese ancestry was accused or convicted of espionage or sabotage after Pearl Harbor while they were still free, a fact which is some evidence of the loyalty of the vast majority of these individuals and of the effectiveness of the established methods of combatting these evils. It seems incredible that under these circumstances it would have been impossible to hold loyalty hearings for the mere 112,000 persons involved—or at least for the 70,000 American citizens—especially when a large part of this number represented children and elderly men and women. Any inconvenience that may have accompanied an attempt to conform to procedural due process cannot be said to justify violations of constitutional rights of individuals.

I dissent, therefore, from this legalization of racism. Racial discrimination in any form and in any degree has no justifiable part whatever in our democratic way of life. It is unattractive in any setting but it is utterly revolting among a free people who have embraced the principles set forth in the Constitution of the United States. All residents of this nation are kin in some way by blood or culture to a foreign land. Yet they are primarily and necessarily a part of the new and distinct civilization of the United States. They must accordingly be treated at all times as the heirs of the American experiment and as entitled to all the rights and freedoms guaranteed by the Constitution.

Mr. Justice Jackson, dissenting.

Korematsu was born on our soil, of parents born in Japan. The Constitution makes him a citizen of the United States by nativity and a citizen of California by residence. No claim is made that he is not loyal to this country. There is no suggestion that apart from the matter involved here he is not law-abiding and well disposed. Korematsu, however, has been convicted of an act not commonly a crime. It consists merely of being present in the state whereof he is a citizen, near the place where he was born, and where all his life he has lived.

Even more unusual is the series of military orders which made this conduct a crime. They forbid such a one to remain, and they also forbid him to leave. They were so drawn that the only way Korematsu could avoid violation was to give himself up to the military authority. This meant submission to custody, examination, and transportation out of the territory, to be followed by indeterminate confinement in detention camps.

A citizen's presence in the locality, however, was made a crime only if his parents were of Japanese birth. Had Korematsu been one of four —the others being, say, a German alien enemy, an Italian alien enemy, and a citizen of American-born ancestors, convicted of treason but out on parole—only Korematsu's presence would have violated the order. The difference between their innocence and his crime would result, not from anything he did, said, or thought, different than they, but only in that he was born of different racial stock.

Now, if any fundamental assumption underlies our system, it is that guilt is personal and not inheritable. Even if all of one's antecedents had been convicted of treason, the Constitution forbids its penalties to be visited upon him, for it provides that "no attainder of treason shall work corruption of blood, or forfeiture except during the life of the person attained." But here is an attempt to make an otherwise innocent act a crime merely because this prisoner is the son of parents as to whom he had no choice, and belongs to a race from which there is no way to resign. If Congress in peace-time legislation should enact such a criminal law, I should suppose this Court would refuse to enforce it.

But the "law" which this prisoner is convicted of disregarding is not found in an act of Congress, but in a military order. Neither the Act of Congress nor the Executive Order of the President, nor both together, would afford a basis for this conviction. It rests on the orders of General DeWitt. And it is said that if the military commander had reasonable military grounds for promulgating the orders, they are constitutional and become law, and the Court is required to enforce them. There are several reasons why I cannot subscribe to this doctrine.

It would be impracticable and dangerous idealism to expect or insist that each specific military command in an area of probable operations will conform to conventional tests of constitutionality. When an area is so beset that it must be put under military control at all, the paramount consideration is that its measures be successful, rather than legal. The armed services must protect a society, not merely its Constitution. The very essence of the military job is to marshal physical force, to remove every obstacle to its effectiveness, to give it every strategic advantage. Defense measures will not, and often should not, be held within the limits that bind civil authority in peace. No court can require such a commander in such circumstances to act as a reasonable man; he may be unreasonably cautious and exacting. Perhaps he should be. But a commander in temporarily focusing the life of a community on defense is carrying out a military program; he is not making law in the sense the courts know the term. He issues orders, and they may have a certain authority as military commands, although they may be very bad as constitutional law.

But if we cannot confine military expedients by the Constitution, neither would I distort the Constitution to approve all that the military may deem expedient. That is what the Court appears to be doing, whether consciously or not. I cannot say, from any evidence before me, that the orders of General DeWitt were not reasonably expedient military precautions, nor could I say that they were. But even if they were permissible military procedures, I deny that it follows that they are constitutional. If, as the Court holds, it does follow, then we may as well say that any military order will be constitutional and have done with it.

The limitation under which courts always will labor in examining the necessity for a military order are illustrated by this case. How does the Court know that these orders have a reasonable basis in necessity? No evidence whatever on that subject has been taken by this or any other court. There is sharp controversy as to the credibility of the DeWitt report. So the Court, having no real evidence before it, has no choice but to accept General DeWitt's own unsworn, self-serving statement, untested by any cross-examination, that what he did was reasonable. And thus it will always be when courts try to look into the reasonableness of a military order.

In the very nature of things, military decisions are not susceptible of intelligent judicial appraisal. They do not pretend to rest on evidence, but are made on information that often would not be admissible and on assumptions that could not be proved. Information in support of an order could not be disclosed to courts without danger that it would reach the enemy. Neither can courts act on communications made in confidence. Hence courts can never have any real alternative to accepting the mere declaration of the authority that issued the order that it was reasonably necessary from a military viewpoint.

Much is said of the danger to liberty from the Army program for deporting and detaining these citizens of Japanese extraction. But a judicial construction of the due process clause that will sustain this order is a far more subtle blow to liberty than the promulgation of the order itself. A military order, however unconstitutional, is not apt to last longer than the military emergency. Even during that period a succeeding commander may revoke it all. But once a judicial opinion rationalizes such an order to show that it conforms to the Constitution, or rather rationalizes the Constitution to show that the Constitution sanctions such an order, the Court for all time has validated the principle of racial discrimination in criminal procedure and of transplanting American citizens. The principle then lies about like a loaded weapon ready for the hand of any authority that can bring forward a plausible claim of an urgent need. Every repetition imbeds that principle more deeply in our law and thinking and expands it to new purposes. All who observe the work of courts are familiar with what Judge Cardozo described as "the tendency of a principle to expand itself to the limit of its logic." A military commander may overstep the bounds of constitutionality, and it is an incident. But if we review and approve, that passing incident becomes the doctrine of the Constitution. There it has a generative power of its own, and all that it creates will be in its own image. Nothing better illustrates this danger than does the Court's opinion in this case.

It argues that we are bound to uphold the conviction of Korematsu because we upheld one in *Hirabayashi* v. *United States,* when we sustained these orders in so far as they applied a curfew requirement to a citizen of Japanese ancestry. I think we should learn something from that experience.

In that case we were urged to consider only the curfew feature, that being all that technically was involved, because it was the only count necessary to sustain Hirabayashi's conviction and sentence. We yielded, and the Chief Justice guarded the opinion as carefully as language will do. He said: "Our investigation here does not go beyond the inquiry whether, in the light of all the relevant circumstances preceding and attending their promulgation, the challenged orders and statute *afforded a reasonable basis for the action taken in imposing the curfew*." "We decide only the issue as we have defined it—we decide only that the *curfew order* as applied, and at the time it was applied, was within the boundaries of the war power." And again: "It is unnecessary to consider whether or to what extent *such findings would support orders differing from the curfew order*." (Italics supplied.) However, in spite of our limiting words we did validate a discrimination on the basis of ancestry for mild and temporary deprivation of liberty. Now the principle of racial discrimination is pushed from support of mild measures to very harsh ones, and from temporary deprivations to indeterminate ones. And the precedent which it is said requires us to do so is *Hirabayashi*. The Court is now saying that in *Hirabayashi* we did decide the very things we there said we were not deciding. Because we said that these citizens could be made to stay in their homes during the hours of dark, it is said we must require them to leave home entirely; and if that, we are told they may also be taken into custody for deportation; and if that, it is argued they may also be held for some undetermined time in detention camps. How far the principle of this case would be extended before plausible‑ reasons would play out, I do not know.

I should hold that a civil court cannot be made to enforce an order which violates constitutional limitations even if it is a reasonable exercise of military authority. The courts can exercise only the judicial power, can apply only law, and must abide by the Constitution, or they cease to be civil courts and become instruments of military policy.

Of course the existence of a military power resting on force, so vagrant, so centralized, so necessarily heedless of the individual, is an inherent threat to liberty. But I would not lead people to rely on this Court for a review that seems to me wholly delusive. The military reasonableness of these orders can only be determined by military superiors. If the people ever let command of the war power fall into irresponsible and unscrupulous hands, the courts wield no power equal to its restraint. The chief restraint upon those who command the physical forces of the country, in the future as in the past, must be their responsibility to the political judgments of their contemporaries and to the moral judgments of history.

My duties as a justice as I see them do not require me to make a military judgment as to whether General DeWitt's evacuation and detention program was a reasonable military necessity. I do not suggest that the courts should have attempted to interfere with the Army in carrying out its task. But I do not think they may be asked to execute a military expedient that has no place in law under the Constitution. I would reverse the judgment and discharge the prisoner.

Part V

DISCRIMINATION AND LIVELIHOOD

The cases in this group involve, in various ways, the problem of racial discrimination as it bears on access to working opportunities.

Yick Wo v. Hopkins
118 U. S. 356   1886

Mr. Justice Matthews delivered the opinion of the Court.

In the case of the petitioner, brought here by writ of error to the Supreme Court of California, our jurisdiction is limited to the question, whether the plaintiff in error has been denied a right in violation of the Constitution, laws, or treaties of the United States. The question whether his imprisonment is illegal, under the constitution and laws of the State, is not open to us. And although that question might have been considered in the Circuit Court in the application made to it, and by this court on appeal from its order, yet judicial propriety is best consulted by accepting the judgment of the State court upon the points involved in that inquiry.

That, however, does not preclude this court from putting upon the ordinances of the supervisors of the county and city of San Francisco an independent construction; for the determination of the question whether the proceedings under these ordinances and in enforcement of them are in conflict with the Constitution and laws of the United States, necessarily involves the meaning of the ordinances, which, for that purpose, we are required to ascertain and adjudge.

We are consequently constrained, at the outset, to differ from the Supreme Court of California upon the real meaning of the ordinances in question. That court considered these ordinances as vesting in the board of supervisors a not unusual discretion in granting or withholding their assent to the use of wooden buildings as laundries, to be exercised in reference to the circumstances of each case, with a view to the protection of the public against the dangers of fire. We are not able to concur in that interpretation of the power conferred upon the supervisors. There is nothing in the ordinances which points to such a regulation of the business of keeping and conducting laundries. They seem intended to confer, and actually do confer, not a discretion to be exercised upon a consideration of the circumstances of each case, but a naked and arbitrary power to give or withhold consent, not only as to places, but as to persons. So that, if an applicant for such consent, being in every way a competent and qualified person, and having complied with every reasonable condition demanded by any public interest, should, failing to obtain the requisite consent of the supervisors to the prosecution of his business, apply for redress by the judicial process of *mandamus,* to require the supervisors to consider and act upon his case, it would be a sufficient answer for them to say that the law had conferred upon them authority to withhold their assent, without reason and without responsibility. The power given to them is not confided to their discretion in the legal sense of that term, but is granted to their mere will. It is purely arbitrary, and acknowledges neither guidance nor restraint.

This erroneous view of the ordinances in question led the Supreme Court of California into the further error of holding that they were justified by the decisions of this court in the cases of *Barbier* v. *Connolly* and *Soon Hing* v. *Crowley*. In both of these cases the ordinance involved was simply a prohibition to carry on the washing and ironing of clothes in public laundries and washhouses, within certain prescribed limits of the city and county of San Francisco, from ten o'clock at night until six o'clock in the morning of the following day. This provision was held to be purely a police regulation, within the competency of any municipality possessed of the ordinary powers belonging to such bodies; a necessary measure of precaution in a city composed largely of wooden buildings like San Francisco, in the application of which there was no invidious discrimination against any one within the prescribed limits, all persons engaged in the same business being treated alike, and subject to the same restrictions, and entitled to the same privileges, under similar conditions.

For these reasons, that ordinance was adjudged not to be within the prohibitions of the Fourteenth Amendment to the Constitution of the United States, which, it was said, in the first case cited, "undoubtedly intended not only that there should be no arbitrary deprivation of life or liberty, or arbitrary spoliation of property, but that equal protection and security should be given to all under like circumstances in the enjoyment of their personal and civil rights; that all persons should be equally entitled to pursue their happiness and acquire and enjoy property; that they should have like access to the courts of the country for the protection of their persons and property, the prevention and redress of wrongs, and the enforcement of contracts; that no impediment should be interposed to the pursuits of any one, except as applied to the same pursuits by others under like circumstances; that no greater burdens should be laid upon one than are laid upon others in the same calling and condition; and that in the administration of criminal justice no different or higher punishment should be imposed upon one than such as is prescribed to all for like offences." "Class legislation, discriminating against some and favoring others, is prohibited, but legislation which, in carrying out a public purpose, is limited in its application, if within the sphere of its operation it affects alike all persons similarly situated, is not within the amendment."

The ordinance drawn in question in the present case is of a very different character. It does not prescribe a rule and conditions for the regulation of the use of property for laundry purposes, to which all similarly situated may conform. It allows without restriction the use for such purposes of buildings of brick or stone; but, as to wooden buildings, constituting nearly all those in previous use, it divides the owners or occupiers into two classes, not having respect to their personal character and qualifications for the business, nor the situation and nature and adaptation of the buildings themselves, but merely by an arbitrary line, on one side of which are those who are permitted to pursue their industry by the mere will and consent of the supervisors, and on the other those from whom that consent is withheld, at their mere will and pleasure. And both classes are alike only in this, that they are tenants at will, under the supervisors, of their means of living. The ordinance, therefore, also differs from the not unusual case, where discretion is lodged by law in public officers or bodies to grant or withhold licenses to keep taverns, or places for the sale of spirituous liquors, and the like, when one of the conditions is that the applicant shall be a fit person for the exercise of the privilege, because in such cases the fact of fitness is submitted to the judgment of the officer, and calls for the exercise of a discretion of a judicial nature.

The rights of the petitioners, as affected by the proceedings of which they complain, are not less, because they are aliens and subjects of the Emperor of China. By the third article of the treaty between this Government and that of China, concluded November 17, 1880, it is stipulated: "If Chinese laborers, or Chinese of any other class, now either permanently or temporarily residing in the territory of the United States, meet with ill treatment at the hands of any other persons, the Government of the United States will exert all its powers to devise measures for their protection, and to secure to them the same rights, privileges, immunities and exemptions as may be enjoyed by the citizens or subjects of the most favored nation, and to which they are entitled by treaty."

The Fourteenth Amendment to the Constitution is not confined to the protection of citizens. It says: "Nor shall any State deprive any person of life, liberty, or property without due process of law; nor deny to any person within its jurisdiction the equal protection of the laws." These provisions are universal in their application, to all persons within the territorial jurisdiction, without regard to any differences of race, of color, or of nationality; and the equal protection of the laws is a pledge of the protection of equal laws. It is accordingly enacted by § 1977 of the Revised Statutes, that "all persons within the jurisdiction of the United States shall have the same right in every State and Territory to make and enforce contracts, to sue, be parties, give evidence, and to the full and equal benefit of all laws and proceedings for the security of persons and property as is enjoyed by white citizens and shall be subject to like punishment, pains, penalties, taxes, licenses, and exactions of every kind, and to no other." The questions we have to consider and decide in these cases, therefore, are to be treated as involving the rights of every citizen of the United States equally with those of the strangers and aliens who now invoke the jurisdiction of the court.

It is contended on the part of the petitioners, that the ordinances for violations of which they are severally sentenced to imprisonment, are void on their face, as being within the prohibitions of the Fourteenth Amendment; and, in the alternative, if not so, that they are void by reason of their administration, operating unequally, so as to punish in the present petitioners what is permitted to others as lawful, without any distinction of circumstances—an unjust and illegal discrimination, it is claimed, which, though not made expressly by the ordinances is made possible by them.

When we consider the nature and the theory of our institutions of government, the principles upon which they are supposed to rest, and review the history of their development, we are constrained to conclude that they do not mean to leave room for the play and action of purely personal and arbitrary power. Sovereignty itself is, of course, not subject to law, for it is the author and source of law; but in our system, while sovereign powers are delegated to the agencies of government, sovereignty itself remains with the people, by whom and for whom all government exists and acts. And the law is the definition and limitation of power. It is, indeed, quite true, that there must always be lodged somewhere, and in some person or body, the authority of final decision; and in many cases of mere administration the responsibility is purely political, no appeal lying except to the ultimate tribunal of the public judgment, exercised either in the pressure of opinion or by means of the suffrage. But the fundamental rights to life, liberty, and the pursuit of happiness, considered as individual possessions, are secured by those maxims of constitutional law which are the monuments showing the victorious progress of the race in securing to men the blessings of civilization under the reign of just and equal laws, so that, in the famous language of the Massachusetts Bill of Rights, the government of the commonwealth "may be a government of laws and not of men." For, the very idea that one man may be compelled to hold his life, or the means of living, or any material right essential to the enjoyment of life, at the mere will of another, seems to be intolerable in any country where freedom prevails, as being the essence of slavery itself.

There are many illustrations that might be given of this truth, which would make manifest that it was self-evident in the light of our system of jurisprudence. The case of the political franchise of voting is one. Though not regarded strictly as a natural right, but as a privilege merely conceded by society according to its will, under certain conditions, nevertheless it is regarded as a fundamental political right, because preservative of all rights.

In reference to that right, it was declared by the Supreme Judicial Court of Massachusetts, in *Capen* v. *Foster,* in the words of Chief Justice Shaw, "that in all cases where the constitution has conferred a political right or privilege, and where the constitution has not particularly designated the manner in which that right is to be exercised, it is clearly within the just and constitutional limits of the legislative power, to adopt any reasonable and uniform regulations, in regard to the time and mode of exercising that right, which are designed to secure and facilitate the exercise of such right, in a prompt, orderly, and convenient manner"; nevertheless, "such a construction would afford no warrant for such an exercise of legislative power, as, under the pretence and color of regulating, should subvert or injuriously restrain the right itself." It has accordingly been held generally in the States, that, whether the particular provisions of an act of legislation, establishing means for ascertaining the qualifications of those entitled to vote, and making previous registration in lists of such, a condition precedent to the exercise of the right, were or were not reasonable regulations, and accordingly valid or void, was always open to inquiry, as a judicial question.

The same principle has been more freely extended to the quasi-legislative acts of inferior municipal bodies, in respect to which it is an ancient jurisdiction of judicial tribunals to pronounce upon the reasonableness and consequent validity of their by-laws. In respect to these, it was the doctrine, that every by-law must be reasonable, not inconsistent with the charter of the corporation, nor with any statute of Parliament, nor with the general principles of the common law of the land, particularly those having relation to the liberty of the subject or the rights of private property. Accordingly, in the case of *The State of Ohio ex rel. &c.* v. *The Cincinnati Gas-Light and Coke Company,* an ordinance of the city council purporting to fix the price to be charged for gas, under an authority of law giving discretionary power to do so, was held to be bad, if passed in bad faith, fixing an unreasonable price, for the fraudulent purpose of compelling the gas company to submit to an unfair appraisement of their works. And a similar question, very pertinent to the one in the present cases, was decided by the Court of Appeals of Maryland, in the case of the *City of Baltimore* v. *Radecke.* In that case the defendant had erected and used a steam engine, in the prosecution of his business as a carpenter and box-maker in the city of Baltimore, under a permit from the mayor and city council, which contained a condition that the engine was "to be removed after six months' notice to that effect from the mayor." After such notice and refusal to conform to it, a suit was instituted to recover the penalty provided by the ordinance, to restrain the prosecution of which a bill in equity was filed. The court holding the opinion that "there may be a case in which an ordinance, passed under grants of power like those we have cited, is so clearly unreasonable, so arbitrary, oppressive, or partial, as to raise the presumption that the legislature never intended to confer the power to pass it, and to justify the courts in interfering and setting it aside as a plain abuse of authority," it proceeds to speak, with regard to the ordinance in question, in relation to the use of steam engines, as follows: "It does not profess to prescribe *regulations* for their construction, location, or use, nor require such precautions and safeguards to be provided by those who own and use them as are best calculated to render them less dangerous to life and property, nor does it restrain their use in box factories and other similar establishments within certain defined limits, nor in any other way attempt to promote their safety and security without destroying their usefulness. But it commits to the unrestrained will of a single public officer the power to notify every person who now employs a steam engine in the prosecution of any business in the city of Baltimore, to cease to do so, and, by providing compulsory fines for every day's disobedience of such notice and order of removal, renders his power over the use of steam in that city practically absolute, so that he may prohibit its use altogether. But if he should not choose to do this, but only to act in particular cases, there is nothing in the ordinance to guide or control his action. It lays down no *rules* by which its *impartial execution* can be secured or partiality and oppression prevented. It is clear that giving and enforcing these notices may, and quite likely will, bring ruin to the business of those against whom they are directed, while others, from whom they are withheld, may be actually benefited by what is thus done to their neighbors; and, when we remember that this action or non-action may proceed from enmity or prejudice, from partisan zeal or animosity, from favoritism and other improper influences and motives easy of concealment and difficult to be detected and exposed, it becomes unnecessary to suggest or to comment upon the injustice capable of being brought under cover of such a power, for that becomes apparent to every one who gives to the subject a moment's consideration. In fact, an ordinance which clothes a single individual with such power hardly falls within the *domain of law,* and we are constrained to pronounce it inoperative and void."

This conclusion, and the reasoning on which it is based, are deductions from the face of the ordinance, as to its necessary tendency and ultimate actual operation. In the present cases we are not obliged to reason from the probable to the actual, and pass upon the validity of the ordinances complained of, as tried merely by the opportunities which their terms afford, of unequal and unjust discrimination in their administration. For the cases present the ordinances in actual operation, and the facts shown establish an administration directed so exclusively against a particular class of persons as to warrant and require the conclusion, that, whatever may have been the intent of the ordinances as adopted, they are applied by the public authorities charged with their administration, and thus representing the State itself, with a mind so unequal and oppressive as to amount to a practical denial by the State of that equal protection of the laws which is secured to the petitioners, as to all other persons, by the broad and benign provisions of the Fourteenth Amendment to the Constitution of the United States. Though the law itself be fair on its face and impartial in appearance, yet, if it is applied and administered by public authority with an evil eye and an unequal hand, so as practically to make unjust and illegal discriminations between persons in similar circumstances, material to their rights, the denial of equal justice is still within the prohibition of the Constitution. This principle of interpretation has been sanctioned by this court in *Henderson* v. *Mayor of New York; Chy Lung* v. *Freeman; Ex parte Virginia; Neal* v. *Delaware;* and *Soon Hing* v. *Crowley.*

The present cases, as shown by the facts disclosed in the record, are within this class. It appears that both petitioners have complied with every requisite, deemed by the law or by the public offices charged with its administration, necessary for the protection of neighboring property from fire, or as a precaution against injury to the public health. No reason whatever, except the will of the supervisors, is assigned why they should not be permitted to carry on, in the accustomed manner, their harmless and useful occupation, on which they depend for a livelihood. And while this consent of the supervisors is withheld from them and from two hundred others who have also petitioned, all of whom happen to be Chinese subjects, eighty others, not Chinese subjects, are permitted to carry on the same business under similar conditions. The fact of this discrimination is admitted. No reason for it is shown, and the conclusion cannot be resisted, that no reason for it exists except hostility to the race and nationality to which the petitioners belong, and which in the eye of the law is not justified. The discrimination is, therefore, illegal, and the public administration which enforces it is a denial of the equal protection of the laws and a violation of the Fourteenth Amendment of the Constitution. The imprisonment of the petitioners is, therefore, illegal, and they must be discharged. To this end,

The judgment of the Supreme Court of California in the case of Yick Wo, and that of the Circuit Court of the United States for the District of California in the case of Wo Lee, are severally reversed, and the cases remanded, each to the proper court, with directions to discharge the petitioners from custody and imprisonment.

New Negro Alliance v. Grocery Company
303 U. S. 552   1938

Mr. Justice Roberts delivered the opinion of the Court.

The matter in controversy is whether the case made by the pleadings involves or grows out of a labor dispute within the meaning of § 13 of the Norris-LaGuardia Act.

The respondent, by bill filed in the District Court of the District of Columbia, sought an injunction restraining the petitioners and their agents from picketing its stores and engaging in other activities injurious to its business. The petitioners answered, the cause was heard upon bill and answer, and an injunction was awarded. The United States Court of Appeals for the District of Columbia affirmed the decree. The importance of the question presented and asserted conflict with the decisions of this and other federal courts moved us to grant certiorari.

As the case was heard upon the bill and a verified answer the facts upon which decision must rest are those set forth in the bill and admitted or not denied by the answer and those affirmatively set up in the answer.

The following facts alleged in the bill are admitted by the answer. Respondent, a Delaware corporation, operates 255 retail grocery, meat, and vegetable stores, a warehouse and a bakery in the District of Columbia and employs both white and colored persons. April 3, 1936, it opened a new store at 1936 Eleventh Street, N. W., installing personnel having an acquaintance with the trade in the vicinity. Petitioner, The New Negro Alliance, is a corporation composed of colored persons, organized for the mutual improvement of its members and the promotion of civic, educational, benevolent, and charitable enterprises. The individual petitioners are officers of the corporation. The relation of employer and employes does not exist between the respondent and the petitioners or any of them. The petitioners are not engaged in any business competitive with that of the respondent, and the officers, members, or representatives of the Alliance are not engaged in the same business or occupation as the respondent or its employes.

As to other matters of fact, the state of the pleadings may be briefly summarized. The bill asserts: the petitioners have made arbitrary and summary demands upon the respondent that it engage and employ colored persons in managerial and sales positions in the new store and in various other stores; it is essential to the conduct of the business that respondent employ experienced persons in its stores and compliance with the arbitrary demands of defendants would involve the discharge of white employes and their replacement with colored; it is imperative that respondent be free in the selection and control of persons employed by it without interference by the petitioners or others; petitioners have written respondent letters threatening boycott and ruination of its business and notices that by means of announcements, meetings and advertising the petitioners will circulate statements that respondent is unfair to colored people and to the colored race and, contrary to fact, that respondent does not employ colored persons; respondent has not acceded to these demands. The answer admits the respondent has not acceded to the petitioners' demands, but denies the other allegations and states that the Alliance and its agents have requested only that respondent, in the regular course of personnel changes in its retail stores, give employment to Negroes as clerks, particularly in stores patronized largely by colored people; that the petitioners have not requested the discharge of white employes nor sought action which would involve their discharge. It denies the making of the threats described and alleges the only representations threatened by the Alliance or its authorized agents are true representations that named stores of the respondent do not employ Negroes as sales persons and that the petitioners have threatened no more than the use of lawful and peaceable persuasion of members of the community to withhold patronage from particular stores after the respondent's refusal to acknowledge petitioner's requests that it adopt a policy of employing Negro clerks in such stores in the regular course of personnel changes.

The bill further alleges that the petitioners and their authorized representatives "have unlawfully conspired with each other to picket, patrol, boycott, and ruin the Plaintiff's business in said stores, and particularly in the store located at 1936 Eleventh Street, Northwest" and, "in an effort to fulfill their threats of coercion and intimidation, actually have caused the said store to be picketed or patrolled during hours of business of the plaintiff, by their members, representatives, officers, agents, servants, and employees"; the pickets carrying large placards charging respondent with being unfair to Negroes and reading: "Do Your Part! Buy Where You Can Work! No Negroes Employed Here!" for the purpose of intimidating and coercing prospective customers from entering the respondent's store until the respondent accedes to the petitioners' demands. "Said defendants, their pickets or patrols or some of them have jostled and collided with persons in front of the said store and have physically hindered, obstructed, interfered with, delayed, molested, and harassed persons desiring to enter the place of business of the Plaintiff Corporation; said pickets, or some of them, have attempted to dissuade and prevent persons from entering plaintiff's place of business; said defendants, their pickets or patrols are disorderly while picketing or patrolling, and attract crowds to gather in front of said store, and encourage the crowds or members thereof to become disorderly, and to harass, and otherwise annoy, interfere with and attempt to dissuade, and to prevent persons from entering the place of business of the plaintiff, the disorder thereby preventing the proper conduct of and operation of the plaintiff's business. Defendants have threatened to use similar tactics of picketing and patrolling as aforesaid in front of the several other stores of the plaintiff." Four photographs alleged to portray the picketing are annexed as exhibits to the bill. One of them shows a man carrying a sandwich placard on the sidewalk and no one else within the range of the camera. In another, two children are seen beside the picket; in another, two adults; in the fourth, one adult entering respondent's store at a distance from the picket and without apparent interference. The answer denies all these allegations save that it admits the petitioners did, during April 4, 1936, and at no other time, cause the store at 1936 Eleventh Street, N. W., to be continuously picketed by a single person carrying a placard exhibiting the words quoted by the bill; and the petitioners, prior to the acts complained of in the bill, picketed, or expressed the intention of picketing, two other stores. It admits that the photographs correctly represent the picketing of April 4, 1936. The answer avers the information carried on the placards was true, was not intended to, and did not in fact, intimidate customers; there was no physical obstruction, interference or harassment of anyone desiring to enter the store; there was no disorderly conduct, and the picketing did not cause or encourage crowds to gather in front of the store.

The bill states: "As evidence of the widespread and concerted action planned by the Defendants herein, they have caused to be placed or have permitted to appear in the Washington Tribune . . . the following statements . . ." There follow quotations from articles appearing in the newspaper purporting to report meetings of the Alliance and speeches made thereat. There is no statement that the facts reported in the articles are true. The answer denies that any of the petitioners is connected with or exercises any control over the Washington Tribune or caused or permitted that newspaper to publish any article or news item whatsoever or in any way acted in concert with the newspaper in those publications.

The bill asserts that petitioners and their representatives, officers, and agents, unlawfully conspired to picket, boycott, and ruin the respondent's business in its stores, particularly the store at 1936 Eleventh Street. This is denied by the answer.

The bill says that the described conduct of petitioners will continue until respondent complies with petitioners' demands; is and will continue to be dangerous to the life and health of persons on the highway, to property thereon, and to respondent's employes, its property, and business and will cause respondent irreparable injury; the petitioners' acts are unlawful, constitute a conspiracy in restraint of trade, and, if continued, will ruin the respondent's business. The answer denies these allegations so far as they constitute assertions of fact.

The case, then, as it stood for judgment, was this: The petitioners requested the respondent to adopt a policy of employing Negro clerks in certain of its stores in the course of personnel changes; the respondent ignored the request and the petitioners caused one person to patrol in front of one of the respondent's stores on one day carrying a placard which said: "Do Your Part! Buy Where You Can Work! No Negroes Employed Here!" and caused or threatened a similar patrol of two other stores of respondent. The information borne by the placard was true. The patrolling did not coerce or intimidate respondent's customers; did not physically obstruct, interfere with, or harass persons desiring to enter the store, the picket acted in an orderly manner, and his conduct did not cause crowds to gather in front of the store.

The trial judge was of the view that the laws relating to labor disputes had no application to the case. He entered a decree enjoining the petitioners and their agents and employes from picketing or patrolling any of the respondent's stores, boycotting or urging others to boycott respondent; restraining them, whether by inducements, threats, intimidation or actual or threatened physical force from hindering any person entering respondent's places of business, from destroying or damaging or threatening to destroy or damage respondent's property and from aiding or abetting others in doing any of the prohibited things. The

Court of Appeals thought that the dispute was not a labor dispute within the Norris-LaGuardia Act because it did not involve terms and conditions of employment such as wages, hours, unionization or betterment of working conditions, and that the trial court, therefore, had jurisdiction to issue the injunction. We think the conclusion that the dispute was not a labor dispute within the meaning of the Act, because it did not involve terms and conditions of employment in the sense of wages, hours, unionization or betterment of working conditions is erroneous.

Subsection (a) of § 13 provides: "A case shall be held to involve or to grow out of a labor dispute when the case involves persons who are engaged in the same industry, trade, craft, or occupation; or have direct or indirect interests therein; . . . or when the case involves any conflicting or competing interests in a 'labor dispute' (as hereinafter defined) of 'persons participating or interested' therein (as hereinafter defined)." Subsection (b) characterizes a person or association as participating or interested in a labor dispute "if relief is sought against him or it and if he or it . . . has a direct or indirect interest therein, . . ." Subsection (c) defines the term "labor dispute" as including "any controversy concerning terms or conditions of employment, . . . regardless of whether or not the disputants stand in the proximate relation of employer and employee." These definitions plainly embrace the controversy which gave rise to the instant suit and classify it as one arising out of a dispute defined as a labor dispute. They leave no doubt that The New Negro Alliance and the individual petitioners are, in contemplation of the Act, persons interested in the dispute.

In quoting the clauses of § 13 we have omitted those that deal with disputes between employers and employes and disputes between associations of persons engaged in a particular trade or craft, and employers in the same industry. It is to be noted, however, that the inclusion in the definitions of such disputes, and the persons interested in them, serves to emphasize the fact that the quoted portions were intended to embrace controversies other than those between employers and employes; between labor unions seeking to represent employes and employers; and between persons seeking employment and employers.

The Act does not concern itself with the background or the motives of the dispute. The desire for fair and equitable conditions of employment on the part of persons of any race, color, or persuasion, and the removal of discriminations against them by reason of their race or religious beliefs is quite as important to those concerned as fairness and equity in terms and conditions of employment can be to trade or craft unions or any form of labor organization or association. Race discrimination by an employer may reasonably be deemed more unfair and less excusable than discrimination against workers on the ground of union affiliation. There is no justification in the apparent purposes or the express terms of the Act for limiting its definition of labor disputes and cases arising therefrom by excluding those which arise with respect to discrimination in terms and conditions of employment based upon differences of race or color. . . .

The legislative history of the Act demonstrates that it was the purpose of the Congress further to extend the prohibitions of the Clayton Act respecting the exercise of jurisdiction by federal courts and to obviate the results of the judicial construction of that Act. It was intended that peaceful and orderly dissemination of information by those defined as persons interested in a labor dispute concerning "terms and conditions of employment" in an industry or a plant or a place of business should be lawful; that, short of fraud, breach of the peace, violence, or conduct otherwise unlawful, those having a direct or indirect interest in such terms and conditions of employment should be at liberty to advertise and disseminate facts and information with respect to terms and conditions of employment, and peacefully to persuade others to concur in their views respecting an employer's practices. The District Court erred in not complying with the provisions of the Act.

The decree must be reversed and the cause remanded to the District Court for further proceedings in conformity with this opinion.

Mr. Justice Cardozo took no part in the consideration or decision of this case.

Mr. Justice McReynolds, dissenting.

Mr. Justice Butler and I cannot accept the view that a "labor dispute" emerges whenever an employer fails to respond to a communication from A, B and C—irrespective of their race, character, reputation, fitness, previous or present employment—suggesting displeasure because of his choice of employes and their expectation that in the future he will not fail to select men of their complexion.

It seems unbelievable that, in all such circumstances, Congress intended to inhibit courts from extending protection long guaranteed by law and thus, in effect, encourage mobbish interference with the individual's liberty of action. Under the tortured meaning now attributed to the words "labor dispute," no employer—merchant, manufacturer, builder, cobbler, housekeeper or what not—who prefers helpers of one color or class can find adequate safeguard against intolerable violations of his freedom if members of some other class, religion, race or color demand that he give them precedence.

Design thus to promote strife, encourage trespass and stimulate intimidation, ought not to be admitted where, as here, not plainly avowed. The ultimate result of the view now approved to the very people whom present petitioners claim to represent, it may be, is prefigured by the grievous plight of minorities in lands where the law has become a mere political instrument.

Steele v. L. and N.R. Company
323 U. S. 192   1944

Mr. Chief Justice Stone delivered the opinion of the Court.

The question is whether the Railway Labor Act imposes on a labor organization, acting by authority of the statute as the exclusive bargaining representative of a craft or class of railway employees, the duty to represent all the employees in the craft without discrimination because of their race, and, if so, whether the courts have jurisdiction to protect the minority of the craft or class from the violation of such obligation.

The issue is raised by demurrer to the substituted amended bill of complaint filed by petitioner, a locomotive fireman, in a suit brought in the Alabama Circuit Court against his employer, the Louisville & Nashville Railroad Company, the Brotherhood of Locomotive Firemen and Enginemen, an unincorporated labor organization, and certain individuals representing the Brotherhood. The Circuit Court sustained the demurrer, and the Supreme Court of Alabama affirmed. We granted certiorari, the question presented being one of importance in the administration of the Railway Labor Act.

The allegations of the bill of complaint, so far as now material, are as follows: Petitioner, a Negro, is a locomotive fireman in the employ of respondent Railroad, suing on his own behalf and that of his fellow employees who, like petitioner, are Negro firemen employed by the Railroad. Respondent Brotherhood, a labor organization, is, as provided under § 2, Fourth of Railway Labor Act, the exclusive bargaining representative of the craft of firemen employed by the Railroad and is recognized as such by it and the members of the craft. The majority of the firemen employed by the Railroad are white and are members of the Brotherhood, but a substantial minority are Negroes who, by the constitution and ritual of the Brotherhood, are excluded from its membership. As the membership of the Brotherhood constitutes a majority of all firemen employed on respondent Railroad, and as under § 2, Fourth the members because they are the majority have the right to choose and have chosen the Brotherhood to represent the craft, petitioner and other Negro firemen on the road have been required to accept the Brotherhood as their representative for the purposes of the Act.

On March 28, 1940, the Brotherhood, purporting to act as representative of the entire craft of firemen, without informing the Negro firemen or giving them opportunity to be heard, served a notice on respondent Railroad and on twenty other railroads operating principally in the southeastern part of the United States. The notice announced the Brotherhood's desire to amend the existing collective bargaining agreement in such manner as ultimately to exclude all Negro firemen from the service. By established practice on the several railroads so notified only white firemen can be promoted to serve as engineers, and the notice proposed that only "promotable," i. e. white, men should be employed as firemen or assigned to new runs or jobs or permanent vacancies in established runs or jobs.

On February 18, 1941, the railroads and the Brotherhood, as representative of the craft, entered into a new agreement which provided that not more than 50% of the firemen in each class of service in each seniority district of a carrier should be Negroes; that until such percentage should be reached all new runs and all vacancies should be filled by white men; and that the agreement did not sanction the employment of Negroes in any seniority district in which they were not working. The agreement reserved the right of the Brotherhood to negotiate for further restrictions on the employment of Negro firemen on the individual railroads. On May 12, 1941, the Brotherhood entered into a supplemental agreement with respondent Railroad further controlling the seniority rights of Negro firemen and restricting their employment. The Negro firemen were not given notice or opportunity to be heard with respect to either of these agreements, which were put into effect before their existence was disclosed to the Negro firemen.

Until April 8, 1941, petitioner was in a "passenger pool," to which one white and five Negro firemen were assigned. These jobs were highly desirable in point of wages, hours and other considerations. Petitioner had performed and was performing his work satisfactorily. Following a reduction in the mileage covered by the pool, all jobs in the pool were, about April 1, 1941, declared vacant. The Brotherhood and the Railroad, acting under the agreement, disqualified all the Negro firemen and replaced them with four white men, members of the Brotherhood, all junior in seniority to petitioner and no more competent or worthy. As a consequence petitioner was deprived of employment for sixteen days and then was assigned to more arduous, longer, and less remunerative work in local freight service. In conformity to the agreement, he was later replaced by a Brotherhood member junior to him, and assigned work on a switch engine, which was still harder and less remunerative, until January 3, 1942. On that date, after the bill of complaint in the present suit had been filed, he was reassigned to passenger service.

Protests and appeals of petitioner and his fellow Negro firemen, addressed to the Railroad and the Brotherhood, in an effort to secure relief and redress, have been ignored. Respondents have expressed their intention to enforce the agreement of February 18, 1941 and its subsequent modifications. The Brotherhood has acted and asserts the right to act as exclusive bargaining representative of the firemen's craft. It is alleged that in that capacity it is under an obligation and duty imposed by the Act to represent the Negro firemen impartially and in good faith; but instead, in its notice to and contracts with the railroads, it has been hostile and disloyal to the Negro firemen, has deliberately discriminated against them, and has sought to deprive them of their seniority rights and to drive them out of employment in their craft, all in order to create a monopoly of employment for Brotherhood members.

The bill of complaint asks for discovery of the manner in which the agreements have been applied and in other respects; for an injunction against enforcement of the agreements made between the Railroad and the Brotherhood; for an injunction against the Brotherhood and its agents from purporting to act as representative of petitioner and others similarly situated under the Railway Labor Act, so long as the discrimination continues, and so long as it refuses to give them notice and hearing with respect to proposals affecting their interests; for a declaratory judgment as to their rights; and for an award of damages against the Brotherhood for its wrongful conduct.

The Supreme Court of Alabama took jurisdiction of the cause but held on the merits that petitioner's complaint stated no cause of action. It pointed out that the Act places a mandatory duty on the Railroad to treat with the Brotherhood as the exclusive representative of the employees in a craft, imposes heavy criminal penalties for willful failure to comply with its command, and provides that the majority of any craft shall have the right to determine who shall be the representative of the class for collective bargaining with the employer. It thought that the Brotherhood was empowered by the statute to enter into the agreement of February 18, 1941, and that by virtue of the statute the Brotherhood has power by agreement with the Railroad both to create the seniority rights of petitioner and his fellow Negro employees and to destroy them. It construed the statute, not as creating the relationship of principal and agent between the members of the craft and the Brotherhood, but as conferring on the Brotherhood plenary authority to treat with the Railroad and enter into contracts fixing rates of pay and working conditions for the craft as a whole without any legal obligation or duty to protect the rights of minorities from discrimination or unfair treatment, however gross. Consequently it held that neither the Brotherhood nor the Railroad violated any rights of petitioner or his fellow Negro employees by negotiating the contracts discriminating against them.

If, as the state court has held, the Act confers this power on the bargaining representative of a craft or class of employees without any commensurate statutory duty toward its members, constitutional questions arise. For the representative is clothed with power not unlike that of a legislature which is subject to constitutional limitations on its power to deny, restrict, destroy or discriminate against the rights of those for whom it legislates and which is also under an affirmative constitutional duty equally to protect those rights. If the Railway Labor Act purports to impose on petitioner and the other Negro members of the craft the legal duty to comply with the terms of a contract whereby the representative has discriminatorily restricted their employment for the benefit and advantage of the Brotherhood's own members, we must decide the constitutional questions which petitioner raises in his pleading.

But we think that Congress, in enacting the Railway Labor Act and authorizing a labor union, chosen by a majority of a craft, to represent the craft, did not intend to confer plenary power upon the union to sacrifice, for the benefit of its members, rights of the minority of the craft, without imposing on it any duty to protect the minority. Since petitioner and the other Negro members of the craft are not members of the Brotherhood or eligible for membership, the authority to act for them is derived not from their action or consent but wholly from the command of the Act. Section 2, Fourth provides: "Employees shall have the right to organize and bargain collectively through representatives of their own choosing. The majority of any craft or class of employees shall have the right to determine who shall be the representative of the craft or class for the purposes of this Act. . . ." Under §§ 2, Sixth and Seventh, when the representative bargains for a change of working conditions, the latter section specifies that they are the working conditions of employees "as a class." Section 1, Sixth of the Act defines "representative" as meaning "Any person or . . . labor union . . . designated either by a carrier or group of carriers or by its or their employees, to act for it or them." The use of the word "representative," as thus defined and in all the contexts in which it is found, plainly implies that the representative is to act on behalf of all the employees which, by virtue of the statute, it undertakes to represent.

By the terms of the Act, § 2, Fourth, the employees are permitted to act "through" their representative, and it represents them "for the purposes of" the Act. The purposes of the Act declared by § 2 are the avoidance of "any interruption to commerce or to the operation of any carrier engaged therein," and this aim is sought to be achieved by encouraging "the prompt and orderly settlement of all disputes concerning rates of pay, rules, or working conditions." These purposes would hardly be attained if a substantial minority of the craft were denied the right to have their interests considered at the conference table and if the final result of the bargaining process were to be the sacrifice of the interests of the minority by the action of a representative chosen by the majority. The only recourse of the minority would be to strike, with the attendant interruption of commerce, which the Act seeks to avoid.

Section 2, Second, requiring carriers to bargain with the representative so chosen, operates to exclude any other from representing a craft. The minority members of a craft are thus deprived by the statute of the right, which they would otherwise possess, to choose a representative of their own, and its members cannot bargain individually on behalf of themselves as to matters which are properly the subject of collective bargaining.

The labor organization chosen to be the representative of the craft or class of employees is thus chosen to represent all of its members, regardless of their union affiliations or want of them. As we have pointed out with respect to the like provision of the National Labor Relations Act in *J. I. Case Co.* v. *Labor Board,* "The very purpose of providing by statute for the collective agreement is to supersede the terms of separate agreements of employees with terms which reflect the strength and bargaining power and serve the welfare of the group. Its benefits and advantages are open to every employee of the represented unit. . . ." The purpose of providing for a representative is to secure those benefits for those who are represented and not to deprive them or any of them of the benefits of collective bargaining for the advantage of the representative or those members of the craft who selected it.

As the National Mediation Board said in In The Matter of Representation of Employees of the St. Paul Union Depot Company, Case No. R–635: "Once a craft or class has designated its representative, such representative is responsible under the law to act for all employees within the craft or class, those who are not members of the represented organization, as well as those who are members."

Unless the labor union representing a craft owes some duty to represent non-union members of the craft, at least to the extent of not discriminating against them as such in the contracts which it makes as their representative, the minority would be left with no means of protecting their interests or, indeed, their right to earn a livelihood by pursuing the occupation in which they are employed. While the majority of the craft chooses the bargaining representative, when chosen it represents, as the Act by its terms makes plain, the craft or class, and not the majority. The fair interpretation of the statutory language is that the organization chosen to represent a craft is to represent all its members, the majority as well as the minority, and it is to act for and not against those whom it represents. It is a principle of general application that the exercise of a granted power to act in behalf of others involves the assumption toward them of a duty to exercise the power in their interest and behalf, and that such a grant of power will not be deemed to dispense with all duty toward those for whom it is exercised unless so expressed.

We think that the Railway Labor Act imposes upon the statutory representative of a craft at least as exacting a duty to protect equally the interests of the members of the craft as the Constitution imposes upon a legislature to give equal protection to the interests of those for whom it legislates. Congress has seen fit to clothe the bargaining representative with powers comparable to those possessed by a legislative body both to create and restrict the rights of those whom it represents, but it has also imposed on the representative a corresponding duty. We hold that the language of the Act to which we have referred, read in the light of the purposes of the Act, expresses the aim of Congress to impose on the bargaining representative of a craft or class of employees the duty to exercise fairly the power conferred upon it in behalf of all those for whom it acts, without hostile discrimination against them.

This does not mean that the statutory representative of a craft is barred from making contracts which may have unfavorable effects on some of the members of the craft represented. Variations in the terms of the contract based on differences relevant to the authorized purposes of the contract in conditions to which they are to be applied, such as differences in seniority, the type of work performed, the competence and skill with which it is performed, are within the scope of the bargaining representation of a craft, all of whose members are not identical in their interest or merit. Without attempting to mark the allowable limits of differences in the terms of contracts based on differences of conditions to which they apply, it is enough for present purposes to say that the statutory power to represent a craft and to make contracts as to wages, hours and working conditions does not include the authority to make among members of the craft discriminations not based on such relevant differences. Here the discriminations based on race alone are obviously irrelevant and invidious. Congress plainly did not undertake to authorize the bargaining representative to make such discriminations.

The representative which thus discriminates may be enjoined from so doing, and its members may be enjoined from taking the benefit of such discriminatory action. No more is the Railroad bound by or entitled to take the benefit of a contract which the bargaining representative is prohibited by the statute from making. In both cases the right asserted, which is derived from the duty imposed by the statute on the bargaining representative, is a federal right implied from the statute and the policy which it has adopted. It is the federal statute which condemns as unlawful the Brotherhood's conduct. "The extent and nature of the legal consequences of this condemnation, though left by the statute to judicial determination, are nevertheless to be derived from it and the federal policy which it has adopted."

So long as a labor union assumes to act as the statutory representative of a craft, it cannot rightly refuse to perform the duty, which is inseparable from the power of representation conferred upon it, to represent the entire membership of the craft. While the statute does not deny to such a bargaining labor organization the right to determine eligibility to its membership, it does require the union, in collective bargaining and in making contracts with the carrier, to represent non-union or minority union members of the craft without hostile discrimination, fairly, impartially, and in good faith. Wherever necessary to that end, the union is required to consider requests of non-union members of the craft and expressions of their views with respect to collective bargaining with the employer and to give to them notice of and opportunity for hearing upon its proposed action. . . .

In the absence of any available administrative remedy, the right here asserted, to a remedy for breach of the statutory duty of the bargaining representative to represent and act for the members of a craft, is of judicial cognizance. That right would be sacrificed or obliterated if it were without the remedy which courts can give for breach of such a duty or obligation and which it is their duty to give in cases in which they have jurisdiction. . . .

We conclude that the duty which the statute imposes on a union representative of a craft to represent the interests of all its members stands on no different footing and that the statute contemplates resort to the usual judicial remedies of injunction and award of damages when appropriate for breach of that duty.

The judgment is accordingly reversed and remanded for further proceedings not inconsistent with this opinion.

Mr. Justice Black concurs in the result.

Mr. Justice Murphy, concurring.

The economic discrimination against Negroes practiced by the Brotherhood and the railroad under color of Congressional authority raises a grave constitutional issue that should be squarely faced.

The utter disregard for the dignity and the well-being of colored citizens shown by this record is so pronounced as to demand the invocation of constitutional condemnation. To decide the case and to analyze the statute solely upon the basis of legal niceties, while remaining mute and placid as to the obvious and oppressive deprivation of constitutional guarantees, is to make the judicial function something less than it should be.

The constitutional problem inherent in this instance is clear. Congress, through the Railway Labor Act, has conferred upon the union selected by a majority of a craft or class of railway workers the power to represent the entire craft or class in all collective bargaining matters. While such a union is essentially a private organization, its power to represent and bind all members of a class or craft is derived solely from Congress. The Act contains no language which directs the manner in which the bargaining representative shall perform its duties. But it cannot be assumed that Congress meant to authorize the representative to act so as to ignore rights guaranteed by the Constitution. Otherwise the Act would bear the stigma of unconstitutionality under the Fifth Amendment in this respect. For that reason I am willing to read the statute as not permitting or allowing any action by the bargaining representative in the exercise of its delegated powers which would in effect violate the constitutional rights of individuals.

If the Court's construction of the statute rests upon this basis, I agree. But I am not sure that such is the basis. Suffice it to say, however, that this constitutional issue cannot be lightly dismissed. The cloak of racism surrounding the actions of the Brotherhood in refusing membership to Negroes and in entering into and enforcing agreements discriminating against them, all under the guise of Congressional authority, still remains. No statutory interpretation can erase this ugly example of economic cruelty against colored citizens of the United States. Nothing can destroy the fact that the accident of birth has been used as the basis to abuse individual rights by an organization purporting to act in conformity with its Congressional mandate. Any attempt to interpret the Act must take that fact into account and must realize that the constitutionality of the statute in this respect depends upon the answer given.

The Constitution voices its disapproval whenever economic discrimination is applied under authority of law against any race, creed or color. A sound democracy cannot allow such discrimination to go unchallenged.

Racism is far too virulent today to permit the slightest refusal, in the light of a Constitution that abhors it, to expose and condemn it wherever it appears in the course of a statutory interpretation.

Railway Mail Association v. Corsi
326 U. S. 88 1945

Mr. Justice Reed delivered the opinion of the Court.

The appellant, Railway Mail Association, questioned the validity of Section 43, and related Sections 41 and 45, of the New York Civil Rights Law which provide, under penalty against its officers and members, that no labor organization shall deny a person membership by reason of race, color or creed, or deny to any of its members, by reason of race, color or creed, equal treatment in the designation of its members for employment, promotion or dismissal by an employer. Appellant contended that it was not a "labor organization" subject to these sections, and that if they were held to apply to it, they violated the due process and equal protection clauses of the Fourteenth Amendment of the federal Constitution and were in conflict with the federal power over post offices and post roads. The New York Court of Appeals rejected these contentions. On appeal to this Court, consideration of the question of jurisdiction was postponed to the hearing on the merits for determination of whether the case presented a "case or controversy" within the meaning of the federal Constitution. The jurisdiction of this Court rests on § 237 (a) of the Judicial Code.

The appellant, Railway Mail Association, a New Hampshire corporation, is an organization with a membership of some 22,000 regular and substitute postal clerks of the United States Railway Mail Service. It has division and branch associations, thirteen of such branch associations being located in different parts of New York. Article III of appellant's constitution limits membership in the association to eligible postal clerks who are of the Caucasian race, or native American Indians. Certain officers and members of one of appellant's branch associations raised the question of the validity of Article III of appellant's constitution with the appellee, the Industrial Commissioner of the State of New York, who was charged with enforcement of § 43. Faced with the threat of enforcement of the statute against it, the appellant filed suit against the Industrial Commissioner in a state court for a declaratory judgment to determine the validity of § 43, and related provisions, and for an injunction restraining its enforcement against the appellant. A state Supreme Court entered judgment for the appellant, finding that it was not a "labor organization" as defined in § 43 of the state statute. On appeal to the Appellate Division, this judgment was reversed, the appellate court finding that appellant was covered by § 43 and that § 43 as applied to appellant did not violate the federal Constitution.

On appeal to the New York Court of Appeals, the judgment against the appellant was affirmed. The Court of Appeals noted that appellant's constitution provided that one of the objects of the association was to enable railway postal clerks "to perfect any movement that may be for their benefit as a class or for the benefit of the Railway Mail Service . . ."; that the Industrial Secretary of the Association was to assist in the presentation of grievances pertaining to service conditions and endeavor to secure adjustment of such through administrative action. It was pointed out that appellant was affiliated with the American Federation of Labor and that the appellant was designated a "labor union" in the Bulletin of the United States Department of Labor as well as in various trade union publications and reports. Appellant's own publications claimed credit for bringing "to every railway postal clerk many material benefits" and "many additional millions of dollars brought to the pockets of railway postal clerks each year by the efforts of the Association," and pointed out that "Reforms always come as a result of demands from the worker. If better conditions are worth securing, they must come as the result of organized effort." In the light of this evidence, the Court of Appeals held appellant to be a "labor organization" as defined in § 43. As heretofore stated, it rejected appellant's contentions that the statute, as applied to it, violated the federal Constitution.

Prior to consideration of the issues, it is necessary to determine whether appeal from this state court declaratory judgment proceeding presents a justiciable "case or controversy" under §§ 1 and 2 of Article III of the federal Constitution. We are of the opinion that it does. The conflicting contentions of the parties in this case as to the validity of the state statute present a real, substantial controversy between parties having adverse legal interests, a dispute definite and concrete, not hypothetical or abstract. Legal rights asserted by appellant are threatened with imminent invasion by appellees and will be directly affected to a specific and substantial degree by decision of the questions of law.

Appellant first contends that § 43 and related §§ 41 and 45 of the New York Civil Rights Law, as applied to appellant, offends the due process clause of the Fourteenth Amendment as an interference with its right of selection to membership and abridgment of its property rights and liberty of contract. We have here a prohibition of discrimination in membership or union services on account of race, creed or color. A judicial determination that such legislation violated the Fourteenth Amendment would be a distortion of the policy manifested in that amendment, which was adopted to prevent state legislation designed to perpetuate discrimination on the basis of race or color. We see no constitutional basis for the contention that a state cannot protect workers from exclusion solely on the basis of race, color or creed by an organization, functioning under the protection of the state, which holds itself out to represent the general business needs of employees.

To deny a fellow-employee membership because of race, color or creed may operate to prevent that employee from having any part in the determination of labor policies to be promoted and adopted in the industry and deprive him of all means of protection from unfair treatment arising out of the fact that the terms imposed by a dominant union apply to all employees, whether union members or not. In their very nature, racial and religious minorities are likely to be so small in number in any particular industry as to be unable to form an effective organization for securing settlement of their grievances and consideration of their group aims with respect to conditions of employment. The fact that the employer is the Government has no significance from this point of view. . . .

The judgment is

Affirmed.

Mr. Justice Rutledge concurs in the result.

Mr. Justice Frankfurter, concurring.

The Railway Mail Association is a union of railway clerks. To operate as a union in New York it must obey the New York Civil Rights Law. That law prohibits such an organization from denying membership in the union by reason of race, color or creed, with all the economic consequences that such denial entails.

Apart from other objections, which are too unsubstantial to require consideration, it is urged that the Due Process Clause of the Fourteenth Amendment precludes the State of New York from prohibiting racial and religious discrimination against those seeking employment. Elaborately to argue against this contention is to dignify a claim devoid of constitutional substance. Of course a State may leave abstention from such discriminations to the conscience of individuals. On the other hand, a State may choose to put its authority behind one of the cherished aims of American feeling by forbidding indulgence in racial or religious prejudice to another's hurt. To use the Fourteenth Amendment as a sword against such State power would stultify that Amendment. Certainly the insistence by individuals on their private prejudices as to race, color or creed, in relations like those now before us, ought not to have a higher constitutional sanction than the determination of a State to extend the area of non-discrimination beyond that which the Constitution itself exacts.

Takahashi v. Fish and Game Commission
334 U. S. 410   1948

Mr. Justice Black delivered the opinion of the Court.

The respondent, Torao Takahashi, born in Japan, came to this country and became a resident of California in 1907. Federal laws, based on distinctions of "color" and race," have permitted Japanese and certain other non-white racial groups to enter and reside in the country, but have made them ineligible for United States citizenship. The question presented is whether California can, consistently with the Federal Constitution and laws passed pursuant to it, use this federally created racial ineligibility for citizenship as a basis for barring Takahashi from earning his living as a commercial fisherman in the ocean waters off the coast of California.

Prior to 1943 California issued commercial fishing licenses to all qualified persons without regard to alienage or ineligibility to citizenship. From 1915 to 1942 Takahashi, under annual commercial fishing licenses issued by the State, fished in ocean waters off the California coast, apparently both within and without the three-mile coastal belt, and brought his fresh fish ashore for sale. In 1942, while this country was at war with Japan, Takahashi and other California residents of Japanese ancestry were evacuated from the State under military orders. In 1943, during the period of war and evacuation, an amendment to the California Fish and Game Code was adopted prohibiting issuance of a license to any "alien Japanese." In 1945, the state code was again amended by striking the 1943 provision for fear that it might be "declared unconstitutional" because directed only "against alien Japanese"; the new amendment banned issuance of licenses to any "person ineligible to citizenship," which classification included Japanese. Because of this state provision barring issuance of commercial fishing licenses to persons ineligible for citizenship under federal law, Takahashi, who met all other state requirements, was denied a license by the California Fish and Game Commission upon his return to California in 1945.

Takahashi brought this action for mandamus in the Superior Court of Los Angeles County, California, to compel the Commission to issue a license to him. That court granted the petition for mandamus. It held that lawful alien inhabitants of California, despite their ineligibility to citizenship, were entitled to engage in the vocation of commercial fishing on the high seas beyond the three-mile belt on the same terms as other lawful state inhabitants, and that the California code provision denying them this right violated the equal protection clause of the Fourteenth Amendment. The State Supreme Court, three judges dissenting, reversed, holding that California had a proprietary interest in fish in the ocean waters within three miles of the shore, and that this interest justified the State in barring all aliens in general and aliens ineligible to citizenship in particular from catching fish within or without the three-mile coastal belt and bringing them to California for commercial purposes. To review this question of importance in the fields of federal-state relationships and of constitutionally protected individual equality and liberty, we granted certiorari.

We may well begin our consideration of the principles to be applied in this case by a summary of this Court's holding in *Truax* v. *Raich,* not deemed controlling by the majority of the California Supreme Court, but regarded by the dissenters as requiring the invalidation of the California law. That case involved an attack upon an Arizona law which required all Arizona employers of more than five workers to hire not less than eighty (80) per cent qualified electors or native-born citizens of the United States. Raich, an alien who worked as a cook in a restaurant which had more than five employees, was about to lose his job solely because of the state law's coercive effect on the restaurant owner. This Court, in upholding Raich's contention that the Arizona law was invalid, declared that Raich, having been lawfully admitted into the country under federal law, had a federal privilege to enter and abide in "any State in the Union" and thereafter under the Fourteenth Amendment to enjoy the equal protection of the laws of the state in which he abided; that this privilege to enter in and abide in any state carried with it the "right to work for a living in the common occupations of the community," a denial of which right would make of the Amendment "a barren form of words." In answer to a contention that Arizona's restriction upon the employment of aliens was "reasonable" and therefore permissible, this Court declared:

"It must also be said that reasonable classification implies action consistent with the legitimate interests of the State, and it will not be disputed that these cannot be so broadly conceived as to bring them into hostility to exclusive Federal power. The authority to control immigration—to admit or exclude aliens—is vested solely in the Federal Government. The assertion of an authority to deny to aliens the opportunity of earning a livelihood when lawfully admitted to the State would be tantamount to the assertion of the right to deny them entrance and abode, for in ordinary cases they cannot live where they cannot work. And, if such a policy were permissible, the practical result would be that those lawfully admitted to the country under the authority of the acts of Congress, instead of enjoying in a substantial sense and in their full scope the privileges conferred by the admission, would be segregated in such of the States as chose to offer hospitality."

Had the *Truax* decision said nothing further than what is quoted above, its reasoning, if followed, would seem to require invalidation of this California code provision barring aliens from the occupation of fishing as inconsistent with federal law, which is constitutionally declared to be "the supreme Law of the Land." However, the Court there went on to note that it had on occasion sustained state legislation that did not apply alike to citizens and non-citizens, the ground for the distinction being that such laws were necessary to protect special interests either of the state or of its citizens as such. The *Truax* opinion pointed out that the Arizona law, aimed as it was against employment of aliens in *all* vocations, failed to show a "special public interest with respect to any particular business . . . that could possibly be deemed to support the enactment." The Court noted that it had previously upheld various state laws which restricted the privilege of planting oysters in the tidewater rivers of a state to citizens of that state, and which denied to aliens within a state the privilege of possessing a rifle and of shooting game within that state; it also referred to decisions recognizing a state's broad powers, in the absence of overriding treaties, to restrict the devolution of real property to non-aliens.

California now urges, and the State Supreme Court held, that the California fishing provision here challenged falls within the rationale of the "special public interest" cases distinguished in the *Truax* opinion, and thus that the state's ban upon commercial fishing by aliens ineligible to citizenship is valid. The contention is this: California owns the fish within three miles of its coast as a trustee for all California citizens as distinguished from its non-citizen inhabitants; as such trustee-owner, it has complete power to bar any or all aliens from fishing in the three-mile belt as a means of conserving the supply of fish; since migratory fish caught while swimming in the three-mile belt are indistinguishable from those caught while swimming in the adjacent high seas, the State, in order to enforce its three-mile control, can also regulate the catching and delivery to its coast of fish caught beyond the three-mile belt under this Court's decision in *Bayside Fish Co.* v. *Gentry*. Its law denying fishing licenses to aliens ineligible for citizenship, so the state's contention goes, tends to reduce the number of commercial fishermen and therefore is a proper fish conservation measure; in the exercise of its power to decide what groups will be denied licenses, the State has a right, if not a duty, to bar first of all aliens, who have no community interest in the fish owned by the State. Finally, the legislature's denial of licenses to those aliens who are "ineligible to citizenship" is defended as a reasonable classification, on the ground that California has simply followed the Federal Government's lead in adopting that classification from the naturalization laws.

First. The state's contention that its law was passed solely as a fish conservation measure is vigorously denied. The petitioner argues that it was the outgrowth of racial antagonism directed solely against the Japanese, and that for this reason alone it cannot stand. We find it unnecessary to resolve this controversy concerning the motives that prompted enactment of the legislation. Accordingly, for purposes of our decision we may assume that the code provision was passed to conserve fish in the California coastal waters, or to protect California citizens engaged in commercial fishing from competition by Japanese aliens, or for both reasons.

Second. It does not follow, as California seems to argue, that because the United States regulates immigration and naturalization in part on the basis of race and color classifications, a state can adopt one or more of the same classifications to prevent lawfully admitted aliens within its borders from earning a living in the same way that other state inhabitants earn their living. The Federal Government has broad constitutional powers in determining what aliens shall be admitted to the United States, the period they may remain, regulation of their conduct before naturalization, and the terms and conditions of their naturalization. Under the Constitution the states are granted no such powers; they can neither add to nor take from the conditions lawfully imposed by Congress upon admission, naturalization and residence of aliens in the United States or the several states. State laws which impose discriminatory burdens upon the entrance or residence of aliens lawfully within the United States conflict with this constitutionally derived federal power to regulate immigration, and have accordingly been held invalid. Moreover, Congress, in the enactment of a comprehensive legislative plan for the nation-wide control and regulation of immigration and naturalization, has broadly provided:

"All persons within the jurisdiction of the United States shall have the same right in every State and Territory to make and enforce contracts, to sue, be parties, give evidence, and to the full and equal benefit of all laws and proceedings for the security of persons and property as is enjoyed by white citizens, and shall be subject to like punishment, pains, penalties, taxes, licenses, and exactions of every kind, and to no other."

The protection of this section has been held to extend to aliens as well as to citizens. Consequently the section and the Fourteenth Amendment on which it rests in part protect "all persons" against state legislation bearing unequally upon them either because of alienage or color. The Fourteenth Amendment and the laws adopted under its authority thus embody a general policy that all persons lawfully in this country shall abide "in any state" on an equality of legal privileges with all citizens under non-discriminatory laws.

All of the foregoing emphasizes the tenuousness of the state's claim that it has power to single out and ban its lawful alien inhabitants, and particularly certain racial and color groups within this class of inhabitants, from following a vocation simply because Congress has put some such groups in special classifications in exercise of its broad and wholly distinguishable powers over immigration and naturalization. The state's law here cannot be supported in the employment of this legislative authority because of policies adopted by Congress in the exercise of its power to treat separately and differently with aliens from countries composed of peoples of many diverse cultures, races, and colors. For these reasons the power of a state to apply its laws exclusively to its alien inhabitants as a class is confined within narrow limits.

Third. We are unable to find that the "special public interest" on which California relies provides support for this state ban on Takahashi's commercial fishing. As before pointed out, California's claim of "special public interest" is that its citizens are the collective owners of fish swimming in the three-mile belt. It is true that this Court did long ago say that the citizens of a state collectively own "the tide-waters . . . and the fish in them, so far as they are capable of ownership while running." The *McCready* case upheld a Virginia law which prohibited citizens of other states from planting oysters in a Virginia tidewater river. Though the *McCready* case has been often distinguished, its rationale has been relied on in other cases, including *Geer* v. *Connecticut.* That decision, where only the commerce clause was involved, sustained a state law that, in order to restrict the use of game to the people of the state, prohibited the out-of-state transportation of game killed within the state. On the other hand, where Louisiana laws declared that the state owned all shrimp within the waters of the state, but permitted ultimate sale and shipment of shrimp for consumption outside that state's boundaries, Louisiana was denied power under the commerce clause to require the local processing of shrimp taken from Louisiana marshes as a prerequisite to out-of-state transportation. In the absence of overriding federal treaties, this Court sustained a state law barring aliens from hunting wild game in the interest of conserving game for citizens of the state against due process and equal protection challenges. Later, however, the Federal Migratory Bird Treaty Act of 1918 was sustained as within federal power despite the claim of Missouri of ownership of birds within its boundaries based on prior statements as to state ownership of game and fish in the *Geer* case. The Court was of opinion that "To put the claim of the State upon title is to lean upon a slender reed." We think that same statement is equally applicable here. To whatever extent the fish in the three-mile belt off California may be "capable of ownership" by California, we think that "ownership" is inadequate to justify California in excluding any or all aliens who are lawful residents of the State from making a living by fishing in the ocean off its shores while permitting all others to do so.

This leaves for consideration the argument that this law should be upheld on authority of those cases which have sustained state laws barring aliens ineligible to citizenship from land ownership. Assuming the continued validity of those cases, we think they could not in any event be controlling here. They rested solely upon the power of states to control the devolution and ownership of land within their borders, a power long exercised and supported on reasons peculiar to real property. They cannot be extended to cover this case.

The judgment is reversed and remanded for proceedings not inconsistent with this opinion.

Mr. Justice Murphy, with whom Mr. Justice Rutledge agrees, concurring.

The opinion of the Court, in which I join, adequately expresses my views as to all but one important aspect of this case. That aspect relates to the fact that § 990 of the California Fish and Game Code, barring those ineligible to citizenship from securing commercial fishing licenses, is the direct outgrowth of antagonism toward persons of Japanese ancestry. Even the most cursory examination of the background of the statute demonstrates that it was designed solely to discriminate against such persons in a manner inconsistent with the concept of equal protection of the laws. Legislation of that type is not entitled to wear the cloak of constitutionality.

The statute in question is but one more manifestation of the anti-Japanese fever which has been evident in California in varying degrees since the turn of the century. That fever, of course, is traceable to the refusal or the inability of certain groups to adjust themselves economically and socially relative to residents of Japanese ancestry. For some years prior to the Japanese attack on Pearl Harbor, these protagonists of intolerance had been leveling unfounded accusations and innuendoes against Japanese fishing crews operating off the coast of California. These fishermen numbered about a thousand and most of them had long resided in that state. It was claimed that they were engaged not only in fishing but in espionage and other illicit activities on behalf of the Japanese Government. As war with Japan approached and finally became a reality, these charges were repeated with increasing vigor. Yet full investigations by appropriate authorities failed to reveal any competent supporting evidence; not even one Japanese fisherman was arrested for alleged espionage. Such baseless accusations can only be viewed as an integral part of the long campaign to undermine the reputation of persons of Japanese background and to discourage their residence in California.

More specifically, these accusations were used to secure the passage of discriminatory fishing legislation. But such legislation was not immediately forthcoming. The continued presence in California of the Japanese fishermen without the occurrence of any untoward incidents on their part served for a time as adequate and living refutation of the propaganda. Then came the evacuation of all persons of Japanese ancestry from the West Coast. Once evacuation was achieved, an intensive campaign was begun to prevent the return to California of the evacuees. All of the old charges, including the ones relating to the fishermen, were refurbished and augmented. This time the Japanese were absent and were unable to provide effective opposition. The winds of racial animosity blew unabated.

During the height of this racial storm in 1943, numerous anti-Japanese bills were considered by the California legislators. Several amendments to the Alien Land Law were enacted. And § 990 of the Fish and Game Code was altered to provide that "A commercial fishing license may be issued to any person other than an alien Japanese." No pretense was made that this alteration was in the interests of conservation. It was made at a time when all alien Japanese were excluded from California, with no immediate return indicated; thus the banning of fishing licenses for them could have no early effect upon the conservation of fish. Moreover, the period during which this amendment was passed was one in which both federal and state authorities were doing their utmost to encourage greater food production for wartime purposes. The main desire at this time was to increase rather than to decrease the catch of fish. Certainly the contemporaneous bulletins and reports of the Bureau of Marine Fisheries of California did not indicate the existence of any conservation problem due to an excess number of fishermen.

These circumstances only confirm the obvious fact that the 1943 amendment to § 990 was intended to discourage the return to California of Japanese aliens. By taking away their commercial fishing rights, the lives of those aliens who plied the fisherman's trade would be made more difficult and unremunerative. And the non-Japanese fishermen would thereby be free from the competition afforded by these aliens. The equal protection clause of the Fourteenth Amendment, however, does not permit a state to discriminate against resident aliens in such a fashion, whether the purpose be to give effect to racial animosity or to protect the competitive interests of other residents.

The 1945 amendment to § 990 which is now before us stands in no better position than the 1943 amendment. This later alteration eliminated the reference to "alien Japanese" and substituted therefor "a person ineligible to citizenship." Adoption of this change also occurred during a period when anti-Japanese agitation in California had reached one of its periodic peaks. The announcement of the end of the Japanese exclusion orders, plus this Court's decision in *Ex parte Endo,* made the return to California of many of the evacuees a reasonable certainty. The prejudices, the antagonisms and the hatreds were once again aroused, punctuated this time by numerous acts of violence against the returning Japanese Americans. Another wave of anti-Japanese proposals marked the 1945 legislative session. It was in this setting that the amendment to § 990 was proposed and enacted in 1945.

It is of interest and significance that the amendment in question was proposed by a legislative committee devoted to Japanese resettlement problems, not by a committee concerned with the conservation of fish. The Senate Fact-Finding Committee on Japanese Resettlement issued a report on May 1, 1945. This report dealt with such matters as the Alien Land Law, the Japanese language schools, dual citizenship and the Tule Lake riot. And under the heading "Japanese Fishing Boats" appeared this explanation of the proposed amendment to § 990:

"The committee gave little consideration to the problems of the use of fishing vessels on our coast owned and operated by Japanese, since this matter seems to have previously been covered by legislation. The committee, however, feels that there is danger of the present statute being declared unconstitutional, on the grounds of discrimination, since it is directed against alien Japanese. It is believed that this legal question can probably be eliminated by an amendment which has been proposed to the bill which would make it apply to any alien who is ineligible to citizenship. The committee has introduced Senate Bill 413 to make this change in the statute."

Not a word was said in this report regarding the need for the conservation of fish or the necessity of limiting the number of fishermen. The obvious thought behind the amendment was to attempt to legalize the discrimination against Japanese alien fishermen by dropping the specific reference to them.

The proposed revision was adopted. The trial court below correctly described the situation as follows: "As it was commonly known to the legislators of 1945 that Japanese were the only aliens ineligible to citizenship who engaged in commercial fishing in ocean waters bordering on California, and as the Court must take judicial notice of the same fact, it becomes manifest that in enacting the present version of Section 990, the Legislature intended thereby to eliminate alien Japanese from those entitled to a commercial fishing license by means of description rather than by name. To all intents and purposes and in effect the provision in the 1943 and 1945 amendments are the same, the thin veil used to conceal a purpose being too transparent. Under each and both, alien Japanese are denied a right to a license to catch fish on the high seas for profit, and to bring them to shore for the purpose of selling the same in a fresh state . . . this discrimination constitutes an unequal exaction and a greater burden upon the persons of the class named than that imposed upon others in the same calling and under the same conditions, and amounts to prohibition. This discrimination, patently hostile, is not based upon a reasonable ground of classification and, to that extent, the section is in violation of Section 1 of the Fourteenth Amendment to the Constitution of the United States, ..."

We should not blink at the fact that § 990, as now written, is a discriminatory piece of legislation having no relation whatever to any constitutionally cognizable interest of California. It was drawn against a background of racial and economic tension. It is directed in spirit and in effect solely against aliens of Japanese birth. It denies them commercial fishing rights not because they threaten the success of any conservation program, not because their fishing activities constitute a clear and present danger to the welfare of California or of the nation, but only because they are of Japanese stock, a stock which has had the misfortune to arouse antagonism among certain powerful interests. We need but unbutton the seemingly innocent words of § 990 to discover beneath them the very negation of all the ideals of the equal protection clause. No more is necessary to warrant a reversal of the judgment below.

Mr. Justice Reed, dissenting.

The reasons which lead me to conclude that the judgment of the Supreme Court of California should be affirmed may be briefly stated. As fishing rights have been treated traditionally as a natural resource, in the absence of federal regulation, California as a sovereign state has power to regulate the taking and handling of fish in the waters bordering its shores. It is, I think, one of the natural resources of the state that may be preserved from exploitation by aliens. The ground for this power in the absence of any exercise of federal authority is California's authority over its fisheries.

The right to fish is analogous to the right to own land, a privilege which a state may deny to aliens as to land within its borders. It is closely akin to the right to hunt, a privilege from which a state may bar aliens, if reasonably deemed advantageous to its citizens. A state's power has even been held to extend to the exclusion of aliens from the operation of pool and billiard halls when a city deemed them not as well qualified as citizens for the conduct of a business thought to have harmful tendencies.

The Federal Government has not pursued a policy of equal treatment of aliens and citizens. Citizens have rights superior to those of aliens in the ownership of land and in exploiting natural resources. Perhaps Congress as a matter of immigration policy may require that states open every door of opportunity in America to all resident aliens, but until Congress so determines as to fisheries, I do not feel that the judicial arm of the Government should require the states to admit all aliens to this privilege.

Certainly *Truax* v. *Raich,* upon which the majority opinion appears to rely in holding that the California statute denies equal protection in attempting to classify aliens by putting restrictions on their right to land fish, is not an authority for such a decision. The power of a state to discriminate against aliens on public works and the exploitation of natural resources was recognized in that case. And, at the very time that it was under consideration, this Court also had before it *Heim* v. *McCall.* In that case, Heim attacked the constitutionality of a New York statute which provided that "In the construction of public works by the State or a municipality, or by persons contracting with the state or such municipality, only citizens of the United States shall be employed; and in all cases where laborers are employed on any such public works, preference shall be given citizens of the State of New York." A unanimous court held that the statute, which was attacked on the ground that it denied aliens their rights under the privileges and immunities, due process, and equal protection clauses of the Constitution, was a constitutional exercise of state power as applied to the construction of New York City subways by private contractors. The Constitution that permits the bar of aliens from public works surely must permit their bar from state fishing rights. A state has power to exclude from enjoyment of its natural resources those who are unwilling or unable to become citizens.

If aliens, as I think they can, may be excluded by a state from fishing privileges, I see no reason why the classification established by California excluding only aliens ineligible to citizenship is prohibited by the Constitution. Whatever we may think of the wisdom of California's statute, we should intervene only when we conclude the state statute passes constitutional limits.

Mr. Justice Jackson joins in this dissent.

Hughes v. Superior Court of California
339 U. S. 460   1950

Mr. Justice Frankfurter delivered the opinion of the Court.

Does the Fourteenth Amendment of the Constitution bar a State from use of the injunction to prohibit picketing of a place of business solely in order to secure compliance with a demand that its employees be in proportion to the racial origin of its then customers? Such is the broad question of this case.

The petitioners, acting on behalf of a group calling themselves Progressive Citizens of America, demanded of Lucky Stores, Inc., that it hire Negroes at its grocery store near the Canal Housing Project in Richmond, California, as white clerks quit or were transferred, until the proportion of Negro clerks to white clerks approximated the proportion of Negro to white customers. At the time in controversy about 50% of the customers of the Canal store were Negroes. Upon refusal of this demand and in order to compel compliance, the Canal store was systematically patrolled by pickets carrying placards stating that Lucky refused to hire Negro clerks in proportion to Negro customers.

Suit was begun by Lucky to enjoin the picketing on appropriate allegations for equitable relief. The Superior Court of Contra Costa County issued a preliminary injunction restraining petitioners and others from picketing any of Lucky's stores to compel "the selective hiring of negro clerks, such hiring to be based on the proportion of white and negro customers who patronize plaintiff's stores." In the face of this injunction, petitioners continued to picket the Canal store, carrying placards reading: "Lucky Won't Hire Negro Clerks in Proportion to Negro Trade—Don't Patronize." In conformity with State procedure, petitioners were found guilty of contempt for "wilfully disregarding" the injunction and were sentenced to imprisonment for two days and fined $20 each. They defended their conduct by challenging the injunction as a deprivation of the liberty assured them by the Due Process Clause of the Fourteenth Amendment. The intermediate appellate court annulled the judgment of contempt but it was reinstated on review by the Supreme Court of California. That court held that the conceded purpose of the picketing in this case—to compel the hiring of Negroes in proportion to Negro customers—was unlawful even though pursued in a peaceful manner. Having violated a valid injunction petitioners were properly punishable for contempt. "The controlling points," according to the decision of the Supreme Court of California, "are that the injunction is limited to prohibiting picketing for a specific unlawful purpose and that the evidence justified the trial court in finding that such narrow prohibition was deliberately violated." We brought the case here to consider claims of infringement of the right of freedom of speech as guaranteed by the Due Process Clause of the Fourteenth Amendment.

First. Discrimination against Negroes in employment has brought a variety of legal issues before this Court in recent years. Such discrimination raises sociological problems which in some aspects and within limits have received legal solutions. California has been sensitive to these problems and decisions of its Supreme Court have been hostile to discrimination on the basis of color. This background of California's legal policy is relevant to the conviction of its court that it would encourage discriminatory hiring to give constitutional protection to petitioners' efforts to subject the opportunity of getting a job to a quota system. The view of that court is best expressed in its own words:

"It was just such a situation—an arbitrary discrimination upon the basis of race and color alone, rather than a choice based solely upon individual quali-fication for the work to be done—which we condemned in the Marinship case. The fact that those seeking such discrimination do not demand that it be practiced as to all employes of a particular employer diminishes in no respect the unlawfulness of their purpose; they would, to the extent of the fixed proportion, make the right to work for Lucky dependent not on fitness for the work nor on an equal right of all, regardless of race, to compete in an open market, but, rather, on membership in a particular race. If petitioners were upheld in their demand then other races, white, yellow, brown and red, would have equal rights to demand discriminatory hiring on a racial basis. Yet that is precisely the type of discrimination to which petitioners avowedly object."

These considerations are most pertinent in regard to a population made up of so many diverse groups as ours. To deny to California the right to ban picketing in the circumstances of this case would mean that there could be no prohibition of the pressure of picketing to secure proportional employment on ancestral grounds of Hungarians in Cleveland, of Poles in Buffalo, of Germans in Milwaukee, of Portuguese in New Bedford, of Mexicans in San Antonio, of the numerous minority groups in New York, and so on through the whole gamut of racial and religious concentrations in various cities. States may well believe that such constitutional sheltering would inevitably encourage use of picketing to compel employment on the basis of racial discrimination. In disallowing such picketing States may act under the belief that otherwise community tensions and conflicts would be exacerbated. The differences in cultural traditions instead of adding flavor and variety to our common citizenry might well be hardened into hostilities by leave of law. The Constitution does not demand that the element of communication in picketing prevail over the mischief furthered by its use in these situations.

Second. "[T]he domain of liberty, withdrawn by the Fourteenth Amendment from encroachment by the states" no doubt includes liberty of thought and appropriate means for expressing it. But while picketing is a mode of communication it is inseparably something more and different. Industrial picketing "is more than free speech, since it involves patrol of a particular locality and since the very presence of a picket line may induce action of one kind or another, quite irrespective of the nature of the ideas which are being disseminated." Mr. Justice Douglas, joined by Black and Murphy, JJ., concurring in *Bakery & Pastry Drivers & Helpers Local v. Wohl.* Publication in a newspaper, or by distribution of circulars, may convey the same information or make the same charge as do those patrolling a picket line. But the very purpose of a picket line is to exert influences, and it produces consequences, different from other modes of communication. The loyalties and responses evoked and exacted by picket lines are unlike those flowing from appeals by printed word.

Third. A State may constitutionally permit picketing despite the ingredients in it that differentiate it from speech in its ordinary context. And we have found that because of its element of communication picketing under some circumstances finds sanction in the Fourteenth Amendment. However general or loose the language of opinions, the specific situations have controlled decision. It has been amply recognized that picketing, not being the equivalent of speech as a matter of fact, is not its inevitable legal equivalent. Picketing is not beyond the control of a State if the manner in which picketing is conducted or the purpose which it seeks to effectuate gives ground for its disallowance. "A state is not required to tolerate in all places and all circumstances even peaceful picketing by an individual.

The constitutional boundary line between the competing interests of society involved in the use of picketing cannot be established by general phrases. Picketing when not in numbers that of themselves carry a threat of violence may be a lawful means to a lawful end. The California Supreme Court suggested a distinction between picketing to promote discrimination, as here, and picketing against discrimination: "It may be assumed for the purposes of this decision, without deciding, that if such discrimination exists, picketing to protest it would not be for an unlawful objective." We cannot construe the Due Process Clause as precluding California from securing respect for its policy against involuntary employment on racial lines by prohibiting systematic picketing that would subvert such policy.

Fourth. The fact that California's policy is expressed by the judicial organ of the State rather than by the legislature we have repeatedly ruled to be immaterial. For the Fourteenth Amendment leaves the States free to distribute the powers of government as they will between their legislative and judicial branches. "[R]ights under that amendment turn on the power of the State, no matter by what organ it acts."

It is not for this Court to deny to a State the right, or even to question the desirability, of fitting its law "to a concrete situation through the authority given . . . to its courts." It is particularly important to bear this in mind in regard to matters affecting industrial relations which, until recently, have "been left largely to judicial lawmaking and not to legislation." In charging its courts with evolving law instead of formulating policy by statute, California has availed itself of the variety of law-making sources, and has recognized that in our day as in Coke's "the law hath provided several weapons of remedy." California chose to strike at the discrimination inherent in the quota system by means of the equitable remedy of injunction to protect against unwilling submission to such a system. It is not for this Court to deny to California that choice from among all "the various weapons in the armory of the law."

The policy of a State may rely for the common good on the free play of conflicting interests and leave conduct unregulated. Contrariwise, a State may deem it wiser policy to regulate. Regulation may take the form of legislation, *e.g.*, restraint of trade statutes, or be left to the *ad hoc* judicial process, *e.g.*, common law mode of dealing with restraints of trade. Either method may outlaw an end not in the public interest or merely address itself to the obvious means toward such end. The form the regulation should take and its scope are surely matters of policy and, as such, within a State's choice.

If because of the compulsive features inherent in picketing, beyond the aspect of mere communication as an appeal to reason, a State chooses to enjoin picketing to secure submission to a demand for employment proportional to the racial origin of the then customers of a business, it need not forbid the employer to adopt such a quota system of his own free will. A State is not required to exercise its intervention on the basis of abstract reasoning. The Constitution commands neither logical symmetry nor exhaustion of a principle. "The problems of government are practical ones and may justify, if they do not require, rough accommodations—illogical, it may be, and unscientific." A State may "direct its law against what it deems the evil as it actually exists without covering the whole field of possible abuses, and it may do so none the less that the forbidden act does not differ in kind from those that are allowed." Lawmaking is essentially empirical and tentative, and in adjudication as in legislation the Constitution does not forbid "cautious advance, step by step, and the distrust of generalities."

The injunction here was drawn to meet what California deemed the evil of picketing to bring about proportional hiring. We do not go beyond the circumstances of the case. Generalizations are treacherous in the application of large constitutional concepts.

Affirmed.

Mr. Justice Black and Mr. Justice Minton are of the opinion that this case is controlled by the principles announced in *Giboney* v. *Empire Storage & Ice Co.* and therefore concur in the Court's judgment.

Mr. Justice Reed, concurring.

I read the opinion of the Supreme Court of California to hold that the pickets sought from Lucky Stores, Inc., discrimination in favor of persons of the Negro race, a discrimination unlawful under California law. Such picketing may be barred by a State.

Mr. Justice Douglas took no part in the consideration or decision of this case.

Railroad Trainmen v. Howard
343 U. S. 768   1951

Mr. Justice Black delivered the opinion of the Court.

This case raises questions concerning the power of courts to protect Negro railroad employees from loss of their jobs under compulsion of a bargaining agreement which, to avoid a strike, the railroad made with an exclusively white man's union. Respondent Simon Howard, a Frisco train employee for nearly forty years, brought this action on behalf of himself and other colored employees similarly situated.

In summary the complaint alleged: Negro employees such as respondent constituted a group called "train porters" although they actually performed all the duties of white "brakemen"; the Brotherhood of Railroad Trainmen, bargaining representative of "brakemen" under the Railway Labor Act, had for years used its influence in an attempt to eliminate Negro trainmen and get their jobs for white men who, unlike colored "train porters," were or could be members of the Brotherhood; on March 7, 1946, the Brotherhood finally forced the Frisco to agree to discharge the colored "train porters" and fill their jobs with white men who, under the agreement, would do less work but get more pay. The complaint charged that the Brotherhood's "discriminatory action" violated the train porters' rights under the Railway Labor Act and under the

Constitution; that the agreement was void because against public policy, prejudicial to the public interest, and designed to deprive Negro trainmen of their right to earn a livelihood because of their race or color. The prayers were that the court adjudge and decree that the contract was void and unenforceable for the reasons stated; that the Railroad be "enjoined from discontinuing the jobs known as Train Porters" and "from hiring white Brakemen to replace or displace plaintiff and other Train Porters as planned in accordance with said agreement."

The facts as found by the District Court, affirmed with emphasis by the Court of Appeals, substantially established the truth of the complaint's material allegations. These facts showed that the Negro train porters had for a great many years served the Railroad with loyalty, integrity and efficiency; that "train porters" do all the work of brakemen; that the Government administrator of railroads during World War I had classified them as brakemen and had required that they be paid just like white brakemen; that when the railroads went back to their owners, they redesignated these colored brakemen as "train porters," "left their duties untouched," and forced them to accept wages far below those of white "brakemen" who were Brotherhood members; that for more than a quarter of a century the Brotherhood and other exclusively white rail unions had continually carried on a program of aggressive hostility to employment of Negroes for train, engine and yard service; that the agreement of March 7, 1946, here under attack, provides that train porters shall no longer do any work "generally recognized as brakeman's duties"; that while this agreement did not in express words compel discharge of "train porters," the economic unsoundness of keeping them after transfer of their "brakemen" functions made complete abolition of the "train porter" group inevitable; that two days after "the Carriers reluctantly, and as a result of the strike threats" signed the agreement, they notified train porters that "Under this agreement we will, effective April 1, 1946, discontinue all train porter positions." Accordingly, respondent Howard, and others, were personally notified to turn in their switch keys, lanterns, markers and other brakemen's equipment, and notices of job vacancies were posted to be bid in by white brakemen only.

The District Court held that the complaint raised questions which Congress by the Railway Labor Act had made subject to the exclusive jurisdiction of the National Mediation Board and the National Railroad Adjustment Board. The Court of Appeals reversed this holding. It held that the agreement, as construed and acted upon by the Railroad, was an "attempted predatory appropriation" of the "train porters'" jobs, and was to this extent illegal and unenforceable. It therefore ordered that the Railroad must keep the "train porters" as employees; it permitted the Railroad and the Brotherhood to treat the contract as valid on condition that the Railroad would recognize the colored "train porters" as members of the craft of "brakemen" and that the Brotherhood would fairly represent them as such. We granted certiorari.

While different in some respects, the basic pattern of racial discrimination in this case is much the same as that we had to consider in *Steele v. L. & N.R. Co.* In this case, as was charged in the *Steele* case, a Brotherhood acting as a bargaining agent under the Railway Labor Act has been hostile to Negro employees, has discriminated against them, and has forced the Railroad to make a contract which would help Brotherhood members take over the jobs of the colored "train porters."

There is a difference in the circumstances of the two cases, however, which it is contended requires us to deny the judicial remedy here that was accorded in the *Steele* case. That difference is this: Steele was admittedly a locomotive fireman although not a member of the Brotherhood of Locomotive Firemen and Enginemen which under the Railway Labor Act was the exclusive bargaining representative of the entire craft of firemen. We held that the language of the Act imposed a duty on the craft bargaining representative to exercise the power conferred upon it in behalf of all those for whom it acts, without hostile discrimination against any of them. Failure to exercise this duty was held to give rise to a cause of action under the Act. In this case, unlike the *Steele* case, the colored employees have for many years been treated by the carriers and the Brotherhood as a separate class for representation purposes and have in fact been represented by another union of their own choosing. Since the Brotherhood has discriminated against "train porters" instead of minority members of its own "craft," it is argued that the Brotherhood owed no duty at all to refrain from using its statutory bargaining power so as to abolish the jobs of the colored porters and drive them from the railroads. We think this argument is unsound and that the opinion in the *Steele* case points to a breach of statutory duty by this Brotherhood.

As previously noted, these train porters are threatened with loss of their jobs because they are not white and for no other reason. The job they did hold under its old name would be abolished by the agreement;

their color alone would disqualify them for the old job under its new name. The end result of these transactions is not in doubt; for precisely the same reasons as in the *Steele* case "discriminations based on race alone are obviously irrelevant and invidious. Congress plainly did not undertake to authorize the bargaining representative to make such discriminations." The Federal Act thus prohibits bargaining agents it authorizes from using their position and power to destroy colored workers' jobs in order to bestow them on white workers. And courts can protect those threatened by such an unlawful use of power granted by a federal act.

Here, as in the *Steele* case, colored workers must look to a judicial remedy to prevent the sacrifice or obliteration of their rights under the Act. For no adequate administrative remedy can be afforded by the National Railroad Adjustment or Mediation Board. The claims here cannot be resolved by interpretation of a bargaining agreement so as to give jurisdiction to the Adjustment Board under our holding in *Slocum v. Delaware, L. & W. R. Co.* This dispute involves the validity of the contract, not its meaning. Nor does the dispute hinge on the proper craft classification of the porters so as to call for settlement by the National Mediation Board under our holding in *Switchmen's Union v. National Mediation Board.* For the contention here with which we agree is that the racial discrimination practiced is unlawful, whether colored employees are classified as "train porters," "brakemen," or something else. Our conclusion is that the District Court has jurisdiction and power to issue necessary injunctive orders notwithstanding the provisions of the Norris-LaGuardia Act. We need add nothing to what was said about inapplicability of that Act in the *Steele* case and in *Graham v. Brotherhood of Firemen.*

Bargaining agents who enjoy the advantages of the Railway Labor Act's provisions must execute their trust without lawless invasions of the rights of other workers. We agree with the Court of Appeals that the District Court had jurisdiction to protect these workers from the racial discrimination practiced against them. On remand, the District Court should permanently enjoin the Railroad and the Brotherhood from use of the contract or any other similar discriminatory bargaining device to oust the train porters from their jobs. In fashioning its decree the District Court is left free to consider what provisions are necessary to afford these employees full protection from future discriminatory practices of the Brotherhood. However, in drawing its decree, the District Court must bear in mind that *disputed* questions of reclassification of the craft of "train porters" are committed by the Railway Labor Act to the National Mediation Board.

The judgment of the Court of Appeals reversing that of the District Court is affirmed, and the cause is remanded to the District Court for further proceedings in accordance with this opinion.

Mr. Justice Minton, with whom The Chief Justice and Mr. Justice Reed join, dissenting.

The right of the Brotherhood to represent railroad employees existed before the Railway Labor Act was passed. The Act simply protects the employees when this right of representation is exercised. If a labor organization is designated by a majority of the employees in a craft or class as bargaining representative for that craft or class and is so recognized by the carrier, that labor organization has a duty to represent in good faith all workers of the craft. In the *Steele* case, the complainant was a locomotive fireman; his duties were wholly those of a fireman. The Brotherhood in that case represented the "firemen's craft," but would not admit Steele as a member because he was a Negro. As the legal representative of his craft of firemen, the Brotherhood made a contract with the carrier that discriminated against him because of his race. This Court held the contract invalid. It would have been the same if the Brotherhood had discriminated against him on some other ground, unrelated to race. It was the Brotherhood's duty "to act on behalf of all the employees which, by virtue of the statute, it undertakes to represent."

In the instant case the Brotherhood has never purported to represent the train porters. The train porters have never requested that the Brotherhood represent them. Classification of the job of "train porter" was established more than forty years ago and has never been disputed. At that time, the principal duties of the train porters were cleaning the cars, assisting the passengers, and helping to load and unload baggage; only a small part of the duties were those of brakemen, who were required to have higher educational qualifications. As early as 1921, the train porters organized a separate bargaining unit through which they have continuously bargained with the carrier here involved; they now have an existing contract with this carrier. Although the carriers gradually imposed upon the train porters more of the duties of brakemen until today most of their duties are those of brakemen, they have never been classified as brakemen.

The majority does not say that the train porters are brakemen and therefore the Brotherhood must represent them fairly, as was held in *Steele*. Whether they belong to the Brotherhood is not determinative of the latter's duties of representation, if it represents the craft of brakemen and if the train porters are brakemen. Steele was not a member of the Brotherhood of Locomotive Firemen and Enginemen and could not be because of race—the same reason that the train porters cannot belong to the Brotherhood of Trainmen. But Steele was a fireman, while the train porters are not brakemen.

The Brotherhood stoutly oppose the contention that it is the representative of the train porters. For the Court so to hold would be to fly in the face of the statute and the holding of this Court in *General Committee* v. *Missouri-K.-T. R. Co.* The majority avoids the dispute in terms but embraces it in fact by saying it is passing on the validity of the contract. If this is true, it is done at the instance of persons for whom the Brotherhood was not contracting and was under no duty to contract. The train porters had a duly elected bargaining representative, which fact operated to exclude the Brotherhood from representing the craft.

The majority reaches out to invalidate the contract, not because the train porters are brakemen entitled to fair representation by the Brotherhood, but because they are Negroes who were discriminated against by the carrier at the behest of the Brotherhood. I do not understand that private parties such as the carrier and the Brotherhood may not discriminate on the ground of race. Neither a state government nor the Federal Government may do so, but I know of no applicable federal law which says that private parties may not. That is the whole problem underlying the proposed Federal Fair Employment Practices Code. Of course, this Court by sheer power can say this case is *Steele,* or even lay down a code of fair employment practices. But sheer power is not a substitute for legality. I do not have to agree with the discrimination here indulged in to question the legality of today's decision.

I think there was a dispute here between employees of the carrier as to whether the Brotherhood was the representative of the train porters, and that this is a matter to be resolved by the National Mediation Board, not the courts. I would remand this case to the District Court to be dismissed as nonjusticiable.

Part VI

RESTRICTIVE COVENANTS

Buchanan v. Warley

Corrigan v. Buckley

Shelley v. Kraemer

Hurd v. Hodge

Barrows v. Jackson

These cases, dealing with restrictive covenants, raise some difficult questions about "state action" and "private action."

Buchanan v. Warley

245 U. S. 60   1917

Mr. Justice Day delivered the opinion of the court.

. . . We pass, then, to a consideration of the case upon its merits. This ordinance prevents the occupancy of a lot in the city of Louisville by a person of color in a block where the greater number of residences are occupied by white persons; where such a majority exists, colored persons are excluded. This interdiction is based wholly upon color; simply that, and nothing more. In effect, premises situated as are those in question in the so-called white block are effectively debarred from sale to persons of color, because, if sold, they cannot be occupied by the purchaser nor by him sold to another of the same color.

This drastic measure is sought to be justified under the authority of the state in the exercise of the police power. It is said such legislation tends to promote the public peace by preventing racial conflicts; that it tends to maintain racial purity; that it prevents the deterioration of property owned and occupied by white people, which deterioration, it is contended, is sure to follow the occupancy of adjacent premises by persons of color.

The authority of the state to pass laws in the exercise of the police power, having for their object the promotion of the public health, safety, and welfare, is very broad, as has been affirmed in numerous and recent decisions of this court. Furthermore, the exercise of this power, embracing nearly all legislation of a local character, is not to be interfered with by the courts where it is within the scope of legislative authority and the means adopted reasonably tend to accomplish a lawful purpose. But it is equally well established that the police power, broad as it is, cannot justify the passage of a law or ordinance which runs counter to the limitations of the Federal Constitution; that principle has been so frequently affirmed in this court that we need not stop to cite the cases.

The Federal Constitution and laws passed within its authority are, by the express terms of that instrument, made the supreme law of the land. The 14th Amendment protects life, liberty, and property from invasion by the states without due process of law. Property is more than the mere thing which a person owns. It is elementary that it includes the right to acquire, use, and dispose of it. The Constitution protects these essential attributes of property. Property consists of the free use, enjoyment, and disposal of a person's acquisitions without control or diminution save by the law of the land.

True it is that dominion over property springing from ownership is not absolute and unqualified. The disposition and use of property may be controlled, in the exercise of the police power, in the interest of the public health, convenience, or welfare. Harmful occupations may be controlled and regulated. Legitimate business may also be regulated in the interest of the public. Certain uses of property may be confined to portions of the municipality other than the residence district, such as livery stables, brickyards, and the like, because of the impairment of the health and comfort of the occupants of neighboring property. Many illustrations might be given from the decisions of this court and other courts, of this principle, but these cases do not touch the one at bar.

The concrete question here is: May the occupancy, and, necessarily, the purchase and sale of property of which occupancy is an incident, be inhibited by the states, or by one of its municipalities, solely because of the color of the proposed occupant of the premises? That one may dispose of his property, subject only to the control of lawful enactments curtailing that right in the public interest, must be conceded. The question now presented makes it pertinent to inquire into the constitutional right of the white man to sell his property to a colored man, having in view the legal status of the purchaser and occupant.

Following the Civil War certain amendments to the Federal Constitution were adopted, which have become an integral part of that instrument, equally binding upon all the states and fixing certain fundamental rights which all are bound to respect. The 13th Amendment abolished slavery in the United States and in all places subject to their jurisdiction, and gave Congress power to enforce the Amendment by appropriate legislation. The 14th Amendment made all persons born or naturalized in the United States, citizens of the United States and of the states in which they reside, and provided that no state shall make or enforce any law which shall abridge the privileges or immunities of citizens of the United States, and that no state shall deprive any person of life, liberty, or property without due process of law, nor deny to any person the equal protection of the laws.

The effect of these Amendments was first dealt with by this court in Slaughter-House Cases. The reasons for the adoption of the Amendments were elaborately considered by a court familiar with the times in which the necessity for the Amendments arose and with the circumstances which impelled their adoption. In that case Mr. Justice Miller, who spoke for the majority, pointed out that the colored race, having been freed from slavery by the 13th Amendment, was raised to the dignity of citizenship and equality of civil rights by the 14th Amendment, and the states were prohibited from abridging the privileges and immunities of such citizens, or depriving any person of life, liberty, or property without due process of law. While a principal purpose of the latter Amendment was to protect persons of color, the broad language used was deemed sufficient to protect all persons, white or black, against discriminatory legislation by the states. This is now the settled law. In many of the cases since arising the question of color has not been involved, and the cases have been decided upon alleged violations of civil or property rights, irrespective of the race or color of the complainant. In Slaughter-House Cases it was recognized that the chief inducement to the passage of the Amendment was the desire to extend Federal protection to the recently emancipated race from unfriendly and discriminating legislation by the states.

In Strauder, v. West Virginia this court held that a colored person charged with an offense was denied due process of law by a statute which prevented colored men from sitting on the jury which tried him. Mr. Justice Strong, speaking for the court, again reviewed the history of the Amendments, and, among other things, in speaking of the 14th Amendment, said:

"It [the 14th Amendment] was designed to assure to the colored race the enjoyment of all the civil rights that, under the law, are enjoyed by white persons, and to give to that race the protection of the general government in that enjoyment, whenever it should be denied by the states. It not only gave citizenship and privileges of citizenship to persons of color, but it denied to any state the power to withhold from them the equal protection of the laws, and authorized Congress to enforce its provisions by appropriate legislation. . . . It ordains that no state shall make or enforce any laws which shall abridge the privileges or immunities of citizens of the United States. . . . It ordains that no state shall deprive any person of life, liberty, or property without due process of law, or deny to any person within its jurisdiction the equal protection of the laws.

"What is this but declaring that the law in the states shall be the same for the black as for the white—that all persons, whether colored or white, shall stand equal before the laws of the states, and, in regard to the colored race, for whose protection the Amendment was primarily designed, that no discrimination shall be made against them by law because of their color? . . .

"The 14th Amendment makes no attempt to enumerate the rights it designs to protect. It speaks in general terms and those are as comprehensive as possible. Its language is prohibitory; but every prohibition implies the existence of rights and immunities, prominent among which is an immunity from inequality of legal protection either for life, liberty, or property. Any state action that denies this immunity to a colored man is in conflict with the Constitution."

Again, this court in Ex parte Virginia, speaking of the 14th Amendment, said:

"Whoever, by virtue of public position under a state government, deprives another of property, life, or liberty, without due process of law, or denies or takes away the equal protection of the laws, violates the constitutional inhibition; and as he acts in the name and for the state and is clothed with the state's power, his act is that of the state."

In giving legislative aid to these constitutional provisions Congress enacted in 1866 that:

"All citizens of the United States shall have the same right in every state and territory, as is enjoyed by white citizens thereof to inherit, purchase, lease, sell, hold, and convey real and personal property."

And in 1870 that:

"All persons within the jurisdiction of the United States shall have the same right in every state and territory to make and enforce contracts, to sue, be parties, give evidence, and to the full and equal benefit of all laws and proceedings for the security of persons and property as is enjoyed by white citizens, and shall be subject to like punishment, pains, penalties, taxes, licenses and exactions of every kind, and no other."

In the face of these constitutional and statutory provisions, can a white man be denied, consistently with due process of law, the right to dispose of his property to a purchaser by prohibiting the occupation of it for the sole reason that the purchaser is a person of color, intending to occupy the premises as a place of residence?

The statute of 1866, originally passed under sanction of the 13th Amendment, and practically re-enacted after the adoption of the 14th Amendment, expressly provided that all citizens of the United States in any state shall have the same right to purchase property as is enjoyed by white citizens. Colored persons are citizens of the United States and have the right to purchase property and enjoy and use the same without laws discriminating against them solely on account of color. These enactments did not deal with the social rights of men, but with those fundamental rights in property which it was intended to secure upon the same terms to citizens of every race and color. The 14th Amendment and these statutes enacted in furtherance of its purpose operate to qualify and entitle a colored man to acquire property without state legislation discriminating against him solely because of color.

The defendant in error insists that Plessy v. Ferguson is controlling in principle in favor of the judgment of the court below. In that case this court held that a provision of a statute of Louisiana requiring railway companies carrying passengers to provide in their coaches equal but separate accommodations for the white and colored races did not run counter to the provisions of the 14th Amendment. It is to be observed that in that case there was no attempt to deprive persons of color of transportation in the coaches of the public carrier, and the express requirements were for equal though separate accommodations for the white and colored races. In Plessy v. Ferguson, classification of accommodations was permitted upon the basis of equality for both races.

In the Berea College Case a state statute was sustained in the courts of Kentucky, which, while permitting the education of white persons and negroes in different localities by the same incorporated institution, prohibited their attendance at the same place, and in this court the judgment of the court of appeals of Kentucky was affirmed solely upon the reserved authority of the legislature of Kentucky to alter, amend, or repeal charters of its own corporations, and the question here involved was neither discussed nor decided.

In Carey v. Atlanta the supreme court of Georgia, holding an ordinance, similar in principle to the one herein involved, to be invalid, dealt with Plessy v. Ferguson and the Berea College Case in language so apposite that we quote a portion of it:

"In each instance the complaining person was afforded the opportunity to ride, or to attend institutions of learning, or afforded the thing of whatever nature to which in the particular case he was entitled. The most that was done was to require him, as a member of a class, to conform with reasonable rules in regard to the separation of the races. In none of them was he denied the right to use, control, or dispose of his property, as in this case. Property of a person, whether as a member of a class or as an individual, cannot be taken without due process of law. In the recent case of McCabe v. Atchison, T. & S. F. R. Co. where the court had under consideration a statute which allowed railroad companies to furnish dining cars for white people and to refuse to furnish dining cars altogether for colored persons, this language was used in reference to the contentions of the attorney general: 'This argument with respect to volume of traffic seems to us to be without merit. It makes the constitutional right depend upon the number of persons who may be discriminated against, whereas the essence of the constitutional right is that it is a personal one.' . . .

"The effect of the ordinance under consideration was not merely to regulate a business or the like, but was to destroy the right of the individual to acquire, enjoy, and dispose of his property. Being of this character it was void as being opposed to the due-process clause of the Constitution."

That there exists a serious and difficult problem arising from a feeling of race hostility which the law is powerless to control, and to which it must give a measure of consideration, may be freely admitted. But its solution cannot be promoted by depriving citizens of their constitutional rights and privileges.

As we have seen, this court has held laws valid which separated the races on the basis of equal accommodations in public conveyances, and courts of high authority have held enactments lawful which provide for separation in the public schools of white and colored pupils where equal privileges are given. But, in view of the rights secured by the 14th Amendment to the Federal Constitution, such legislation must have its limitations, and cannot be sustained where the exercise of authority exceeds the restraints of the Constitution. We think these limitations are exceeded in laws and ordinances of the character now before us.

It is the purpose of such enactments, and it is frankly avowed it will be their ultimate effect, to require by law, at least in residential districts, the compulsory separation of the races on account of color. Such action is said to be essential to the maintenance of the purity of the races, although it is to be noted in the ordinance under consideration that the employment of colored servants in white families is permitted, and nearby residences of colored persons not coming within the blocks, as defined in the ordinance, are not prohibited.

The case presented does not deal with an attempt to prohibit the amalgamation of the races. The right which the ordinance annulled was the civil right of a white man to dispose of his property if he saw fit to do so to a person of color, and of a colored person to make such disposition to a white person.

It is urged that this proposed segregation will promote the public peace by preventing race conflicts. Desirable as this is, and important as is the preservation of the public peace, this aim cannot be accomplished by laws or ordinances which deny rights created or protected by the Federal Constitution.

It is said that such acquisitions by colored persons depreciate property owned in the neighborhood by white persons. But property may be acquired by undesirable white neighbors, or put to disagreeable though lawful uses with like results.

We think this attempt to prevent the alienation of the property in question to a person of color was not a legitimate exercise of the police power of the state, and is in direct violation of the fundamental law enacted in the 14th Amendment of the Constitution preventing state interference with property rights except by due process of law. That being the case, the ordinance cannot stand.

Reaching this conclusion it follows that the judgment of the Kentucky Court of Appeals must be reversed, and the cause remanded to that court for further proceedings not inconsistent with this opinion.

Corrigan v. Buckley

271 U. S. 323   1926

Mr. Justice Sanford delivered the opinion of the Court.

This is a suit in equity brought by John J. Buckley in the supreme court of the District of Columbia against Irene H. Corrigan and Helen Curtis, to enjoin the conveyance of certain real estate from one to the other of the defendants.

The case made by the bill is this: The parties are citizens of the United States, residing in the District. The plaintiff and the defendant Corrigan are white persons, and the defendant Curtis is a person of the negro race. In 1921, thirty white persons, including the plaintiff and the defendant Corrigan, owning twenty-five parcels of land, improved by dwelling houses, situated on S street, between 18th and New Hampshire avenue, in the city of Washington, executed an indenture, duly recorded, in which they recited that for their mutual benefit and the best interests of the neighborhood comprising these properties, they mutually covenanted and agreed that no part of these properties should ever be used or occupied by, or sold, leased or given to, any person of the negro race or blood; and that this covenant should run with the land and bind their respective heirs and assigns for twenty-one years from and after its date.

In 1922, the defendants entered into a contract by which the defendant Corrigan, although knowing the defendant Curtis to be a person of the negro race, agreed to sell her a certain lot, with dwelling house, including within the terms of the indenture, and the defendant Curtis, although knowing of the existence and terms of the indenture, agreed to purchase it. The defendant Curtis demanded that this contract of sale be carried out, and, despite the protest of other parties to the indenture, the defendant Corrigan had stated that she would convey the lot to the defendant Curtis.

The bill alleged that this would cause irreparable injury to the plaintiff and the other parties to the indenture, and that the plaintiff, having no adequate remedy at law, was entitled to have the covenant of the defendant Corrigan specifically enforced in equity by an injunction preventing the defendants from carrying the contract of sale into effect; and prayed, in substance, that the defendant Corrigan be enjoined during twenty-one years from the date of the indenture, from conveying the lot to the defendant Curtis, and that the defendant Curtis be enjoined from taking title to the lot during such period, and from using or occupying it.

The defendant Corrigan moved to dismiss the bill on the grounds that the "indenture or covenant made the basis of said bill" is (1) "void in that the same is contrary to and in violation of the Constitution of the United States," and (2) "is void in that the same is contrary to public policy." And the defendant Curtis moved to dismiss the bill on the ground that it appears therein that the indenture or covenant "is void, in that it attempts to deprive the defendant, the said Helen Curtis, and others of property, without due process of law; abridges the privilege and immunities of citizens of the United States, including the defendant, Helen Curtis, and other persons within this jurisdiction [and denies them] the equal protection of the law, and therefore, is forbidden by the Constitution of the United States, and especially by the 5th, 13th, and 14th Amendments thereof, and the Laws enacted in aid and under the sanction of the said 13th and 14th Amendments."

. . . The mere assertion that the case is one involving the construction or application of the Constitution, and in which the construction of Federal laws is drawn in question, does not, however, authorize this court to entertain the appeal; and it is our duty to decline jurisdiction if the record does not present such a constitutional or statutory question substantial in character and properly raised below. And under well-settled rules jurisdiction is wanting if such questions are so unsubstantial as to be plainly without color of merit and frivolous.

Under the pleadings in the present case the only constitutional question involved was that arising under the assertions in the motions to dismiss that the indenture or covenant which is the basis of the bill, is "void" in that it is contrary to and forbidden by the 5th, 13th, and 14th Amendments. This contention is entirely lacking in substance or color of merit. The 5th Amendment "is a limitation only upon the powers of the general government," and is not directed against the action of individuals. The 13th Amendment denouncing slavery and involuntary servitude, that is, a condition of enforced compulsory service of one to another, does not in other matters protect the individual rights of persons of the negro race. And the prohibitions of the 14th Amendment "have reference to state action exclusively, and not to any action of private individuals." "It is state action of a particular character that is prohibited. Individual invasion of individual rights is not the subject-matter of the Amendment." It is obvious that none of these Amendments prohibited private individuals from entering into contracts respecting the control and disposition of their own property; and there is no color whatever for the contention that they rendered the indenture void. And, plainly, the claim urged in this court that they were to be looked to, in connection with the provisions of the Revised Statutes and the decisions of the courts, in determining the contention, earnestly pressed, that the indenture is void as being "against public policy," does not involve a constitutional question within the meaning of the Code provision.

. . . We therefore conclude that neither the constitutional nor statutory questions relied on as grounds for the appeal to this court have any substantial quality or color of merit, or afford any jurisdictional basis for the appeal.

And while it was further urged in this court that the decrees of the courts below in themselves deprived the defendants of their liberty and property without due process of law, in violation of the 5th and 14th Amendments, this contention likewise cannot serve as a jurisdictional basis for the appeal. Assuming that such a contention, if of a substantial character, might have constituted ground for an appeal under ¶ 3 of the Code provision, it was not raised by the petition for the appeal or by any assignment of error, either in the court of appeals or in this court; and it likewise is lacking in substance. The defendants were given a full hearing in both courts; they were not denied any constitutional or statutory right; and there is no semblance of ground for any contention that the decrees were so plainly arbitrary and contrary to law as to be acts of mere spoliation. Mere error of a court, if any there be, in a judgment entered after a full hearing, does not constitute a denial of due process of law.

It results that, in the absence of any substantial constitutional or statutory question giving us jurisdiction of this appeal under the provisions of § 250 of the Judicial Code, we cannot determine upon the merits the contentions earnestly pressed by the defendants in this court that the indenture is not only void because contrary to public policy, but is also of such a discriminatory character that a court of equity will not lend its aid by enforcing the specific performance of the covenant. These are questions involving a consideration of rules not expressed in any constitutional or statutory provision, but claimed to be a part of the common or general law in force in the District of Columbia; and, plainly, they may not be reviewed under this appeal unless jurisdiction of the case is otherwise acquired.

Hence, without a consideration of these questions, the appeal must be, and is dismissed for want of jurisdiction.

Shelley v. Kraemer
334 U. S. 1   1948

Mr. Chief Justice Vinson delivered the opinion of the Court.

These cases present for our consideration questions relating to the validity of court enforcement of private agreements, generally described as restrictive covenants, which have as their purpose the exclusion of persons of designated race or color from the ownership or occupancy of real property. Basic constitutional issues of obvious importance have been raised.

The first of these cases comes to this Court on certiorari to the Supreme Court of Missouri. On February 16, 1911, thirty out of a total of thirty-nine owners of property fronting both sides of Labadie Avenue between Taylor Avenue and Cora Avenue in the city of St. Louis, signed an agreement, which was subsequently recorded, providing in part:

". . . the said property is hereby restricted to the use and occupancy for the term of Fifty (50) years from this date, so that it shall be a condition all the time and whether recited and referred to as [sic] not in subsequent conveyances and shall attach to the land as a condition precedent to the sale of the same, that hereafter no part of said property or any portion thereof shall be, for said term of Fifty-years, occupied by any person not of the Caucasian race, it being intended hereby to restrict the use of said property for said period of time against the occupancy as owners or tenants of any portion of said property for resident or other purpose by people of the Negro or Mongolian Race."

The entire district described in the agreement included fifty-seven parcels of land. The thirty owners who signed the agreement held title to forty-seven parcels, including the particular parcel involved in this case. At the time the agreement was signed, five of the parcels in the district were owned by Negroes. One of those had been occupied by Negro families since 1882, nearly thirty years before the restrictive agreement was executed. The trial court found that owners of seven out of nine homes on the south side of Labadie Avenue, within the restricted district and "in the immediate vicinity" of the premises in question, had failed to sign the restrictive agreement in 1911. At the time this action was brought, four of the premises were occupied by Negroes, and had been so occupied for periods ranging from twenty-three to sixty-three years. A fifth parcel had been occupied by Negroes until a year before this suit was instituted.

On August 11, 1945, pursuant to a contract of sale, petitioners Shelley, who are Negroes, for valuable consideration received from one Fitzgerald a warranty deed to the parcel in question. The trial court found that petitioners had no actual knowledge of the restrictive agreement at the time of the purchase.

On October 9, 1945, respondents, as owners of other property subject to the terms of the restrictive covenant, brought suit in the Circuit Court of the city of St. Louis praying that petitioners Shelley be restrained from taking possession of the property and that judgment be entered divesting title out of petitioners Shelley and revesting title in the immediate grantor or in such other person as the court should direct. The trial court denied the requested relief on the ground that the restrictive agreement, upon which respondents based their action, had never become final and complete because it was the intention of the parties to that agreement that it was not to become effective until signed by all property owners in the district, and signatures of all the owners had never been obtained.

The Supreme Court of Missouri sitting *en banc* reversed and directed the trial court to grant the relief for which respondents had prayed. That court held the agreement effective and concluded that enforcement of its provisions violated no rights guaranteed to petitioners by the Federal Constitution. At the time the court rendered its decision, petitioners were occupying the property in question.

The second of the cases under consideration comes to this Court from the Supreme Court of Michigan. The circumstances presented do not differ materially from the Missouri case. In June, 1934, one Ferguson and his wife, who then owned the property located in the city of Detroit which is involved in this case, executed a contract providing in part:

"This property shall not be used or occupied by any person or persons except those of the Caucasian race.

"It is further agreed that this restriction shall not be effective unless at least eighty percent of the property fronting on both sides of the street in the block where our land is located is subjected to this or a similar restriction."

The agreement provided that the restrictions were to remain in effect until January 1, 1960. The contract was subsequently recorded; and similar agreements were executed with respect to eighty percent of the lots in the block in which the property in question is situated.

By deed dated November 30, 1944, petitioners, who were found by the trial court to be Negroes, acquired title to the property and thereupon entered into its occupancy. On January 30, 1945, respondents, as owners of property subject to the terms of the restrictive agreement, brought suit against petitioners in the Circuit Court of Wayne County. After a hearing, the court entered a decree directing petitioners to move from the property within ninety days. Petitioners were further enjoined and restrained from using or occupying the premises in the future. On appeal, the Supreme Court of Michigan affirmed, deciding adversely to petitioners' contentions that they had been denied rights protected by the Fourteenth Amendment.

Petitioners have placed primary reliance on their contentions, first raised in the state courts, that judicial enforcement of the restrictive agreements in these cases has violated rights guaranteed to petitioners by the Fourteenth Amendment of the Federal Constitution and Acts of Congress passed pursuant to that Amendment. Specifically, petitioners urge that they have been denied the equal protection of the laws, deprived of property without due process of law, and have been denied privileges and immunities of citizens of the United States. We pass to a consideration of those issues.

I

Whether the equal protection clause of the Fourteenth Amendment inhibits judicial enforcement by state courts of restrictive covenants based on race or color is a question which this Court has not heretofore been called upon to consider. Only two cases have been decided by this Court which in any way have involved the enforcement of such agreements. The first of these was the case of *Corrigan* v. *Buckley*. There, suit was brought in the courts of the District of Columbia to enjoin a threatened violation of certain restrictive covenants relating to lands situated in the city of Washington. Relief was granted, and the case was brought here on appeal. It is apparent that that case, which had originated in the federal courts and involved the enforcement of covenants on land located in the District of Columbia, could present no issues under the Fourteenth Amendment; for that Amendment by its terms applies only to the States. Nor was the question of the validity of court enforcement of the restrictive covenants under the Fifth Amendment properly before the Court, as the opinion of this Court specifically recognizes. The only constitutional issue which the appellants had raised in the lower courts, and hence the only constitutional issue before this Court on appeal, was the validity of the covenant agreements as such. This Court concluded that since the inhibitions of the constitutional provisions invoked apply only to governmental action, as contrasted to action of private individuals, there was no showing that the covenants, which were simply agreements between private property owners, were invalid. Accordingly, the appeal was dismissed for want of a substantial question. Nothing in the opinion of this Court, therefore, may properly be regarded as an adjudication on the merits of the constitutional issues presented by these cases, which raise the question of the validity, not of the private agreements as such, but of the judicial enforcement of those agreements.

The second of the cases involving racial restrictive covenants was *Hansberry* v. *Lee*. In that case, petitioners, white property owners, were enjoined by the state courts from violating the terms of a restrictive agreement. The state Supreme Court had held petitioners bound by an earlier judicial determination, in litigation in which petitioners were not parties, upholding the validity of the restrictive agreement, although, in fact, the agreement had not been signed by the number of owners necessary to make it effective under state law. This Court reversed the judgment of the state Supreme Court upon the ground that petitioners had been denied due process of law in being held estopped to challenge the validity of the agreement on the theory, accepted by the state court, that the earlier litigation, in which petitioners did not participate, was in the nature of a class suit. In arriving at its result, this Court did not reach the issues presented by the cases now under consideration.

It is well, at the outset, to scrutinize the terms of the restrictive agreements involved in these cases. In the Missouri case, the covenant declares that no part of the affected property shall be "occupied by any person not of the Caucasian race, it being intended hereby to restrict the use of said property . . . against the occupancy as owners or tenants of any portion of said property for resident or other purpose by people of the Negro or Mongolian Race." Not only does the restriction seek to proscribe use and occupancy of the affected properties by members of the excluded class, but as construed by the Missouri courts, the agreement requires that title of any person who uses his property in violation of the restriction shall be divested. The restriction of the covenant in the Michigan case seeks to bar occupancy by persons of the excluded class. It provides that "This property shall not be used or occupied by any person or persons except those of the Caucasian race."

It should be observed that these covenants do not seek to proscribe any particular use of the affected properties. Use of the properties for residential occupancy, as such, is not forbidden. The restrictions of these agreements, rather, are directed toward a designated class of persons and seek to determine who may and who may not own or make use of the properties for residential purposes. The excluded class is defined wholly in terms of race or color; "simply that and nothing more."

It cannot be doubted that among the civil rights intended to be protected from discriminatory state action by the Fourteenth Amendment are the rights to acquire, enjoy, own and dispose of property. Equality in the enjoyment of property rights was regarded by the framers of that Amendment as an essential pre-condition to the realization of other basic civil rights and liberties which the Amendment was intended to guarantee. Thus, § 1978 of the Revised Statutes, derived from § 1 of the Civil Rights Act of 1866 which was enacted by Congress while the Fourteenth Amendment was also under consideration, provides:

"All citizens of the United States shall have the same right, in every State and Territory, as is enjoyed by white citizens thereof to inherit, purchase, lease, sell, hold, and convey real and personal property."

This Court has given specific recognition to the same principle.

It is likewise clear that restrictions on the right of occupancy of the sort sought to be created by the private agreements in these cases could not be squared with the requirements of the Fourteenth Amendment if imposed by state statute or local ordinance. We do not understand respondents to urge the contrary. In the case of *Buchanan* v. *Warley* a unanimous Court declared unconstitutional the provisions of a city ordinance which denied to colored persons the right to occupy houses in blocks in which the greater number of houses were occupied by white persons, and imposed similar restrictions on white persons with respect to blocks in which the greater number of houses were occupied by colored persons. During the course of the opinion in that case, this Court stated: "The Fourteenth Amendment and these statutes enacted in furtherance of its purpose operate to qualify and entitle a colored man to acquire property without state legislation discriminating against him solely because of color."

In *Harmon* v. *Tyler* a unanimous court, on the authority of *Buchanan* v. *Warley,* declared invalid an ordinance which forbade any Negro to establish a home on any property in a white community or any white person to establish a home in a Negro community, "except on the written consent of a majority of the persons of the opposite race inhabiting such community or portion of the City to be affected."

The precise question before this Court in both the *Buchanan* and *Harmon* cases involved the rights of white sellers to dispose of their properties free from restrictions as to potential purchasers based on considerations of race or color. But that such legislation is also offensive to the rights of those desiring to acquire and occupy property and barred on grounds of race or color is clear, not only from the language of the opinion in *Buchanan* v. *Warley,* but from this Court's disposition of the case of *Richmond* v. *Deans*. There, a Negro, barred from the occupancy of certain property by the terms of an ordinance similar to that in the *Buchanan* case, sought injunctive relief in the federal courts to enjoin the enforcement of the ordinance on the grounds that its provisions violated the terms of the Fourteenth Amendment. Such relief was granted, and this Court affirmed, finding the citation of *Buchanan* v. *Warley,* and *Harmon* v. *Tyler,* sufficient to support its judgment.

But the present cases, unlike those just discussed, do not involve action by state legislatures or city councils. Here the particular patterns of discrimination and the areas in which the restrictions are to operate, are determined, in the first instance, by the terms of agreements among private individuals. Participation of the State consists in the enforcement of the restrictions so defined. The crucial issue with which we are here confronted is whether this distinction removes these cases from the operation of the prohibitory provisions of the Fourteenth Amendment.

Since the decision of this Court in the *Civil Rights Cases* the principle has become firmly embedded in our constitutional law that the action inhibited by the first section of the Fourteenth Amendment is only such action as may fairly be said to be that of the States. That Amendment erects no shield against merely private conduct, however discriminatory or wrongful.

We conclude, therefore, that the restrictive agreements standing alone cannot be regarded as violative of any rights guaranteed to petitioners by the Fourteenth Amendment. So long as the purposes of those agreements are effectuated by voluntary adherence to their terms, it would appear clear that there has been no action by the State and the provisions of the Amendment have not been violated.

But here there was more. These are cases in which the purposes of the agreements were secured only by judicial enforcement by state courts of the restrictive terms of the agreements. The respondents urge that judicial enforcement of private agreements does not amount to state action; or, in any event, the participation of the State is so attenuated in character as not to amount to state action within the meaning of the Fourteenth Amendment. Finally, it is suggested, even if the States in these cases may be deemed to have acted in the constitutional sense, their action did not deprive petitioners of rights guaranteed by the Fourteenth Amendment. We move to a consideration of these matters.

II

That the action of state courts and judicial officers in their official capacities is to be regarded as action of the State within the meaning of the Fourteenth Amendment, is a proposition which has long been established by decisions of this Court. That principle was given expression in the earliest cases involving the construction of the terms of the Fourteenth Amendment. Thus, in *Virginia* v. *Rives,* this Court stated: "It is doubtless true that a State may act through different agencies—either by its legislative, its executive, or its judicial authorities; and the prohibitions of the amendment extend to all action of the State denying equal protection of the laws, whether it be action by one of these agencies or by another." In *Ex parte Virginia,* the Court observed: "A State acts by its legislative, its executive, or its judicial authorities. It can act in no other way." In the *Civil Rights Cases,* this Court pointed out that the Amendment makes void "State action of every kind" which is inconsistent with the guaranties therein contained, and extends to manifestations of "State authority in the shape of laws, customs, or judicial or executive proceedings." Language to like effect is employed no less than eighteen times during the course of that opinion.

Similar expressions, giving specific recognition to the fact that judicial action is to be regarded as action of the State for the purposes of the Fourteenth Amendment, are to be found in numerous cases which have been more recently decided. In *Twining* v. *New Jersey,* the Court said: "The judicial act of the highest court of the State, in authoritatively construing and enforcing its laws, is the act of the State." In *Brinkerhoff-Faris Trust & Savings Co.* v. *Hill,* the Court, through Mr. Justice Brandeis, stated: "The federal guaranty of due process extends to state action through its judicial as well as through its legislative, executive or administrative branch of government." Further examples of such declarations in the opinions of this Court are not lacking.

One of the earliest applications of the prohibitions contained in the Fourteenth Amendment to action of state judicial officials occurred in cases in which Negroes had been excluded from jury service in criminal prosecutions by reason of their race or color. These cases demonstrate, also, the early recognition by this Court that state action in violation of the Amendment's provisions is equally repugnant to the constitutional commands whether directed by state statute or taken by a judicial official in the absence of statute. Thus, in *Strauder* v. *West Virginia,* this Court declared invalid a state statute restricting jury service to white persons as amounting to a denial of the equal protection of the laws to the colored defendant in that case. In the same volume of the reports, the Court in *Ex parte Virginia* held that a similar discrimination imposed by the action of a state judge denied rights protected by the Amendment, despite the fact that the language of the state statute relating to jury service contained no such restrictions.

The action of state courts in imposing penalties or depriving parties of other substantive rights without providing adequate notice and opportunity to defend, has, of course, long been regarded as a denial of the due process of law guaranteed by the Fourteenth Amendment.

In numerous cases, this Court has reversed criminal convictions in state courts for failure of those courts to provide the essential ingredients of a fair hearing. Thus it has been held that convictions obtained in state courts under the domination of a mob are void. Convictions obtained by coerced confessions, by the use of perjured testimony known by the prosecution to be such, or without the effective assistance of counsel, have also been held to be exertions of state authority in conflict with the fundamental rights protected by the Fourteenth Amendment.

But the examples of state judicial action which have been held by this Court to violate the Amendment's commands are not restricted to situations in which the judicial proceedings were found in some manner to be procedurally unfair. It has been recognized that the action of state courts in enforcing a substantive common-law rule formulated by those courts, may result in the denial of rights guaranteed by the Fourteenth Amendment, even though the judicial proceedings in such cases may have been in complete accord with the most rigorous conceptions of procedural due process. Thus, in *American Federation of Labor* v. *Swing,* enforcement by state courts of the common-law policy of the State, which resulted in the restraining of peaceful picketing, was held to be state action of the sort prohibited by the Amendment's guaranties of freedom of discussion. In *Cantwell* v. *Connecticut* a conviction in a state court of the common-law crime of breach of the peace was, under the circumstances of the case, found to be a violation of the Amendment's commands relating to freedom of religion. In *Bridges* v. *California* enforcement of the state's common-law rule relating to contempts by publication was held to be state action inconsistent with the prohibitions of the Fourteenth Amendment.

The short of the matter is that from the time of the adoption of the Fourteenth Amendment until the present, it has been the consistent ruling of this Court that the action of the States to which the Amendment has reference includes action of state courts and state judicial officials. Although, in construing the terms of the Fourteenth Amendment, differences have from time to time been expressed as to whether particular types of state action may be said to offend the Amendment's prohibitory provisions, it has never been suggested that state court action is immunized from the operation of those provisions simply because the act is that of the judicial branch of the state government.

III

Against this background of judicial construction, extending over a period of some three-quarters of a century, we are called upon to consider whether enforcement by state courts of the restrictive agreements in these cases may be deemed to be the acts of those States; and, if so, whether that action has denied these petitioners the equal protection of the laws which the Amendment was intended to insure.

We have no doubt that there has been state action in these cases in the full and complete sense of the phrase. The undisputed facts disclose that petitioners were willing purchasers of properties upon which they desired to establish homes. The owners of the properties were willing sellers; and contracts of sale were accordingly consummated. It is clear that but for the active intervention of the state courts, supported by the full panoply of state power, petitioners would have been free to occupy the properties in question without restraint.

These are not cases, as has been suggested, in which the States have merely abstained from action, leaving private individuals free to impose such discriminations as they see fit. Rather, these are cases in which the States have made available to such individuals the full coercive power of government to deny to petitioners, on the grounds of race or color, the enjoyment of property rights in premises which petitioners are willing and financially able to acquire and which the grantors are willing to sell. The difference between judicial enforcement and non-enforcement of the restrictive covenants is the difference to petitioners between being denied rights of property available to other members of the community and being accorded full enjoyment of those rights on an equal footing.

The enforcement of the restrictive agreements by the state courts in these cases was directed pursuant to the common-law policy of the States as formulated by those courts in earlier decisions. In the Missouri case, enforcement of the covenant was directed in the first instance by the highest court of the State after the trial court had determined the agreement to be invalid for want of the requisite number of signatures. In the Michigan case, the order of enforcement by the trial court was affirmed by the highest state court. The judicial action in each case bears the clear and unmistakable imprimatur of the State. We have noted that previous decisions of this Court have established the proposition that judicial action is not immunized from the operation of the Fourteenth Amendment simply because it is taken pursuant to the state's common-law policy. Nor is the Amendment ineffective simply because the particular pattern of discrimination, which the State has enforced, was defined initially by the terms of a private agreement. State action, as that phrase is understood for the purposes of the Fourteenth Amendment, refers to exertions of state power in all forms. And when the effect of that action is to deny rights subject to the protection of the Fourteenth Amendment, it is the obligation of this Court to enforce the constitutional commands.

We hold that in granting judicial enforcement of the restrictive agreements in these cases, the States have denied petitioners the equal protection of the laws and that, therefore, the action of the state courts cannot stand. We have noted that freedom from discrimination by the States in the enjoyment of property rights was among the basic objectives sought to be effectuated by the framers of the Fourteenth Amendment. That such discrimination has occurred in these cases is clear. Because of the race or color of these petitioners, they have been denied rights of ownership or occupancy enjoyed as a matter of course by other citizens of different race or color. The Fourteenth Amendment declares "that all persons, whether colored or white, shall stand equal before the laws of the States, and, in regard to the colored race, for whose protection the amendment was primarily designed, that no discrimination shall be made against them by law because of their color." Only recently this Court had occasion to declare that a state law which denied equal enjoyment of property rights to a designated class of citizens of specified race and ancestry, was not a legitimate exercise of the state's police power but violated the guaranty of the equal protection of the laws. Nor may the discriminations imposed by the state courts in these cases be justified as proper exertions of state police power.

Respondents urge, however, that since the state courts stand ready to enforce restrictive covenants excluding white persons from the ownership or occupancy of property covered by such agreements, enforcement of covenants excluding colored persons may not be deemed a denial of equal protection of the laws to the colored persons who are thereby affected. This contention does not bear scrutiny. The parties have directed our attention to no case in which a court, state or federal, has been called upon to enforce a covenant excluding members of the white majority from ownership or occupancy of real property on grounds of race or color. But there are more fundamental considerations. The rights created by the first section of the Fourteenth Amendment are, by its terms, guaranteed to the individual. The rights established are personal rights. It is, therefore, no answer to these petitioners to say that the courts may also be induced to deny white persons rights of ownership and occupancy on grounds of race or color. Equal protection of the laws is not achieved through indiscriminate imposition of inequalities.

Nor do we find merit in the suggestion that property owners who are parties to these agreements are denied equal protection of the laws if denied access to the courts to enforce the terms of restrictive covenants and to assert property rights which the state courts have held to be created by such agreements. The Constitution confers upon no individual the right to demand action by the State which results in the denial of equal protection of the laws to other individuals. And it would appear beyond question that the power of the State to create and enforce property interests must be exercised within the boundaries defined by the Fourteenth Amendment.

The problem of defining the scope of the restrictions which the Federal Constitution imposes upon exertions of power by the States has given rise to many of the most persistent and fundamental issues which this Court has been called upon to consider. That problem was foremost in the minds of the framers of the Constitution, and, since that early day, has arisen in a multitude of forms. The task of determining whether the action of a State offends constitutional provisions is one which may not be undertaken lightly. Where, however, it is clear that the action of the State violates the terms of the fundamental charter, it is the obligation of this Court so to declare.

The historical context in which the Fourteenth Amendment became a part of the Constitution should not be forgotten. Whatever else the framers sought to achieve, it is clear that the matter of primary concern was the establishment of equality in the enjoyment of basic civil and political rights and the preservation of those rights from discriminatory action on the part of the States based on considerations of race or color. Seventy-five years ago this Court announced that the provisions of the Amendment are to be construed with this fundamental purpose in mind. Upon full consideration, we have concluded that in these cases the States have acted to deny petitioners the equal protection of the laws guaranteed by the Fourteenth Amendment. Having so decided, we find it unnecessary to consider whether petitioners have also been deprived of property without due process of law or denied privileges and immunities of citizens of the United States.

For the reasons stated, the judgment of the Supreme Court of Missouri and the judgment of the Supreme Court of Michigan must be reversed.

Mr. Justice Reed, Mr. Justice Jackson, and Mr. Justice Rutledge took no part in the consideration or decision of these cases.

Hurd v. Hodge

334 U. S. 24   1948

Mr. Chief Justice Vinson delivered the opinion of the Court.

These are companion cases to *Shelley* v. *Kraemer* and *McGhee* v. *Sipes,* and come to this Court on certiorari to the United States Court of Appeals for the District of Columbia.

In 1906, twenty of thirty-one lots in the 100 block of Bryant Street, Northwest, in the City of Washington, were sold subject to the following covenant:

". . . that said lot shall never be rented, leased, sold, transferred or conveyed unto any Negro or colored person, under a penalty of Two Thousand Dollars ($2,000), which shall be a lien against said property."

The covenant imposes no time limitation on the restriction.

Prior to the sales which gave rise to these cases, the twenty lots which are subject to the covenants were at all times owned and occupied by white persons, except for a brief period when three of the houses were occupied by Negroes who were eventually induced to move without legal action. The remaining eleven lots in the same block, however, are not subject to a restrictive agreement and, as found by the District Court, were occupied by Negroes for the twenty years prior to the institution of this litigation.

These cases involve seven of the twenty lots which are subject to the terms of the restrictive covenants. In No. 290, petitioners Hurd, found by the trial court to be Negroes, purchased one of the restricted properties from the white owners. In No. 291, petitioner Urciolo, a white real estate dealer, sold and conveyed three of the restricted properties to the Negro petitioners Rowe, Savage, and Stewart. Petitioner Urciolo also owns three other lots in the block subject to the covenants. In both cases, the Negro petitioners are presently occupying as homes the respective properties which have been conveyed to them.

Suits were instituted in the District Court by respondents, who own other property in the block subject to the terms of the covenants, praying for injunctive relief to enforce the terms of the restrictive agreement. The cases were consolidated for trial, and after a hearing, the court entered a judgment declaring null and void the deeds of the Negro petitioners; enjoining petitioner Urciolo and one Ryan, the white property owners who had sold the houses to the Negro petitioners, from leasing, selling or conveying the properties to any Negro or colored person; enjoining the Negro petitioners from leasing or conveying the properties and directing those petitioners "to remove themselves and all of their personal belongings" from the premises within sixty days.

The United States Court of Appeals for the District of Columbia, with one justice dissenting, affirmed the judgment of the District Court. The majority of the court was of the opinion that the action of the District Court was consistent with earlier decisions of the Court of Appeals and that those decisions should be held determinative in these cases.

Petitioners have attacked the judicial enforcement of the restrictive covenants in these cases on a wide variety of grounds. Primary reliance, however, is placed on the contention that such governmental action on the part of the courts of the District of Columbia is forbidden by the due process clause of the Fifth Amendment of the Federal Constitution.

Whether judicial enforcement of racial restrictive agreements by the federal courts of the District of Columbia violates the Fifth Amendment has never been adjudicated by this Court. In *Corrigan* v. *Buckley* an appeal was taken to this Court from a judgment of the United States Court of Appeals for the District of Columbia which had affirmed an order of the lower court granting enforcement to a restrictive covenant. But as was pointed out in our opinion in *Shelley* v. *Kraemer,* the only constitutional issue which had been raised in the lower courts in the *Corrigan* case, and, consequently, the only constitutional question before this Court on appeal, related to the validity of the private agreements as such. Nothing in the opinion of this Court in that case, therefore, may properly be regarded as an adjudication of the issue presented by petitioners in this case which concerns, not the validity of the restrictive agreements standing alone, but the validity of court enforcement of the restrictive covenants under the due process clause of the Fifth Amendment.

This Court has declared invalid municipal ordinances restricting occupancy in designated areas to persons of specified race and color as denying rights of white sellers and Negro purchasers of property, guaranteed by the due process clause of the Fourteenth Amendment. Petitioners urge that judicial enforcement of the restrictive covenants by courts of the District of Columbia should likewise be held to deny rights of white sellers and Negro purchasers of property, guaranteed by the due process clause of the Fifth Amendment. Petitioners point out that this Court in *Hirabayashi* v. *United States* reached its decision in a case in which issues under the Fifth Amendment were presented, on the assumption that "racial discriminations are in most circumstances irrelevant and therefore prohibited . . . ."

Upon full consideration, however, we have found it unnecessary to resolve the constitutional issue which petitioners advance; for we have concluded that judicial enforcement of restrictive covenants by the courts of the District of Columbia is improper for other reasons hereinafter stated.

Section 1978 of the Revised Statutes, derived from § 1 of the Civil Rights Act of 1866, provides:

"All citizens of the United States shall have the same right, in every State and Territory, as is enjoyed by white citizens thereof to inherit, purchase, lease, sell, hold, and convey real and personal property."

All the petitioners in these cases, as found by the District Court, are citizens of the United States. We have no doubt that, for the purposes of this section, the District of Columbia is included within the phrase "every State and Territory." Nor can there be doubt of the constitutional power of Congress to enact such legislation with reference to the District of Columbia.

We may start with the proposition that the statute does not invalidate private restrictive agreements so long as the purposes of those agreements are achieved by the parties through voluntary adherence to the terms. The action toward which the provisions of the statute under consideration is directed is governmental action. Such was the holding of *Corrigan* v. *Buckley*.

In considering whether judicial enforcement of restrictive covenants is the kind of governmental action which the first section of the Civil Rights Act of 1866 was intended to prohibit, reference must be made to the scope and purposes of the Fourteenth Amendment; for that statute and the Amendment were closely related both in inception and in the objectives which Congress sought to achieve.

Both the Civil Rights Act of 1866 and the joint resolution which was later adopted as the Fourteenth Amendment were passed in the first session of the Thirty-Ninth Congress. Frequent references to the Civil

Rights Act are to be found in the record of the legislative debates on the adoption of the Amendment. It is clear that in many significant respects the statute and the Amendment were expressions of the same general congressional policy. Indeed, as the legislative debates reveal, one of the primary purposes of many members of Congress in supporting the adoption of the Fourteenth Amendment was to incorporate the guaranties of the Civil Rights Act of 1866 in the organic law of the land. Others supported the adoption of the Amendment in order to eliminate doubt as to the constitutional validity of the Civil Rights Act as applied to the States.

The close relationship between § 1 of the Civil Rights Act and the Fourteenth Amendment was given specific recognition by this Court in *Buchanan* v. *Warley*. There, the Court observed that, not only through the operation of the Fourteenth Amendment, but also by virtue of the "statutes enacted in furtherance of its purpose," including the provisions here considered, a colored man is granted the right to acquire property free from interference by discriminatory state legislation. In *Shelley* v. *Kraemer* we have held that the Fourteenth Amendment also forbids such discrimination where imposed by state courts in the enforcement of restrictive covenants. That holding is clearly indicative of the construction to be given to the relevant provisions of the Civil Rights Act in their application to the Courts of the District of Columbia.

Moreover, the explicit language employed by Congress to effectuate its purposes leaves no doubt that judicial enforcement of the restrictive covenants by the courts of the District of Columbia is prohibited by the Civil Rights Act. That statute, by its terms, requires that all citizens of the United States shall have the same right "as is enjoyed by white citizens . . . to inherit, purchase, lease, sell, hold, and convey real and personal property." That the Negro petitioners have been denied that right by virtue of the action of the federal courts of the District is clear. The Negro petitioners entered into contracts of sale with willing sellers for the purchase of properties upon which they desired to establish homes. Solely because of their race and color they are confronted with orders of court divesting their titles in the properties and ordering that the premises be vacated. White sellers, one of whom is a petitioner here, have been enjoined from selling the properties to any Negro or colored person. Under such circumstances, to suggest that the Negro petitioners have been accorded the same rights as white citizens to purchase, hold, and convey real property is to reject the plain meaning of language. We hold that the action of the District Court directed against the Negro purchasers and the white sellers denies rights intended by Congress to be protected by the Civil Rights Act and that, consequently, the action cannot stand.

But even in the absence of the statute, there are other considerations which would indicate that enforcement of restrictive covenants in these cases is judicial action contrary to the public policy of the United States, and as such should be corrected by this Court in the exercise of its supervisory powers over the courts of the District of Columbia. The power of the federal courts to enforce the terms of private agreements is at all times exercised subject to the restrictions and limitations of the public policy of the United States as manifested in the Constitution, treaties, federal statutes, and applicable legal precedents. Where the enforcement of private agreements would be violative of that policy, it is the obligation of courts to refrain from such exertions of judicial power.

We are here concerned with action of federal courts of such a nature that if taken by the courts of a State would violate the prohibitory provisions of the Fourteenth Amendment. It is not consistent with the public policy of the United States to permit federal courts in the Nation's capital to exercise general equitable powers to compel action denied the state courts where such state action has been held to be violative of the guaranty of the equal protection of the laws. We cannot presume that the public policy of the United States manifests a lesser concern for the protection of such basic rights against discriminatory action of federal courts than against such action taken by the courts of the States.

Reversed.

Mr. Justice Reed, Mr. Justice Jackson, and Mr. Justice Rutledge took no part in the consideration or decision of these cases.

Mr. Justice Frankfurter, concurring.

In these cases, the plaintiffs ask equity to enjoin white property owners who are desirous of selling their houses to Negro buyers simply because the houses were subject to an original agreement not to have them pass into Negro ownership. Equity is rooted in conscience. An injunction is, as it always has been, "an extraordinary remedial process which is granted, not as a matter of right but in the exercise of a sound judicial discretion." In good conscience, it cannot be "the exercise of a sound judicial discretion" by a federal court to grant the relief here asked for when the authorization of such an injunction by the States of the Union violates the Constitution—and violates it, not for any narrow technical reason, but for considerations that touch rights so basic to our society that, after the Civil War, their protection against invasion by the States was safeguarded by the Constitution. This is to me a sufficient and conclusive ground for reaching the Court's result.

Barrows v. Jackson
346 U. S. 249   1953

Mr. Justice Minton delivered the opinion of the Court.

This Court held in *Shelley* v. *Kraemer* that racial restrictive covenants could not be enforced in equity against Negro purchasers because such enforcement would constitute state action denying equal protection of the laws to the Negroes, in violation of the Fourteenth Amendment to the Federal Constitution. The question we now have is: Can such a restrictive covenant be enforced at law by a suit for damages against a co-covenantor who allegedly broke the covenant?

Petitioners sued respondent at law for damages for breach of a restrictive covenant the parties entered into as owners of residential real estate in the same neighborhood in Los Angeles, California. The petitioners' complaint alleged in part:

"That by the terms of said Agreement each of the signers promised and agreed in writing and bound himself, his heirs, executors, administrators, successors, and assigns, by a continuing covenant that no part of his said real property, described therein, should ever at any time be used or occupied by any person or persons not wholly of the white or Caucasian race, and also agreed and promised in writing that this restriction should be incorporated in all papers and transfers of lots or parcels of land hereinabove referred to; provided, however, that said restrictions should not prevent the employment by the owners or tenants of said real property of domestic servants or other employees who are not wholly of the white or Caucasian race; provided, further, however, that such employees shall be permitted to occupy said real property only when actively engaged in such employment. That said Agreement was agreed to be a covenant running with the land. That each provision in said Agreement was for the benefit for all the lots therein described."

The complaint further alleged that respondent broke the covenant in two respects: (1) by conveying her real estate without incorporating in the deed the restriction contained in the covenant; and (2) by permitting non-Caucasians to move in and occupy the premises. The trial court sustained a demurrer to the complaint, the District Court of Appeal for the Second Appellate District affirmed, and the Supreme Court of California denied hearing. We granted certiorari because of the importance of the constitutional question involved and to consider the conflict which has arisen in the decisions of the state courts since our ruling in the *Shelley* case. Like the California court in the instant case, the Supreme Court of Michigan sustained the dismissal of a claim for damages for breach of a racial restrictive covenant. The Supreme Court of Missouri reached a contrary result, while the Supreme Court of Oklahoma has held that a claim for damages may be maintained against a white seller, an intermediate straw man, and a non-Caucasian purchaser for a conspiracy to violate the covenant.

The trial court in the case here held that a party to a covenant restricting use and occupancy of real estate to Caucasians could not maintain a suit at law against a co-covenantor for breach of the covenant because of our ruling in *Shelley*. In *Shelley*, this Court held that the action of the lower courts in granting equitable relief in the enforcement of such covenants constituted state action denying to Negroes, against whom the covenant was sought to be enforced, equal protection of the laws in violation of the Fourteenth Amendment. This Court said:

"We conclude, therefore, that the restrictive agreements standing alone cannot be regarded as violative of any rights guaranteed to petitioners by the Fourteenth Amendment. So long as the purposes of those agreements are effectuated by voluntary adherence to their terms, it would appear clear that there has been no action by the State and the provisions of the Amendment have not been violated. . . ."

That is to say, the law applicable in that case did not make the covenant itself invalid, no one would be punished for making it, and no one's constitutional rights were violated by the covenantor's voluntary adherence thereto. Such voluntary adherence would constitute individual action only. When, however, the parties cease to rely upon voluntary action to carry out the covenant and the State is asked to step in and give its sanction to the enforcement of the covenant, the first question that arises is whether a court's awarding damages constitutes state action under the Fourteenth Amendment. To compel respondent to respond in damages would be for the State to punish her for her failure to perform her covenant to continue to discriminate against non-Caucasians in the use of her property. The result of that sanction by the State would be to encourage the use of restrictive covenants. To that extent, the State would act to put its sanction behind the covenants. If the State may thus punish respondent for her failure to carry out her covenant, she is coerced to continue to use her property in a discriminatory manner, which in essence is the purpose of the covenant. Thus, it becomes not respondent's voluntary choice but the State's choice that she observe her covenant or suffer damages. The action of a state court at law to sanction the validity of the restrictive covenant here involved would constitute state action as surely as it was state action to enforce such covenants in equity, as in *Shelley*.

The next question to emerge is whether the state action in allowing damages deprives anyone of rights protected by the Constitution. If a state court awards damages for breach of a restrictive covenant, a prospective seller of restricted land will either refuse to sell to non-Caucasians or else will require non-Caucasians to pay a higher price to meet the damages which the seller may incur. Solely because of their race, non-Caucasians will be unable to purchase, own, and enjoy property on the same terms as Caucasians. Denial of this right by state action deprives such non-Caucasians, unidentified but identifiable, of equal protection of the laws in violation of the Fourteenth Amendment.

But unlike *Shelley*, no non-Caucasian is before the Court claiming to have been denied his constitutional rights. May respondent, whom petitioners seek to coerce by an action to pay damages for her failure to honor her restrictive covenant, rely on the invasion of the rights of others in her defense to this action?

Ordinarily, one may not claim standing in this Court to vindicate the constitutional rights of some third party. Reference to this rule is made in varied situations. The requirement of standing is often used to describe the constitutional limitation on the jurisdiction of this Court to "cases" and "controversies." Apart from the jurisdictional requirement, this Court has developed a complementary rule of self-restraint for its own governance (not always clearly distinguished from the constitutional limitation) which ordinarily precludes a person from challenging the constitutionality of state action by invoking the rights of others. The common thread underlying both requirements is that a person cannot challenge the constitutionality of a statute unless he shows that he himself is injured by its operation. This principle has no application to the instant case in which respondent has been sued for damages totaling $11,600, and in which a judgment against respondent would constitute a direct, pocketbook injury to her.

There are still other cases in which the Court has held that even though a party will suffer a direct substantial injury from application of a statute, he cannot challenge its constitutionality unless he can show that he is within the class whose constitutional rights are allegedly infringed. One reason for this ruling is that the state court, when actually faced with the question, might narrowly construe the statute to obliterate the objectionable feature, or it might declare the unconstitutional provisions separable. It would indeed be undesirable for this Court to consider every conceivable situation which might possibly arise in the application of complex and comprehensive legislation. Nor are we so ready to frustrate the expressed will of Congress or that of the state legislatures.

This is a salutary rule, the validity of which we reaffirm. But in the instant case, we are faced with a unique situation in which it is the action of the state *court* which might result in a denial of constitutional rights and in which it would be difficult if not impossible for the persons whose rights are asserted to present their grievance before any court. Under the peculiar circumstances of this case, we believe the reasons which underlie our rule denying standing to raise another's rights, which is only a rule of practice, are outweighed by the need to protect the fundamental rights which would be denied by permitting the damages action to be maintained.

In other unique situations which have arisen in the past, broad constitutional policy has led the Court to proceed without regard to its usual rule. In *Pierce* v. *Society of Sisters* a state statute required all parents (with certain immaterial exceptions) to send their children to public schools. A private and a parochial school brought suit to enjoin enforcement of the act on the ground that it violated the constitutional rights of parents and guardians. No parent or guardian to whom the act applied was a party or before the Court. The Court held that the act was unconstitutional because it "unreasonably interferes with the liberty of parents and guardians to direct the upbringing and education of children under their control." In short, the schools were permitted to assert in defense of their property rights the constitutional rights of the parents and guardians.

There is such a close relationship between the restrictive covenant here and the sanction of a state court which would punish respondent for not going forward with her covenant, and the purpose of the covenant itself, that relaxation of the rule is called for here. It sufficiently appears that mulcting in damages of respondent will be solely for the purpose of giving vitality to the restrictive covenant, that is to say, to punish respondent for not continuing to discriminate against non-Caucasians in the use of her property. This Court will not permit or require California to coerce respondent to respond in damages for failure to observe a restrictive covenant that this Court would deny California the right to enforce in equity, *Shelley;* or that this Court would deny California the right to incorporate in a statute, *Buchanan* v. *Warley;* or that could not be enforced in a federal jurisdiction because such a covenant would be contrary to public policy:

"It is not consistent with the public policy of the United States to permit federal courts in the Nation's capital to exercise general equitable powers to compel action denied the state courts where such state action has been held to be violative of the guaranty of the equal protection of the laws. We cannot presume that the public policy of the United States manifests a lesser concern for the protection of such basic rights against discriminatory action of federal courts than against such action taken by the courts of the States." *Hurd* v. *Hodge.*

Consistency in the application of the rules of practice in this Court does not require us in this unique set of circumstances to put the State in such an equivocal position simply because the person against whom the injury is directed is not before the Court to speak for himself. The law will permit respondent to resist any effort to compel her to observe such a covenant, so widely condemned by the courts, since she is the one in whose charge and keeping reposes the power to continue to use her property to discriminate or to discontinue such use. The relation between the coercion exerted on respondent and her possible pecuniary loss thereby is so close to the purpose of the restrictive covenant, to violate the constitutional rights of those discriminated against, that respondent is the only effective adversary of the unworthy covenant in its last stand. She will be permitted to protect herself and, by so doing, close the gap to the use of this covenant, so universally condemned by the courts.

Petitioners argue that the right to equal protection of the laws is a "personal" right, guaranteed to the individual rather than to groups or classes. For instance, discriminatory denial of sleeping-car and dining-car facilities to an individual Negro cannot be justified on the ground that there is little demand for such facilities by Negroes as a group. This description of the right as "personal," when considered in the context in which it has been used, obviously has no bearing on the question of standing. Nor do we violate this principle by protecting the rights of persons not identified in this record. For instance, in the *Pierce* case, the persons whose rights were invoked were identified only as "present and prospective patrons" of the two schools. In the present case, it is not non-Caucasians as a group whose rights are asserted by respondent, but the rights of particular non-Caucasian would-be users of restricted land.

It is contended by petitioners that for California courts to refuse to enforce this covenant is to impair the obligation of their contracts. Article I, § 10, of the Federal Constitution provides: "No State shall . . . pass any . . . Law impairing the Obligation of Contracts . . . ." The short answer to this contention is that this provision, as its terms indicate, is directed against legislative action only.

"It has been settled by a long line of decisions, that the provision of § 10, Article I, of the Federal Constitution, protecting the obligation of contracts against state action, is directed only against impairment by legislation and not by judgments of courts. . . ."

It is finally contended that petitioners are denied due process and equal protection of the laws by the failure to enforce the covenant. The answer to that proposition is stated by the Court in *Shelley* in these words:

"The Constitution confers upon no individual the right to demand action by the State which results in the denial of equal protection of the laws to other individuals. . . ."

The judgment is

Affirmed.

Mr. Justice Reed and Mr. Justice Jackson took no part in the consideration or decision of this case.

Mr. Chief Justice Vinson, dissenting.

This case, we are told, is "unique." I agree with the characterization. The Court, by a unique species of arguments, has developed a unique exception to an otherwise easily understood doctrine. While I may hope that the majority's use of "unique" is but another way of saying that the decision today will be relegated to its precise facts tomorrow, I must voice my dissent.

The majority seems to recognize, albeit ignores, a proposition which I thought was made plain in the *Shelley* case. That proposition is this: these racial restrictive covenants, whatever we may think of them, are not legal nullities so far as any doctrine of federal law is concerned; it is not unlawful to make them; it is not unlawful to enforce them unless the method by which they are enforced in some way contravenes the Federal Constitution or a federal statute.

Thus, in the *Shelley* case, it was not the covenants which were struck down but judicial enforcement of them against Negro vendees. The question which we decided was simply whether a state court could decree the ouster of Negroes from property which they had purchased and which they were enjoying. We held that it could not. We held that such judicial action, which operated directly against the Negro petitioners and deprived them of their right to enjoy their property solely because of their race, was state action and constituted a denial of "equal protection."

This case is different.

The majority identifies no non-Caucasian who has been injured or could be injured if damages are assessed against respondent for breaching the promise which she willingly and voluntarily made to petitioners, a promise which neither the federal law nor the Constitution proscribes. Indeed, the non-Caucasian occupants of the property involved in this case will continue their occupancy undisturbed, regardless of the outcome of the suit. The state court was asked to do nothing which would impair their rights or their enjoyment of the property.

The plain, admitted fact that there is no identifiable non-Caucasian before this Court who will be denied any right to buy, occupy or otherwise enjoy the properties involved in this lawsuit, or any other particular properties, is decisive to me. It means that the constitutional defect, present in the *Shelley* case, is removed from this case. It means that this Court has no power to deal with the constitutional issue which respondent seeks to inject in this litigation as a defense to her breach of contract. It means that the covenant, valid on its face, can be enforced between the parties—unless California law or California policy forbids its enforcement—without running afoul of any doctrine ever promulgated by this Court, without any interference from this Court.

I turn, first, to the matter of our power to decide this case. The majority states the issue:

". . . May respondent, whom petitioners seek to coerce by an action to pay damages for her failure to honor her restrictive covenant, rely on the invasion of the rights of others in her defense to this action?"

Logically this issue should be met where such an issue is usually met—at the "threshold"; this decision should precede any discussion of the merits of respondent's constitutional claim. Yet it is not amiss to point out that the majority has failed to put first things first; it decides the merits and then, comforted by its decision on the merits, resolves its doubts that it has power to decide the merits.

A line of decisions—long enough to warrant the respect of even the most hardened skeptic of the strength of *stare decisis* as an effective limitation upon this Court's exercise of jurisdiction in constitutional cases —establishes the principle which should stay this Court from deciding what it decides today—from doing what it does today—from imposing a novel constitutional limitation upon the power of the courts of the several states to enforce their own contract laws as they choose. This deep-rooted, vital doctrine demands that the Court refrain from deciding a constitutional issue until it has a party before it who has standing to raise the issue. The majority agrees that this is a "salutary" principle, and supplies us with but a small sampling of the cases to show that it has been rigorously applied in many varied situations, and surely no sophistry is required to apply it to this case. Accordingly, respondent must show, at the outset, that she, herself, and not some unnamed person in an amorphous class, is the victim of the unconstitutional discrimination of which she complains.

Respondent makes no such showing. She does not ask the Court to protect her own constitutional rights, nor even the rights of the persons who now occupy her property. Instead, she asks the Court to protect the rights of those non-Caucasians—whoever they may be—who might, at some point, be prospective vendees of some other property encumbered by some other similar covenant. Had respondent failed to designate herself as the agent of this anonymous, amorphous class, the majority certainly would have no power to vindicate its rights. Yet, because respondent happens to have decided to act as the self-appointed agent of these principals whom she cannot identify—in order to relieve herself of the obligations of her own covenant—the majority finds itself able to assert the power over state courts which it asserts today. I do not think that such tenuous circumstances can spawn the broad constitutional limitation upon state courts which springs from today's decision.

Yet we are told that the rule which restricts our power to impose this constitutional limitation is but a rule of "self-restraint." So is every other jurisdictional limitation which depends, in the last analysis, solely upon this Court's willingness to govern its own exercise of power. And certainly to characterize the rule as self-imposed does not mean that it is self-removable by a simple self-serving process of argument. Yet the majority's logic, reduced to its barest outlines, seems to proceed in that fashion. We are told that the reasons for the self-imposed rule, which precludes us from reaching the merits, have been dissipated in this case, but the only reason why the reasons do not exist is because the Court first holds for respondent, and, having thus decided the merits, it feels free to abandon the rule which should preclude it from reaching the merits. In my view, respondent cannot surmount the hurdle of our well-established rule by proceeding with an argument which carries her in a circle right back to her precise point of departure. If it should be, as the majority assumes, that there is no other way that the rights of unidentified non-Caucasians can be vindicated in court, that is only an admission that there is no way in which a substantial case or controversy can be predicated upon the right which the majority is so anxious to pass upon. I cannot assent to a manner of vindicating the constitutional rights of persons unknown which puts personal predisposition in a paramount position over well-established proscriptions on power.

But even if the merits are to be reached, even if we must decide whether enforcement of this covenant in a lawsuit of this kind is state action which contravenes the Fourteenth Amendment, I think that the absence of any direct injury to any identifiable non-Caucasian is decisive. The *Shelley* case, resting on the express determination that restrictive covenants are valid between the parties, dealt only with a state court's attempt to enforce them directly against innocent third parties whose right to enjoy their property would suffer immediate harm.

In this case, the plaintiffs have not sought such relief. The suit is directed against the very person whose solemn promise helped to bring the covenant into existence. The plaintiffs ask only that respondent do what she in turn had a right to ask of plaintiffs—indemnify plaintiffs for the bringing about of an event which she recognized would cause injury to the plaintiffs. We need not concern ourselves now with any question of whether this injury is fancied or real. The short of that matter is that the parties thought that any influx of non-Caucasian neighbors would impair their enjoyment of their properties, and, whether right or wrong, each had the right to control the use of his property against that event and to exact a promise from his or her neighbor that he or she would act accordingly. And that is precisely what petitioners and respondent did. Moreover, we must, at this pleading stage of the case, accept it as a fact that respondent has thus far profited from the execution of this bargain; observance of the covenant by petitioners raised the value of respondent's properties. By this suit, the plaintiffs sought only to have respondent disgorge that which was gained at the expense of depreciation in her neighbors' property.

The majority speaks of this as an attempt to "coerce" respondent to continue to abide by her agreement. Yet the contract has already been breached. The non-Caucasians are in undisturbed occupancy. Furthermore, the respondent consented to the "coercion"—if "coercion" there be —by entering into the covenant. Plaintiffs ask only that respondent now pay what she legally obligated herself to pay for an injury which she recognized would occur if she did what she did.

Of course, there may be other elements of coercion. Coercion might result on the minds of some Caucasian property owners who have signed a covenant such as this, for they may now feel an economic compulsion to abide by their agreements. But visiting coercion upon the minds of some unidentified Caucasian property owners is not at all the state action which was condemned in the *Shelley* case. In that case, the state court had directed "the full coercive power of government" against the Negro petitioners—forcefully removing them from their property because they fell in a class discriminatorily defined. But in this case, where no identifiable third person can be directly injured if respondent is made to disgorge enough to indemnify petitioners, the Court should not undertake to hold that the Fourteenth Amendment stands as a bar to the state court's enforcement of its contract law.

Obviously we can only interfere in this case if the Fourteenth Amendment compels us to do so, for that is the only basis upon which respondent seeks to sustain her defense. While we are limited to enforcement of the Fourteenth Amendment, the state courts are not; they may decline to recognize the covenants for other reasons. Since we must rest our decision on the Constitution alone, we must set aside predilections on social policy and adhere to the settled rules which restrict the exercise of our power of judicial review—remembering that the only restraint upon this power is our own sense of self-restraint.

Because I cannot see how respondent can avail herself of the Fourteenth Amendment rights of total strangers—the only rights which she has chosen to assert—and since I cannot see how the Court can find that those rights would be impaired in this particular case by requiring respondent to pay petitioners for the injury which she recognizes that she has brought upon them, I am unwilling to join the Court in today's decision.

Part VII

DISCRIMINATION AND THE JURY

Although racial discrimination in the selection of jurors has consistently been held to be a violation of the Fourteenth Amendment, the determination of whether or not a particular method of selecting jurors is discriminatory has presented difficulties. Here are some typical cases chosen from a great many dealing with this problem.

Part VII

DISCRIMINATION AND THE JURY

Strauder v. W. Virginia

Smith v. Texas

Brown v. Mississippi

Cassell v. Texas

Avery v. Georgia

Hernandez v. Texas

Eubanks v. Louisiana

Although racial discrimination in the selection of jurors has repeatedly been held to be a violation of the Fourteenth Amendment, the determination of whether or not a particular method of selecting jurors is discriminatory has presented difficulties. Here are some typical cases chosen from a great many dealing with this problem.

Strauder v. W. Virginia
100 U. S. 303   1880

Mr. Justice Strong delivered the opinion of the Court.

. . . It is to be observed that the first of these questions is not whether
a colored man, when an indictment has been preferred against him,
has a right to a grand or a petit jury composed in whole or in part of
persons of his own race or color, but it is whether, in the composition
or selection of jurors by whom he is to be indicted or tried, all persons
of his race or color may be excluded by law, solely because of their race
or color, so that by no possibility can any colored man sit upon the jury.

The questions are important, for they demand a construction of the
recent amendments of the Constitution. If the defendant has a right to
have a jury selected for the trial of his case without discrimination
against all persons of his race or color, because of their race or color,
the right, if not created, is protected by those amendments, and the
legislation of Congress under them. The Fourteenth Amendment ordains
that "all persons born or naturalized in the United States and subject
to the jurisdiction thereof are citizens of the United States and of the
State wherein they reside. No State shall make or enforce any laws which
shall abridge the privileges or immunities of citizens of the United States,
nor shall any State deprive any person of life, liberty, or property, without due process of law, nor deny to any person within its jurisdiction
the equal protection of the laws."

This is one of a series of constitutional provisions having a common
purpose; namely, securing to a race recently emancipated, a race that
through many generations had been held in slavery, all the civil rights
that the superior race enjoy. The true spirit and meaning of the amendments, as we said in the *Slaughter-House Cases,* cannot be understood
without keeping in view the history of the times when they were adopted,
and the general objects they plainly sought to accomplish. At the time

when they were incorporated into the Constitution, it required little knowledge of human nature to anticipate that those who had long been regarded as an inferior and subject race would, when suddenly raised to the rank of citizenship, be looked upon with jealousy and positive dislike, and that State laws might be enacted or enforced to perpetuate the distinctions that had before existed. Discriminations against them had been habitual. It was well known that in some States laws making such discriminations then existed, and others might well be expected. The colored race, as a race, was abject and ignorant, and in that condition was unfitted to command the respect of those who had superior intelligence. Their training had left them mere children, and as such they needed the protection which a wise government extends to those who are unable to protect themselves. They especially needed protection against unfriendly action in the States where they were resident. It was in view of these considerations the Fourteenth Amendment was framed and adopted. It was designed to assure to the colored race the enjoyment of all the civil rights that under the law are enjoyed by white persons, and to give to that race the protection of the general government, in that enjoyment, whenever it should be denied by the States. It not only gave citizenship and the privileges of citizenship to persons of color, but it denied to any State the power to withhold from them the equal protection of the laws, and authorized Congress to enforce its provisions by appropriate legislation. To quote the language used by us in the *Slaughter-House Cases,* "No one can fail to be impressed with the one pervading purpose found in all the amendments, lying at the foundation of each, and without which none of them would have been suggested—we mean the freedom of the slave race, the security and firm establishment of that freedom, and the protection of the newly made freeman and citizen from the oppressions of those who had formerly exercised unlimited dominion over them." So again: "The existence of laws in the States where the newly emancipated negroes resided, which discriminated with gross injustice and hardship against them as a class, was the evil to be remedied, and by it [the Fourteenth Amendment] such laws were forbidden. If, however, the States did not conform their laws to its requirements, then, by the fifth section of the article of amendment, Congress was authorized to enforce it by suitable legislation." And it was added, "We doubt very much whether any action of a State, not directed by way of discrimination against the negroes, as a class, will ever be held to come within the purview of this provision."

If this is the spirit and meaning of the amendment, whether it means more or not, it is to be construed liberally, to carry out the purposes of its framers. It ordains that no State shall make or enforce any laws which shall abridge the privileges or immunities of citizens of the United States (evidently referring to the newly made citizens, who, being citizens of the United States, are declared to be also citizens of the State in which they reside). It ordains that no State shall deprive any person of life, liberty, or property, without due process of law, or deny to any person within its jurisdiction the equal protection of the laws. What is this but declaring that the law in the States shall be the same for the black as for the white; that all persons, whether colored or white, shall stand equal before the laws of the States, and, in regard to the colored race, for whose protection the amendment was primarily designed, that no discrimination shall be made against them by law because of their color? The words of the amendment, it is true, are prohibitory, but they contain a necessary implication of a positive immunity, or right, most valuable to the colored race—the right to exemption from unfriendly legislation against them distinctively as colored—exemption from legal discriminations, implying inferiority in civil society, lessening the security of their enjoyment of the rights which others enjoy, and discriminations which are steps towards reducing them to the condition of a subject race.

That the West Virginia statute respecting juries—the statute that controlled the selection of the grand and petit jury in the case of the plaintiff in error—is such a discrimination ought not to be doubted. Nor would it be if the persons excluded by it were white men. If in those States where the colored people constitute a majority of the entire population a law should be enacted excluding all white men from jury service, thus denying to them the privilege of participating equally with the blacks in the administration of justice, we apprehend no one would be heard to claim that it would not be a denial to white men of the equal protection of the laws. Nor if a law should be passed excluding all naturalized Celtic Irishmen, would there be any doubt of its inconsistency with the spirit of the amendment. The very fact that colored people are singled out and expressly denied by a statute all right to participate in the administration of the law, as jurors, because of their color, though they are citizens, and may be in other respects fully qualified, is practically a brand upon them, affixed by the law, an assertion of their inferiority, and a stimulant to that race prejudice which is an impediment to securing to individuals of the race that equal justice which the law aims to secure to all others.

The right to a trial by jury is guaranteed to every citizen of West Virginia by the Constitution of that State, and the constitution of juries is a very essential part of the protection such a mode of trial is intended to secure. The very idea of a jury is a body of men composed of the peers or equals of the person whose rights it is selected or summoned to determine, that is, of his neighbors, fellows, associates, persons having the same legal status in society as that which he holds. Blackstone, in his Commentaries, says, "The right of trial by jury on the country, is a trial by the peers of every Englishman, and is the grand bulwark of his liberties, and is secured to him by the Great Charter." It is also guarded by statutory enactments intended to make impossible what Mr. Bentham called "packing juries." It is well known that prejudices often exist against particular classes in the community, which sway the judgment of jurors, and which, therefore, operate in some cases to deny to persons of those classes the full enjoyment of that protection which others enjoy. Prejudice in a local community is held to be a reason for a change of venue. The framers of the constitutional amendment must have known full well the existence of such prejudice and its likelihood to continue against the manumitted slaves and their race, and that knowledge was doubtless a motive that led to the amendment. By their manumission and citizenship the colored race became entitled to the equal protection of the laws of the States in which they resided; and the apprehension that through prejudice they might be denied that equal protection, that is, that there might be discrimination against them, was the inducement to bestow upon the national government the power to enforce the provision that no State shall deny to them the equal protection of the laws. Without the apprehended existence of prejudice that portion of the amendment would have been unnecessary, and it might have been left to the States to extend equality of protection.

In view of these considerations, it is hard to see why the statute of West Virginia should not be regarded as discriminating against a colored man when he is put upon trial for an alleged criminal offence against the State. It is not easy to comprehend how it can be said that while every white man is entitled to a trial by a jury selected from persons of his own race or color, or, rather, selected without discrimination against his color, and a negro is not, the latter is equally protected by the law with the former. Is not protection of life and liberty against race or color prejudice a right, a legal right, under the constitutional amendment? And how can it be maintained that compelling a colored man to submit to a trial for his life by a jury drawn from a panel from which the State has expressly excluded every man of his race, because of color alone, however well qualified in other respects, is not a denial to him of equal legal protection?

We do not say that within the limits from which it is not excluded by the amendment a State may not prescribe the qualifications of its jurors, and in so doing make discriminations. It may confine the selection to males, to freeholders, to citizens, to persons within certain ages, or to persons having educational qualifications. We do not believe the Fourteenth Amendment was ever intended to prohibit this. Looking at its history, it is clear it had no such purpose. Its aim was against discrimination because of race or color. As we have said more than once, its design was to protect an emancipated race, and to strike down all possible legal discriminations against those who belong to it. To quote further from 16 Wall. "In giving construction to any of these articles [amendments], it is necessary to keep the main purpose steadily in view." "It is so clearly a provision for that race and that emergency, that a strong case would be necessary for its application to any other." We are not now called upon to affirm or deny that it had other purposes.

The Fourteenth Amendment makes no attempt to enumerate the rights it designed to protect. It speaks in general terms, and those are as comprehensive as possible. Its language is prohibitory; but every prohibition implies the existence of rights and immunities, prominent among which is an immunity from inequality of legal protection, either for life, liberty, or property. Any State action that denies this immunity to a colored man is in conflict with the Constitution . . . .

Smith v. Texas

311 U. S. 128   1940

Mr. Justice Black delivered the opinion of the Court.

In Harris County, Texas, where petitioner, a negro, was indicted and convicted of rape, negroes constitute over 20% of the population, and almost 10% of the poll-tax payers; a minimum of from three to six thousand of them measure up to the qualifications prescribed by Texas statutes for grand jury service. The court clerk, called as a state witness and testifying from court records covering the years 1931 through 1938, showed that only 5 of the 384 grand jurors who served during that period were negroes; that of 512 persons summoned for grand jury duty, only 18 were negroes; that of these 18, the names of 13 appeared as the last name on the 16 man jury list, the custom being to select the 12 man grand jury in the order that the names appeared on the list; that of the 5 negroes summoned for grand jury service who were not given the number 16, 4 were given numbers between 13 and 16, and 1 was number 6; that the result of this numbering was that of the 18 negroes summoned, only 5 ever served, whereas 379 of the 494 white men summoned actually served; that of 32 grand juries empanelled, only 5 had negro members, while 27 had none; that of these 5, the same individual served 3 times, so that only 3 individual negroes served at all; that there had been no negroes on any of the grand juries in 1938, the year petitioner was indicted; that there had been none on any of the grand juries in 1937; that the service of negroes by years had been: 1931, 1; 1932, 2; 1933, 1; 1934, 1; 1935, none; 1936, 1; 1937, none; 1938, none.

It is petitioner's contention that his conviction was based on an indictment obtained in violation of the provision of the Fourteenth Amendment that "No State shall . . . deny to any person within its jurisdiction the equal protection of the laws." And the contention that equal protection was denied him rests on a charge that negroes were, in 1938 and long prior thereto, intentionally and systematically excluded from grand jury service solely on account of their race and color. That a conviction based upon an indictment returned by a jury so selected is a denial of equal protection is well settled, and is not challenged by the state. But both the trial court and the Texas Criminal Court of Appeals were of opinion that the evidence failed to support the charge of racial discrimination. For that reason the Appellate Court approved the trial court's action in denying petitioner's timely motion to quash the indictment. But the question decided rested upon a charge of denial of equal protection, a basic right protected by the Federal Constitution. And it is therefore our responsibility to appraise the evidence as it relates to this constitutional right.

It is part of the established tradition in the use of juries as instruments of public justice that the jury be a body truly representative of the community. For racial discrimination to result in the exclusion from jury service of otherwise qualified groups not only violates our Constitution and the laws enacted under it but is at war with our basic concepts of a democratic society and a representative government. We must consider this record in the light of these important principles. The fact that the written words of a state's laws hold out a promise that no such discrimination will be practiced is not enough. The Fourteenth Amendment requires that equal protection to all must be given—not merely promised.

Here, the Texas statutory scheme is not in itself unfair; it is capable of being carried out with no racial discrimination whatsoever. But by reason of the wide discretion permissible in the various steps of the plan, it is equally capable of being applied in such a manner as practically to proscribe any group thought by the law's administrators to be undesirable. And from the record before us the conclusion is inescapable that it is the latter application that has prevailed in Harris County. Chance and accident alone could hardly have brought about the listing for grand jury service of so few negroes from among the thousands shown by the undisputed evidence to possess the legal qualifications for jury service. Nor could chance and accident have been responsible for the combination of circumstances under which a negro's name, when listed at all, almost invariably appeared as number 16, and under which number 16 was never called for service unless it proved impossible to obtain the required jurors from the first 15 names on the list.

The state argues that the testimony of the commissioners themselves shows that there was no arbitrary or systematic exclusion. And it is true that two of the three commissioners who drew the September, 1938, panel testified to that effect. Both of them admitted that they did not select any negroes, although the subject was discussed, but both categorically denied that they intentionally, arbitrarily or systematically discriminated against negro jurors as such. One said that their failure to select negroes was because they did not know the names of any who were qualified and the other said that he was not personally acquainted with any member of the negro race. This is, at best, the testimony of two individuals who participated in drawing 1 out of the 32 jury panels discussed in the record. But even if their testimony were given the greatest possible effect, and their situation considered typical of that of the 94 commissioners who did not testify, we would still feel compelled to reverse the decision below. What the Fourteenth Amendment prohibits is racial discrimination in the selection of grand juries. Where jury commissioners limit those from whom grand juries are selected to their own personal acquaintance, discrimination can arise from commissioners who know no negroes as well as from commissioners who know but eliminate them. If there has been discrimination, whether accomplished ingeniously or ingenuously, the conviction cannot stand.

Patton v. Mississippi
332 U. S. 463   1947

Mr. Justice Black delivered the opinion of the Court.

The petitioner, a Negro, was indicted in the Circuit Court of Lauderdale County, Mississippi, by an all-white grand jury, charged with the murder of a white man. He was convicted by an all-white petit jury and sentenced to death by electrocution. He had filed a timely motion to quash the indictment alleging that, although there were Negroes in the county qualified for jury service, the venires for the term from which the grand and petit juries were selected did not contain the name of a single Negro. Failure to have any Negroes on the venires, he alleged, was due to the fact that for a great number of years previously and during the then term of court there had been in the county a "systematic, intentional, deliberate and invariable practice on the part of administrative officers to exclude negroes from the jury lists, jury boxes and jury service, and that such practice has resulted and does now result in the denial of the equal protection of the laws to this defendant as guaranteed by the 14th amendment to the U. S. Constitution." In support of his motion petitioner introduced evidence which showed without contradiction that no Negro had served on the grand or petit criminal court juries for thirty years or more. There was evidence that a single Negro had once been summoned during that period but for some undisclosed reason he had not served, nor had he even appeared. And there was also evidence from one jury supervisor that he had, at some indefinite time, placed on the jury lists the names of "two or three" unidentified Negroes. In 1940 the adult colored population of Lauderdale County, according to the United States Census, was 12,511 out of a total adult population of 34,821.

In the face of the foregoing the trial court overruled the motion to quash. The Supreme Court of Mississippi affirmed over petitioner's renewed insistence that he had been denied the equal protection of the laws by the deliberate exclusion of Negroes from the grand jury that indicted and the petit jury that convicted him. We granted certiorari to review this serious contention.

Sixty-seven years ago this Court held that state exclusion of Negroes from grand and petit juries solely because of their race denied Negro defendants in criminal cases the equal protection of the laws required by the Fourteenth Amendment. A long and unbroken line of our decisions since then has reiterated that principle, regardless of whether the discrimination was embodied in statute or was apparent from the administrative practices of state jury selection officials, and regardless of whether the system for depriving defendants of their rights was "ingenious or ingenuous."

Whether there has been systematic racial discrimination by administrative officials in the selection of jurors is a question to be determined from the facts in each particular case. In this case the Mississippi Supreme Court concluded that petitioner had failed to prove systematic racial discrimination in the selection of jurors, but in so concluding it erroneously considered only the fact that no Negroes were on the particular venire lists from which the juries were drawn that indicted and convicted petitioner. It regarded as irrelevant the key fact that for thirty years or more no Negro had served on the grand or petit juries. This omission seriously detracts from the weight and respect that we would otherwise give to its conclusion in reviewing the facts, as we must in a constitutional question like this.

It is to be noted at once that the indisputable fact that no Negro had served on a criminal court grand or petit jury for a period of thirty years created a very strong showing that during that period Negroes were systematically excluded from jury service because of race. When such a showing was made, it became a duty of the State to try to justify such an exclusion as having been brought about for some reason other than racial discrimination. The Mississippi Supreme Court did not conclude, the State did not offer any evidence, and in fact did not make any claim, that its officials had abandoned their old jury selection practices. The State Supreme Court's conclusion of justification rested upon the following reasoning. Section 1762 of the Mississippi Code enumerates the qualifications for jury service, the most important of which apparently are that one must be a male citizen and "a qualified elector." Sections 241, 242, 243 and 244 of the State Constitution set forth the prerequisites for qualified electors. Among other things, these provisions require that each elector shall pay an annual poll tax, produce satisfactory proof of such payment, and be able to read any section of the State Constitution, or to understand the same when read to him, or to give a reasonable interpretation thereof. The evidence showed that a very small number of Negro male citizens (the court estimated about 25), as compared with white male citizens, had met the requirements for qualified electors, and thereby become eligible to be considered under additional tests for jury service. On this subject the State Supreme Court said:

"Of the 25 qualified negro male electors there would be left, therefore, as those not exempt, 12 or 13 available male negro electors as compared with 5,500 to 6,000 male white electors as to whom, after deducting 500 to 1,000 exempt, would leave a proportion of 5,000 nonexempt white jurors to 12 or 13 nonexempt negro jurors, or about one-fourth of one per cent negro jurors, —400 to 1. . . . For the reasons already heretofore stated there was only a chance of 1 in 400 that a negro would appear on such a venire and as this venire was of one hundred jurors, the sheriff, had he brought in a negro, would have had to discriminate against white jurors, not against negroes— he could not be expected to bring in one-fourth of one negro."

The above statement of the Mississippi Supreme Court illustrates the unwisdom of attempting to disprove systematic racial discrimination in the selection of jurors by percentage calculations applied to the composition of a single venire.

The petitioner here points out certain legislative record evidence of which it is claimed we can take judicial notice, and which it is asserted establishes that the reason why there are so few qualified Negro electors in Mississippi is because of discrimination against them in making up the registration lists. But we need not consider that question in this case. For it is clear from the evidence in the record that there were some

Negroes in Lauderdale County on the registration list. In fact, in 1945, the circuit clerk of the county, who is himself charged with duties in administering the jury system, sent the names of eight Negroes to the jury commissioner of the Federal District Court as citizens of Lauderdale County qualified for federal jury service. Moreover, there was evidence that the names of from thirty to several hundred qualified Negro electors were on the registration lists. But whatever the precise number of qualified colored electors in the county, there were some; and if it can possibly be conceived that all of them were disqualified for jury service by reason of the commission of crime, habitual drunkenness, gambling, inability to read and write, or to meet any other or all of the statutory tests, we do not doubt that the State could have proved it.

We hold that the State wholly failed to meet the very strong evidence of purposeful racial discrimination made out by the petitioner upon the uncontradicted showing that for thirty years or more no Negro had served as a juror in the criminal courts of Lauderdale County. When a jury selection plan, whatever it is, operates in such way as always to result in the complete and long-continued exclusion of any representative at all from a large group of Negroes, or any other racial group, indictments and verdicts returned against them by juries thus selected cannot stand. As we pointed out in *Hill* v. *Texas,* our holding does not mean that a guilty defendant must go free. For indictments can be returned and convictions can be obtained by juries selected as the Constitution commands.

The judgment of the Mississippi Supreme Court is reversed and the case is remanded for proceedings not inconsistent with this opinion.

Cassell v. Texas
339 U. S. 282   1950

Mr. Justice Reed announced the judgment of the Court and an opinion in which The Chief Justice, Mr. Justice Black and Mr. Justice Clark concurred.

Review was sought in this case to determine whether there had been a violation by Texas of petitioner's federal constitutional right to a fair and impartial grand jury. The federal question was raised by a motion to quash the indictment on the ground that petitioner, a Negro, suffered unconstitutional discrimination through the selection of white men only for the grand jury that indicted him. After full hearing, the trial court denied the motion, and this action was sustained by the Court of Criminal Appeals of Texas in affirming petitioner's conviction.

The Court of Criminal Appeals accepted the federal rule that a Negro is denied the equal protection of the laws when he is indicted by a grand jury from which Negroes as a race have been intentionally excluded. It was from an examination of facts that the court deduced its conclusion that racial discrimination had not been practiced. Since the result reached may deny a federal right, we may reexamine the facts to determine whether petitioner has sustained by proof his allegation of discrimination. Certiorari was granted to consider petitioner's claim that in this case Negroes were omitted from the list of grand jurymen either because of deliberate limitation by the Dallas County jury commissioners, or because of failure by the commissioners to acquaint themselves with available Negroes.

Acting under the Texas statutes, the Dallas County grand-jury commissioners chose a list of sixteen males for this September 1947 grand jury from citizens eligible under the statute. The judge chose twelve of these for the panel. No challenge is now made to the fairness of this statutory system. We have approved it.

Petitioner's attack is upon the way the statutory method of grand-jury selection has been administered by the jury commissioners. One charge is that discrimination must have been practiced because the Negro proportion of grand jurors is less than the Negro proportion of the county's population. Under the 1940 census the total population of Dallas County was 398,564, of whom 61,605 were Negroes. This is about 15.5%. In weighing this matter of custom, we limit ourselves, as do the parties, to the period between June 1, 1942, when *Hill* v. *Texas* was decided, and November 1947, when petitioner was indicted. There were 21 grand juries in this period; of the 252 members of the panels, 17, or 6.7%, were Negroes. But this apparent discrepancy may be explained by the fact that Texas grand jurors must possess certain statutory qualifications. Grand jurors must ordinarily be eligible to vote; eligibility requires payment of a poll tax; and the validity of the poll-tax requirement is not challenged. The record shows 5,500 current Negro poll-tax payers in Dallas County in 1947, and nothing indicates that this number varied substantially from year to year. The corresponding figure for all poll-tax payers, male and female, is 83,667. These figures would indicate that as a proportional matter 6.5% of grand jurors would be Negroes, a percentage approximating the ratio of Negroes actually sitting on the 21 grand jury panels. Without more it cannot be said that Negroes had been left off grand-jury panels to such a degree as to establish a *prima facie* case of discrimination.

A different question is presented by petitioner's next charge that subsequent to the *Hill* case the Dallas County grand-jury commissioners for 21 consecutive lists had consistently limited Negroes selected for grand-jury service to not more than one on each grand jury. The contention is that the *Akins* case has been interpreted in Dallas County to allow a limitation of the number of Negroes on each grand jury, provided the limitation is approximately proportional to the number of Negroes eligible for grand-jury service. Since the *Hill* case the judges of the trial court have been careful to instruct their jury commissioners that discrimination on grounds of race or color is forbidden. The judge did so here. If, notwithstanding this caution by the trial court judges, commissioners should limit proportionally the number of Negroes selected for grand-jury service, such limitation would violate our Constitution. Jurymen should be selected as individuals, on the basis of individual qualifications, and not as members of a race.

We have recently written why proportional representation of races on a jury is not a constitutional requisite. Succinctly stated, our reason was that the Constitution requires only a fair jury selected without regard to race. Obviously the number of races and nationalities appearing in the ancestry of our citizens would make it impossible to meet a requirement of proportional representation. Similarly, since there can be no exclusion of Negroes as a race and no discrimination because of color, proportional limitation is not permissible. That conclusion is compelled by the United States Code, Title 18, § 243, based on § 4 of the Civil Rights Act of 1875. While the language of the section directs attention to the right to serve as a juror, its command has long been recognized also to assure rights to an accused. Prohibiting racial disqualification of Negroes for jury service, this congressional enactment under the Fourteenth Amendment has been consistently sustained and its violation held to deny a proper trial to a Negro accused. Proportional racial limitation is therefore forbidden. An accused is entitled to have charges against him considered by a jury in the selection of which there has been neither inclusion nor exclusion because of race.

Our holding that there was discrimination in the selection of grand jurors in this case, however, is based on another ground. In explaining the fact that no Negroes appeared on this grand-jury list, the commissioners said that they knew none available who qualified; at the same time they said they chose jurymen only from those people with whom they were personally acquainted. It may be assumed that in ordinary activities in Dallas County, acquaintanceship between the races is not on a sufficiently familiar basis to give citizens eligible for appointment as jury commissioners an opportunity to know the qualifications for grand-jury service of many members of another race. An individual's qualifications for grand-jury service, however, are not hard to ascertain, and with no evidence to the contrary, we must assume that a large proportion of the Negroes of Dallas County met the statutory requirements for jury service. When the commissioners were appointed as judicial administrative officials, it was their duty to familiarize themselves fairly with the qualifications of the eligible jurors of the county without regard to race and color. They did not do so here, and the result has been racial discrimination. We repeat that recent statement of Chief Justice Stone in *Hill* v. *Texas:*

"Discrimination can arise from the action of commissioners who exclude all negroes whom they do not know to be qualified and who neither know nor seek to learn whether there are in fact any qualified to serve. In such a case, discrimination necessarily results where there are qualified negroes available for jury service. With the large number of colored male residents of the county who are literate, and in the absence of any countervailing testimony, there is no room for inference that there are not among them householders of good moral character, who can read and write, qualified and available for grand jury service."

The existence of the kind of discrimination described in the *Hill* case does not depend upon systematic exclusion continuing over a long period and practiced by a succession of jury commissioners. Since the issue must be whether there has been discrimination in the selection of the jury that his indicted petitioner, it is enough to have direct evidence based on the statements of the jury commissioners in the very case. Discrimination may be proved in other ways than by evidence of long-continued unexplained absence of Negroes from many panels. The statements of the jury commissioners that they chose only whom they knew, and that they knew no eligible Negroes in an area where Negroes made up so large a proportion of the population, prove the intentional exclusion that is discrimination in violation of petitioner's constitutional rights.

The judgment of the Court of Criminal Appeals of Texas is

Reversed.

Mr. Justice Douglas took no part in the consideration or decision of this case.

Mr. Justice Frankfurter, whom Mr. Justice Burton and Mr. Justice Minton join, concurring in the judgment.

It has been settled law since 1880 that the Civil War Amendments barred the States from discriminating because of race in the selection of juries, whether grand or petty. As a result, a conviction cannot stand which is based on an indictment found by a grand jury from which Negroes were kept because of discrimination. We ought not to reverse a course of decisions of long standing directed against racial discrimination in the administration of justice. But discrimination in this context means purposeful, systematic non-inclusion because of color. It does not mean an absence of proportional representation of the various racial components of the relevant political unit from which a grand jury is drawn or an isolated instance of disparity among such components. Assuming that the grand-jury pool fairly enough reflects the racial composition of the community, there is no basis for a claim of constitutional discrimination if without design it comes to pass that a particular grand jury has no representation of a particular race. The Civil War Amendments did not deprive the States of their power to define qualifications for grand-jury service relevant to the functions of a grand jury, nor did they turn matters that are inherently incommensurable into mere matters of arithmetic. The Constitution has not withdrawn the administration of criminal justice, of which the jury system is a part, from the States. It does command that no State purposefully make jury service turn on color.

A claim that the constitutional prohibition of discrimination was disregarded calls for ascertainment of two kinds of issues which ought not to be confused by being compendiously called "facts." The demonstrable, outward events by which a grand jury came into being raise issues quite different from the fair inferences to be drawn from what took place in determining the constitutional question: was there a purposeful non-inclusion of Negroes because of race or a merely symbolic representation, not the operation of an honest exercise of relevant judgment or the uncontrolled caprices of chance?

This Court does not sit as a jury to weigh conflicting evidence on underlying details, as for instance what steps were taken to make up the jury list, why one person was rejected and another taken, whether names were picked blindly or chosen by judgment. This is not the place for disputation about what really happened. On that we accept the findings of the State court. But it is for this Court to define the constitutional standards by which those findings are to be judged. Thereby the duty of securing observance of these standards may fall upon this Court. The meaning of uncontrovertible facts in relation to the ultimate issue of discrimination is precisely the constitutional issue on which this Court must pass. Of course even as to this, as always when a State court judgment is claimed to be in disregard of the Constitution, appropriate respect should be given to the judgment of the State court. And so we are brought to this case.

If the record here showed no more than that the grand-jury commissioners had considered the Negroes with whom they were acquainted— just as they considered white persons whom they knew—and had found them to be either unqualified for grand-jury service or qualified but unavailable, and did so not designedly to exclude Negroes, the State court's validation of the local procedure would have to prevail. We ought not to go behind such a conscientious process, however rough and ready the procedure of selection by jury commissioners. To find in such honest even if pragmatic selection of grand jurors the operation of unconstitutional standards would turn this Court into an agency for supervising the criminal procedure of the forty-eight States. Such an assumption of authority by this Court would jeopardize the practical functioning of grand juries throughout the country in view of the great variety of minority groups that compose our society.

A different situation would be presented by an unquestioned showing that jury commissioners had such a limited personal knowledge of potentially qualified Negro jurors that their purposeful limitation of choice to the negligibly few Negroes known to them would inevitably imply designed exclusion of eligible Negroes. The record here affords no basis whatever for such a finding. It indicates the contrary.

The record does disclose stark facts requiring reversal on a very different basis. If one factor is uniform in a continuing series of events that are brought to pass through human intervention, the law would have to have the blindness of indifference rather than the blindness of impartiality not to attribute the uniform factor to man's purpose. The purpose may not be of evil intent or in conscious disregard of what is conceived to be a binding duty. Prohibited conduct may result from misconception of what duty requires. Such misconception I believe to be the real situation on the record before us.

The governing facts are briefly stated. In *Hill* v. *Texas* this Court found discrimination in the selection of grand jurors in Dallas County, Texas, by virtue of the fact that, despite a large number of Negroes qualified for grand-jury service, none had been drawn. In the course of the five and a half years between that decision and the time of the drawing of the grand jury which found the indictment now challenged, there were twenty-one grand-jury panels. On each of these twenty-one consecutive panels there was never more than one Negro. This selection was made from lists which were not the result of a drawing of lots but the personal choice of the grand-jury commissioners. The available evidence clearly indicates that no more than one Negro was chosen by the commissioners for each of the twenty-one lists. Only one Negro was placed on the list—he did not serve on the panel—for the second grand jury in Dallas County after the decision in *Hill* v. *Texas*. Again, as to the grand jury which figured in *Akins* v. *Texas* only one Negro was placed on the list, and he served as a grand juror. And in *Weems* v. *State* it was stipulated that only one Negro, who did not serve on the panel, was on the list. In the present case it is conceded that no Negro was placed on the list. The State makes no contrary claim as to any of the other grand-jury lists though the facts regarding them are peculiarly within the State's knowledge. In view of this background, the assumption that more than one Negro was placed on the lists is inconceivable.

To assume that the commissioners did tender to the judges lists containing more than one Negro would lead inescapably to the conclusion that the judges systematically discriminated against Negroes. This is so because it just does not happen that from lists of sixteen it is always Negroes (barring one) that judges unpurposefully reject. I cannot attribute such discrimination to the trial judges of Dallas County. I can decline to attribute such discrimination to these judges only by concluding that the judges were never given the opportunity to select more than one Negro.

The grand-jury commissioners here received instructions from the judge not to "discriminate," and I have no doubt that they tried conscientiously to abide by them. The difficulty lies in what they conceived to be the standard for determining discrimination, as revealed by their action. The number of Negroes both qualified and available for jury service in Dallas County precluded such uniform presence of never more than one Negro on any other basis of good faith than that the commissioners were guided by the belief that one Negro on the grand jury satisfied the prohibition against discrimination in *Hill* v. *Texas*. That this was their view is compelled by their testimony at the hearing on the motion to quash the indictment.

This is of course a misconception. The prohibition of the Constitution against discrimination because of color does not require in and of itself the presence of a Negro on a jury. But neither is it satisfied by Negro representation arbitrarily limited to one. It is not a question of presence on a grand jury nor absence from it. The basis of selection cannot consciously take color into account. Such is the command of the Constitution. Once that restriction upon the State's freedom in devising and administering its jury system is observed, the States are masters in their own household. If it is observed, they cannot be charged with discrimination because of color, no matter what the composition of a grand jury may turn out to be.

On this record I cannot escape the conclusion that the judgment below is not based on an allowable finding of facts behind which this Court cannot go. It derives from the ultimate constitutional significance of undisputed facts. These bear no other rational meaning than purposeful discrimination. It does not neutralize the discrimination that it may well have been due to a misconception by the grand-jury commissioners of the requirements of this Court's decisions.

This compels reversal of the judgment.

Mr. Justice Clark, concurring.

For the reasons stated by Mr. Justice Jackson, it seems to me quite doubtful as an original issue whether a conviction should be reversed because of purposeful exclusion of the members of a race from the grand jury which returned the indictment. However, I think we must adhere to the settled course of decision by this Court with respect to such exclusion.

I am unable to conclude that from the date of the decision in *Hill* v.

Texas to the date of the trial of this case there has been purposeful systematic limitation of the number of Negroes on grand juries in Dallas County. The only evidence relied upon to establish such limitation is with regard to the composition of the twenty-one grand juries, including the jury returning the indictment of petitioner, which were impaneled during this period. But each of these grand juries of twelve persons was selected by a judge from a list of sixteen persons prepared by commissioners. The record shows only those Negroes who have actually served on the grand juries and not those who were on the commissioners' lists. We cannot conclude that there has been uniformity as to race in the selections of commissioners when we do not know how many Negroes have been on their lists. Even if judicial notice is taken of the racial composition of three lists during the period in question, which are reported in *Akins* v. *Texas* and in *Weems* v. *State,* there remain sixty-eight persons on the lists whose race is not ascertainable from the record or from any concession of counsel. Nor do I think that alternatively we are compelled by the statistics relied upon by petitioner to conclude that the judges purposefully discriminated during this period. Any presumption as to the purpose of the judges, or of the commissioners whom the judges appointed, instructed and supervised, must be that they intended no racial limitation. And the testimony of the judge who impaneled the grand jury in this case and a number of other grand juries during the period under review, as well as the testimony of the commissioners in this case as to the judge's instructions to them, indicates that he has not purposefully limited participation on account of race. In the face of this presumption and testimony, I think that, even if there were more than one Negro on each of the commissioners' lists, we could not infer any purpose on the part of the judges to limit Negro participation solely because of race. The burden of showing facts which permit an inference of purposeful limitation is on the defendant. I do not find the present record persuasive that there was such limitation.

The difficulties facing grand-jury commissioners are well illustrated by this case. On the one hand they are told that purposeful discrimination is inferred from the available statistics during the previous five and one-half years, showing that no more than one Negro was chosen for each of 21 grand juries; that this indicates that the commissioners must have been guided by the misconceived view that the presence of one Negro on the grand jury satisfied constitutional requirements. But they are also told quite properly that a token representation of a race on a grand jury is not a constitutional requisite; that in fact it may reach the point of illegality; that representation on the grand jury by race in proportion to population is not permissible for there must be "neither inclusion nor exclusion because of race." Under these circumstances one may, like Job's comforter, only add to the commissioners' distress by writing further. But it does appear to me from this record that their responsibility is broader than they understood it to be. They frankly stated that in making up the list they discussed only those persons whom they knew personally, and that they considered only one Negro, a school principal who could not serve. The record indicates clearly that there were Negroes qualified and available whom the commissioners did not know but whom upon inquiry they should have considered. Their responsibility was to learn whether there were persons among the Negroes they did not know who were qualified and available for service. The elimination of this large group in the community from the commissioners' consideration deprived petitioner of constitutional safeguards as defined in the decisions of this Court. For this reason I concur in the opinion of Mr. Justice Reed and in the judgment of reversal.

Mr. Justice Jackson, dissenting.

The case before us is that of a Negro convicted of murder by crushing the skull of a sleeping watchman with a piece of iron pipe to carry out a burglary. No question is here as to his guilt. We are asked to order his release from this conviction upon the sole ground that Negroes were purposefully discriminated against in selection of the grand jury that indicted him. It is admitted that Negroes were not excluded from the trial jury by which he was convicted.

In setting aside this conviction, the Court is moved by a desire to enforce equality in that realm where, above all, it must be enforced— in our judicial system. But this conviction is reversed for errors that have nothing to do with the defendant's guilt or innocence, or with a fair trial of that issue. This conflicts with another principle important to our law, *viz.*, that no conviction should be set aside for errors not affecting substantial rights of the accused.

This Court has never weighed these competing considerations in cases of this kind. The use of objections to the composition of juries is lately so much resorted to for purposes of delay, however, and the spectacle of a defendant putting the grand jury on trial before he can be tried for a crime is so discrediting to the administration of justice, that it is time to examine the basis for the practice.

I

It is the command of the Fourteenth Amendment that Negro citizens be afforded the same opportunities to serve upon grand juries as are afforded white citizens. Moreover, Congress, which is authorized to provide for its enforcement, has enacted that "no citizen possessing all other qualifications which are or may be prescribed by law shall be disqualified for service as grand or petit juror in any court of the United States, or of any State, on account of race, color, or previous condition of servitude; . . . ."

The substantive right is thus clear. But whose right is it? The right is conferred upon the qualified colored citizen to serve on equal terms with the qualified white citizen. This defendant is not here asking that right for himself. He claims that failure to give other Negroes an equal right to sit on the grand jury gives him quite a different right—a right not to be indicted by it. Two reasons occur to me which could justify this Court in translating the wrong to those Negroes excluded from a grand jury into a right of this defendant to void an indictment. One is that the absence of Negroes on the grand jury prejudiced this defendant. The other is that it is the only practicable method for enforcing the right of qualified Negroes to serve on grand juries. It is doubtful if either of these can be sustained.

II

Congress, which has implemented the right of Negroes to serve on juries, had also commanded all United States Courts to give judgment "without regard to technical errors, defects, or exceptions which do not affect the substantial rights of the parties." And this same congressional policy was manifested in a provision directing that no indictment found and presented by a grand jury in United States Courts "shall be deemed insufficient, nor shall the trial, judgment, or other proceeding thereon be affected by reason of any defect or imperfection in matter of form only, which shall not tend to the prejudice of the defendant"; and also in the provision that a motion to quash an indictment shall fail where the ground is that one or more members of the grand jury were unqualified, but where it appears that twelve or more qualified jurors concurred in the finding of the indictment.

This Court never has explained how discrimination in the selection of a grand jury, illegal though it be, has prejudiced a defendant whom a trial jury, chosen with no discrimination, has convicted. The reason this question was not considered perhaps is that, in the earlier cases where convictions were set aside, the discrimination condemned was present in selecting *both grand and trial jury* and, while the argument was chiefly based on the latter, the language of the opinions made no differentiation, nor for their purpose did they need to. Only within the last few years have convictions been set aside for discrimination in composition of the grand jury alone, and in these the question now under consideration was not discussed.

It is obvious that discriminatory exclusion of Negroes from a trial jury does, or at least may, prejudice a Negro's right to a fair trial, and that a conviction so obtained should not stand. The trial jury hears the evidence of both sides and chooses what it will believe. In so deciding, it is influenced by imponderables—unconscious and conscious prejudices and preferences—and a thousand things we cannot detect or isolate in its verdict and whose influence we cannot weigh. A single juror's dissent is generally enough to prevent conviction. A trial jury on which one of the defendant's race has no chance to sit may not have the substance, and cannot have the appearance, of impartiality, especially when the accused is a Negro and the alleged victim is not.

The grand jury is a very different institution. The States are not required to use it at all. Its power is only to accuse, not to convict. Its indictment does not even create a presumption of guilt; all that it charges must later be proved before the trial jury, and then beyond a reasonable doubt. The grand jury need not be unanimous. It does not hear both sides but only the prosecution's evidence, and does not face the problem of a choice between two adversaries. Its duty is to indict if the prosecution's evidence, unexplained, uncontradicted and unsupplemented, would warrant a conviction. If so, its indictment merely puts the accused to trial. The difference between the function of the trial jury and the function of the grand jury is all the difference between deciding a case and merely deciding that a case should be tried.

It hardly lies in the mouth of a defendant whom a fairly chosen trial jury has found guilty beyond reasonable doubt, to say that his indictment is attributable to prejudice. In this case a trial judge heard the prosecution's evidence, ruled it sufficient to warrant a conviction, appellate courts have held the same, and no further question about it is before us. Moreover, a jury admittedly chosen without racial discrimination has heard the prosecution's and defendant's evidence and has held that guilt beyond a reasonable doubt has been proved. That finding, too, has been affirmed on appeal and is not here. Under such circumstances, it is frivolous to contend that any grand jury, however constituted, could have done its duty in any way other than to indict.

III

Congress has provided means other than release of convicted defendants to enforce this right of the Negro community to participate in grand jury service; and they are, if used, direct and effective remedies to accomplish this purpose.

"[W]hoever, being an officer or other person charged with any duty in the selection or summoning of jurors, excludes or fails to summon any citizen" because of his color or race has committed a federal crime and is subject to a fine of not more than $5,000.

Congress has also provided that "every person who, under color of any statute, ordinance, regulation, custom, or usage, of any State or Territory, subjects, or causes to be subjected, any citizen of the United States or other person within the jurisdiction thereof to the deprivation of any rights, privileges, or immunities secured by the Constitution and laws, shall be liable to the party injured in an *action at law, suit in equity,* or *other proper proceeding for redress."* (Emphasis supplied.)

These criminal and civil remedies for discriminatory exclusions from the jury have been almost totally neglected both by the Federal Government and by Negro citizens entitled to sit as jurors. Back in 1878 a state judge was indicted in federal court for violation of the Act and this Court sustained it. That case has been allowed to stand as solitary and neglected authority for direct enforcement of the Negro's right to sit on juries.

Qualified Negroes excluded by discrimination have available, in addition, remedies in courts of equity. I suppose there is no doubt, and if there is this Court can dispel it, that a citizen or a class of citizens unlawfully excluded from jury service could maintain in a federal court an individual or a class action for an injunction or mandamus against the state officers responsible. If the order were evaded or disobeyed, imprisonment for contempt could follow.

IV

It is implicit in the Court's decision that the federal penal statute has been violated. So in effect it holds that the crime of discrimination offsets the crime of murder and that the State must start over again, if death of witnesses, loss of evidence or other conditions wrought by time do not prevent.

I do not see how this Court can escape the conclusion that any discrimination in selection of the grand jury in this case, however great the wrong toward qualified Negroes of the community, was harmless to this defendant. To conclude otherwise is to assume that Negroes qualified to sit on a grand jury would refuse even to put to trial a man whom a lawfully chosen trial jury found guilty beyond a reasonable doubt.

The Negro's right to be selected for grand jury service is unquestionable and should be directly and uncompromisingly enforced. But I doubt if any good purpose will be served in the long run by identifying the right of the most worthy Negroes to serve on grand juries with the efforts of the least worthy to defer or escape punishment for crime. I cannot believe that those qualified for grand jury service would fail to return a true bill against a murderer because he is a Negro. But unless they would, this defendant has not been harmed.

I would treat this as a case where the irregularity is not shown to have harmed this defendant, and affirm the conviction. But in this and similar cases, I would send a copy of the record to the Department of Justice for investigation as to whether there have been violations of the statute and, if so, for prosecution.

Avery v. Georgia
345 U. S. 559 1953

Mr. Chief Justice Vinson delivered the opinion of the Court.

Petitioner was tried for rape in the Superior Court of Fulton County, Georgia. He was convicted and sentenced to death. The Supreme Court of Georgia affirmed after overruling petitioner's contention that the jury which convicted him had been selected by a means repugnant to the Equal Protection Clause of the Fourteenth Amendment. We granted certiorari to review this claim.

The indictment, upon which petitioner was tried, was returned by a grand jury in Walker County, Georgia. A change of venue was granted and the cause removed to Fulton County. By proper pleadings petitioner, a Negro, challenged the array of petit jurors selected to try his case; he charged that discrimination had been practiced against members of his race. Testimony was then taken, and thereafter the trial court overruled the challenge.

The salient facts, developed in this hearing, are undisputed. Under Georgia law the task of organizing panels of petit jurors for criminal cases falls upon a county Board of Jury Commissioners. In discharging this responsibility the Commissioners, at stated intervals, select prospective jurors from the county tax returns. Their list is then printed; the names of white persons on this list are printed on white tickets; the names of Negroes are printed on yellow tickets. These tickets—white and yellow—are placed in a jury box. A judge of the Superior Court then draws a number of tickets from the box. The tickets are handed to a sheriff who in turn entrusts them to a clerk. It is the clerk's duty to "arrange" the tickets and to type up, in final form, the list of persons to be called to serve on the panel.

Approximately sixty persons were selected to make up the panel from which the jury in this particular case was drawn. The judge who picked out the tickets—bearing the names of persons composing the panel—testified that he did not, nor had he ever, practiced discrimination in any way, in the discharge of that duty. There is no contradictory evidence. Yet the fact remains that there was not a single Negro in that panel. The State concedes that Negroes are available for jury service in Fulton County, and we are told that Negroes generally do serve on juries in the courts of that county. The question we must decide, based upon our independent analysis of the record, is whether petitioner has made a sufficient showing of discrimination in the organization of this particular panel. We think he has.

The Jury Commissioners, and the other officials responsible for the selection of this panel, were under a constitutional duty to follow a procedure—"a course of conduct"—which would not "operate to discriminate in the selection of jurors on racial grounds." If they failed in that duty, then this conviction must be reversed—no matter how strong the evidence of petitioner's guilt. That is the law established by decisions of this Court spanning more than seventy years of interpretation of the meaning of "equal protection."

Petitioner's charge of discrimination in the jury selection in this case springs from the Jury Commissioners' use of white and yellow tickets. Obviously that practice makes it easier for those to discriminate who are of a mind to discriminate. Further, the practice has no authorization in the Georgia statutes—which simply enjoin the Commissioners to select "upright and intelligent men to serve as jurors . . . ." It is important to note that the Supreme Court of Georgia, in this case, specifically disapproved of the use of separately colored tickets in Fulton County, saying that it constituted "prima facie evidence of discrimination."

We agree. Even if the white and yellow tickets were drawn from the jury box without discrimination, opportunity was available to resort to it at other stages in the selection process. And, in view of the case before us, where not a single Negro was selected to serve on a panel of sixty—though many were available—we think that petitioner has certainly established a prima facie case of discrimination.

The court below affirmed, however, because petitioner had failed to prove some particular act of discrimination by some particular officer responsible for the selection of the jury; and the State now argues that it is petitioner's burden to fill this "factual vacuum." We cannot agree. If there is a "vacuum" it is one which the State must fill, by moving in with sufficient evidence to dispel the prima facie case of discrimination. We have held before, and the Georgia Supreme Court, itself, recently followed these decisions, that when a prima facie case of discrimination is presented, the burden falls, forthwith, upon the State to overcome it. The State failed to meet this test.

Reversed.

Mr. Justice Black concurs in the result.

Mr. Justice Jackson took no part in the consideration or decision of this case.

Mr. Justice Reed, concurring.

I concur in the reversal. My concurrence is based on the undisputed facts presented by the record. The facts that make a prima facie case of discrimination in the selection of petitioner's jury are as follows. The population of Fulton County is 691,797. Negroes comprise 25% or 165,814. The tax receiver's digest from which the jury list is selected has 105,035 white citizens and 17,736 Negroes—14%. The jury list for the year in question had 20,509 white and 1,115 Negroes—5%. From that list a number, 150 to 200, were drawn for service on each of the divisions of the court. Evidently these were for a week or a term's service. The venire from which the trial jury for Avery was selected numbered 60. All were white.

These facts establish a prima facie case of discrimination which the record does not rebut.

Mr. Justice Frankfurter, concurring.

It is undisputed that the drawings here were made from a box containing white and colored slips differentiated according to racial lines, white for white veniremen and yellow for colored. The slips were indiscriminately placed in the box and were drawn from the box by a county court judge. There was testimony from a recent member of the county Board of Jury Commissioners that the use of these white and yellow slips was designed for purposes of racial discrimination, and it has not been shown that they could serve any other purpose. So far as the particular facts of this case are concerned, we may accept the testimony of the judge who drew the slips from the box as to the honesty of his purpose; that testimoney does not refute the fact that there were opportunities to discriminate, as experience tells us there will inevitably be when such differentiating slips are used. In this case the opportunities are obvious, partly because the aperture in the box was sufficiently wide to make open to view the color of the slips and partly because of the subsequent use or abuse that could be made of the slips however fairly drawn. However that may be, opportunity for working of a discriminatory system exists whenever the mechanism for jury selection has a component part, such as the slips here, that differentiates between white and colored; such a mechanism certainly cannot be countenanced when a discriminatory result is reached. The stark resulting phenomenon here was that somehow or other, despite the fact that over 5% of the slips were yellow, no Negro got onto the panel of 60 jurors from which Avery's jury was selected. The mind of justice, not merely its eyes, would have to be blind to attribute such an occurrence to mere fortuity.

Accordingly, I concur in the judgment.

Hernandez v. Texas
347 U. S. 475 1954

Mr. Chief Justice Warren delivered the opinion of the Court.

The petitioner, Pete Hernandez, was indicted for the murder of one Joe Espinosa by a grand jury in Jackson County, Texas. He was convicted and sentenced to life imprisonment. The Texas Court of Criminal Appeals affirmed the judgment of the trial court. Prior to the trial, the petitioner, by his counsel, offered timely motions to quash the indictment and the jury panel. He alleged that persons of Mexican descent were systematically excluded from service as jury commissioners, grand jurors, and petit jurors, although there were such persons fully qualified to serve residing in Jackson County. The petitioner asserted that exclusion of this class deprived him, as a member of the class, of the equal protection of the laws guaranteed by the Fourteenth Amendment of the Constitution. After a hearing, the trial court denied the motions. At the trial, the motions were renewed, further evidence taken, and the motions again denied. An allegation that the trial court erred in denying the motions was the sole basis of petitioner's appeal. In affirming the judgment of the trial court, the Texas Court of Criminal Appeals considered and passed upon the substantial federal question raised by the petitioner. We granted a writ of certiorari to review that decision.

In numerous decisions, this Court has held that it is a denial of the equal protection of the laws to try a defendant of a particular race or color under an indictment issued by a grand jury, or before a petit jury, from which all persons of his race or color have, solely because of that race or color, been excluded by the State, whether acting through its legislature, its courts, or its executive or administrative officers. Although the Court has had little occasion to rule on the question directly, it has been recognized since *Strauder* v. *West Virginia* that the exclusion of a class of persons from jury service on grounds other than race or color may also deprive a defendant who is a member of that class of the constitutional guarantee of equal protection of the laws. The State of Texas would have us hold that there are only two classes—white and Negro—within the contemplation of the Fourteenth Amendment. The decisions of this Court do not support that view. And, except where the question presented involves the exclusion of persons of Mexican descent from juries, Texas courts have taken a broader view of the scope of the equal protection clause.

Throughout our history differences in race and color have defined easily identifiable groups which have at times required the aid of the courts in securing equal treatment under the laws. But community prejudices are not static, and from time to time other differences from the community norm may define other groups which need the same protection. Whether such a group exists within a community is a question of fact. When the existence of a distinct class is demonstrated, and it is further shown that the laws, as written or as applied, single out that class for different treatment not based on some reasonable classification, the guarantees of the Constitution have been violated. The Fourteenth Amendment is not directed solely against discrimination due to a "two-class theory"—that is, based upon differences between "white" and Negro.

As the petitioner acknowledges, the Texas system of selecting grand and petit jurors by the use of jury commissions is fair on its face and capable of being utilized without discrimination. But as this Court has held, the system is susceptible to abuse and can be employed in a discriminatory manner. The exclusion of otherwise eligible persons from jury service solely because of their ancestry or national origin is discrimination prohibited by the Fourteenth Amendment. The Texas statute makes no such discrimination, but the petitioner alleges that those administering the law do.

The petitioner's initial burden in substantiating his charge of group discrimination was to prove that persons of Mexican descent constitute a separate class in Jackson County, distinct from "whites." One method by which this may be demonstrated is by showing the attitude of the community. Here the testimony of responsible officials and citizens contained the admission that residents of the community distinguished between "white" and "Mexican." The participation of persons of Mexican descent in business and community groups were shown to be slight. Until very recent times, children of Mexican descent were required to attend a segregated school for the first four grades. At least one restaurant in town prominently displayed a sign announcing "No Mexicans Served." On the courthouse grounds at the time of the hearing, there were two men's toilets, one unmarked, and the other marked "Colored Men" and "Hombres Aqui" ("Men Here"). No substantial evidence was offered to rebut the logical inference to be drawn from these facts, and it must be concluded that petitioner succeeded in his proof.

Having established the existence of a class, petitioner was then charged with the burden of proving discrimination. To do so, he relied on the pattern of proof established by *Norris* v. *Alabama*. In that case, proof that Negroes constituted a substantial segment of the population of the jurisdiction, that some Negroes were qualified to serve as jurors, and that none had been called for jury service over an extended period of time, was held to constitute prima facie proof of the systematic exclusion of Negroes from jury service. This holding, sometimes called the "rule of exclusion," has been applied in other cases, and it is available in supplying proof of discrimination against any delineated class.

The petitioner established that 14% of the population of Jackson County were persons with Mexican or Latin-American surnames, and that 11% of the males over 21 bore such names. The County Tax Assessor testified that 6 or 7 percent of the freeholders on the tax rolls of the County were persons of Mexican descent. The State of Texas stipulated that "for the last twenty-five years there is no record of any person with a Mexican or Latin-American name having served on a jury commission, grand jury or petit jury in Jackson County." The parties also stipulated that "there are some male persons of Mexican or Latin American descent in Jackson County who, by virtue of being citizens, householders, or freeholders, and having all other legal prerequisites to jury service, are eligible to serve as members of a jury commission, grand jury and/or petit jury."

The petitioner met the burden of proof imposed in *Norris* v. *Alabama*. To rebut the strong prima facie case of the denial of the equal protection of the laws guaranteed by the Constitution thus established, the State offered the testimony of five jury commissioners that they had not discriminated against persons of Mexican or Latin-American descent in selecting jurors. They stated that their only objective had been to select those whom they thought were best qualified. This testimony is not enough to overcome the petitioner's case. As the Court said in *Norris* v. *Alabama:*

"That showing as to the long-continued exclusion of negroes from jury service, and as to the many negroes qualified for that service, could not be met by mere generalities. If, in the presence of such testimony as defendant adduced, the mere general assertions by officials of their performance of duty were to be accepted as an adequate justification for the complete exclusion of negroes from jury service, the constitutional provision . . . would be but a vain and illusory requirement."

The same reasoning is applicable to these facts.

Circumstances or chance may well dictate that no persons in a certain class will serve on a particular jury or during some particular period. But it taxes our credulity to say that mere chance resulted in there being no members of this class among the over six thousand jurors called in the past 25 years. The result bespeaks discrimination, whether or not it was a conscious decision on the part of any individual jury commissioner. The judgment of conviction must be reversed.

To say that this decision revives the rejected contention that the Fourteenth Amendment requires proportional representation of all the component ethnic groups of the community on every jury ignores the facts. The petitioner did not seek proportional representation, nor did he claim a right to have persons of Mexican descent sit on the particular juries which he faced. His only claim is the right to be indicted and tried by juries from which all members of his class are not systematically excluded—juries selected from among all qualified persons regardless of national origin or descent. To this much, he is entitled by the Constitution.

Eubanks v. Louisiana
356 U. S. 584   1958

Mr. Justice Black delivered the opinion of the Court.

In an unbroken line of cases stretching back almost 80 years this Court has held that a criminal defendant is denied the equal protection of the laws guaranteed by the Fourteenth Amendment if he is indicted by a grand jury or tried by a petit jury from which members of his race have been excluded because of their race. Our only concern here is with the application of this established principle to the facts disclosed by the record now before us.

The petitioner, a young Negro, was indicted by an all-white grand jury in the Parish of Orleans, Louisiana, for murder of a white woman. He moved to quash the indictment on the ground that Negroes had been systematically excluded from grand juries in the parish, including the grand jury which returned the indictment against him. After a hearing, his motion was overruled, and he was tried, convicted and sentenced to death. The Louisiana Supreme Court affirmed, holding that the record disclosed no discriminatory exclusion of Negroes from his grand jury. We granted certiorari.

The method by which grand juries are selected in the parish is not controverted. A jury commission is required to select, "impartially, from the citizens of the Parish of Orleans having the qualifications requisite to register as voters, the names of not less than seven hundred and fifty persons competent . . . to serve as jurors." Twice each year the Commissioners draw the names of 75 persons from this group. The list of 75 is then submitted to one of the six judges of the local criminal court who, in rotation, choose a new grand jury of 12 every six months. Obviously the judges have broad discretion in selecting from the list provided by the Commission. Several of them interview a substantial number of prospective jurors before making their choice. Others, including the judge who chose the jury that indicted petitioner, testified that they usually selected on the basis of personal knowledge or reputation in the community. Petitioner does not challenge this system of choosing grand jurors, as such, but he does contend that it has been administered by the local judges so that members of the Negro race have been systematically excluded from grand jury service.

346

Although Negroes comprise about one-third of the population of the parish, the uncontradicted testimony of various witnesses established that only one Negro had been picked for grand jury duty within memory. And this lone exception apparently resulted from the mistaken impression that the juror was white. From 1936, when the Commission first began to include Negroes in the pool of potential jurors, until 1954, when petitioner was indicted, 36 grand juries were selected in the parish. Six or more Negroes were included in each list submitted to the local judges. Yet out of the 432 jurors selected only the single Negro was chosen. Undisputed testimony also proved that a substantial number of the large Negro population in the parish were educated, registered to vote and possessed the qualifications required for jury service, all of which is emphasized by the fact that since 1936 the Commission has regularly selected Negroes for the grand jury panel. Indeed, Negroes have served on the federal grand jury in the parish for many years.

In *Patton* v. *Mississippi* this Court declared, in a unanimous opinion, that "When a jury selection plan, whatever it is, operates in such way as always to result in the complete and long-continued exclusion of any representative at all from a large group of Negroes, or any other racial group, indictments and verdicts returned against them by juries thus selected cannot stand." This is essentially the situation here. True, the judges now serving on the local court testified generally that they had not discriminated against Negroes in choosing grand juries, and had only tried to pick the best available jurors. But as Chief Justice Hughes said for the Court in *Norris* v. *Alabama,* "If, in the presence of such testimony as defendant adduced, the mere general assertions by officials of their performance of duty were to be accepted as an adequate justification for the complete exclusion of negroes from jury service, the [Equal Protection Clause]—adopted with special reference to their protection—would be but a vain and illusory requirement." This is particularly true here where several of the parish judges apparently have never even interviewed a Negro in selecting grand jurors. We are reluctantly forced to conclude that the uniform and long-continued exclusion of Negroes from grand juries shown by this record cannot be attributed to chance, to accident, or to the fact that no sufficiently qualified Negroes have ever been included in the lists submitted to the various local judges. It seems clear to us that Negroes have been consistently barred from jury service because of their race.

It may well be, as one of the parish judges recently stated, that "the selection of grand juries in this community throughout the years has been controlled by a tradition and the general thinking of the community as a whole is under the influence of that tradition." But local tradition cannot justify failure to comply with the constitutional mandate requiring equal protection of the laws.

"A prisoner whose conviction is reversed by this Court need not go free if he is in fact guilty, for [the State] may indict and try him again by the procedure which conforms to constitutional requirements. But no State is at liberty to impose upon one charged with crime a discrimination in its trial procedure which the Constitution, and an Act of Congress passed pursuant to the Constitution, alike forbid. Nor is this Court at liberty to grant or withhold the benefits of equal protection, which the Constitution commands for all, merely as we may deem the defendant innocent or guilty." *Hill* v. *Texas*.

The judgment of the Louisiana Supreme Court is reversed and the cause is remanded for further proceedings not inconsistent with this opinion.

Part VIII

VOTING

This group of cases begins with the relatively recent *Smith* v. *Allwright,* in which there is discussion of many of the earlier cases that considerations of space forced us to omit.

Smith v. Allwright

321 U. S. 649   1944

Mr. Justice Reed delivered the opinion of the Court.

This writ of certiorari brings here for review a claim for damages in the sum of $5,000 on the part of petitioner, a Negro citizen of the 48th precinct of Harris County, Texas, for the refusal of respondents, election and associate election judges respectively of that precinct, to give petitioner a ballot or to permit him to cast a ballot in the primary election of July 27, 1940, for the nomination of Democratic candidates for the United States Senate and House of Representatives, and Governor and other state officers. The refusal is alleged to have been solely because of the race and color of the proposed voter.

The actions of respondents are said to violate §§ 31 and 43 of Title 8 of the United States Code in that petitioner was deprived of rights secured by §§ 2 and 4 of Article I and the Fourteenth, Fifteenth and Seventeenth Amendments to the United States Constitution. The suit was filed in the District Court of the United States for the Southern District of Texas, which had jurisdiction under Judicial Code § 24, subsection 14.

The District Court denied the relief sought and the Circuit Court of Appeals quite properly affirmed its action on the authority of *Grovey* v. *Townsend*. We granted the petition for certiorari to resolve a claimed inconsistency between the decision in the *Grovey* case and that of *United States* v. *Classic*.

The State of Texas by its Constitution and statutes provides that every person, if certain other requirements are met which are not here in issue, qualified by residence in the district or county "shall be deemed a qualified elector." Primary elections for United States Senators, Congressmen and state officers are provided for by Chapters Twelve and Thirteen of the statutes. Under these chapters, the Democratic party was required to hold the primary which was the occasion of the alleged wrong to petitioner. A summary of the state statutes regulating primaries appears in the footnote. These nominations are to be made by the qualified voters of the party.

The Democratic party of Texas is held by the Supreme Court of that State to be a "voluntary association," protected by § 27 of the Bill of Rights, Art. 1, Constitution of Texas, from interference by the State except that:

"In the interest of fair methods and a fair expression by their members of their preferences in the selection of their nominees, the State may regulate such elections by proper laws."

That court stated further:

"Since the right to organize and maintain a political party is one guaranteed by the Bill of Rights of this State, it necessarily follows that every privilege essential or reasonably appropriate to the exercise of that right is likewise guaranteed—including, of course, the privilege of determining the policies of the party and its membership. Without the privilege of determining the policy of a political association and its membership, the right to organize such an association would be a mere mockery. We think these rights—that is, the right to determine the membership of a political party and to determine its policies, of necessity are to be exercised by the state convention of such party, and cannot, under any circumstances, be conferred upon a state or governmental agency."

The Democratic party on May 24, 1932, in a state convention adopted the following resolution, which has not since been "amended, abrogated, annulled or avoided":

"Be it resolved that all white citizens of the State of Texas who are qualified to vote under the Constitution and laws of the State shall be eligible to membership in the Democratic party and, as such, entitled to participate in its deliberations."

It was by virtue of this resolution that the respondents refused to permit the petitioner to vote.

Texas is free to conduct her elections and limit her electorate as she may deem wise, save only as her action may be affected by the prohibitions of the United States Constitution or in conflict with powers delegated to and exercised by the National Government. The Fourteenth Amendment forbids a State from making or enforcing any law which abridges the privileges or immunities of citizens of the United States and the Fifteenth Amendment specifically interdicts any denial or abridgement by a State of the right of citizens to vote on account of color. Respondents appeared in the District Court and the Circuit Court of Appeals and defended on the ground that the Democratic party of Texas is a voluntary organization with members banded together for the purpose of selecting individuals of the group representing the common political beliefs as candidates in the general election. As such a voluntary organization, it was claimed, the Democratic party is free to select its own membership and limit to whites participation in the party primary. Such action, the answer asserted, does not violate the Fourteenth, Fifteenth or Seventeenth Amendment as officers of government cannot be chosen at primaries and the Amendments are applicable only to general elections where governmental officers are actually elected. Primaries, it is said, are political party affairs, handled by party, not governmental, officers. No appearance for respondents is made in this Court. Arguments presented here by the Attorney General of Texas and the Chairman of the State Democratic Executive Committee of Texas, as amici curiae, urged substantially the same grounds as those advanced by the respondents.

The right of a Negro to vote in the Texas primary has been considered heretofore by this Court. The first case was *Nixon* v. *Herndon*. At that time, 1924, the Texas statute, Art. 3093a, afterwards numbered Art. 3107 declared "in no event shall a Negro be eligible to participate in a Democratic Party primary election in the State of Texas." Nixon was refused the right to vote in a Democratic primary and brought a suit for damages against the election officers under R. S. §§ 1979 and 2004, the present §§ 43 and 31 of Title 8, U. S. C., respectively. It was urged to this Court that the denial of the franchise to Nixon violated his Constitutional rights under the Fourteenth and Fifteenth Amendments. Without consideration of the Fifteenth, this Court held that the action of Texas in denying the ballot to Negroes by statute was in violation of the equal protection clause of the Fourteenth Amendment and reversed the dismissal of the suit.

The legislature of Texas reenacted the article but gave the State Executive Committee of a party the power to prescribe the qualifications of its members for voting or other participation. This article remains in the statutes. The State Executive Committee of the Democratic party adopted a resolution that white Democrats and none other might participate in the primaries of that party. Nixon was refused again the privilege of voting in a primary and again brought suit for damages by virtue of § 31, Title 8, U. S. C. This Court again reversed the dismissal of the suit for the reason that the Committee action was deemed to be state action and invalid as discriminatory under the Fourteenth Amendment. The test was said to be whether the Committee operated as representative of the State in the discharge of the State's authority. *Nixon* v. *Condon.* The question of the inherent power of a political party in Texas "without restraint by any law to determine its own membership" was left open.

In *Grovey* v. *Townsend,* this Court had before it another suit for damages for the refusal in a primary of a county clerk, a Texas officer with only public functions to perform, to furnish petitioner, a Negro, an absentee ballot. The refusal was solely on the ground of race. This case differed from *Nixon* v. *Condon* in that a state convention of the Democratic party had passed the resolution of May 24, 1932, hereinbefore quoted. It was decided that the determination by the state convention of the membership of the Democratic party made a significant change from a determination by the Executive Committee. The former was party action, voluntary in character. The latter, as had been held in the *Condon* case, was action by authority of the State. The managers of the primary election were therefore declared not to be state officials in such sense that their action was state action. A state convention of a party was said not to be an organ of the State. This Court went on to announce that to deny a vote in a primary was a mere refusal of party membership with which "the State need have no concern," while for a State to deny a vote in a general election on the ground of race or color violated the Constitution. Consequently, there was found no ground for holding that the county clerk's refusal of a ballot because of racial ineligibility for party membership denied the petitioner any right under the Fourteenth or Fifteenth Amendment.

Since *Grovey* v. *Townsend* and prior to the present suit, no case from Texas involving primary elections has been before this Court. We did decide, however, *United States* v. *Classic.* We there held that § 4 of Article I of the Constitution authorized Congress to regulate primary as well as general elections "where the primary is by law made an integral part of the election machinery." Consequently, in the *Classic* case, we upheld the applicability to frauds in a Louisiana primary of §§ 19 and 20 of the Criminal Code. Thereby corrupt acts of election officers were subjected to Congressional sanctions because that body had power to protect rights of federal suffrage secured by the Constitution in primary as in general elections. This decision depended, too, on the determination that under the Louisiana statutes the primary was a part of the procedure for choice of federal officials. By this decision the doubt as to whether or not such primaries were a part of "elections" subject to federal control, which had remained unanswered since *Newberry* v. *United States* was erased. The *Nixon Cases* were decided under the equal protection clause of the Fourteenth Amendment without a determination of the status of the primary as a part of the electoral process. The exclusion of Negroes from the primaries by action of the State was held invalid under that Amendment. The fusing by the *Classic* case of the primary and general elections into a single instrumentality for choice of officers has a definite bearing on the permissibility under the Constitution of excluding Negroes from primaries. This is not to say that the *Classic* case cuts directly into the rationale of *Grovey* v. *Townsend*. This latter case was not mentioned in the opinion. *Classic* bears upon *Grovey* v. *Townsend* not because exclusion of Negroes from primaries is any more or less state action by reason of the unitary character of the electoral process but because the recognition of the place of the primary in the electoral scheme makes clear that state delegation to a party of the power to fix the qualifications of primary elections is delegation of a state function that may make the party's action the action of the State. When *Grovey* v. *Townsend* was written, the Court looked upon the denial of a vote in a primary as a mere refusal by a party of party membership. As the Louisiana statutes for holding primaries are similar to those of Texas, our ruling in *Classic* as to the unitary character of the electoral process calls for a reexamination as to whether or not the exclusion of Negroes from a Texas party primary was state action.

The statutes of Texas relating to primaries and the resolution of the Democratic party of Texas extending the privileges of membership to white citizens only are the same in substance and effect today as they were when *Grovey* v. *Townsend* was decided by a unanimous Court. The question as to whether the exclusionary action of the party was the action of the State persists as the determinative factor. In again entering upon consideration of the inference to be drawn as to state action from a substantially similar factual situation, it should be noted that *Grovey* v. *Townsend* upheld exclusion of Negroes from primaries through the denial of party membership by a party convention. A few years before, this Court refused approval of exclusion by the State Executive Committee of the party. A different result was reached on the theory that the Committee action was state authorized and the Convention action was unfettered by statutory control. Such a variation in the result from so slight a change in form influences us to consider anew the legal validity of the distinction which has resulted in barring Negroes from participating in the nominations of candidates of the Democratic party in Texas. Other precedents of this Court forbid the abridgement of the right to vote.

It may now be taken as a postulate that the right to vote in such a primary for the nomination of candidates without discrimination by the State, like the right to vote in a general election, is a right secured by the Constitution. By the terms of the Fifteenth Amendment that right may not be abridged by any State on account of race. Under our Constitution the great privilege of the ballot may not be denied a man by the State because of his color.

We are thus brought to an examination of the qualifications for Democratic primary electors in Texas, to determine whether state action or private action has excluded Negroes from participation. Despite Texas' decision that the exclusion is produced by private or party action, federal courts must for themselves appraise the facts leading to that conclusion. It is only by the performance of this obligation that a final and uniform interpretation can be given to the Constitution, the "supreme Law of the Land." Texas requires electors in a primary to pay a poll tax. Every person who does so pay and who has the qualifications of age and residence is an acceptable voter for the primary. As appears above in the summary of the statutory provisions set out in note 6, Texas requires by the law the election of the county officers of a party. These compose the county executive committee. The county chairmen so selected are members of the district executive committee and choose the chairman for the district. Precinct primary election officers are named by the county executive committee. Statutes provide for the election by the voters of precinct delegates to the county convention of a party and the selection of delegates to the district and state conventions by the county convention. The state convention selects the state executive committee. No convention may place in platform or resolution any demand for specific legislation without endorsement of such legislation by the voters in a primary. Texas thus directs the selection of all party officers.

Primary elections are conducted by the party under state statutory authority. The county executive committee selects precinct election officials and the county, district or state executive committees, respectively, canvass the returns. These party committees or the state convention certify the party's candidates to the appropriate officers for inclusion on the official ballot for the general election. No name which has not been so certified may appear upon the ballot for the general election as a candidate of a political party. No other name may be printed on the ballot which has not been placed in nomination by qualified voters who must take oath that they did not participate in a primary for the selection of a candidate for the office for which the nomination is made.

The state courts are given exclusive original jurisdiction of contested elections and of mandamus proceedings to compel party officers to perform their statutory duties.

We think that this statutory system for the selection of party nominees for inclusion on the general election ballot makes the party which is required to follow these legislative directions an agency of the State in so far as it determines the participants in a primary election. The party takes its character as a state agency from the duties imposed upon it by state statutes; the duties do not become matters of private law because they are performed by a political party. The plan of the Texas primary follows substantially that of Louisiana, with the exception that in Louisiana the State pays the cost of the primary while Texas assesses the cost against candidates. In numerous instances, the Texas statutes fix or limit the fees to be charged. Whether paid directly by the State or through state requirements, it is state action which compels. When primaries become a part of the machinery for choosing officials, state and national, as they have here, the same tests to determine the character of discrimination or abridgement should be applied to the primary as are applied to the general election. If the State requires a certain electoral procedure, prescribes a general election ballot made up of party nominees so chosen and limits the choice of the electorate in general elections for state offices, practically speaking, to those whose names appear on such a ballot, it endorses, adopts and enforces the discrimination against Negroes, practiced by a party entrusted by Texas law with the determination of the qualifications of participants in the primary. This is state action within the meaning of the Fifteenth Amendment.

The United States is a constitutional democracy. Its organic law grants to all citizens a right to participate in the choice of elected officials without restriction by any State because of race. This grant to the people of the opportunity for choice is not to be nullified by a State through casting its electoral process in a form which permits a private organization to practice racial discrimination in the election. Constitutional rights would be of little value if they could be thus indirectly denied.

The privilege of membership in a party may be, as this Court said in *Grovey* v. *Townsend* no concern of a State. But when, as here, that privilege is also the essential qualification for voting in a primary to select nominees for a general election, the State makes the action of the party the action of the State. In reaching this conclusion we are not unmindful of the desirability of continuity of decision in constitutional questions. However, when convinced of former error, this Court has never felt constrained to follow precedent. In constitutional questions, where correction depends upon amendment and not upon legislative action this Court throughout its history has freely exercised its power to reexamine the basis of its constitutional decisions. This has long been accepted practice, and this practice has continued to this day. This is particularly true when the decision believed erroneous is the application of a constitutional principle rather than an interpretation of the Constitution to extract the principle itself. Here we are applying, contrary to the recent decision in *Grovey* v. *Townsend,* the well-established principle of the Fifteenth Amendment, forbidding the abridgement by a State of a citizen's right to vote. *Grovey* v. *Townsend* is overruled.

Judgment reversed.

Mr. Justice Frankfurter concurs in the result.

Mr. Justice Roberts:

In *Mahnich* v. *Southern Steamship Co.* I have expressed my views with respect to the present policy of the court freely to disregard and to overrule considered decisions and the rules of law announced in them. This tendency, it seems to me, indicates an intolerance for what those who have composed this court in the past have conscientiously and deliberately concluded, and involves an assumption that knowledge and wisdom reside in us which was denied to our predecessors. I shall not repeat what I there said for I consider it fully applicable to the instant decision, which but points the moral anew.

A word should be said with respect to the judicial history forming the background of *Grovey* v. *Townsend* which is now overruled.

In 1923 Texas adopted a statute which declared that no negro should be eligible to participate in a Democratic primary election in that State. A negro, a citizen of the United States and of Texas, qualified to vote, except for the provisions of the statute, was denied the opportunity to vote in a primary election at which candidates were to be chosen for the offices of senator and representative in the Congress of the United States. He brought action against the judges of election in a United States court for damages for their refusal to accept his ballot. This court unanimously reversed a judgment dismissing the complaint and held that the judges acted pursuant to state law and that the State of Texas, by its statute, had denied the voter the equal protection secured by the Fourteenth Amendment.

In 1927 the legislature of Texas repealed the provision condemned by this court and enacted that every political party in the State might, through its Executive Committee, prescribe the qualifications of its own members and determine in its own way who should be qualified to vote or participate in the party, except that no denial of participation could be decreed by reason of former political or other affiliation. Thereupon the State Executive Committee of the Democratic party in Texas adopted a resolution that white Democrats, and no other, should be allowed to participate in the party's primaries.

A negro, whose primary ballot was rejected pursuant to the resolution, sought to recover damages from the judges who had rejected it. The United States District Court dismissed his action, and the Circuit Court of Appeals affirmed; but this court reversed the judgment and sustained the right of action by a vote of 5 to 4.

The opinion was written with care. The court refused to decide whether a political party in Texas had inherent power to determine its membership. The court said, however: "Whatever inherent power a state political party has to determine the content of its membership resides in the state convention," and referred to the statutes of Texas to demonstrate that the State had left the Convention free to formulate the party faith. Attention was directed to the fact that the statute under attack did not leave to the party convention the definition of party membership but placed it in the party's State Executive Committee which could not, by any stretch of reasoning, be held to constitute the party. The court held, therefore, that the State Executive Committee acted solely by virtue of the statutory mandate and as delegate of state power, and again struck down the discrimination against negro voters as deriving force and virtue from state action—that is, from statute.

In 1932 the Democratic Convention of Texas adopted a resolution that "all white citizens of the State of Texas who are qualified to vote under the Constitution and laws of the State shall be eligible to membership in the Democratic party and as such entitled to participate in its deliberations."

A negro voter qualified to vote in a primary election, except for the exclusion worked by the resolution, demanded an absentee ballot which he was entitled to mail to the judges at a primary election except for the resolution. The county clerk refused to furnish him a ballot. He brought an action for damages against the clerk in a state court. That court, which was the tribunal having final jurisdiction under the laws of Texas, dismissed his complaint and he brought the case to this court for review. After the fullest consideration by the whole court an opinion was written representing its unanimous views and affirming the judgment. *Grovey* v. *Townsend.*

I believe it will not be gainsaid the case received the attention and consideration which the questions involved demanded and the opinion represented the views of all the justices. It appears that those views do not now commend themselves to the court. I shall not restate them. They are exposed in the opinion and must stand or fall on their merits. Their soundness, however, is not a matter which presently concerns me.

The reason for my concern is that the instant decision, overruling that announced about nine years ago, tends to bring adjudications of this tribunal into the same class as a restricted railroad ticket, good for this day and train only. I have no assurance, in view of current decisions, that the opinion announced today may not shortly be repudiated and overruled by justices who deem they have new light on the subject. In the present term the court has overruled three cases.

In the present case, as in *Mahnich* v. *Southern S. S. Co.,* the court below relied, as it was bound to, upon our previous decision. As that court points out, the statutes of Texas have not been altered since *Grovey* v. *Townsend* was decided. The same resolution is involved as was drawn in question in *Grovey* v. *Townsend.* Not a fact differentiates that case from this except the names of the parties.

It is suggested that *Grovey* v. *Townsend* was overruled *sub silentio* in *United States* v. *Classic.* If so, the situation is even worse than that exhibited by the outright repudiation of an earlier decision, for it is the fact that, in the *Classic* case, *Grovey* v. *Townsend* was distinguished in brief and argument by the Government without suggestion that it was wrongly decided, and was relied on by the appellees, not as a controlling decision, but by way of analogy. The case is not mentioned in either of the opinions in the *Classic* case. Again and again it is said in the opinion of the court in that case that the voter who was denied the right to vote was a fully qualified voter. In other words, there was no question of his being a person entitled under state law to vote in the primary. The offense charged was the fraudulent denial of his conceded right by an election officer because of his race. Here the question is altogether different. It is whether, in a Democratic primary, he who tendered his vote was a member of the Democratic party.

I do not stop to call attention to the material differences between the primary election laws of Louisiana under consideration in the *Classic* case and those of Texas which are here drawn in question. These differences were spelled out in detail in the Government's brief in the *Classic* case and emphasized in its oral argument. It is enough to say that the Louisiana statutes required the primary to be conducted by state officials and made it a state election, whereas, under the Texas statute, the primary is a party election conducted at the expense of members of the party and by officials chosen by the party. If this court's opinion in the *Classic* case discloses its method of overruling earlier decisions, I can only protest that, in fairness, it should rather have adopted the open and frank way of saying what it was doing than, after the event, characterize its past action as overruling *Grovey* v. *Townsend* though those less sapient never realized the fact.

It is regrettable that in an era marked by doubt and confusion, an era whose greatest need is steadfastness of thought and purpose, this court, which has been looked to as exhibiting consistency in adjudication, and a steadiness which would hold the balance even in the face of temporary ebbs and flows of opinion, should now itself become the breeder of fresh doubt and confusion in the public mind as to the stability of our institutions.

Terry v. Adams
345 U. S. 461 1953

Mr. Justice Black announced the judgment of the Court and an opinion in which Mr. Justice Douglas and Mr. Justice Burton join.

In *Smith* v. *Allwright*, 321 U. S. 649, we held that rules of the Democratic Party of Texas excluding Negroes from voting in the party's primaries violated the Fifteenth Amendment. While no state law directed such exclusion, our decision pointed out that many party activities were subject to considerable statutory control. This case raises questions concerning the constitutional power of a Texas county political organization called the Jaybird Democratic Association or Jaybird Party to exclude Negroes from its primaries on racial grounds. The Jaybirds deny that their racial exclusions violate the Fifteenth Amendment. They contend that the Amendment applies only to elections or primaries held under state regulation, that their association is not regulated by the state at all, and that it is not a political party but a self-governing voluntary club. The District Court held the Jaybird racial discriminations invalid and entered judgment accordingly. The Court of Appeals reversed, holding that there was no constitutional or congressional bar to the admitted discriminatory exclusion of Negroes because Jaybird's primaries were not to any extent state controlled. We granted certiorari.

There was evidence that:

The Jaybird Association or Party was organized in 1889. Its membership was then and always has been limited to white people; they are automatically members if their names appear on the official list of county voters. It has been run like other political parties with an executive committee named from the county's voting precincts. Expenses of the party are paid by the assessment of candidates for office in its primaries. Candidates for county offices submit their names to the Jaybird Committee in accordance with the normal practice followed by regular political parties all over the country. Advertisements and posters proclaim that these candidates are running subject to the action of the Jaybird primary. While there is no legal compulsion on successful Jaybird candidates to enter Democratic primaries, they have nearly always done so and with few exceptions since 1889 have run and won without opposition in the Democratic primaries and the general elections that followed. Thus the party has been the dominant political group in the county since organization, having endorsed every county-wide official elected since 1889.

It is apparent that Jaybird activities follow a plan purposefully designed to exclude Negroes from voting and at the same time to escape the Fifteenth Amendment's command that the right of citizens to vote shall neither be denied nor abridged on account of race. These were the admitted party purposes according to the following testimony of the Jaybird's president:

Q. . . . Now Mr Adams, will you tell me specifically what is the specific purpose of holding these elections and carrying on this organization like you do?

A. Good government.

Q. Now I will ask you to state whether or not it is the opinion and policy of the Association that to carry on good government they must exclude negro citizens?

A. Well, when we started it was and it is still that way, I think.

Q. And then one of the purposes of your organization is for the specific purpose of excluding negroes from voting, isn't it?

A. Yes.

Q. And that is your policy?

A. Yes.

Q. I will ask you, that is the reason you hold your election in May rather than in June or July, isn't it?

A. Yes.

Q. Because if you held it in July you would have to abide by the statutes and the law by letting them vote?

A. They do vote in July.

Q. And if you held yours at that time they would have to vote too, wouldn't they?

A. Why sure.

Q. And you hold it in May so they won't have to?

A. Well, they don't vote in ours but they can vote on anybody in the July election they want to.

Q. But you are not answering my question. My question is that you hold yours in May so you won't have to let them vote, don't you?

A. Yes.

Q. And that is your purpose?

A. Yes.

Q. And your intention?

A. Yes.

Q. And to have a vote of the white population at a time when the negroes can't vote, isn't that right?

A. That's right.

Q. That is the whole policy of your Association?

A. Yes.

Q. And that is its purpose?

A. Yes.

The District Court found that the Jaybird Association was a political organization or party; that the majority of white voters generally abide by the results of its primaries and support in the Democratic primaries the persons endorsed by the Jaybird primaries; and that the chief object of the Association has always been to deny Negroes any voice or part in the election of Fort Bend County officials.

The facts and findings bring this càse squarely within the reasoning and holding of the Court of Appeals for the Fourth Circuit in its two recent decisions about excluding Negroes from Democratic primaries in South Carolina. South Carolina had repealed every trace of statutory or constitutional control of the Democratic primaries. It did this in the hope that thereafter the Democratic Party or Democratic "Clubs" of South Carolina would be free to continue discriminatory practices against Negroes as voters. The contention there was that the Democratic "Clubs" were mere private groups; the contention here is that the Jaybird Association is a mere private group. The Court of Appeals in invalidating the South Carolina practices answered these formalistic arguments by holding that no election machinery could be sustained if its purpose or effect was to deny Negroes on account of their race an effective voice in the governmental affairs of their country, state, or community. In doing so the Court relied on the principle announced in *Smith* v. *Allwright* that the constitutional right to be free from racial discrimination in voting ". . . is not to be nullified by a State through casting its electoral process in a form which permits a private organization to practice racial discrimination in the election."

The South Carolina cases are in accord with the commands of the Fifteenth Amendment and the laws passed pursuant to it. That Amendment provides as follows:

"The right of citizens of the United States to vote shall not be denied or abridged by the United States or by any State on account of race, color, or previous condition of servitude."

The Amendment bans racial discrimination in voting by both state and nation. It thus establishes a national policy, obviously applicable to the right of Negroes not to be discriminated against as voters in elections to determine public governmental policies or to select public officials, national, state, or local. Shortly after its adoption Mr. Chief Justice Waite speaking for this Court said:

"It follows that the amendment has invested the citizens of the United States with a new constitutional right which is within the protecting power of Congress. That right is exemption from discrimination in the exercise of the elective franchise on account of race, color, or previous condition of servitude." *United States* v. *Reese.*

Other cases have reemphasized the Fifteenth Amendment's specific grant of this new constitutional right. Not content to rest congressional power to protect this new constitutional right on the necessary and proper clause of the Constitution, the Fifteenth Amendment's framers added § 2, reading:

"The Congress shall have power to enforce this article by appropriate legislation."

And Mr. Justice Miller speaking for this Court declared that the Amendment's granted right to be free from racial discrimination ". . . should be kept free and pure by congressional enactments whenever that is necessary." Acting pursuant to the power granted by the second section of the Fifteenth Amendment, Congress in 1870 provided as follows:

"All citizens of the United States who are otherwise qualified by law to vote at any election by the people in any State, Territory, district, county, city, parish, township, school district, municipality, or other territorial subdivision, shall be entitled and allowed to vote at all such elections, without distinction of race, color, or previous condition of servitude; any constitution, law, custom, usage, or regulation of any State or Territory, or by or under its authority, to the contrary notwithstanding."

The Amendment, the congressional enactment and the cases make explicit the rule against racial discrimination in the conduct of elections. Together they show the meaning of "elections." Clearly the Amendment includes any election in which public issues are decided or public officials selected. Just as clearly the Amendment excludes social or business clubs. And the statute shows the congressional mandate against discrimination whether the voting on public issues and officials is conducted in community, state or nation. Size is not a standard.

It is significant that precisely the same qualifications as those prescribed by Texas entitling electors to vote at county-operated primaries are adopted as the sole qualifications entitling electors to vote at the county-wide Jaybird primaries with a single proviso—Negroes are excluded. Everyone concedes that such a proviso in the county-operated primaries would be unconstitutional. The Jaybird Party thus brings into being and holds precisely the kind of election that the Fifteenth Amendment seeks to prevent. When it produces the equivalent of the prohibited election, the damage has been done.

For a state to permit such a duplication of its election processes is to permit a flagrant abuse of those processes to defeat the purposes of the Fifteenth Amendment. The use of the county-operated primary to ratify the result of the prohibited election merely compounds the offense. It violates the Fifteenth Amendment for a state, by such circumvention, to permit within its borders the use of any device that produces an equivalent of the prohibted election.

The only election that has counted in this Texas county for more than fifty years has been that held by the Jaybirds from which Negroes were excluded. The Democratic primary and the general election have become no more than the perfunctory ratifiers of the choice that has already been made in Jaybird elections from which Negroes have been excluded. It is immaterial that the state does not control that part of this elective process which it leaves for the Jaybirds to manage. The Jaybird primary has become an integral part, indeed the only effective part, of the elective process that determines who shall rule and govern in the county. The effect of the whole procedure, Jaybird primary plus Democratic primary plus general election, is to do precisely that which the Fifteenth Amendment forbids—strip Negroes of every vestige of influence in selecting the officials who control the local county matters that intimately touch the daily lives of citizens.

We reverse the Court of Appeals' judgment reversing that of the District Court. We affirm the District Court's holding that the combined Jaybird-Democratic-general election machinery has deprived these petitioners of their right to vote on account of their race and color. The case is remanded to the District Court to enter such orders and decrees as are necessary and proper under the jurisdiction it has retained under 28 U. S. C. § 2202. In exercising this jurisdiction, the Court is left free to hold hearings to consider and determine what provisions are essential to afford Negro citizens of Fort Bend County full protection from future discriminatory Jaybird-Democratic-general election practices which deprive citizens of voting rights because of their color.

Mr. Justice Frankfurter.

Petitioners are Negroes who claim that they and all Negroes similarly situated in Fort Bend County, Texas, are denied all voice in the primary elections for county offices by the activities of respondent association, the Jaybird Democratic Association. The Jaybird Association was organized in 1889 and from that time until the present has selected, first in mass meetings but for some time by ballot of its members, persons whom the organization indorses for election in the Democratic primary for county office. The Association has never permitted Negroes to participate in its selection of the candidates to be indorsed; balloting is open only to all white citizens of the county qualified under State law to vote. The District Court granted a declaratory judgment that Negroes in the county be allowed to participate in the balloting of the Association. The Court of Appeals reversed, saying that although the white voters in the county are "vainly holding" to "outworn and outmoded" practices, the action of the Association was not "action under color of state law" and therefore not in violation of federal law.

The evidence, summarized by formal stipulation, shows that all rules of the Association are made by its members themselves or by its Executive Committee. Membership, defined by the rules of the Association, consists of the entire white voting population as shown in poll lists prepared by the county. The time of balloting, in what are called the Jaybird primaries, is set by the Executive Committee of the Association for a day early in May of each election year. The expenses of these primaries, the officiating personnel, the balloting places, the determination of the winner—all aspects of these primaries are exclusively controlled by the Association. The balloting rules in general follow those prescribed by the State laws regulating primaries. But formal State action, either by way of legislative recognition or official authorization, is wholly wanting.

The successful candidates in the Jaybird primaries, in formal compliance with State rules in that regard, file individually as candidates in the Democratic primary held on the fourth Saturday in July. No mention is made in the filing or in the listing of the candidates on the Democratic primary ballot that they are the Jaybird indorsees. That fact is conveyed to the public by word of mouth, through newspapers, and by other private means. There is no restriction on filing by anyone else as a candidate in the Democratic primary, nor on voting by Negroes in that official primary.

For the sixty years of the Association's existence, the candidate ultimately successful in the Democratic primary for every county-wide office was the man indorsed by the Jaybird Association. Indeed, other candidates almost never file in the Democratic primary. This continuous success over such a period of time has been the result of action by practically the entire qualified electorate of the county, barring Negroes.

This case is for me by no means free of difficulty. Whenever the law draws a line between permissive and forbidden conduct cases are bound to arise which are not obviously on one side or the other. These dubious situations disclose the limited utility of the figure of speech, a "line," in the law. Drawing a "line" is necessarily exercising a judgment, however confined the conscientious judgment may be within the bounds of constitutional and statutory provisions, the course of decisions, and the presuppositions of the judicial process. If "line" is in the main a fruitful tool for dividing the sheep from the goats, it must not be forgotten that since the "line" is figurative the place of this or that case in relation to it cannot be ascertained externally but is a matter of the mind.

Close analysis of what it is that the Fifteenth Amendment prohibits must be made before it can be determined what the relevant line is in the situation presented by this case. The Fifteenth Amendment, not the Fourteenth, outlawed discrimination on the basis of race or color with respect to the right to vote. Concretely, of course, it was directed against attempts to bar Negroes from having the same political franchise as white folk. "The right of citizens of the United States to vote shall not be denied or abridged by the United States or by any State on account of race, color, or previous condition of servitude." The command against such denial or abridgment is directed to the United States and to the individual States. Therefore, violation of this Amendment and the enactments passed in enforcement of it must involve the United States or a State. In this case the conduct that is assailed pertains to the election of local Texas officials. To find a denial or abridgment of the guaranteed voting right to colored citizens of Texas solely because they are colored, one must find that the State has had a hand in it.

The State, in these situations, must mean not private citizens but those clothed with the authority and the influence which official position affords. The application of the prohibition of the Fifteenth Amendment to "any State" is translated by legal jargon to read "State action." This phrase gives rise to a false direction in that it implies some impressive machinery or deliberative conduct normally associated with what orators call a sovereign state. The vital requirement is State responsibility—that somewhere, somehow, to some extent, there be an infusion of conduct by officials, panoplied with State power, into any scheme by which colored citizens are denied voting rights merely because they are colored.

As the action of the entire white voting community, the Jaybird primary is as a practical matter the instrument of those few in this small county who are politically active—the officials of the local Democratic party and, we may assume, the elected officials of the county. As a matter of practical politics, those charged by State law with the duty of assuring all eligible voters an opportunity to participate in the selection of candidates at the primary—the county election officials who are normally leaders in their communities—participate by voting in the Jaybird primary. They join the white voting community in proceeding with elaborate formality, in almost all respects parallel to the procedures dictated by Texas law for the primary itself, to express their preferences in a wholly successful effort to withdraw significance from the State-prescribed primary, to subvert the operation of what is formally the law of the State for primaries in this county.

The legal significance of the Jaybird primary must be tested against the cases which, in an endeavor to screen what is effectively an exertion of State authority in preventing Negroes from exercising their constitutional right of franchise, have pierced the various manifestations of astuteness. In the last of the series, *Smith* v. *Allwright,* we held that the State regulation there of primaries conducted by a political party made the party "required to follow these legislative directions an agency of the State in so far as it determines the participants in a primary election." Alternative routes have been suggested for concluding that the Jaybird primary is "so slight a change in form" that the result should not differ in substance from that of *Smith* v. *Allwright*. The District Court found that the Jaybird Association is a political party within the meaning of the Texas legislation regulating the administration of primaries by political parties; it said that the Association could not avoid that result by holding its primary on a different date and by utilizing different methods than those prescribed by the statutes.

Whether the Association is a political party regulated by Texas and thus subject to a duty of nondiscrimination, or is, as it claims, clearly not a party within the meaning of that legislation, failing as it does to attempt to comply with a number of the State requirements, particularly as to the date of the "primary," is a question of State law not to be answered in the first instance by a federal court. We do not know what the Texas Supreme Court would say. An operation such as the Jaybird primary may be found by the Texas court to satisfy Texas law although it does not come within the formal definition; it may so be found because long-accepted customs and the habits of a people may generate "law" as surely as a formal legislative declaration, and indeed, sometimes even in the face of it. But even if the Jaybird Association is a political party, a federal court cannot say that a political party in Texas is to hold a primary open to all on a day other than that fixed by Texas statute. This would be an inadmissible intervention of the federal judiciary into the political process of a State. If such a remedy is to be derived from a finding that the Jaybird Association is a political party, it is one that must be devised by the Texas courts. For the same reason, we cannot say that the Jaybird primary is a "primary" within the meaning of Texas law and so regulated by Texas law that *Smith* v. *Allwright* would apply.

But assuming, as I think we must, that the Jaybird Association is not a political party holding a State-regulated primary, we should nonetheless decide this case against respondents on the ground that in the precise situation before us the State authority has come into play.

The State of Texas has entered into a comprehensive scheme of regulation of political primaries, including procedures by which election officials shall be chosen. The county election officials are thus clothed with the authority of the State to secure observance of the State's interest in "fair methods and a fair expression" of preferences in the selection of nominees. If the Jaybird Association, although not a political party, is a device to defeat the law of Texas regulating primaries, and if the electoral officials, clothed with State power in the county, share in that subversion, they cannot divest themselves of the State authority and help as participants in the scheme. Unlawful administration of a State statute fair on its face may be shown "by extrinsic evidence showing a discriminatory design to favor one individual or class over another not to be inferred from the action itself"; here, the county election officials aid in this subversion of the State's official scheme of which they are trustees, by helping as participants in the scheme.

This is not a case of occasional efforts to mass voting strength. Nor is this a case of boss-control, whether crudely or subtly exercised. Nor is this a case of spontaneous efforts by citizens to influence votes or even continued efforts by a fraction of the electorate in support of good government. This is a case in which county election officials have participated in and condoned a continued effort effectively to exclude Negroes from voting. Though the action of the Association as such may not be proscribed by the Fifteenth Amendment, its role in the entire scheme to subvert the operation of the official primary brings it "within reach of the law. . . . [T]hey are bound together as the parts of a single plan. The plan may make the parts unlawful." Mr. Justice Holmes, speaking for the Court, in *Swift and Company* v. *United States*.

The State here devised a process for primary elections. The right of all citizens to share in it, and not to be excluded by unconstitutional bars, is emphasized by the fact that in Texas nomination in the Democratic primary is tantamount to election. The exclusion of the Negroes from meaningful participation in the only primary scheme set up by the State was not an accidental, unsought consequence of the exercise of civic rights by voters to make their common viewpoint count. It was the design, the very purpose of this arrangement that the Jaybird primary in May exclude Negro participation in July. That it was the action in part of the election officials charged by Texas law with the fair administration of the primaries, brings it within the reach of the law. The officials made themselves party to means whereby the machinery with which they are entrusted does not discharge the functions for which it was designed.

It does not follow, however, that the relief granted below was proper. Since the vice of this situation is not that the Jaybird primary itself is the primary discriminatorily conducted under State law but is that the determination there made becomes, in fact, the determination in the Democratic primary by virtue of the participation and acquiescence of State authorities, a federal court cannot require that petitioners be al- lowed to vote in the Jaybird primary. The evil here is that the State, through the action and abdication of those whom it has clothed with authority, has permitted white voters to go through a procedure which predetermines the legally devised primary. To say that Negroes should be allowed to vote in the Jaybird primary would be to say that the State is under a duty to see to it that Negroes may vote in that primary. We cannot tell the State that it must participate in and regulate this primary; we cannot tell the State what machinery it will use. But a court of equity can free the lawful political agency from the combination that subverts its capacity to function. What must be done is that this country be rid of 'the means by which the unlawful "usage" in this case asserts itself.

Mr. Justice Clark, with whom The Chief Justice, Mr. Justice Reed, and Mr. Justice Jackson join, concurring.

The issue is whether the Jaybird Democratic Association of Fort Bend County, Texas, by excluding Negroes from its primaries has denied to Negro citizens of the county a right to vote secured by the Fifteenth Amendment. On March 16, 1950, petitioners on behalf of themselves and similarly situated Negro citizens in Fort Bend County instituted a class action against respondents individually and as officers of the Jaybird Democratic Association. The complaint, in substance, charged that the Negro petitioners were duly qualified voters of the State of Texas who for many years and solely because of their race and color had been denied the right to vote in the primaries of the Association, a political party. Contending that these practices transgressed the Constitution and laws of the United States, petitioners sought declaratory and injunctive relief. Respondents insisted that the Jaybird Democratic Association was not a political party regulated by Texas statutes but merely a private voluntary group. The District Court held that the Jaybird Democratic Association was a political party, and ruled its discriminatory exclusion of Negroes from the primary invalid. Judgment accordingly entered declared petitioners legally entitled to vote in the Jaybird primary. The District Court refused an injunction but retained jurisdiction to grant further appropriate relief. The Court of Appeals reversed; in its view the discriminatory exclusions were not reached by the terms of the Constitution and congressional enactments.

An old pattern in new guise is revealed by the record. The Jaybird Democratic Association of Fort Bend County was founded in 1889 to promote "good government" in the post-Reconstruction period. During its entire life span the Association has restricted membership to whites. In earlier years, the members at mass meetings determined their choice of candidates to support at forthcoming official elections. Subsequently the Association developed a system closely paralleling the structure of the Democratic Party. The Association is governed by an Executive Committee of twenty-two persons, one from each voting precinct in the county. The Committee in each election year sets the date of the Jaybird primary for selecting by ballot the candidates to be endorsed by the Association for public office in the county. The machinery of the Jaybird Democratic Association primary now differs from the state-regulated Democratic Party primary mainly in the Association's prohibition of more than two consecutive terms for officeholders, the absence of a pledge on the ballot at the Jaybird primary, and the Association's practice of not officially filing as a ticket the names of candidates successful in its balloting. And for more than a half century the Association has adhered to its guiding principle: to deny the Negro voters of Fort Bend County any effective voice in their government.

The Court of Appeals, in reversing the District Court, largely relied on what it deemed "the settled course of decision culminating in Collins v. Hardyman . . . that it was not against individual, but against state, action that the Fourteenth and Fifteenth Amendments and 8 U. S. C. A. §§ 43 and 47 were, and are, directed." But *Collins* dealt not with racial discrimination at the ballot box but merely "a lawless political brawl, precipitated by a handful of white citizens against other white citizens." In any event, *Collins* adjudicated that Congress in the narrow class of conspiracies defined by the Civil Rights Statutes had not included the conspiracy charged in that particular complaint; expressly refraining from constitutional questions, that case cannot be held controlling here.

In our view, the Court of Appeals has misconceived the thrust of our recent decisions. The Fifteenth Amendment secures the franchise exercised by citizens of the United States against abridgment by any state on the basis of race or color. In *Smith* v. *Allwright* this Court held that the Democratic Party of itself, and perforce any other political party, is prohibited by that Amendment from conducting a racially discriminatory primary election. By the rule of that case, any "part of the machinery for choosing officials" becomes subject to the Constitution's restraints. There, as here, we dealt with an organization that took the form of "voluntary association" of unofficial character. But because in fact it functioned as a part of the state's electoral machinery, we held it controlled by the same constitutional limitations that ruled the official general election.

We agree with Chief District Judge Kennerly that the Jaybird Democratic Association is a political party whose activities fall within the Fifteenth Amendment's self-executing ban. Not every private club, association or league organized to influence public candidacies or political action must conform to the Constitution's restrictions on political parties. Certainly a large area of freedom permits peaceable assembly and concerted private action for political purposes to be exercised separately by white and colored citizens alike. More, however, is involved here.

The record discloses that the Jaybird Democratic Association operates as part and parcel of the Democratic Party, an organization existing under the auspices of Texas law. Each maintains the same basic qualification for membership: eligibility to vote under Texas law. Although the state Democratic Party in Texas since *Smith* v. *Allwright* no longer can restrict its membership to whites, the Jaybird Democratic Association bars Negroes from its ranks. In May of each election year it conducts a full-scale white primary in which each candidate campaigns for his candidacy subject to the action of that primary *and the Democratic primary of July,* linking the two primaries together. After gaining the Jaybird Democratic Association's endorsement, the announced winners after full publicity then file in the July Democratic primary. The record reveals that 3,910 eligible voters were listed in Fort Bend County in the presidential year 1944; though only 2,032 participated in the July primary under the Democratic banner, 3,790 members voted in the May balloting of the Jaybird Democratic Association. In 1946, an off-year for presidential balloting, eligible voters numbered 4,460; the Association's May primary polled 3,309 votes, and the Democratic July primary counted but 2,996. And while the lists in 1948, again a presidential year, show only 3,856 eligible electors in the County, the Jaybird primary mustered a total vote of 4,055, compared with 3,108 in the primary voting in July. Significantly, since 1889 the winners of the Jaybird Democratic Association balloting, with but a single exception shown by this record, ran unopposed and invariably won in the Democratic July primary and the subsequent general elections for county-wide office.

Quite evidently the Jaybird Democratic Association operates as an auxiliary of the local Democratic Party organization, selecting its nominees and using its machinery for carrying out an admitted design of destroying the weight and effect of Negro ballots in Fort Bend County. To be sure, the Democratic primary and the general election are nominally open to the colored elector. But his must be an empty vote cast after the real decisions are made. And because the Jaybird-indorsed nominee meets no opposition in the Democratic primary, the Negro minority's vote is nullified at the sole stage of the local political process where the bargaining and interplay of rival political forces would make it count.

The Jaybird Democratic Association device, as a result, strikes to the core of the electoral process in Fort Bend County. Whether viewed as a separate political organization or as an adjunct of the local Democratic Party, the Jaybird Democratic Association is the decisive power in the county's recognized electoral process. Over the years its balloting has emerged as the locus of effective political choice. Consonant with the broad and lofty aims of its Framers, the Fifteenth Amendment, as the Fourteenth, "refers to exertions of state power in all forms." Accordingly, when a state structures its electoral apparatus in a form which devolves upon a political organization the uncontested choice of public officials, that organization itself, in whatever disguise, takes on those attributes of government which draw the Constitution's safeguards into play.

In sum, we believe that the activities of the Jaybird Democratic Association fall within the broad principle laid down in *Smith* v. *Allwright*. For that reason we join the judgment of the Court.

Mr. Justice Minton, dissenting.

I am not concerned in the least as to what happens to the Jaybirds or their unworthy scheme. I am concerned about what this Court says is state action within the meaning of the Fifteenth Amendment to the Constitution. For, after all, this Court has power to redress a wrong under that Amendment only if the wrong is done by the State. That has been the holding of this Court since the earliest cases. The Chief Justice for a unanimous Court in the recent case of *Shelley* v. *Kraemer* stated the law as follows:

"Since the decision of this Court in the *Civil Rights Cases* the principle has become firmly embedded in our constitutional law that the action inhibited by the first section of the Fourteenth Amendment is only such action as may fairly be said to be that of the States. *That Amendment erects no shield against merely private conduct, however discriminatory or wrongful.*" (Emphasis supplied.)

As I understand Mr. Justice Black's opinion, he would have this Court redress the wrong even if it was individual action alone. I can understand that praiseworthy position, but it seems to me it is not in accord with the Constitution. State action must be shown.

Mr. Justice Frankfurter recognizes that it must be state action but he seems to think it is enough to constitute state action if a state official participates in the Jaybird primary. That I cannot follow. For it seems clear to me that everything done by a person who is an official is not done officially and as a representative of the State. However, I find nothing in this record that shows the state or county officials participating in the Jaybird primary.

Mr. Justice Clark seems to recognize that state action must be shown. He finds state action in assumption, not in facts. This record will be searched in vain for one iota of state action sufficient to support an anemic inference that the Jaybird Association is in any way associated with or forms a part of or cooperates in any manner with the Democratic Party of the County or State, or with the State. It calls itself the Jaybird Democratic Association because its interest is only in the candidates of the Democratic Party in the county, a position understandable in Texas. It as a gratuitous asumption on the part of Mr. Justice Clark that: "Quite evidently the Jaybird Democratic Association operates as an auxiliary of the local Democratic Party organization, selecting its nominees and using its machinery for carrying out an admitted design of destroying the weight and effect of Negro ballots in Fort Bend County." The following stipulation in the record shows the unsubstantiality of that statement just quoted from Mr. Justice Clark's opinion. I quote the stipulation:

"There is no compulsion upon any person who receives the indorsement of the Jaybird Democratic Association of Fort Bend County, Texas, for a particular office, to run for that office or any other office. In the event such indorsee of the Association does desire to run for such office he may do so; but if he does so run for such office he must himself file his application with the Executive Chairman or Committee of the Democratic Party for the position on the Democratic Party ballot for the July primary of such Democratic Party, and must himself pay the fee as provided by law. Neither the Jaybird Democratic Association nor its Executive Committee files an application with the Democratic Party Executive Committee or Chairman that the Jaybird Democratic Association nominee be placed on the ballot for the Democratic Party July primary election. There is nothing on the ballot of the Democratic

Party primary to indicate that any person appearing thereon does or does not have the indorsement of the Jaybird Democratic Association.

"The name of the applicant for a place on the Democratic Party ballot is not placed on said ballot unless he complies with the laws of the State of Texas, even though such applicant were indorsed by the Jaybird Democratic Association; and every qualified applicant who makes the required application to the Democratic Executive Committee and pays the requisite fee is placed on the Democratic Party primary ballot for the July Democratic primary though not indorsed by the Jaybird Democratic Association.

"No member of the Negro race, nor any other person qualified under the laws of the State of Texas to become a candidate, has been refused a place on the Democratic Party primary ballot for Fort Bend County, Texas, by the Democratic Party."

Neither is there any more evidence that the Jaybird Association avails itself of or conforms in any manner to any law of the State of Texas. As to the Jaybird Association's relation to the State, I again quote the stipulation in the record:

"There is no political organization in Fort Bend County, Texas, by the official name or designation 'Jaybird Party'. At all times since 1889, however, there has been and still is, an organization in Fort Bend County, Texas, by the name of 'Jaybird Democratic Association of Fort Bend County, Texas'. Said Association, however, has not since 1938, and it does not : (a) Have a State organization; (b) Follow or attempt to comply with any of the provisions of Article 3163 of the Revised Statutes of Texas, or of any other statutes of the State of Texas with reference to primary elections or general elections; (c) Hold any convention or 'primary election' on the legal primary election day, to-wit: The fourth Saturday in July or the fourth Saturday in August, of any year; (d) Hold any primary convention in any precinct on the Saturday preceding a legal primary election day; (e) By the chairman of a county committee, or otherwise, certify to the County Clerk of Fort Bend County, Texas, or to the County Judge thereof, or to any official committee or other representative of the Democratic or Republican party, any nominations or indorsements made by the Association; (f) Have, or cause to be, printed in a separate column headed by the Association name any nominations on any official ballot used, or for use in, a primary or general election held on a legal primary election day or general election day; (nor does the name, Jaybird Democratic Association of Fort Bend County, Texas, or any part or indication thereof, appear on any ballot in any election other than the primaries, or other special voting occasions, held by the Association itself and alone); (g) Make, or cause to be made, a written application to the County Judge for such printing, signed and sworn to by 3% of the entire vote cast in Fort Bend County at the last preceding general election.

·   ·   ·   ·   ·

"No officer nor Committee of such Association certifies the result of the Association membership vote, nor any nominations of the Association, to the County Clerk of Fort Bend County, Texas, nor to the Democratic Party Executive Committee nor to the Committee or official of any party with a state-wide organization.

.   .   .   .   .

"In the last few years some of the members of the Negro race have offered to vote in the Democratic Party primaries and no member of the Negro race who had qualified under the laws of the State of Texas to vote has been refused the right to vote. Some of the members of the Negro race have offered to vote in a general election in Fort Bend County, Texas, and no member of the Negro race qualified to vote has been refused a vote.

.   .   .   .   .

"The Jaybird Democratic Association of Fort Bend County, Texas, is not, and does not have, a state organization, but limits its May and June Association primaries to only the county and precinct offices, except that the membership of the Association does vote its preference for the office of District Clerk in Fort Bend County.

"The persons seeking the indorsement of the Jaybird Democratic Association of Fort Bend County, Texas, at its May or June Primaries are not required by the Association to file any expense account and do not file expense accounts with any State or local official, Committee or Board."

These stipulations from the record show the complete absence of any compliance with the state law or practice, or cooperation by or with the State. Even if it be said to be a political organization, the Jaybird Association avails itself of no state law open to political organizations, such as Art. 3163.

However, its action is not forbidden by the law of the State of Texas. Does such failure of the State to act to prevent individuals from doing what they have the right as individuals to do amount to state action? I venture the opinion it does not.

Mr. Justice Clark's opinion agrees with District Judge Kennerly that this Jaybird Democratic Association is a political party whose activities fall within the Fifteenth Amendment's self-executing ban. In the same paragraph, he admits that not all meetings for political action come under the constitutional ban. Surely white or colored members of any political faith or economic belief may hold caucuses. It is only when the State by action of its legislative bodies or action of some of its officials in their official capacity cooperates with such political party or gives it direction in its activities that the Federal Constitution may come into play. A political organization not using state machinery or depending upon state law to authorize what it does could not be within the ban of the Fifteenth Amendment. As the stipulation quoted shows, the Jaybird Association did not attempt to conform or in any way to comply with the statutes of Texas covering primaries. No action of any legislative or quasi-legislative body or of any state official or agency ever in any manner denied the vote to Negroes, even in the Jaybird primaries.

So it seem to me clear there is no state action, and the Jaybird Democratic Association is in no sense a part of the Democratic Party. If it is a political organization, it has made no attempt to use the State, or the State to use it, to carry on its poll.

Rice v. *Elmore* is cited as authority for the position of the petitioners. In that case, South Carolina had repealed all its laws relating to the conduct of primaries. The only primary conducted was by the Democratic Party of South Carolina in accordance with rules adopted by the Party. It was stipulated on the trial of that case that the Democratic Party "conducts nominating primaries and thereafter prints its ballots for use in the General Elections with the names of its nominees thereon which ballots are distributed by party officials and placed at the General Election precincts in South Carolina for use by any electors who choose to use such ballot in voting in any such General Election in South Carolina." The District Court specifically found in Finding 19: "There is no General Election ballot in South Carolina. The only printed ballots available in General Elections in South Carolina are ballots prepared by the political parties giving only the names of their respective candidates." Finding 14 stated: "During the past 25 years the Democratic Party of South Carolina has been the only political party in South Carolina which has held state-wide primaries for nomination of candidates for Federal and State offices."

Thus it will be seen that there the Democratic Party furnished not only the candidate in the general election, but it also furnished the only ballot one could vote in that election. So the State in the general election accepted the ballot of the Democratic Party as its official ballot, and on that ballot no Negro had been permitted to vote. Clearly, the State adopted the Democratic Party's procedure as its action. The State and the Democratic Party effectively cooperated to carry on this two-step election procedure.

No such action is taken by the Jaybird Association. It neither files, certifies, nor supplies anything for the primary or election. The winner of the poll in the Jaybird Association contest files in the Democratic primary, where he may and sometimes has received opposition, and successful opposition, in precinct contests for County Commissioner, Justice of the Peace and Constable. There is no rule of the Jaybird Association that requires the successful party in its poll to file in the Democratic primary or elsewhere. It is all individual, voluntary action. Neither the State nor the Democratic Party avails itself of the action of or cooperates in any manner with the Jaybird Association.

Smith v. *Allwright* is in no manner controlling. In that case, the State had set up the machinery for the Democratic Party to conduct its primary. The State of Texas made the Democratic Party its agent for the conducting of a Democratic primary. Of course, the Democratic Party could not run that primary, set up under the auspices of the State, in a manner to exclude citizens of Texas therefrom because of their race. That such is the basis of the Court's opinion in *Smith* v. *Allwright* is apparent from the following quotation taken from that case:

"Primary elections are conducted by the party under state statutory authority. The county executive committee selects precinct election officials and the county, district or state executive committees, respectively, canvass the returns. These party committees or the state convention certify the party's candidates to the appropriate officers for inclusion on the official ballot for the general election. No name which has not been so certified may appear upon the ballot for the general election as a candidate of a political party. . . .

. . . . .

"We think that this statutory system for the selection of party nominees for inclusion on the general election ballot makes the party *which is required* to follow these legislative directions an agency of the State in so far as it determines the participants in a primary election. The party takes its character as a state agency from the duties imposed upon it by state statutes; the duties do not become matters of private law because they are performed by a political party." (Emphasis supplied.)

This case does not hold that a group of Democrats, white, black, male, female, native-born or foreign, economic royalists or workingmen, may not caucus or conduct a straw vote. What the Jaybird Association did here was to conduct as individuals, separate and apart from the Democratic Party or the State, a straw vote as to who should receive the Association's endorsement for county and precinct offices. It has been successful in seeing that those who receive its endorsement are nominated and elected. That is true of concerted action by any group. In numbers there is strength. In organization there is effectiveness. Often a small minority of stockholders control a corporation. Indeed, it is almost an axiom of corporate management that a small, cohesive group may control, especially in the larger corporations where the holdings are widely diffused.

I do not understand that concerted action of individuals which is successful somehow becomes state action. However, the candidates endorsed by the Jaybird Association have several times been defeated in primaries and elections. Usually but not always since 1938, only the Jaybird-endorsed candidate has been on the Democratic official ballot in the County.

In the instant case, the State of Texas has provided for elections and primaries. This is separate and apart and wholly unrelated to the Jaybird Association's activities. Its activities are confined to one County where a group of citizens have appointed themselves the censors of those who would run for public offices. Apparently so far they have succeeded in convincing the voters of this County in most instances that their supported candidates should win. This seems to differ very little from situations common in many other places far north of the Mason-Dixon line, such as areas where a candidate must obtain the approval of a religious group. In other localities, candidates are carefully selected by both parties to give proper weight to Jew, Protestant and Catholic, and certain posts are considered the sole possession of certain ethnic groups. The propriety of these practices is something the courts sensibly have left to the good or bad judgment of the electorate. It must be recognized that elections and other public business are influenced by all sorts of pressures from carefully organized groups. We have pressure from labor unions, from the National Association of Manufacturers, from the Silver Shirts, from the National Association for the Advancement of Colored People, from the Ku Klux Klan and others. Far from the activities of these groups being properly labeled as state action, under either the Fourteenth or the Fifteenth Amendment, they are to be considered as attempts to influence or obtain state action.

The courts do not normally pass upon these pressure groups, whether their causes are good or bad, highly successful or only so-so. It is difficult for me to see how this Jaybird Association is anything but such a pressure group. Apparently it is believed in by enough people in Fort

Bend County to obtain a majority of the votes for its approved candidates. This differs little from the situation in many parts of the "Bible Belt" where a church stamp of approval or that of the Anti-Saloon League must be put on any candidate who does not want to lose the election.

The State of Texas in its elections and primaries takes no cognizance of this Jaybird Association. The State treats its decisions apparently with the same disdain as it would the approval or condemnation of judicial candidates by a bar association poll of its members.

In this case the majority have found that this pressure group's work does constitute state action. The basis of this conclusion is rather difficult to ascertain. Apparently it derives mainly from a dislike of the goals of the Jaybird Association. I share that dislike. I fail to see how it makes state action. I would affirm.

Lassiter v. Northampton Election Board
360 U. S. 45   1959

Mr. Justice Douglas delivered the opinion of the Court.

This controversy started in a Federal District Court. Appellant, a Negro citizen of North Carolina, sued to have the literacy test for voters prescribed by that State declared unconstitutional and void. A three-judge court was convened. That court noted that the literacy test was part of a provision of the North Carolina Constitution that also included a grandfather clause. It said that the grandfather clause plainly would be unconstitutional under *Guinn* v. *United States*. It noted, however, that the North Carolina *statute* which enforced the registration requirements contained in the State Constitution had been superseded by a 1957 Act and that the 1957 Act does not contain the grandfather clause or any reference to it. But being uncertain as to the significance of the 1957 Act and deeming it wise to have all administrative remedies under that Act exhausted before the federal court acted, it stayed its action, retaining jurisdiction for a reasonable time to enable appellant to exhaust her administrative remedies and obtain from the state courts an interpretation of the statute in light of the State Constitution.

Thereupon the instant case was commenced. It started as an administrative proceeding. Appellant applied for registration as a voter. Her registration was denied by the registrar because she refused to submit to a literacy test as required by the North Carolina statute. She appealed to the County Board of Elections. On the *de novo* hearing before that Board appellant again refused to take the literacy test and she was again denied registration for that reason. She appealed to the Superior Court which sustained the Board against the claim that the requirement of the literacy test violated the Fourteenth, Fifteenth, and Seventeenth Amendments of the Federal Constitution. Preserving her federal question, she appealed to the North Carolina Supreme Court which affirmed the lower court. The case came here by appeal and we noted probable jurisdiction.

The literacy test is a part of § 4 of Art. VI of the North Carolina Constitution. That test is contained in the first sentence of § 4. The second sentence contains a so-called grandfather clause. The entire § 4 reads as follows:

"Every person presenting himself for registration shall be able to read and write any section of the Constitution in the English language. But no male person who was, on January 1, 1867, or at any time prior thereto, entitled to vote under the laws of any state in the United States wherein he then resided, and no lineal descendant of any such person, shall be denied the right to register and vote at any election in this State by reason of his failure to possess the educational qualifications herein prescribed: Provided, he shall have registered in accordance with the terms of this section prior to December 1, 1908. The General Assembly shall provide for the registration of all persons entitled to vote without the educational qualifications herein prescribed, and shall, on or before November 1, 1908, provide for the making of a permanent record of such registration, and all persons so registered shall forever thereafter have the right to vote in all elections by the people in this State, unless disqualified under section 2 of this article."

Originally Art. VI contained in § 5 the following provision:

"That this amendment to the Constitution is presented and adopted as one indivisible plan for the regulation of the suffrage, with the intent and purpose to so connect the different parts, and to make them so dependent upon each other, that the whole shall stand or fall together."

But the North Carolina Supreme Court in the instant case held that a 1945 amendment to Article VI freed it of the indivisibility clause. That amendment rephrased § 1 of Art. VI to read as follows:

"Every person born in the United States, and every person who has been naturalized, twenty-one years of age, and possessing the qualifications set out in this article, shall be entitled to vote . . . ."

That court said that "one of those qualifications" was the literacy test contained in § 4 of Art. VI; and that the 1945 amendment "had the effect of incorporating and adopting anew the provisions as to the qualifications required of a voter as set out in Article VI, freed of the indivisibility clause of the 1902 amendment. And the way was made clear for the General Assembly to act."

In 1957 the Legislature rewrote General Statutes § 163–28 as we have noted. Prior to that 1957 amendment § 163–28 perpetuated the grandfather clause contained in § 4 of Art. VI of the Constitution and § 163–32 established a procedure for registration to effectuate it. But the 1957 amendment contained a provision that "All laws and clauses of laws in conflict with this Act are hereby repealed." The federal three-judge court ruled that this 1957 amendment eliminated the grandfather clause from the statute.

The Attorney General of North Carolina, in an *amicus* brief, agrees that the grandfather clause contained in Art. VI is in conflict with the Fifteenth Amendment. Appellee maintains that the North Carolina Supreme Court ruled that the invalidity of that part of Art. VI does not impair the remainder of Art. VI since the 1945 amendment to Art. VI freed it of its indivisibility clause. Under the view Art. VI would impose the same literacy test as that imposed by the 1957 statute and neither would be linked wth the grandfather clause which, though present in print, is separable from the rest and void. We so read the opinion of the North Carolina Supreme Court.

Appellant argues that that is not the end of the problem presented by the grandfather clause. There is a provision in the General Statutes for permanent registration in some counties. Appellant points out that although the cut-off date in the grandfather clause was December 1, 1908, those who registered before then might still be voting. If they were allowed to vote without taking a literacy test and if appellant were denied the right to vote unless she passed it, members of the white race would receive preferential privileges of the ballot contrary to the command of the Fifteenth Amendment. That would be analogous to the problem posed in the classic case of *Yick Wo* v. *Hopkins* where an ordinance unimpeachable on its face was applied in such a way as to violate the guarantee of equal protection contained in the Fourteenth

Amendment. But this issue of discrimination in the actual operation of the ballot laws of North Carolina has not been framed in the issues presented for the state court litigation. So we do not reach it. But we mention it in passing so that it may be clear that nothing we say or do here will prejudice appellant in tendering that issue in the federal proceedings which await the termination of this state court litigation.

We come then to the question whether a State may consistently with the Fourteenth and Seventeenth Amendments apply a literacy test to all voters irrespective of race or color. The Court in *Guinn* v. *United States* disposed of the question in a few words, "No time need be spent on the question of the validity of the literacy test considered alone since as we have seen its establishment was but the exercise by the State of a lawful power vested in it not subject to our supervision, and indeed, its validity is admitted."

The States have long been held to have broad powers to determine the conditions under which the right of suffrage may be exercised, absent of course the discrimination which the Constitution condemns. Article I, § 2 of the Constitution in its provision for the election of members of the House of Representatives and the Seventeenth Amendment in its provision for the election of Senators provide that officials will be chosen "by the People." Each provision goes on to state that "the Electors in each State shall have the Qualifications requisite for Electors of the most numerous Branch of the State Legislature." So while the right of suffrage is established and guaranteed by the Constitution, it is subject to the imposition of state standards which are not discriminatory and which do not contravene any restriction that Congress, acting pursuant to its constitutional powers, has imposed. While § 2 of the Fourteenth Amendment, which provides for apportionment of Representatives among the States according to their respective numbers counting the whole number of persons in each State (except Indians not taxed), speaks of "the right to vote," the right protected "refers to the right to vote as established by the laws and constitution of the State."

We do not suggest that any standards which a State desires to adopt may be required of voters. But there is wide scope for exercise of its jurisdiction. Residence requirements, age, previous criminal record are obvious examples indicating factors which a State may take into consideration in determining the qualifications of voters. The ability to read and write likewise has some relation to standards designed to promote intelligent use of the ballot. Literacy and illiteracy are neutral on race, creed, color, and sex, as reports around the world show. Literacy and intelligence are obviously not synonymous. Illiterate people may be intelligent voters. Yet in our society where newspapers, periodicals, books, and other printed matter canvass and debate campaign issues, a State might conclude that only those who are literate should exercise the franchise. It was said last century in Massachusetts that a literacy test was designed to insure an "independent and intelligent" exercise of the right of suffrage. North Carolina agrees. We do not sit in judgment on the wisdom of that policy. We cannot say, however, that it is not an allowable one measured by constitutional standards.

Of course a literacy test, fair on its face, may be employed to perpetuate that discrimination which the Fifteenth Amendment was designed to uproot. No such influence is charged here. On the other hand, a literacy test may be unconstitutional on its face. In *Davis* v. *Schnell* the test was the citizens' ability to "understand and explain" an article of the Federal Constitution. The legislative setting of that provision and the great discretion it vested in the registrar made clear that a literacy requirement was merely a device to make racial discrimination easy. We cannot make the same inference here. The present requirement, applicable to members of all races, is that the prospective voter "be able to read and write any section of the Constitution of North Carolina in the English language." That seems to us to be one fair way of determining whether a person is literate, not a calculated scheme to lay springes for the citizen. Certainly we cannot condemn it on its face as a device unrelated to the desire of North Carolina to raise the standards for people of all races who cast the ballot.

Affirmed.

Gomillion v. Lightfoot
364 U. S. 339   1960

Mr. Justice Frankfurter delivered the opinion of the Court.

This litigation challenges the validity, under the United States Constitution, of Local Act No. 140, passed by the Legislature of Alabama in 1957, redefining the boundaries of the City of Tuskegee. Petitioners, Negro citizens of Alabama who were, at the time of this redistricting measure, residents of the City of Tuskegee, brought an action in the United States District Court for the Middle District of Alabama for a declaratory judgment that Act 140 is unconstitutional, and for an injunction to restrain the Mayor and officers of Tuskegee and the officials of Macon County, Alabama, from enforcing the Act against them and other Negroes similarly situated. Petitioners' claim is that enforcement of the statute, which alters the shape of Tuskegee from a square to an uncouth twenty-eight-sided figure, will constitute a discrimination against them in violation of the Due Process and Equal Protection Clauses of the Fourteenth Amendment to the Constitution and will deny them the right to vote in defiance of the Fifteenth Amendment.

The respondents moved for dismissal of the action for failure to state a claim upon which relief could be granted and for lack of jurisdiction of the District Court. The court granted the motion, stating, "This Court has no control over, no supervision over, and no power to change any boundaries of municipal corporations fixed by a duly convened and elected legislative body, acting for the people in the State of Alabama." On appeal, the Court of Appeals for the Fifth Circuit, affirmed the judgment, one judge dissenting. We brought the case here since serious questions were raised concerning the power of a State over its municipalities in relation to the Fourteenth and Fifteenth Amendments.

At this stage of the litigation we are not concerned with the truth of the allegations, that is, the ability of petitioners to sustain their allegations by proof. The sole question is whether the allegations entitle them to make good on their claim that they are being denied rights under the United States Constitution. The complaint, charging that Act 140 is a device to disenfranchise Negro citizens, alleges the following facts: Prior to Act 140 the City of Tuskegee was square in shape; the Act transformed it into a strangely irregular twenty-eight-sided figure as indicated in the diagram appended to this opinion. The essential inevitable effect of this redefinition of Tuskegee's boundaries is to remove from the city all save only four or five of its 400 Negro voters while not removing a single white voter or resident. The result of the Act is to deprive the Negro petitioners discriminatorily of the benefits of residence in Tuskegee, including, *inter alia,* the right to vote in municipal elections.

These allegations, if proven, would abundantly establish that Act 140 was not an ordinary geographic redistricting measure even within familiar abuses of gerrymandering. If these allegations upon a trial remained uncontradicted or unqualified, the conclusion would be irresistible, tantamount for all practical purposes to a mathematical demonstration, that the legislation is solely concerned with segregating white and colored voters by fencing Negro citizens out of town so as to deprive them of their pre-existing municipal vote.

It is difficult to appreciate what stands in the way of adjudging a statute having this inevitable effect invalid in light of the principles by which this Court must judge, and uniformly has judged, statutes that, howsoever speciously defined, obviously discriminate against colored citizens. "The [Fifteenth] Amendment nullifies sophisticated as well as simple-minded modes of discrimination." *Lane* v. *Wilson.*

The complaint amply alleges a claim of racial discrimination. Against this claim the respondents have never suggested, either in their brief or in oral argument, any countervailing municipal function which Act 140 is designed to serve. The respondents invoke generalities expressing the State's unrestricted power—unlimited, that is, by the United States Constitution—to establish, destroy, or reorganize by contraction or expansion its political subdivisions, to wit, cities, counties, and other local units. We freely recognize the breadth and importance of this aspect of the State's political power. To exalt this power into an absolute is to misconceive the reach and rule of this Court's decisions in the leading case of *Hunter* v. *Pittsburgh* and related cases relied upon by respondents.

The *Hunter* case involved a claim by citizens of Allegheny, Pennsylvania, that the General Assembly of that State could not direct a consolidation of their city and Pittsburgh over the objection of a majority of the Allegheny voters. It was alleged that while Allegheny already had made numerous civic improvements, Pittsburgh was only then planning to undertake such improvements, and that the annexation would therefore greatly increase the tax burden on Allegheny residents. All that the case held was (1) that there is no implied contract between a city and its residents that their taxes will be spent solely for the benefit of that city, and (2) that a citizen of one municipality is not deprived of property without due process of law by being subjected to increased tax burdens as a result of the consolidation of his city with another. Related cases, upon which the respondents also rely, such as *Trenton* v. *New Jersey, Pawhuska* v. *Pawhuska Oil Co.,* and *Laramie County* v. *Albany County* are far off the mark. They are authority only for the principle that no constitutionally protected contractural obligation arises between a State and its subordinate governmental entities solely as a result of their relationship.

In short, the cases that have come before this Court regarding legislation by States dealing with their political subdivisions fall into two classes: (1) those in which it is claimed that the State, by virtue of the prohibition against impairment of the obligation of contract and of the Due Process Clause of the Fourteenth Amendment, is without power to extinguish, or alter the boundaries of, an existing municipality; and (2) in which it is claimed that the State has no power to change the identity of a municipality whereby citizens of a pre-existing municipality suffer serious economic disadvantage.

Neither of these claims is supported by such a specific limitation upon State power as confines the States under the Fifteenth Amendment. As to the first category, it is obvious that the creation of municipalities— clearly a political act—does not come within the conception of a contract under the *Dartmouth College* case. As to the second, if one principle clearly emerges from the numerous decisions of this Court dealing with taxation it is that the Due Process Clause affords no immunity against mere inequalities in tax burdens, nor does it afford protection against their increase as an indirect consequence of a State's exercise of its political powers.

Particularly in dealing with claims under broad provisions of the Constitution, which derive content by an interpretive process of inclusion and exclusion, it is imperative that generalizations, based on and qualified by the concrete situations that gave rise to them, must not be applied out of context in disregard of variant controlling facts. Thus, a correct reading of the seemingly unconfined dicta of *Hunter* and kindred cases is not that the State has plenary power to manipulate in every conceivable way, for every conceivable purpose, the affairs of its municipal corporations, but rather that the State's authority is unrestrained by the particular prohibitions of the Constitution considered in those cases.

The *Hunter* opinion itself intimates that a state legislature may not be omnipotent even as to the disposition of some types of property owned by municipal corporations. Further, other cases in this Court have refused to allow a State to abolish a municipality, or alter its boundaries, or merge it with another city, without preserving to the creditors of the old city some effective recourse for the collection of debts owed them. For example, in *Mobile* v. *Watson* the Court said:

"Where the resource for the payment of the bonds of a municipal corporation is the power of taxation existing when the bonds were issued, any law which withdraws or limits the taxing power and leaves no adequate means for the payment of the bonds is forbidden by the Constitution of the United States, and is null and void."

This line of authority conclusively shows that the Court has never acknowledged that the States have power to do as they will with municipal corporations regardless of consequences. Legislative control of municipalities, no less than other state power, lies within the scope of relevant limitations imposed by the United States Constitution. The observation in *Graham* v. *Folsom* becomes relevant: "The power of the State to alter or destroy its corporations is not greater than the power of the State to repeal its legislation." In that case, which involved the attempt by state officials to evade the collection of taxes to discharge the obligations of an extinguished township, Mr. Justice McKenna, writing for the Court, went on to point out, with reference to the *Mount Pleasant* and *Mobile* cases:

"It was argued in those cases, as it is argued in this, that such alteration or destruction of the subordinate governmental divisions was a proper exercise of legislative power, to which creditors had to submit. The argument did not prevail. It was answered, as we now answer it, that such power, extensive though it is, is met and overcome by the provision of the Constitution of the United States which forbids a State from passing any law impairing the obligation of contracts. . . ."

If all this is so in regard to the constitutional protection of contracts, it should be equally true that, to paraphrase, such power, extensive though it is, is met and overcome by the Fifteenth Amendment to the

Constitution of the United States, which forbids a State from passing any law which deprives a citizen of his vote because of his race. The opposite conclusion, urged upon us by respondents, would sanction the achievement by a State of any impairment of voting rights whatever so long as it was cloaked in the garb of the realignment of political subdivisions. "It is inconceivable that guaranties embedded in the Constitution of the United States may thus be manipulated out of existence."

The respondents find another barrier to the trial of this case in *Colegrove* v. *Green*. In that case the Court passed on an Illinois law governing the arrangement of congressional districts within that State. The complaint rested upon the disparity of population between the different districts which rendered the effectiveness of each individual's vote in some districts far less than in others. The disparity came to pass solely through shifts in population between 1901, when Illinois organized its congressional districts, and 1946, when the complaint was lodged. During this entire period elections were held under the districting scheme devised in 1901. The Court affirmed the dismissal of the complaint on the ground that it presented a subject not meet for adjudication. The decisive facts in this case, which at this stage must be taken as proved, are wholly different from the considerations found controlling in *Colegrove*.

That case involved a complaint of discriminatory apportionment of congressional districts. The appellants in *Colegrove* complained only of a dilution of the strength of their votes as a result of legislative inaction over a course of many years. The petitioners here complain that affirmative legislative action deprives them of their votes and the consequent advantages that the ballot affords. When a legislature thus singles out a readily isolated segment of a racial minority for special discriminatory treatment, it violates the Fifteenth Amendment. In no case involving unequal weight in voting distribution that has come before the Court did the decision sanction a differentiation on racial lines whereby approval was given to unequivocal withdrawal of the vote solely from colored citizens. Apart from all else, these considerations lift this controversy out of the so-called "political" arena and into the conventional sphere of constitutional litigation.

In sum, as Mr. Justice Holmes remarked, when dealing with a related situation, in *Nixon* v. *Herndon,* "Of course the petition concerns political action," but "The objection that the subject matter of the suit is political is little more than a play upon words." A statute which is alleged to have worked unconstitutional deprivations of petitioners' rights is not immune to attack simply because the mechanism employed by the legislature is a redefinition of municipal boundaries. According to the allegations here made, the Alabama Legislature has not merely redrawn the Tuskegee city limits with incidental inconvenience to the petitioners; it is more accurate to say that it has deprived the petitioners of the municipal franchise and consequent rights and to that end it has incidentally changed the city's boundaries. While in form this is merely an act redefining metes and bounds, if the allegations are established, the inescapable human effect of this essay in geometry and geography is to despoil colored citizens, and only colored citizens, of their theretofore enjoyed voting rights. That was not *Colegrove* v. *Green*.

When a State exercises power wholly within the domain of state interest, it is insulated from federal judicial review. But such insulation is not carried over when state power is used as an instrument for circumventing a federally protected right. This principle has had many applications. It has long been recognized in cases which have prohibited a State from exploiting a power acknowledged to be absolute in an isolated context to justify the imposition of an "unconstitutional condition." What the Court has said in those cases is equally applicable here, *viz.*, that "Acts generally lawful may become unlawful when done to accomplish an unlawful end, and a constitutional power cannot be used by way of condition to attain an unconstitutional result." The petitioners are entitled to prove their allegations at trial.

For these reasons, the principal conclusions of the District Court and the Court of Appeals are clearly erroneous and the decision below must be

Reversed.

Mr. Justice Douglas, while joining the opinion of the Court, adheres to the dissents in *Colegrove* v. *Green* and *South* v. *Peters*.

Mr. Justice Whittaker, concurring.

I concur in the Court's judgment, but not in the whole of its opinion. It seems to me that the decision should be rested not on the Fifteenth Amendment, but rather on the Equal Protection Clause of the Fourteenth Amendment to the Constitution. I am doubtful that the averments of the complaint, taken for present purposes to be true, show a purpose by Act No. 140 to abridge petitioners' "right . . . to vote," in the Fifteenth Amendment sense. It seems to me that the "right . . . to vote" that is guaranteed by the Fifteenth Amendment is but the same right to vote as is enjoyed by all others within the same election precinct, ward or other political division. And, inasmuch as no one has the right to vote in a political division, or in a local election concerning only an area in which he does not reside, it would seem to follow that one's right to vote in Division A is not abridged by a redistricting that places his residence in Division B *if* he there enjoys the same voting privileges as all others in that Division, even though the redistricting was done by the State for the purpose of placing a racial group of citizens in Division B rather than A.

But it does seem clear to me that accomplishment of a State's purpose —to use the Court's phrase—of "fencing Negro citizens out of" Division A and into Division B is an unlawful segregation of races of citizens, in violation of the Equal Protection Clause of the Fourteenth Amendment and, as stated, I would think the decision should be rested on that ground—which, incidentally, clearly would not involve, just as the cited cases did not involve, the *Colegrove* problem.